Sites of Discourse
– Public and Private Spheres –
Legal Culture

Papers from a Conference Held at the Technical University of Dresden, December 2001

64

Internationale Forschungen zur
Allgemeinen und
Vergleichenden Literaturwissenschaft

SITES OF DISCOURSE
– PUBLIC AND PRIVATE SPHERES –
LEGAL CULTURE

PAPERS FROM A CONFERENCE HELD AT THE TECHNICAL UNIVERSITY OF DRESDEN, DECEMBER 2001

Edited by

Uwe Böker
and
Julie A. Hibbard

Amsterdam - New York, NY 2002

Cover: (left) JohnWilkes, satirical print by William Hogarth (1763); (right) page from *The Complete Collection of the Genuine Papers, Letters, &c. in the Case of John Wilkes, Esq. Elected Knight of the Shire of the County of Middlesex* (published in Berlin, 1769, page 17).

Le papier sur lequel le présent ouvrage est imprimé remplit les prescriptions de "ISO 9706:1994, Information et documentation - Papier pour documents - Prescriptions pour la permanence".

The paper on which this book is printed meets the requirements of " ISO 9706:1994, Information and documentation - Paper for documents - Requirements for permanence".

ISBN: 90-420-1550-0

Printed in The Netherlands

CONTENTS

PREFACE

The present collection of essays grew out of a conference, held in Dresden in December 2001, exploring the relationship between the public sphere and legal culture. The conference was held in connection with the ongoing research undertaken by the *Sonderforschungsbereich* 537 (*SFB*) – particularly by the project 'Circulation of Legal Norms and Values in British Culture from 1700 to 1900' – on processes of institutionalisation and historical change.

The conference papers include essays on the theory of the public sphere from a systematic and historical point of view by Gert Melville (head of *SFB*, Dresden), by Peter Uwe Hohendahl (Cornell University) and by Jürgen Schlaeger (Großbritannien Zentrum, Berlin). Alastair Mann's (University of St Andrews, Scotland) contribution investigates the situation in Scotland, particularly the oath of allegiance and censorship. The paper by Annette Pankratz (University of Passau) focuses on the king's body as a site of the public sphere; Heinz-Joachim Müllenbrock (University of Göttingen) looks into the 'culture of contention' at the beginning of the eighteenth century whereas Eckhart Hellmuth (Ludwig-Maximilians University, Munich) considers the reform movement at the end of the century.

Ian Bell (University of Wales, Swansea), who took part in the conference, suggested the inclusion of part of the first chapter of his seminal study *Literature and Crime in Augustan England*. Beth Swan (Chester College, England), Anna-Christina Giovanopoulos (*SFB*, Dresden), and Christoph Houswitschka (University of Bamberg) respectively analyse the ideologies of justice, the interrelation between journalism and crime, and the juridical evaluation of the crime of incest and its representation in public. Greta Olson (University of Freiburg) investigates keyholes as liminal spaces between the public and the private, Juliet Wightman (University of Stirling, Scotland) focuses on theatre and the bear pit, Uwe Böker (*SFB*, Dresden) examines the court room and the prison as public sites of discourse, and York-Gothart Mix (University of Marburg) discusses the German emigrant culture in North America.

U.B.

Gert Melville

INSTITUTIONS AND THE PUBLIC SPHERE: SOME PRELIMINARY REMARKS

From the point of view of the theory of institutionalisation as developed within the *Sonderforschungsbereich* 537 at the Technical University of Dresden, one research problem is without doubt the relationship between the public and the private spheres, irrespective of the historical period investigated. Whether in Greek or Roman antiquity, the Middle Ages, or the early modern or modern ages, the legitimacy of an institutional order or its claims to and fictions of legitimacy depend to a high degree on the ways a historically given cultural system constitutes its public as well as its private spheres, on the institutionalised but historically varying relationships between these different spheres, and on the evaluation of these relationships. And, conversely, historical manifestations of the public and private spheres are shaped and conditioned, respectively, by dominant types of institutionalised concepts of order and stability.

Even if we assume that every human being is in some way or another always part of a public sphere, just as everyone is entitled to and has a claim to a private realm of their own, the public sphere constitutes what is basically open and accessible to everybody and what concerns everybody; whereas the private sphere is restricted insofar as it is only of individual interest and purport. However, in presupposing a dichotomy of a social and an individual human nature, one might get caught up in failures of anthropological essentialism without gaining new insights into cultural history, its developments and structures.

There is no doubt that the public and private spheres are interrelated constituents of social formations, and that their configurations are effective. Every culture, however, generates – from the basis of the private and public spheres as two extreme positions – its own normative values, attributing different social functions to both spheres and postulating this differentiation as a fact that transcends immediate conditions of existence. But every culture draws the line between the public and private spheres in different ways, regulating their respective scopes and dimensions as well as their juxtaposition and/or opposition.

Insights into historical variations might be the starting point for two further questions that have to do with the possible universality of the public sphere and the particularity of the private sphere. Everybody might be a participant in some overarching general system of communication and interaction, the modern concept (or fiction) of the so-called 'international community' constituting one extreme borderline. If we say 'everybody', this might, however, mean 'all members of one segment.' This would, from a formal, though not a functional point of view, have to be defined as a 'partial public sphere' as distinguished from the universal, i.e., '*the* public sphere'. Conversely, the term 'individual' might refer not only to a single person, but also to distinct groups (families, friends, clubs, colleagues, etc.), constituting public spheres by and through themselves. These spheres naturally claim to be differentiated from the external public sphere to such an extent that they might be considered to be private – be it due to secrecy, to their respective functions (through the fulfilment of exceptional roles), or to the insistence on one's own worth and dignity.

In terms of cultural history, the public and the private spheres, then, are not merely dimensions of communication and action to be confined and differentiated alternatively; they are also subject to different valuations. As can be illustrated through some (still very) hypothetically formulated aspects, there is a close relationship between such variable structures and the historical mechanisms of institutional phenomena. The higher the public sphere's estimate and standing, the more given institutions are forced to establish themselves within a public sphere and enhance the effect of their self-symbolisation accordingly. This may be a reason for symbolisations and representations to assume lives of their own, for their 'keeping up appearances', disengaged from the symbolised object, galvanising into the symbolisation of symbolisation. Enough examples for this process may be found within the culture of the aristocracy at the close of medieval times and at the beginning of the modern age. However, since a highly valued public sphere may not only be considered a realm of representation but also a critical authority or even a tribunal of some sort (which is to say that it has a claim upon power), symbols can also become scandalous or offensive, and institutions may be threatened as a direct result of their symbols. If flying a flag is a symbol of institutional sovereignty, an unhoisted flag may be considered a judgement of the public sphere (as evident in recent incidents concerning the English royal family).

On the other hand, the foremost goal of some institutions is to evade the public sphere altogether. Thus, their symbolisations are meant to communicate the cultural significance of the non-public sphere versus the public sphere. This may be illustrated by looking at the history of abbeys and religious orders, which have accommodated the exchange between the internal and external only because they sharply distinguish between both as a matter of principle.

As a rule, however, each institution develops its own public sphere, so that self-symbolisations are equally intended to have an internal effect. Additionally, the ability of institutions to create order causes them to organise their internal public sphere, to provide it with representative forms, and to transform their normative authority into concrete powers of execution. Early European examples are the heads of the religious orders, the synods of the church, and municipal parliaments.

Since it is institutional, such a public sphere is clearly separated from its equally public surrounding sphere; it is also frequently isolated and explicitly referred to as a 'partial' public sphere. This, however, does not mean that institutions principally tend to confine the public sphere as much as possible to narrow and exclusive limits and to leave it at that; on the contrary, they often attempt to monopolise the public sphere. This can lead to an attempt to propagate an institutional, as well as a veritable hermetic 'partial' public sphere, as an articulation of the public sphere as such. Political parties in totalitarian regimes testify to such an attempt.

One may also consider the problem from another point of view: does the public sphere also crystallise into institutional forms when it is understood (by those acting from within) not as a 'partial' public sphere but as a universal one? If one takes the potential of self-symbolisation as a measure, one encounters institutional phenomena such as symbolic acclamations firmly established through the 'people' in electoral rituals. For example, during the middle ages and early modern times, there were ritualised processions in which an entire city participated, conceiving of itself as a universal public sphere. There is also the tradition of naming poet laureates, the symbolic code of which denoted the distinguishing institution of a public sphere embracing the entire cultural domain. These examples also show paradigmatic differences between conceptions of the public sphere.

Certainly, institutions strongly recur to the public sphere just as, conversely, the public sphere recurs to institutions – though only briefly mentioned here and in need of further examination, this leads to the question as to where else the public and private spheres may intersect. Is the private the niche in which to escape from the power of institutions, obtainable only through the asociality of all things secret, intimate and anachoretic, or is it reachable only by means of the deceptive autism of the interior? (Called the *domus interior* by a twelfth century monk in self-reflection, who knew very well to what extent such 'deceptive autism' had been conditioned by institutionalised codes of conduct.) If this is the case, the private sphere should be able to do without the self-symbolisation that is typical of institutions. On the other hand, many examples may be found for symbolic visualisations of the invisibility of the interior (such as clothing for mourning and repentance), or of the secret domain (e.g., the curtain of the confessional) as well as for emblematic embodiments of demands for respective values of cultural validity (such as the 'fathers' in the 'desert'). These examples enable one to recognise levels of symbolic transcendence which seem to be analogous to that of the institutions. If the private sphere must always come to terms with the public sphere, it can only do so if the private sphere provides itself with institutional forms (or at least pretends to have them) so that it can compete with public sphere orientated institutions.

SUGGESTED READING

Melville, Gert, ed. (1992). *Institutionen und Geschichte: Theoretische Aspekte und mittelalterliche Befunde*. Cologne: Böhlau.

________ (2001). *Institutionalität und Symbolisierung: Verstetigungen kultureller Ordnungsmuster in Vergangenheit und Gegenwart*. Cologne: Böhlau.

Rehberg, Karl-Siegbert (1994). 'Institutionen als symbolische Ordnungen: Leitfragen und Grundkategorien zur Theorie und Analyse institutioneller Mechanismen.' In Gerhard Göhler (ed.), *Die Eigenart der Institutionen: Zum Profil politischer Institutionentheorie*. Baden-Baden: Nomos, 47-76.

________ (1995). 'Die "Öffentlichkeit" der Institutionen: Grundbegriffliche Überlegungen im Rahmen der Theorie und Analyse institutioneller Mechanismen.' In Gerhard Göhler (ed.), *Macht der Öffentlichkeit – Öffentlichkeit der Macht*. Baden-Baden: Nomos, 181-211.

Peter Uwe Hohendahl

The Theory of the Public Sphere Revisited

Books, as we all know, have their own fate, sometimes quite independent of their authors. This is certainly true of Horkheimer and Adorno's *Dialektik der Aufklärung*, a study that was largely ignored when it was published in 1947. It took almost two decades before the work had its full impact on the German reading public, and another decade before it received serious attention in the English-speaking world. Jürgen Habermas' *Strukturwandel der Öffentlichkeit*, first published in 1962, needed less time to influence the critical discussion in Germany, but it arrived in the English-speaking world only with considerable delay. Almost three decades had passed when the translation was finally published. At that point, the book's author had significantly changed his position and was clearly reluctant to identify with his early work, which was built on theoretical foundations that he later rejected. This did not stop the rise of an intensive as well as extensive discussion of the text in the United States and other English-speaking countries. The controversial reception can be taken as a clear indication that the text had not lost its appeal for a new generation of readers. Habermas himself has observed this impact with some surprise and resistance, since he is convinced that an appropriate theory of the public sphere would have to be constructed in a different fashion now. It seems that these hesitations have not influenced the reception of the book as much as one might expect. *Strukturwandel* has remained at the centre of the discussion about the public sphere. For this reason, any reassessment of the theory of the public sphere not only has to begin with Habermas' seminal text, but also has to come back to it through its various appropriations. To put it differently, the fact that the work has been severely criticised, even attacked from a variety of positions, has not undermined its attraction for readers in fields as diverse as musicology, anthropology, history, and political science.

Yet, my discussion will not so much focus on its reception than on the development of the theory of the public sphere from the 1960s to the present. While this book is devoted mostly to the English public sphere of the seventeenth and eighteenth centuries, my remarks will concentrate on the structure and evolution of the theory with only occasional references to the specific historical situation in England, an area that is, for the most part, outside of my own expertise. Of course, Habermas himself dealt rather extensively with the European Enlightenment, including the English Enlightenment, but, in the final analysis, the trajectory of his discussion was determined by systematic concerns for which the eighteenth century provided the best examples. In his historical schema, the eighteenth century furnishes the basis for the development of the modern public sphere, which he differentiates very carefully from both the ancient world and the Middle Ages. Yet, it is precisely this normative aspect of his initial theory, his way of merging particular historical patterns and systematic as well as normative questions that have been for the most part rejected by more recent historical research. It seems to me that social and cultural historians have sometimes misunderstood Habermas' approach to the eighteenth century because they disregarded the larger structure of Habermas' theory and, in particular, the political agenda which grew out of the political problems of the 1950s in the Federal Republic of Germany. They mistook for an historical account what was meant as a normative intervention. I will touch on the historical issues only insofar that they are linked to the more fundamental theoretical problems of Habermas' position.

Because of limited space, I will present my findings in the form of a number of points rather than a more elaborate narrative. The first point will summarise and clarify the structure of Habermas' theory; the second thesis will then focus on a particular important aspect of this theory, namely, the tension between its normative and its historical claims. The third thesis will take up shifts in emphasis that occurred during the 1970s and 1980s, first under the aegis of a more orthodox Marxist approach and later in the context of studies on ethnic and gender differences. My final remarks will return to the eighteenth century and try to make sense of the changes that have occurred in the more recent international debate. The present discussion – and Habermas would be the first one to admit this – has moved far beyond the narrative that he presented in 1962; at the same time, the presence of his theory can still be strongly felt, especially when it is explicitly or implicitly critiqued. While feminists such as Joan Landes (1988) and Isabel Hull (1996) have launched their own projects in clear opposition to and confrontation with *Strukturwandel*, at a deeper level, their own work still bears the mark of Habermasian theory.

In my first thesis I will argue that *Strukturwandel* has remained a relevant part of the present understanding of the public sphere, although the work strikes the contemporary reader as outdated and limited in scope in many ways. This assessment would be shared, by the way, by the author himself, who expressed in a new introduction to the 1990 German edition that he was no longer able to identify with parts of his work and was aware that many changes would be necessary to update the theory (Habermas 1990). When we look back at *Strukturwandel* from the distance of almost forty years, it is relatively easy to recognise the historical embeddedness of the work, the way it grew out of and reacted to specific political and cultural conditions in West Germany during the late fifties. Habermas' theory responded to the still uncertain status of democracy in the Federal Republic. While the formal elements – the institutions and procedures – were operative, there was still a suspicion that the commitment of the population to democracy might be relatively weak. Empirical studies that Habermas had been involved with indicated that an emphatic understanding of political participation remained underdeveloped. The plans of the government for *Notstandsgesetze* that would curtail individual freedom could be seen as an indication that older authoritarian traditions continued to influence the political culture of the Federal Republic.

I want to argue that Habermas' inquiry was motivated by these concerns, that is to say, by the lack of an effective public sphere in which political participation would occur through discussions outside the formal channels of parliament. Put differently, the history of the European public sphere that dominates the narrative of the book is the result of a critical question rather than the beginning of the thought process. The point of the investigation was the analysis of the decline of the public sphere, the analysis of the reasons why contemporary societies in the West are unable to live up to the standards of a fully developed democracy. Unlike the later Habermas, who would have chosen a systematic approach, the early Habermas, in part under the influence of his own teachers, looked for a historically-grounded theory. The notion of the decline of the public sphere contained the conception of a historical process that would move from an ideal situation to a deficient one.

In the choice of this perspective, Habermas was stimulated as well as provoked by three texts that shared this approach, although they otherwise maintained very different positions. The obvious ones were Hannah Arendt's *The Human Condition* of 1958 and Reinhart Koselleck's *Kritik und Krise* of 1959; the less obvious text was, in other respects, the most important one; namely, Horkheimer and Adorno's *Dialektik der Aufklärung* of 1947. At the centre of these texts was the analysis of a loss. Arendt's loss of the public sphere, Koselleck's loss of the authority of the state as a wall against chaos, and the loss of reason (*Vernunft*) in *Dialektik der Aufklärung*. Hence, *Strukturwandel* has to be understood as a triple critique. Habermas struggled both with Arendt's concept of the public sphere and with Koselleck's understanding of the process of critique in the eighteenth century. Finally, he had to come to terms with the pessimism of his own teachers concerning the future of Western democracy.

The genesis of Habermas' own theory was clearly influenced by his predecessors, although he did not share their positions. Arendt's attempt to use the public sphere of the Greek *polis* as a model for democratic equality and participation had the disadvantage that it could be applied to the modern world only in a mode of negation. Her critique of the social as a specifically modern phenomenon that undermined the old divide between the public and the private realm could not provide a useful conceptual apparatus for the modern and contemporary world. In this respect, Koselleck's treatment of the process of critique from the late seventeenth to the late eighteenth century, culminating in the French Revolution, was much closer to Habermas' project, although he could not agree with Koselleck's conclusions. Koselleck emphasised the dangers of the enlightenment as the first phase of modernity, leading to the catastrophe of Fascism and Communism as the logical extensions of the Enlightenment. Of course, this line of argument was precisely the position that Habermas wanted to contest. In this respect, Koselleck was the unacknowledged opponent, the neo-conservative who was more interested in the strength of the state than in democratic participation. Still, Habermas could and did appropriate much of Koselleck's historical interpretation of the eighteenth century, in particular, the notion of critique, which reappears as the concept of a critical public sphere. Of course, Habermas' theory reverses the evaluation of the development: where Koselleck saw an increased politicisation leading to hypocrisy, Habermas observed the possibility of emancipation. It is not accidental, therefore, that his treatment of the Enlightenment culminates in his reading of Kant's political writings. By comparison, Hegel and Marx are already seen as critics of the bourgeois public sphere that Kant elaborated.

The much-debated emphasis on the Enlightenment in *Strukturwandel* with a tendency to foreground the bourgeois public sphere is not only the result of Habermas' opposition to Koselleck but also of his struggle with Horkheimer and Adorno. Habermas basically rejected their critique of the historical Enlightenment as necessarily involved in destruction of *Vernunft*. This resistance was motivated by his assessment of the present and his quest for grounding a theory of a critical public sphere in 1962. Kant served as the locus for a normative understanding of the public sphere that would allow Habermas to offer a critical assessment of the present.

It is precisely this tension between the historical analysis of the public sphere on the one hand, and a normative reading of the public sphere on the other, that has kept *Strukturwandel* alive and controversial. Without the normative element, as much as it was criticised by several generations of readers, the book would no longer be part of the present debate. One might put it this way: without the flaw, the book would have been considered as an outdated historical narrative because it lacks refinement and differentiation of its historical categories. The intertwinement of a normative and a historical approach has significantly contributed to the later discussion and the formulation of competing theories.

The continued presence of Habermas in the contemporary public sphere discussion is due to a complex process of reception in which certain themes are rediscovered by different groups of readers. The tension between the historical model and the normative understanding, which was at the centre of the German debate of the 1970s, resurfaced in the American debate of the 1990s, a debate that was not at all connected to the earlier German discussion. Thus, my second thesis can be formulated in the following manner: the history-norm polarity of the original project is an inevitable structural element of a theory of the public sphere that intends to go beyond mere description on the one hand and abstract normative statements on the other. The link between both aspects could be severed only at the expense of a substantive, content-oriented understanding of the public sphere. Luhmann's treatment would be such a restructuring, since he denies the need for a normative concept of the public sphere in a modern, highly-differentiated society that has its internal steering mechanisms (Luhmann 1970). While the later Habermas will acknowledge such steering mechanisms that are independent of communicative action, he will still insist on the need for a civil society with an effective public sphere. He will continue to insist, in other words, on the normative aspect while admitting at the same time that the way in which he dealt with this problem in *Strukturwandel* was not satisfactory.

Briefly put, the early solution left Habermas with two problems. First, given the historical account he had presented, he could not offer a strong reason why the decline of the public sphere could be reversed. Second, by looking back at the development of the public sphere between the eighteenth and the twentieth centuries, he could not help favouring the early period when the public sphere was rising. This led to the idealisation of the bourgeois public sphere, a feature of his theory that was severely criticised by a number of different camps. Yet, in many instances the cause was not fully appreciated. Habermas was, by all means, aware of the ideological nature of the existing eighteenth-century bourgeois public sphere; what mattered to him were the advances in the formation of the theory, for instance, in the work of Rousseau, Diderot, and Kant. These normative advances could be used for the defence of a normative contemporary public sphere. This was crucial for Habermas because his *historical* trajectory did not allow for an abstract normative outlook. The decline of the public sphere, Habermas had argued, was tied to the transformation of capitalism in the nineteenth century, namely, the emergence of organised capitalism. The question of property took on a new meaning. Given the persistence of advanced capitalism in the 1960s, it was difficult to argue, at least within a materialist conception of history, that a revival of a strong public sphere should be possible. This, of course, was the conclusion that Horkheimer and Adorno had already drawn, a conclusion that Habermas found unsatisfactory for political reasons.

This brings me to my third point. The tension between the normative and the historical-empirical understanding of the public sphere could be resolved either by giving up the normative element or by abstracting the concept of the public sphere from its embeddedness in a lifeworld that is concrete and historically specific. The critique of Oskar Negt and Alexander Kluge in their *Öffentlichkeit und Erfahrung* of 1972 emphasised the materialist and historical underpinnings of the public sphere. In this context, the concept loses the autonomy that Habermas wanted it to gain, and becomes re-attached to the development of social and economic history. As a result, the idea of a normative core in such a manner that any idea of a normative core that can be saved from an earlier historical formation became completely futile. For Negt and Kluge, Habermas' emphasis on the public sphere of the eighteenth century was indeed no more than ideology. By insisting on a materialist understanding of history, they eliminated the very possibility of an abstract normative concept of the public sphere. The public sphere was treated as an epi-phenomenon that is dependent on the relations of production. It is noteworthy that Negt and Kluge, anticipating later critics, introduced the notion of different public spheres. Not only did they distinguish the bourgeois and the proletarian public sphere, they also introduced the concept of a public sphere of production, the media public sphere, the public sphere of the state, etc. In short, Negt and Kluge deliberately destroyed the idea of a unified public sphere, the notion of a locus for unrestrained communication and action. Ultimately, it is no longer clear why the book is at all organised around the concept of the public sphere, a concept that is denied both normative and historical validity. Yet, at the same time, their concept of the proletarian public sphere included the same contradiction they criticised in Habermas, since it contains a utopian moment that did not and could not materialise in the actual history of the working class.

Most of Habermas' critics did not go that far. They attacked the normative fixation of Habermas and frequently called for a more differentiated picture of the historical development from the eighteenth to the twentieth century without necessarily focusing on the normative aspect. In fact, in some instances the Habermasian dilemma is reproduced in a different form. Much of the feminist criticism that takes Habermas to task for his blindness to the gendered nature of the European public sphere introduces its own idealised feminist public sphere that is then imposed on the reading of history. Motivated by ethical and political concerns, this move reproduces the fundamental contradiction of Habermasian theory. Joan B. Landes' critique of Habermas' conception of the bourgeois public sphere in her study *Women and the Public Sphere in the Age of the French Revolution* (1988), for example, relies on a strong normative notion of a critical public sphere that can be turned against any exclusionary model of publicity. The ethical and political force of the argument that the modern public sphere, as it was introduced in the French Revolution, excluded women depends on a concept of the public sphere that stresses universal access as a fundamental requirement. A strictly descriptive approach would have noted the tension between the universal claims of the revolutionaries, on the one hand, and the exclusion of women, on the other, without attaching an ethical or political evaluation to this assessment. Despite her critique, Landes shares with Habermas an evolutionary understanding of modern history that contains the possibility of emancipation as well as the idea of a fully-developed public sphere which allows for universal access.

The Habermasian dilemma could be resolved in the context of a different theoretical model. This would entail a form of translation and re-coding that would transfer the concept of the public sphere into a different theoretical environment. Geoff Eley's essay 'Nations, Publics, and Political Cultures' (1992) can be understood as such an attempt. While acknowledging Habermas' historical and theoretical advances, he looks at the problematic from the perspective of Gramscian Marxism, thereby arriving at rather different conclusions in his assessment of the nineteenth century. While the details of the essay do not matter for my argument, Eley's response to Habermas' normative reading does. Eley is suspicious of the implicit idealisation of the public sphere in Habermas' theory and wants to replace it with a clearly materialist understanding. For this purpose, he draws on Gramsci's concept of the civil society and, in particular, on the notion of hegemony. Like Habermas, he distinguishes between the state and the public sphere, but he redirects our attention from the idea of publicness to the concept of hegemony as a way of describing power relations between classes. What interests him is the effect of hegemony as a non-coercive form of political domination that works through the institutions of civil society rather than the state. By equating civil society and the public sphere, Eley arrives at a definition of the public sphere which has radically eliminated all normative aspects that were crucial to Habermas. A materialist reading of social history turns the public sphere into a battlefield for the class struggle.

Eley's critique touches on another aspect of theorising the public sphere as well. Working initially with the German concept of *Öffentlichkeit*, that is, publicness, Habermas approached the public sphere as an abstract idea that would materialise itself historically in the eighteenth century as part of the rising bourgeois society. Although he was aware that the notion of a unified *Öffentlichkeit* did not do justice even to the developments of the eighteenth century, he treated other forms, such as the plebeian public sphere, as subaltern and dependent on the hegemonic bourgeois public sphere. Clearly, this preference was connected with the normative aspect of the public sphere and the political interest in reviving a democratic political culture. I suspect that his assessment of the political configuration of the Federal Republic of Germany during the late fifties narrowed his vision of possible alternatives and reinforced the ideal of an abstract public sphere. On the whole, Habermas has been severely criticised for this position. This critique began with the intervention of Negt and Kluge, who developed a strong case for the existence of a proletarian counter-public sphere that emerged in the late eighteenth century and unfolded during the nineteenth century together with the proletariat as a competing and oppositional class. It is noteworthy that Negt and Kluge did not perceive the public sphere as a space that had to be shared by competing classes but, rather, as distinct spheres in which communication took place primarily among members of the same class. In the more recent discussion, similar tendencies can be observed either with respect to questions of gender or with regard to problems of race and ethnicity. While Negt and Kluge's study clearly did not favour identity politics (in fact, the authors were rather critical of proletarian attempts to develop forms of identity politics through proletarian subcultures), the emphatic concept of a proletarian public sphere they employed opened up the methodological space for a re-conceptualisation of the public sphere, namely, as a plurality of public spheres that are distinct from each other. Their relationship may be that of complete separation, of partial overlap, of competition, of mutual dependence or of domination and dependence. Each of these possibilities would be, of course, the result of specific historical situations and particular social constellations. It goes without saying that this re-configuration of the theory brought to the fore the concept of power that Habermas had treated as a marginal element and that should be absent from the ideal public sphere. Its presence would be an index of structural problems, as Habermas elaborated in the second half of *Strukturwandel.*

The feminist critique of Habermas has consistently emphasised the hidden element of power relations in the bourgeois public sphere, i.e., the historical domination of men over women. Landes, for instance, pointed to the exclusion of women at the very moment when the ideal of universal access became operative during the French Revolution. The critique of the bourgeois public sphere as gender and unequal went hand in hand with the discovery of separate spaces in which women developed their own forms of publicises. Mary R. Ryan's work on women's politics in nineteenth-century America should be mentioned as a prominent example (1990; 1992). On the whole, feminists have resisted the concept of a unified public sphere as ideological and politically fraught with dangers. The same can be said about the discussion of race and ethnicity. In a recent essay, Michael Dawson (1994) makes it quite clear that the possibility of a black identity in the United States is closely connected with the existence of a separate, strong, and independent public sphere for the Afro-American community.

Especially in the United States and Canada, identity politics of the eighties and nineties has favoured an understanding of the public sphere as pluralistic, open-ended, fluid, and as a space where subaltern groups strive for recognition. If dominant forms of the public sphere have been acknowledged, they have been those of the mass media and the government. In other words, the contrast between public sphere and publicness resurfaces as a way of resisting the interference of the capitalist market and the power of the Federal Government. Identity politics has certainly changed the theoretical perception as well. In particular, it has undermined the Habermasian idea of a universal ethical and political program that grounded the concept of a public sphere. While the early Habermas still relied on the concept of totality and the idea of historical development, a notion that would allow him to narrate the rise and fall of the public sphere, the debate of the nineties focused on the particular, that is, specific problems in specific environments in which the concept of the public sphere would be deployed to describe the space in which the struggle takes place. But the question remains: can the idea of the universal be dismissed out of hand and has the idea of publicness as a space for communication in a civil society lost its relevance? In this respect, Habermas has defended his position, while he has modified his original design in the introduction to the eighteenth edition of *Strukturwandel* as well as in more recent publications, such as *Faktizität und Geltung* (1992).

The plurality and heterogeneity of the public sphere that most critics emphasised when they dealt with Habermas were not at the centre of the author's self-critique. Rather, the possibility of such a modification, which he freely acknowledged, grew out of his retreat from the approach of his own teachers, that is, a retreat from a Marxist-Hegelian philosophy of history that had provided him with a notion of social totality as well as the conception of a logical and necessary process of historical progress. The switch to a linguistic grounding of the public sphere via speech-act theory, as it was fully developed in the *Theorie der kommunikativen Handelns* (1981), allowed Habermas to de-emphasise the historical significance of the bourgeois public sphere and, at the same time, to take into consideration the possibility of competing public spheres during the eighteenth and nineteenth centuries. In the final analysis, however, Habermas' revisions foreground, even more than in his early study, the normative aspect of the public sphere in the contemporary situation. In other words, he holds on to the core assumptions of his first book. This means that the search for a radical democratic society is pursued, as before, in universal terms, but now the historical narrative does not claim universality for the bourgeois public sphere anymore. Looking at the work of Günther Lottes (1979) and others, Habermas concedes that the emergence of a civil society in the eighteenth century contained from the very beginning the struggle between different public spheres, among them the plebeian one.

This has become the underlying assumption of the more recent international discussion, in most cases, without awareness of Habermas' revisions. The notion of a unified public sphere with a strong normative emphasis has been replaced by a considerably more differentiated narrative in which the heterogeneity of competing public spheres is brought out. By the same token, the initial interest in a normative concept of the public sphere is clearly less present in more recent historical scholarship. It has found its place in political theory where the debate over the significance and meaning of the public sphere continues, both in Europe and in America. It may suffice to refer to the work of Nancy Fraser (1992), Sheila Benhabib (1995), Max Pensky (1999), and William Scheuerman (1999) to mark the direction of the discussion. What they share is a keen interest in the development of new decentralised forms of democracy. In this debate, the Habermasian position is still important, although by no means the unquestioned standard. Historical research, on the other hand, has loosened the conceptual and methodological ties to the Frankfurt

School. Here, Gramsci's concepts of civil society and hegemony offered interesting alternatives, as Geoff Eley has suggested. Furthermore, while Foucaultians would not get excited about notions of emancipation and liberation, they could and did pick up on the question of inclusion and exclusion of groups such as women or minorities, as one can see in the work of Landes, Fraser, and Benhabib.

This brings me to my final question: how useful is the concept of the public sphere for the examination of the eighteenth century? Disagreement with Habermas' original or revised position does not, of course, eliminate the analysis of the actual historical processes. In this respect, I want to distinguish two levels. The first refers to the term and the concept of the public sphere. This kind of research is concerned with the examination of the history of the term or related terms and, in a broader sense, with the unfolding of the concept in the discourse of the eighteenth century. The second level pertains to the use of the concept as a historical paradigm for the investigation of the relationship between state and society. The first kind of research operates with the tools of philology and conceptual history (*Begriffsgeschichte*); the second is involved in semantic problems of political as well as of social and cultural history. Although, typically, historians are engaged on both levels, the distinction is still valuable since it allows us to differentiate the nature of specific claims.

I want to look at two examples to illustrate my point. The first is taken from French history; the second one is concerned with German history. The work of the American historian Keith Baker has focused on those trends and processes in French history that would ultimately result in the Great Revolution of 1789 (1987; 1992). In this larger context, the development of the public sphere in France plays a significant role. Baker understands his contribution as a correction of Habermas' reading of the Enlightenment, but also as an affirmation of his basic parameters. Thus, he claims that Habermas underestimates the modernity of eighteenth-century France (compared to England) and, furthermore, that Habermas does not fully appreciate the intertwinement between the state and the public sphere. This correction is based on two different kinds of interrogations. First, Baker wants to show that the term and the concept of the public sphere were used in a variety of settings and could therefore not be synthesised as easily as Habermas assumed. Second, he stresses the participation of important state officials in the discussion about the meaning and relevance of the public sphere. The second point is supposed to undermine the fundamental distinction between the state and the public sphere in Habermas' theory. Here, the point of reference is clearly the political structure of France at the end of the eighteenth century rather than the term and the concept of the public sphere. Still, for Baker, both levels must be involved in a full examination of the public sphere. Like Habermas before him, he is convinced that the public sphere is a structurally relevant category of analysis.

My second case is Isabel Hull's study *Sexuality, State, and Civil Society in Germany, 1700-1815* (1996). Her disagreement with Habermas is more fundamental than that of Baker. She argues that the concept of the public sphere is ultimately not a particularly suitable tool for an examination of the changes that occurred in the late eighteenth century since the idea of a public sphere remains at the discursive level without a firm grasp of the structural base. Therefore, she suggests discussing the changing relationship between the state and the activities of the citizens under the category of 'civil society'. Privileging the second level, she argues, in other words, that there is no clear historical referent to the term 'public sphere', although she is, of course, aware of the fact that the term '*Öffentlichkeit*' was used in Germany from the 1760s on. Her critique focuses on what she calls the ahistorical nature of Habermas' conceptual apparatus that 'make[s] his concept of the "public sphere" misleading for the late eighteenth century' (Hull 1996, 204). She continues,

> Three problems are especially grave for our concerns: the too narrowly economic understanding of civil society, the mistaken notion of the (developing) conception of 'private' and its relation to the state or common good, and the too idealized picture of the actual functioning of Enlightened discussion (Öffentlichkeit). (Ibid.)

I will not take up the difficult question as to what extent Hull may have misunderstood Habermas' theory; her main point is the assertion that the strict Habermasian distinction between state and civil society does not reflect the actual debate of the eighteenth century. In the final analysis, her argument is structural rather than '*begriffsgeschichtlich*', although conceptual history plays a limited role in her claim. For Hull's study, the concept of the public sphere is no longer central; instead, it has been replaced by the concept of civil society, a change that some of Habermas' associates, among them Andrew Arato and Jean Cohen (1992), had already suggested in the 1980s when they examined democratic movements in the Eastern Bloc. What is interesting about Hull's approach is her methodological claim that a theory of the public sphere is ultimately not useful for the practising historian because it is ahistorical. This is, of course, a familiar trope. Yet we have to note that her own choice, namely, the use of the concept of civil society as the central category for her analysis, faces similar objections, since, as much as she brings it down to the level of the sources, it also remains abstract *vis-à-vis* the particular historical moment under discussion.

It would have been more fruitful to pose the question in a different way: Is it possible to develop a theory of the public sphere on the basis of the eighteenth-century discourse as it actually occurred in England or Germany – a theory that remains close enough to the material to guide the analysis of the actual social and cultural transformations? I believe that a reconstruction of the discourse is possible; the real challenge would be the connection of this work with the structural level. A number of Habermas' bold original claims would have to be discarded or revised as Habermas realised when he took stock in 1989. However, for historical work, I believe, the public sphere is still an important and useful heuristic category. The fact that its use is now more detached from the current political debate than a generation ago is probably an advantage in methodological terms. We would be less inclined to invoke the eighteenth century as a standard for political ideals than three decades ago. At the same time, there is a potential danger to this methodological refinement, namely the risk of a historicist attitude that has cut itself off from the present. Ultimately the historical debate and the current discussion have to remain in dialogue in order to produce fruitful conclusions.

REFERENCES

Adorno, Theodor W., and Max Horkheimer (1947). *Dialektik der Aufklärung: Philosophische Fragmente*. Amsterdam: Querido.

Arato, Andrew, and Jean Cohen (1992). *Civil Society and Political Theory*. Cambridge, MA: MIT Press.

Arendt, Hannah (1958). *The Human Condition*. Chicago: University of Chicago Press.

Baker, Keith Michael (1992). 'Defining the Public Sphere in Eighteenth-Century France: Variations on a Theme by Habermas.' In Craig Calhoun (ed.), *Habermas and the Public Sphere*. Cambridge, MA: MIT Press, 181-211.

________, ed. (1987). *The French Revolution and the Creation of Modern Political Culture*. Vol. 1: *The Political Culture of the Old Regime*. New York: Pergamon Press.

Benhabib, Seyla (1995). *Feminist Contentions: A Philosophical Exchange*. New York: Routledge.

Dawson, Michael C. (1994). *Behind the Mule: Race and Class in African-American Politics*. Princeton: Princeton University Press.

Eley, Geoff (1992). 'Nations, Publics, and Political Cultures: Placing Habermas in the Nineteenth Century.' In Craig Calhoun (ed.), *Habermas and the Public Sphere*. Cambridge, MA: MIT Press, 289-339.

Fraser, Nancy (1992). 'Rethinking the Public Sphere: A Contribution to the Critique of Actually Existing Democracies.' In Craig Calhoun (ed.), *Habermas and the Public Sphere*. Cambridge, MA: MIT Press, 109-142.

Habermas, Jürgen (1981). *Theorie der kommunikativen Handelns*. 2 vols. Frankfurt/Main: Suhrkamp.

________ (1990). *Strukturwandel der Öffentlichkeit: Untersuchungen zu einer Kategorie der bürgerlichen Gesellschaft*. Frankfurt/Main: Suhrkamp. Original edition 1962.

________ (1992). *Faktizität und Geltung: Beiträge zur Diskurstheorie des Rechts und des demokratischen Rechtsstaats*. Frankfurt/Main: Suhrkamp.

Hull, Isabel (1996). *Sexuality, State, and Civil Society in Germany, 1700-1815*. Ithaca: Cornell University Press.

Koselleck, Reinhart (1973). *Kritik und Krise: Eine Studie zur Pathogenese der bürgerlichen Welt*. Frankfurt/Main: Suhrkamp. Original edition 1959.

Landes, Joan B. (1988). *Women and the Public Sphere in the Age of the French Revolution*. Ithaca: Cornell University Press.

Lottes, Günther (1979). *Politische Aufklärung und plebejisches Publikum: Zur Theorie und Praxis des englischen Radikalismus im späten 18. Jahrhundert*. Munich: Oldenbourg.

Luhmann, Niklas (1970). 'Öffentliche Meinung.' *Politische Vierteljahrsschrift* 11, 2-28.

Negt, Oskar, and Alexander Kluge (1972). *Öffentlichkeit und Erfahrung: Zur Organisationsanalyse von bürgerlicher und proletarischer Öffentlichkeit*. Frankfurt/Main: Suhrkamp.

Pensky, Max (1999). 'Jürger Habermas and the Antinomies of the Intellectual.' In Peter Dews (ed.), *Habermas: A Critical Reader*. Oxford: Blackwell, 211-240.

Ryan, Mary P. (1990). *Women in Public: Between Banners and Ballots, 1725-1880*. Baltimore: Johns Hopkins University Press.

________ (1992). 'Gender and Public Access: Women's Politics in Nineteenth-Century America.' In Craig Calhoun (ed.), *Habermas and the Public Sphere*. Cambridge, MA: MIT Press, 259-288.

Scheuerman, William S. (1999). 'Between Radicalism and Resignation: Democratic Theory in Habermas's *Between Facts and Norms*.' In Peter Dews (ed.), *Habermas: A Critical Reader*. Oxford: Blackwell, 153-177.

Jürgen Schlaeger

A Reckoning without the Host: Public and Private Spheres in the Eighteenth Century

In most studies about the origin and development of the public sphere and of public opinion in England and, indeed, in the bourgeois western world at large, Locke's famous definition of the 'law of opinion or reputation' as based on the 'consent of private men' justly plays a prominent role. Locke gives this definition in Book 2, Chapter 28 of his *Essay Concerning Human Understanding* under the heading 'Of Other Relations' as if this was a mere afterthought or footnote to the much more important relations of cause and effect, identity and diversity which he had discussed before. This is not, however, what he intended in the overall architecture of his argument: the 'law of opinion' is to hold a place very similar to those other more straightforwardly logical constructs. He is also at pains to convince his readers that this third law earns its place next to divine and to civil law, and is in no way inferior to them in its effectiveness. Locke's arguments are:

> 7. The laws that men generally refer their actions to, to judge of their rectitude or obliquity, seem to me to be these three: (1) The *divine* law. (2) The *civil* law. (3) The law of opinion or reputation, if I may so call it. [...]
>
> 12. If anyone shall imagine that I have forgot my own notion of a law when I make *the law* whereby men judge *of virtue* and *vice* to be nothing else but the consent of private men, who have not authority enough to make a law, especially wanting that which is so necessary and essential to a law, a power to enforce it: I think I may say that he who imagines commendation and disgrace not to be strong motives on men to accommodate themselves to the opinions and rules of those with whom they converse seems little skilled in the nature or history of mankind [...]. (Locke 1961, 1: 296, 300)

If we ask why Locke is so desperate to establish such a logically rather tenuous and institutionally weak law, we will find the answer in his desire to provide a philosophical justification for the constitutional settlement of the Glorious Revolution and the Whig version of history. Against Hobbes who had set the state, the Church, and absolute power against human nature because the animal in man was too strong to be trusted ('*homo homini lupus*'; see Hobbes 1999), Locke reconstructed the relationship between the individual, on the one hand, and the institutions and the moral rules which have to govern society as a close co-operation on the other, as a result of a consensus in the building of which every individual had a say. Private and public were thus ideologically constructed as essentially in harmony. They have a mutual claim upon each other. Society is seen as a self-regulating closed circle of ideally perfect co-operation of the individual and society, of private and public in all matters of morality. The obvious question to ask here is what are the costs of such an ideological construct, what is excluded to make it work? The answer I would like to give is indicated in the title of my paper.

Locke made the reckoning without the host. The bills which he is unable or unwilling to pay are continually presented in the process of modernisation, and Western bourgeois societies are continually under pressure to settle them not only with ever more sophisticated procedures for building a 'consent of private men' but also with ever more encompassing strategies of exclusion and repression. Thus, the undeniable success of the Lockean construction of the relationship between private and public in modern and liberal democracies depends heavily on disciplinary measures taken against the dark and dangerous forces threatening to break the consensus from inside.

Groundbreaking theoretical and historical work on the role of public opinion and the power of censure, on the structure of the public sphere, and on the social and philosophical conditions in which the concept of public opinion arose have been done by Koselleck (1959) and Habermas (1962; and 1991). Recent studies – while acknowledging Koselleck's and Habermas' valuable contributions to this field – have also highlighted some of their shortcomings (Calhoun 1997). They have pointed out that their presentation of the historical developments, particularly in England, was often too narrow; that both have overlooked the importance of religious controversies before, during and after the Civil War. But these are minor flaws in my view. What is more serious is that they pay for the consistency of their arguments in the historical reconstruction and sociological theorising with a simplified psychology. They simply take for granted that the public-private relationship and the development of it in the modern period not only worked but is also already the whole story. The fact that Habermas was criticised for his normative approach in as much as he described an ideal, a type, a prototype of what he thought should govern modern democratic and open societies rather than concentrated on an analysis of the historical specificities, is a case in point.

What I would like to do here is not to add to the array of such studies that have placed the origins of the idea of the public sphere and of the role of public opinion in it in a wider historical context or in relation to different bodies of discourses, or to studies that have given us insight into the material conditions on which it was predicated, including such diverse aspects as the spread of literacy, the increase of paper production and the rise of a market of newspapers and periodicals. Rather, I would like to get at Locke's hidden agenda, at the dynamics whose momentum he was trying to cover up by simply declaring that there is a convergence between the regulatory force society exerts and the voluntary participation of individuals in building and maintaining such a force.

Locke's formula and the individual-society dichotomy which evolved from it, obscures the fact that his category of private men is not only an artificial and ideological construct (private man as the propertied individual), but that it also excludes a large part of the psychological complexities with which western societies and the individuals in it had to come to terms after the dissolution and breakdown of the medieval world picture and its certainties.

I will carry forward my investigation in three steps. First, I would like to establish what is at stake with the advent of the modern world: not only did people perceive their world as 'out of joint' but they also had to look at themselves in radically new ways. This is, of course, a truism, but very often one of the most obvious consequences of this truism is overlooked, i.e., the fact that the dramatic opening of new horizons also involved an opening of a psychological Pandora's Box or, less metaphorically speaking, the fact that the growth of complexities of the outward world produced an equally or even more complex inner world, that outer world and inner self are mutually dependent, and that there is a growing consciousness of this problem and an almost frantic search for solutions and new stability – first in religion and then in a secularised rational conceptualisation of society and the role of the individual in it. And it is within this framework that we have to place and understand Locke's strategic equation between the law of opinion and the consent of private men. The equation is needed to accommodate what is actually a highly-dynamic dialectical process that is forever threatening to run out of control.

Second, I would like to demonstrate that this dynamic cannot be explained in terms of a public-private dichotomy, but requires a tripartite model of explanation. The 'public-private' duet has to be expanded into a trio: secret, private, public; or, if this is considered a still too-rigid construct, one can start from the hypothesis that the operation and success of the private-public partnership as stipulated by the theoreticians of modern democratic societies always has to spend a large part of its energy on controlling and repressing the dark forces that continually threatened it from the dark beyond in the shape of social unrest and psychological restlessness.

And finally, I would like to show that the law of censure was obviously not strong enough to keep the constant threat from the anarchic inner core, the powerful black hole of psychic complexity in the modern self within the field of public consent. The treatment of pornography in the eighteenth century by the law will serve as a case in point.

To my first point: the dynamics of private and public and the perception of it as new and promising as well as dangerous. Early modern man found himself radically dislodged from his traditional foothold in space and time and from the institutions into which he was born. Such dislocation involved a renegotiation of the borderlines between what was familiar and what was new. It also invariably sharpened the awareness of the difference between the self and the other, between one's own inside and the new outside world.

This double process had a double effect: neither the self nor the new versions of the world had it in themselves to accommodate this kind of complexity and provide the stability and security that was needed. The invasion and appropriation of the unknown was not a one-way process, no mere superimposition of a personal or collective world view on hitherto unknown aspects of the world and of the self, but it invariably led to a radical and unending rearrangement and reassessment of attitudes to the world and to the self. Consequently, exploring unknown worlds and exploring unknown dimensions of the self evolved as parallel activities (see Schlaeger 1999).

For evidence of this process, I would like to refer to the parallel application of the language of exploration in the description of maritime enterprises and in discourses about the inner self of man in the late sixteenth and early seventeenth centuries. In this period, both activities – external and internal exploration – were looked at as necessary and highly profitable invasions of unknown territories for which special strategies of mapping, analysis, control and exploitation had to be developed.

Thus, external expansion was paralleled with internal expansion, the assertion of discursive power over what was new out there was intimately bound up with the need to establish discursive control over the complexities of the inner self. It would not be entirely inappropriate to say that exploration and self-exploration, just as colonisation and self-colonisation, exploitation and self-exploitation, were two sides of the same coin in this period of Western history. Without this reciprocity the dynamics and the momentum of the developments in this crucial era of human history must remain a mystery.

If one shifts one's focus from the discourse of maritime exploration back to the broader perspective of the changes in the world picture and the concomitant changes in the perceptions and status of the self, it becomes obvious that more is at stake here than the fortunes of seafarers, merchant adventurers or troubled believers. Without a massive release of mental resources and a rearrangement of the psychic economy, the dramatic drive for new material resources and for knowledge of and power over them would remain inexplicable. From this vantage point, the frequent use of the same set of images for both external and internal exploration is not merely a matter of the metaphorical translation or transposition of one into the other. Rather, it implies mutually reinforcing strategies that have operated at the centre of cultural processes ever since the certainties of the medieval world picture collapsed. The perception of the parallelism between inside and outside is very often accompanied by a growing anxiety about what Young was later to call the 'stranger within thee' (Young 1965, 289).

To give just one example that is not only typical of such metaphorical transfer but also of the anxieties that accompanied it, I would like to take you back to the early seventeenth century. My example is taken from Daniel Dyke's popular treatise *The Mystery of Selfe-Deceiving*, published in 1614. Dyke had been educated in Sidney Sussex College, one of the intellectual centres of Puritanism in England. His puritanical background explains his obsession with the question of how to control the dark forces in the believer's self (Dyke 1614; see Schlaeger 1993).

Dyke's treatise is pervaded by phrases and images that point to a highly complex state of affairs. The excessively pictorial language, which is not exactly in line with the plain-style ideal which Puritans professed to use as evidence for their truthfulness, is a clear sign that the author is here moving on uncertain, unmapped ground. Two quotations may serve to illustrate this point. Dyke tries to come to grips with the evasiveness and threatening complexity of the early modern inner self in the following words: 'O ye many blind corners, the secret turnings and windings, the perplex labyrinths, the close lurking-holes that are here! ... So mysticall are these hearts of ours. So deepe and abstruse are [their] mysteries of deceit' (Dyke 1614, 7).

Such an unstable and dangerous inner state cannot be tolerated. For the sake of salvation – and, in a secularised phase of the development, for the sake of public order and social welfare – it has to be kept under constant surveillance. Therefore, Dyke categorically demands: 'Never then trust thou this heart of thine' (348).

It is therefore all the more important to become literate in these matters, i.e., to be able to discern the large variety of tricks and deceptions, the whispering voices and subtle temptations the inner self has in store. Learning how to discover them is tantamount to learning how to avoid them – and this is Dyke's ultimate pedagogic aim.

The treatise also reveals a growing anxiety about the risks of continual self-examination. To get this message across, Dyke used the image of an exploratory voyage, thus, linking the fascination and the horror of unknown territory with an uncensored vision of one's own dark depths:

> Well then, since the word is that *light which shineth in this darkness*, having it with us, venter we to descend downe into this deepe dungeon, and to launch out into this vast *Ocean*, having this plummet to sound the bottome thereof. *They that goe downe into the deepes*, saith the prophet, *they see the workes and wonders of the Lord.* But they that goe downe into this deepe are not now like to see any thing, but the *deepnesse of Sathan*, the workes and wonders of the Divel, the *Liviathan* that sporteth himself in these waters, or rather a *Neptune* triumphing here, as in his kingdome: [...]. (10)

If we remove the biblical rhetoric from this passage, we have a sort of early Freudian scenario of the inner self. Inside and outside are, as it were, two sides of the same coin.

In many religious tracts, conduct books, and spiritual autobiographies, the authors are obsessed with the fear that inside and outside may not be brought together, that control over one's conduct and control over one's innermost thoughts and feelings could not be achieved, that the innermost self would remain a constant source of anxiety and despair. Against this background, Locke's solution of declaring the law of opinion as the consent of private men provided the perfect secularised ideology for covering up the fact that perfect control could never be achieved. He simply sweeps a large part of the complexities, which the dramatic changes in the early modern world had produced, under the carpet of his streamlined ideal of the rational individual.

My second point is to demonstrate briefly that, with growing confidence and self-reliance, a sense of the darker forces in human nature grew stronger as well. Optimistic and pessimistic anthropologies went hand in hand. Dyke's picturesque and forceful description of that vast Ocean within is a good case in point. Sir Thomas Browne's characterisation of the 'Cosmography of my self' is another one: 'we carry with us the wonders, we seeke without us: There is all Africa, and her prodigies in us' (Browne 1984, 78).

The Africa of the self is dark and propitious, threatening and promising at the same time. Equally telling is Bunyan's endlessly spiralling vacillation between hope and doubt in his *Grace Abounding*, in which he circumscribes the inner centre of his own self as a source of perpetual worry and anxiety until he finally reaches the *certitudo salutis* (see Schlaeger 1987).

Even such enlightenment prophets and representatives of the new middle-class ideals as Steele and Addison cannot but occasionally admit that there is much more than meets the eye when one takes a careful look at one's private self. Here is an example from Steele's *Tatler*, No. 172 of 16 May 1710:

> When a man is in a serious mood, and ponders upon his own make, with a retrospect to the actions of his life, and the many fatal miscarriages in it, which he owes to ungoverned passions, he is then apt to say to himself, that experience has guarded him against such errors for the future: but nature often recurs in spite of his best resolutions, and it is to the very end of our days a struggle between our reason and our temper, which shall have the empire over us.
>
> But however I have rambled on in this libertine manner of writing by way of essay, I now sat down with an intention to represent to my readers, how pernicious, how sudden, and how fatal surprises of passion are to the mind of man; and that in the more intimate commerces of life they are most liable to arise, even in our most sedate and indolent hours. Occurrences of this kind have had very terrible effects; and when one reflects upon them, we cannot but tremble to consider what we are capable of being wrought up to against all the ties of nature, love, honour, reason, and religion, though the man who breaks through them all, had, an hour before he did so, a lively and virtuous sense of their dictates. (Aitken 1898, 3: 303-305)

My best witness for the complex structure that evolved out of the dynamics between outer world and inner self, is, however, Samuel Pepys who, in his diary, allows us a surprisingly unimpeded view of the complex strategies an individual has to develop as a response to the different demands which his role as a civil servant and public figure, his role as husband and master in his own house, and his secret desires put upon him (Schlaeger 1987, 194ff.).

Clearly, the structure we see is one of separate strategies for each of these spheres. There is no private individual striving to use a 'public consensus' with which he can discipline and control himself. What we see instead is rather the opposite: a clear division of labour in his mental economy with different sets of values and different registers of conduct for each of the three spheres. In his closet, he does his accounts – financially and morally: he puts down his most secret thoughts, gives an account of his affairs, reads pornographic books, masturbates and indulges in abject self-pity. In the house, he organises everything according to the standards of an important personage, but also acts as the tyrannical master, seducer of servants, and demanding husband. In public, he works hard to conform to the established code of conduct and to present himself as the ideal gentleman.

Read against the background of this evidence, Locke's equation between private individuals and the law of opinion appears, indeed, as a very optimistic projection, as a massive piece of wishful thinking – but also, perhaps, as one of the key political myths which kept bourgeois society going in spite of the massive contradictions in its concepts of the rational relationship between self and society. An extreme point of this historical trajectory in which the 'law of censure' is used to establish firm control over public morality and codes of conduct, is reached in high Victorianism, when public supervision massively invaded the private sphere in order to stabilise the weakening inner front.

However, as Steven Marcus has shown so convincingly in his revealing study *The Other Victorians*, in spite of these various attempts to use the public sphere as a regulatory force to control the private sphere and even the inner self, deviant behaviour of all kinds, prostitution and pornography flourished. For Marcus, this disturbing picture of a society that invests so much to present a homogeneous surface but which cannot control the darker forces is clearly 'inseparable from those vast social processes which brought about the modern world' (Marcus 1966, 282).

If we look at the period under consideration here – the early eighteenth century – the apparent strength but also inner weakness of the Lockean formula can be demonstrated by the growing willingness of the authorities to use the law in order to suppress, regulate and control the dark undercurrent in human thoughts and emotions. If the law of censure had been successful, no need for such drastic measures would have arisen – particularly in an area which had been considered to be outside the law for a very long time: obscenity and pornography.

It is true, up to the eighteenth century, pornography had been looked upon as immoral and contributing to man's depravity (Pepys burns a pornographic book 'so that it may not be found among my books to my shame'), but there was a public interest to use the law against it. In 1707 James Read and Angell Carter were taken to court and sentenced because they had published a series of pornographic poems with the title *The Fifteen Plagues of Maidenhead*. Read protested, saying that obscenity was something that lay clearly outside the jurisdiction of the court. Lord Chief Justice Holt followed his argument and quashed the verdict arguing:

> This is for printing bawdy stuff, that reflects on no person: and a libel must be against some particular person or persons, or against the government. It is stuff not fit to be mentioned publicly.
>
> If there is no remedy in the Spiritual court, it does not follow there must be a remedy here [...]. It tends to the corruption of manners but that is not sufficient for us to punish. (See Thomas 1969, 78)

The law as understood by the Lord Chief Justice Holt is obviously based on other principles than those established by the consent of private men. But this attitude was not to last. Not even twenty years later, law courts began to pass sentence on pornographic publications by treating them as a threat against public order. The notorious publisher Edmund Curll, for instance, was sentenced to a fine and one hour in the stocks for having published two obscene books: *Venus in the Cloister: or, the Nun in her Smock* and a *Treatise of Flogging*. The court argued the case as follows:

> What I insist upon is, that this is an offence at common law, as it tends to corrupt the morals of the king's subjects, and is against the peace of the king. Peace includes good order and government, and that peace may be broken in many instances without actual force. 1. If it be an act against the constitution or civil government. 2. If it be against religion. And, 3. If against morality [...] As to morality, it is destroying the peace of the government; for government is no more than public order which is morality.
>
> My lord chief justice Holt used to say, Christianity is part of the law: and why not morality too? I do not insist that every immoral act is indictable, such as telling a lie, or the like:
>
> But if it is destructive of morality in general; if it does, or may, affect all the king's subjects, it then is an offence of a public nature. (Foxon 1964, 15; see Schlaeger 1981)

Here the policy is clear: to use the strong arm of the state to bolster a publicly established code of morals in order to control and suppress what is an integral part of the inner dynamics of private individuals. One could say that, at this moment of time, Locke's formula celebrated its first great triumph. The other end of the story is the withdrawal of traditional laws against pornography and censorship in the twentieth century. This is a late recognition of the fact that the belief in the regulatory force of the public opinion that masquerades as the consent of private men is no longer valid.

Today we are witnessing a complete breakdown of the belief in the beneficial effect of the Lockean public-private partnership and, consequently, a diffusion and dissolution of public standards. As Richard Sennett has succinctly put it:

> That history is of the erosion of a delicate balance which maintains society in the first flush of its secular and capitalist existence. It was a balance between public and private life, a balance between an impersonal realm in which men could invest one kind of passion and a personal realm in which they could invest another. This geography of society was governed by an image of human nature based on the idea of an natural human character. [...] As both secularity and capitalism arrived at new forms in the last century, this idea of a transcendent nature gradually lost its meaning. [...] Gradually this mysterious, dangerous force which was the self came to define social relations. It became a social principle. (Sennett 1992, 338f.)

Sennett calls this the 'tyranny of intimacies' and implies that a re-establishment of the old neutral ground which was based on the social fiction of a consent of private men might be advisable *vis-à-vis* the dangers of postmodern societies in which exposures of the most secret experiences and fulfilment of the most private desires seem to dominate the public space and action in it. Whether Sennett advocates a return to the Lockean solution or a postmodernised version of it is difficult to tell. What I share and claim in support of my own investigation is the result of his analysis, which shows that, all along a third dimension, a division of labour into secret, private and public domains has played an important role however firmly the public vision of society and the role of the individual in it was based on the assumption that a bi-partite private-public structure was at the heart of the matter.

References

Aitken, George A., ed. (1898). *The Tatler*. 4 Vols. London: Duckworth.

Browne, Sir Thomas (1984). *Religio Medici*. Ed. C.A. Patrides. Harmondsworth: Penguin. Original edition 1643.

Calhoun, Craig, ed. (1997). *Habermas and the Public Sphere*. 5th ed. Cambridge, MA: MIT Press.

Dyke, Daniel (1614). *The Mystery of Selfe-Deceiving – Or A Discourse and discovery of the deceitfullnesse of Mans Heart*. London: Printed by Edward Griffin in St Pauls Church.

Foxon, David (1964). *Libertine Literature in England: 1660–1745*. London: Shand.

Habermas, Jürgen (1962). *Strukturwandel der Öffentlichkeit: Untersuchungen zu einer Kategorie der bürgerlichen Gesellschaft*. Neuwied: Luchterhand.

________ (1991). *The Structural Transformation of the Public Sphere: An Inquiry into a Category of Bourgeois Society*. Cambridge, MA: MIT Press.

Hobbes, Thomas (1999). *Human Nature and De Corpore Politico*. Ed. J.C.A. Gaskin. Oxford: Oxford University Press. Original edition 1650.

Koselleck, Reinhart (1959). *Kritik und Krise: Ein Beitrag zur Pathogenese der bürgerlichen Welt*. Freiburg: Alber.

Locke, John (1961). *An Essay Concerning Human Understanding*. Ed. John W. Yolton. 2 vols. London: Dent. Original edition 1690.

Marcus, Steven (1966). *The Other Victorians*. Frome: Weidenfeld and Nicolson.

Schlaeger, Jürgen (1981). 'Hermeneutique dans le boudoir.' In Manfred Fuhrmann, Hans-Robert Jauß and Wolfhart Pannenberg (eds.), *Text und Applikation: Theologie, Jurisprudenz und Literaturwissenschaft im hermeneutischen Gespräch*. Poetik und Hermeneutik 9. Munich: Fink, 207-223.

________ (1987). 'Literary History and the Rise of Individualism: An Essay in Literary Anthropology.' In Rudolf Böhm and Henning Wode (eds.), *Anglistentag 1986, Kiel*. Giessen: Hoffmann, 187-208.

________ (1993). 'Das Ich als beschreibenes Blatt: Selbstverschriftlichung und Erinnerungsarbeit.' In Anselm Haverkamp and Renate Lachmann (eds.), *Memoria – Vergessen und Erinnern*. Poetik und Hermeneutik 15. Munich: Fink, 315-337.

________ (1999). 'Parallel Explorations.' *Studies in Travel Writing* 3, 27-46.

Sennett, Richard (1992). *The Fall of Public Man*. New York: Norton..

Thomas, Donald (1969). *A Long Time Burning: The History of Literary Censorship in England*. London: Routledge and Kegan Paul.

Young, Edward (1965). 'Conjectures on Original Composition.' In Edmund D. Jones (ed.), *English Critical Essays*. London: Dent, 270-311. Original publication 1759.

Uwe Böker

Institutionalised Rules of Discourse and the Court Room as a Site of the Public Sphere

I. The Concept of Institutionalisation

As Karl-Siegbert Rehberg (1994) has argued, 'institutionalisation' may be defined as social rules and regulations in which, by means of symbolisations and certain leading concepts (*Leitideen*), the underlying principles and legitimacy of a given order are made manifest. Institutionalisation thereby serves to shape the basic orientations of actors in making available relatively permanent and binding norms and values, at the same time mediating between personal and social structures. It is by symbolically embodying or incarnating a given order and its claims of legitimacy that institutions transcend immediate reality in respect to situation, time, place, role patterns, or worlds of existence (*Lebenswelten*). Institutional theory thus aims at analysing everyday reality as a symbolically structured mediator of 'the other' – of seemingly stable and normative arrangements of order that, in some cases, even claim permanency by obfuscating their historical origins. One of the basic assumptions of institutional interpretations is the analytical relevance of *Leitideen* – principles or concepts that are contingent but not obligatory arrangements of order, and which dominate political, economic, or social action *in toto*. A second assumption is that certain groups within a given society aim at legitimising control, power, hegemony or sovereignty by referring to (ultimately fictive) constructions of order which are epitomised in symbols and *Leitideen*. Thus, institutions always directly or indirectly lay permanent claim to authority; they are culturally sanctioned means of generating control and hegemony. This is one of the reasons for investigating the relationship between the public sphere and the legal culture of English society during the seventeenth and eighteenth centuries.

II. The Concept of the Public Sphere

Since the publication of Jürgen Habermas' seminal study *Strukturwandel der Öffentlichkeit* in 1962, there have been countless essays and books on the concept of the public sphere and new ways and approaches to solve the question of the political sphere's historical emergence during the seventeenth and/or eighteenth centuries.[1] During the last decades, research has in many cases concentrated on the uncovering of ever more groups that had been excluded in Habermas' model on the basis of gender, class or race: women, working people, blacks, native Americans, servants, etc. On the other hand, as David Zaret has pointed out, such analyses were often based on

1 E.g., Negt and Kluge 1972; Lottes 1979; Calhoun 1992; Hohendahl 2000. For Habermas' later revaluation of his initial arguments, see Habermas 1992a.

'idealized descriptions of critical uses of public reason, often derived from self-promoting representations by eighteenth-century philosophers who celebrated their kingdom of reason' (Zaret 2000, 16-17; cf. Stallybrass and White 1986, 82). But, as Zaret maintains, 'empirical knowledge of the origins of our democratic culture will not be advanced by interpretations of philosophic or theological texts in order to establish the Enlightenment or Protestant religion as a prototype of the democratic public sphere.'[2]

One of the main goals of research in regard to the institutionalisation and circulation of legal norms and values in seventeenth and eighteenth-century England has been the analysis of the various processes regulating, negotiating, or mediating the transfer of norms between the legal system and the public sphere, as well as the historical reasons for the changing patterns of their institutionalisation (Böker 2001). But instead of re-reading the eminent philosophical texts and unearthing hitherto neglected social groups, this paper will use a different approach. It is based on Stallybrass and White's idea of the ultimately spatial nature of the various public spheres. There are, as these authors maintain, certain distinctive sites and spaces that are subject to hegemonic discourses; the discursive rules do not – at least in certain cases – allow departures from the institutionalised and binding discursive praxis. According to Stallybrass and White:

> patterns of discourse are regulated through the forms of corporate assembly in which they are produced. [...] Each 'site of assembly' constitutes a nucleus of material and cultural conditions which regulate what may and may not be said, who may speak, how people may communicate and what importance must be given to what is said. An utterance is legitimated or disregarded according to its place of production and so, in large part, the history of political struggle has been the history of the attempts made to control significant sites of assembly and spaces of discourse. (Stallybrass and White 1986, 80)

Under certain circumstances and at particular historical moments, such sites of assembly came to be nuclei of a public sphere in England; sites in which the boundaries between oral, scribal, and printed techniques of communication began to overlap, creating an intertextual network in the voicing and distribution of public opinion.

This may be demonstrated by looking into two trials of members of the Society of Friends (Quakers) shortly after 1660. The persecution of the Quakers during the Restoration – which in fact aimed at a stricter enforcement of Anglicanism – began with the 1662 Quaker Act (renewed in 1670) and was considerably reinforced with the Conventicles Act in 1664, which was part of the Clarendon Code.[3] In this context, it

2 See Zaret: 'we should rather look into the historical shifts from norms of secrecy to appeals to public opinion at the level of communicative practice' (2000, 6).

3 See Horle 1988, 50f.; Greaves 1990, 129ff.; and Green 1985, 202: 'By the terms of the act, which elaborated upon the Act of 1662, those convicted of meeting in groups of five or more persons aged sixteen or over under pretense of religion, but not according to the forms of the Anglican Church, were to be imprisoned for three months unless they paid a fine of five pounds. For conviction on a second offense the penalty was more onerous, and those convicted of the third offense would suffer seven years' transportation or a fine of 100 pounds' (Stat. 16 Chas. II, c.4, sects. 1-3, 5). The

can be shown that court rooms, as sites of institutionalised and highly formalised discourse, were used as sites of public utterance by the Quakers, thus constituting a sort of interface between the emerging public sphere and the changing legal culture of Restoration England. It remains to be shown that the participants in legal actions at court had to stick to certain rules and procedures that were institutionalised to a very high degree; that is, re-iterated over and over again and, thus, made stable and permanent as ways of maintaining hegemony and control. However, because they served not only legal but also political aims, these rules came to be challenged by members of religious (and implicitly political) subcultures such as the Quakers, eventually being undermined even in court and, thus, de-institutionalised.

III. LEGAL CULTURE

According to Lawrence Friedman, the concept of legal culture may be defined as a mixture of :

> ideas, attitudes, expectations and opinions about law, held by people in some given society. It is the network of values and attitudes [...] which determines when and why and where people turn to law or government or turn away. It is thus the immediate source of legal change, whatever the ultimate source may be. The term covers those thoughts and ideas which act as motives or incentives for 'legal behaviour' – behaviour oriented toward or away from legal rules, legal institutions, or the uses or nonuses of law. (Friedman 1990, 213)[4]

According to a more recent study by David Nelken and others, the concept of legal culture 'should be treated as a "multi-layered" concept which includes legal norms, salient features of legal institutions and their infrastructure, social behavior in creating, using and not using the law, as well as legal consciousness in the legal professions and amongst the public' (Nelken 1995; 1997).

Friedman's and Nelken's concepts of legal culture are based on a set of other concepts: mentalities (that is, ideas, opinions, values, norms and conscious or unconscious attitudes), the ways people at a given historical moment perceive themselves, their social environment and the universe, the nature of their popular and religious beliefs or superstitions, etc. According to Gaskill, 'historians of mentalities need to ask how life experiences were perceived, and how norms, attitudes, beliefs and ideas were articulated, affirmed and adapted within the real-life contexts of household, neighbourhood, community and wider society' (Gaskill 2000, 14). Thus, the mentalities at the base of a given legal culture are situated somewhere in-between the hard facts or ideas of intellectual history (history from above) and Le Goff's 'everyday automanisms of behaviour' (history from within; Le Goff 1974, 168; see also Böker 1996; Gaskill 2000, ch. 1).

---

meaning of 'seditious conventicles' was 'secret meetings'. See also Horle 1988, 46ff. Andrew Marvell called the 1670 Act the 'quintessence of arbitrary malice' (Horle 1988, 120).

4 See also Friedman's other (and earlier) studies: Friedman 1971; 1975. For criticism of Friedman's concept and its application to literary studies, see Raiser 1987; Rottleuthner 1987; Nelken 1995 and 1997; Schönert 1983 and 1991; Weiler 1998, 13-14.

We cannot speak of mentalities without pointing to the actors that articulate ideas or live their attitudes in everyday life. Thus, the concept of legal culture refers, on the one hand, to those people that are busy on the corridors of political power and the law, who are finding, defining and/or inculcating more or less binding legal norms and values in parliaments, court rooms, prisons and various other places; and, on the other hand, to those members of a society that have been socialised in the historically given private and/or public spaces of discourse that they may act according to already existing laws, regulations, norms, and values – or not. This means that there are at least two interlocking spheres to be considered: the inner legal culture of the 'legal profession' and the outer legal culture(s) of the general public (sphere).

IV. Legal Culture, Public Sphere, and Political Power Structures

Legal culture may be defined as a subsystem of a given society, especially so during the seventeenth and eighteenth centuries, that at certain moments in its historical evolution is more and more in need of legitimisation by the general public. Without going deeper into the analysis of the concept of legitimisation (this has been done, e.g., by Lüderssen 1996, and Habermas 1992b), one might say that strategies of legitimisation depend on power structures and elite authority, and that, as a rule, they aim at the stabilisation of institutionalised practises or leading ideas. Some English examples include practices such as trial by jury or trial by ones peers, and concepts and leading ideas such as 'the ancient constitution', 'the rule of law', or 'artificial [judicial] reason'. As has been shown elsewhere, concepts and leading ideas are narrative constructions or fictions that tell people more or less convincing stories about their own past or future (Böker 2002) and that try to persuade the participants in political or other discourses that there is some sense and meaning to historical decisions, situations, or developments.[5]

In this respect, public spheres serve as open spaces for political or social groups or classes in power (or coalitions of these) that are in need of political or cultural legitimisation and are looking for ways and means to stabilise a certain social order by means of power or persuasion. Historically speaking, the decisive change occurred in England during the seventeenth century with, according to David Zaret, 'the shift from norms of secrecy to appeals to public opinion at the level of communicative practice' (2000, 6).

Recent research on the interrelationship between law and literature has, however, made us aware of the fact that the English legal culture of the centuries under discussion was far from consensus oriented: it was dominated by dissent, by referring to the fundamental rights of the so-called 'ancient constitution', and by the ideology of the 'rule of law', which more often than not was nothing more than the 'colour of law' (Bell 1991; Swan 1997; Dolin 1999; Gladfelder 2001). In the course of the following analysis, I will take into consideration one of the three historical fields of investigation

5 For a psychologically based theory of historical narrativity, see Kraus 2000, and Straub 1998.

that are singled out by Rehberg; that is, the plurality of and competition between pre- and post-revolutionary institutionalisation (Rehberg 1994, 75). Due to the socio-economic and political modernisation in England from the fifteenth to the nineteenth centuries, these processes of institutionalisation were relatively unstable. According to Richard Price, England saw the emergence of a public sphere that resulted in a delicate balance between civil society, the state and the individual at the beginning of the eighteenth century.[6] According to Price, the 'institutional state', the 'public world of civil society', and the 'private world of the individual' are, at least for an analysis of British society since the seventeenth century, the three basic categories or, in terms of institutional analysis, the three basic *Leitideen* manifest in a variety of symbolic representations. The loss of authority that the state experienced for various reasons – a state that had been embodied in the Stuart monarchy throughout the seventeenth century – resulted in a shift of power that favoured Parliament.

The 'old' seventeenth and eighteenth-century society was still 'an open aristocracy based on property and patronage' (Perkin 1969), and law and law enforcement remained, although the English lacked the coercive capacities and institutions of a fully developed and centralised police force (see McMullan 1984; 1987), in the hands of the political elite. Thus, the emerging public sphere, which was a necessary concomitant of economic developments, became the culturally-mediating and legitimising institutional field in which the role of state power and the rights and obligations of the private individual were discussed. This is evident from the numerous trials of Quakers during the 1660s and 1670s.

V. Quaker Orality and Quaker Print Culture

Radical groups such as the Levellers, the Diggers, or the Ranters had not only questioned the rights of property during the 1640s and 1650s, but also attacked the monopoly of language as a form of cultural capital and as a communicative rhetoric in which members of the elite were trained at the universities; instead, they sought to redefine the property of language in terms of a free market of ideas and as a common good (Hazelton 2000, 253). These revolutionary groups had been more or less silenced, but there were others, after 1660, that, on the basis of religious millenarianism, seemed to pose a continuous threat to the new political elite. As has been convincingly argued, the Quakers, diverging in some ways from the ideas and concepts of the Levellers, went on to challenge dominant concepts of language and rhetoric, although, under George Fox's pacifistic leadership, they were less militant

6 'Civil society is bounded on one side by the jurisdiction of the state and on the other side by the private world of the individual. The kinds of institutions that fill the spaces, define the character and determine the values of civil society vary over different historical periods. Similarly, the relationship between the formal structures of the state, the public world of civil society and the intimate world of the individual will vary over time and place. Understanding the dynamics of civil society in any period requires appreciating the arrangements that govern the relationships between three elements: the institutional state, the public world of civil society and the private world of the individual' (Price 1999, 192).

than during the 1650s (Greaves 1990, 134). instead of defining language in terms of a free market, they challenged the application of market principles to free speech, seeking to institutionalise a communism of language (Hazelton 2000, 258f).

Although subject to all sorts of pressure and censorship, itinerant Quaker ministers took over the job of disseminating ideas at local meetings by preaching (orality), by sending letters to local congregations after their departure (scribal techniques) and by distributing religious books (printed media). Thus, they acted according to Richard Hubberthorn's idea of a language free of charge, of 'free Preaching and a free Hearing among all People that so it may be a free Nation' (quoted in Hazelton 2000, 262). In addition to disseminating ideas at local meetings, the Friends developed special ways of reaching a wider and even a non-Quaker audience. One of these was the oral and printed challenge of magistrates.

George Fox had instructed his Quaker followers to record and publicise their sufferings in order to expose their persecution, to influence judges, and to engender popular support.[7] One of the first to suffer but also to notify the public was James Parnell, who in 1654 had been arrested for pinning up a paper denouncing a local magistrate; his trial account was subsequently published by a Quaker printer. Accounts of other prisoners held in local goals were sent to the Quaker gatherings, and printed accounts of their tribulations or 'sufferings' were published.[8] William Penn, who visited Quakers in prison and spoke with magistrates and judges during the time of growing persecution, began to write 'a book against persecution Call'd the Great Case of L[iberty] of C[onscience] Debated and Defended' (diary entry of 19 March 1670; quoted in Bronner and Fraser 1986, 113).

Joseph Besse's martyrological *Collection of the Sufferings of the People Called Quakers*, covering the period from 1650 to 1689 but published almost a century later in 1753, manifests the extent to which magistrates overreacted by breaking the law and instigating Quaker bashing, mob violence of 'rude boys', brutal attacks by soldiers (the militia), demolition of meeting houses, seizure of property, and imprisonment.[9] Included in Besse's *Collection* is an account of the breaking-up of a meeting in Grace Church Street, during which opponents drummed to drown out the speakers, drove a coach and horses through the crowd, and, finally, used their muskets as clubs: '[they] pusht down both men and women with their muskets, and tore Mary Wick's Scarf and Apron, and pincht her' (quoted in Knott 1994, 131). On another occasion, the authorities disrupted a meeting of Friends and:

> had them into a Room, where they were striped naked, & and their necks and armes put in ye stocks, & there cruelly whipped with boards in a bloody manner [...]. And when they had thus

---

7 Fox 1831, 1: 134-136. In reference to Fox, see Knott 1993, 128ff. See also Ingle 1994, 139-140.

8 On the dismal prison conditions and the aggravations of not being tried at the appointed quarter sessions or assizes, see Horle 1988, 103 and 146ff.

9 See Cragg 1971, ch. 2. On the pattern of persecution and for statistics, see Horle 1988, 102; and Greaves 1990, 137ff.

cruelly proceeded, they fastened irons upon them with great cloggs of wood & put them in amongst transgressors.[10]

Quakers practised what they used to call 'bold speaking',[11] that is, challenging ministers in their own pulpits[12] and also judges during examinations and trials. Besse's *Collection* bears witness to the increasing skill of Quakers in using legal tactics as well as the assumptions of some of the justices for their own benefit. This is especially true of the trials of John Crook in 1762 and William Penn and William Meade in 1670.

The 1662 Licensing 'Act for preventing the frequent Abuses in printing seditious, treasonable and unlicensed Books and Pamphlets and for regulating of Printing and Printing Presses' reinforced most of the *provisos* of the 1637 Star Chamber Decree. Licensing and censorship was supervised by the notorious Roger L'Estrange, who did whatever was possible to search for Quaker and Anabaptist printings.[13] The first victim in L'Estrange's campaign against the radical press was the printer John Twyn who, after a trial in February 1664, was hanged, disembowelled, and dismembered (Greaves 1990, 167ff.). L'Estrange later warned others that they would suffer 'like brother Twyn'. Giles Calvert of the Black Spread-Eagle in St Paul's Churchyard, one of the three printers that were responsible for about 800 books and pamphlets before Roger L'Estrange began his work, found himself in gaol. His establishment was likened to an 'Apothecaries shop' that 'keeps open poison, so Giles Calvert doth for soul-poison' (quoted in Fraser 1986, 62). In response, the Friends developed the idea of an 'official' underground press to get their unlicensed writings into print (57ff.). The idea was voiced during a meeting in 1666, but authors were warned to avoid inflammatory publications, so that 'nothing but what is sound and savoury [...] may be exposed by us to public view' (ibid.). They eventually practised their own inner-group censorship, thereby hoping to reach and persuade a wider public. After the start of the so-called Morning Meetings in 1673, the committee responsible for approval was 'especially careful not to approve for the press such sensational reports as visions and prophecies – particularly when most potential converts were approaching religion rather more intellectually than spiritually' (58). Penn suffered no censorship from his brothers, but he had his books and pamphlets all printed anonymously between 1668 and 1680, that is, after the temporary lapse of the licensing act. As printers omitted

---

10 From *A True Declaration of the bloody Proceedings of the Men in Maidstone* (1655); quoted in Fraser 1986, 57. For the law-enforcement officers' reasons for such violence, see Horle 1988, 126.

11 See the accompanying text to the picture of Faithful's trial in Vanity Fair in John Bunyan's *The Pilgrim's Progress* (1688), which reads: 'Now Faithful play the man, speak for thy God: / Fear not the wickeds malice nor their rod: / Speak boldly man, the truth is on thy side: / Die for it, and to life in triumph ride.' See the reproduction in Knott 1993, fig. 8 (between pages 150 and 151).

12 They could be tried, however, for disrupting the routine of ministers and congregations; see Horle 1988, 48.

13 'Identifying Penn's printers requires the kind of ingenuity Sir Roger L'Estrange displayed when he marched up to Simon Dover's typecase in 1663 and plucked out the telltale flower ornament that had appeared in the unauthorized Marprelate Tracts. L'Estrange had struck upon the crime-lab technique for identifying anonymous printers. That flower was Dover's "fingerprint". Refined a bit, L'Estrange's scientific method of type analysis can be used today in assigning Penn's work to his underground printers' (Fraser 1986, 53 and 63).

imprint details for fear of prosecution, we do not know much about the printing and publishing processes.[14]

VI. JOHN CROOK'S 'CRY OF THE INNOCENT FOR JUSTICE': LAYERS OF PUBLICNESS

John Crook (1617-1699) had been a captain in the Parliamentary Army during the Civil War, and later became one of the commissioners for the Assessment in the county of Bedfordshire and Justice of the Peace there. He also held other public offices in Bedfordshire during the fifties, during which time he became a practising Quaker. The Friends' meetings in Bedfordshire were raided in April 1655 (Tibbutt 1947, 113),[15] and Crook lost his post, was arrested, and was kept in Northhampton goal for some time. In 1659 he was one of those Quakers who presented a Declaration to Parliament, offering themselves to be imprisoned for others that were in gaol. He was imprisoned several times after 1660, and thrown into Newgate prison in 1662 and, together with others, put to trial at the Old Bailey.

In order to analyse the texts printed in John Crook's *The Design of Christianity, with other Books, Epistles and Manuscripts, of the Ancient Faithful Servant of Christ Jesus* (1701), we have to distinguish between different layers and manifestations of publicness. The trial account itself ('The Cry of the Innocent for Justice') was first published immediately after the event and was reprinted several times (for a bibliography, see Tibbutt 1947, 132), the trial account of 1662 as such seems to be more or less a verbatim rendering of the interrogations and discussions in court, although we certainly cannot be sure as to what degree the account might provide a biased view (Crook 1662). Crook would have either asked some of his brethren to write everything down in shorthand[16] or he would afterward have used his own notes.[17] As a matter of fact, Crook himself remarks several times that, due to the

14 Those interested might nevertheless have a look at Fraser's careful work of identification of Penn's printers. His information on the well-known Quaker printer Andrew Sowle may be of particular interest (Fraser 1986, 77-78).

15 For Crook's spiritual history, his 'inward distress and trouble' and his 'inward experiences', see Crook, who writes of his first meeting with a Quaker (1706, 22 and 27) and the 'Superfluities in Apparel, Words and Carriages, which was hard for me to do, being then in Commission as Justice of the Peace' (30), and of his experiences in Northampton prison (43). There are some remarks about his prison experiences: 'Ten times [...] have I been in Bonds, and not only incurred the Sentence of Premunire with my Brethren at *London*, but also have been tryed for my Life in the Country, and all for a good Conscience to my God: But this Holy Spirit never left me, but in Prisons many times hath made me sing, and often at the Bar fresh Courage did bring; who by its virtue Judges hath bound, and envious Witnesses quite confound, that thought the Innocent to destroy [...]' (44).

16 The audience included the official state or court personnel as well as an unknown number of interested spectators, even though there were no seats in court until the eighteenth century (Baker 2000, 163, n.147), presumably, some of the spectators were fellow Quakers.

17 See n.37 below on the use of shorthand in connection with Penn's trial accounts.

THE

Cry of the Innocent

FOR

JUSTICE:

BEING

A RELATION of the TRYAL of *JOHN CROOK*, and others, at the *General Sessions*, held in the *Old Bayley*, *London*; beginning the 25*th*. day of the 4*th*. Month, called *June*, in the year, 1662. Before the *Lord Mayor* of the City of *London*, and *Recorder* of the same, Chief Justice *Forster*, and divers other *Judges* and *Justices* of the *Peace*, so called.

Published for no other end but to prevent Mistakes, and to satisfie all moderate Enquirers, concerning the Dealings and Usage that the said *J. C.* and others met withal, from the beginning of the said *Tryals* to the end.

Alitur vitium, vivitq; tegendo.

Eccles. 5. 8. *If thou seest the Oppression of the poor, and violent perverting of Judgment and Justice in a Province, marvel not at the matter; for he that is higher than the highest regardeth, and there be higher than they.*

Printed in the Year, 1662.

confusion caused by the shouting of juries and judges, he had been unable to understand and, thus, unable to record everything that had been spoken. We might therefore consider the reported dialogues as the first layer of oral publicness.

In addition, there is layer of non-orality, as Crook afterwards supplemented the account with sentences and whole passages he would have voiced during the trial had he been allowed to speak[18] or to listen to certain texts being read in court; that is, the transcription of the Latin text of the indictment that Crook was refused a copy of at the beginning of the trial and during the following days.[19] This text, translated by himself into English, was meant for the use of readers later interested in the trial accounts as well as for the book published in 1701; and, in addition to the two versions of the indictment (original and translation), Crook gives the reasons for his defiant attitude in court, that is, '*the Point of Conscience, that I desired to be heard to speak of* (1791, 193); but, as he was not allowed speak about such 'points of conscience', he informed the trial account readers of his original ideas.

The third layer of publicness, directed even more directly at the general reader of the book interested in law, consists of a number of prefaces and postscripts elucidating (from the Quakers' point of view and by referring to or quoting legal authorities and statutes) the religious and juridical problems of being forced to take the Oath of Allegiance, thus, discoursing on the '*illegality of the late aforesaid Proceedings*' (205).

VII. Public Sites and Rules of Discourse

From the beginning of the trial, it is made clear that the court room is a public site that has its own rules of discourse, institutionalised and made permanent, one could say, since 'time immemorial', upheld and redefined through the authority of the king's

18 For example, at one point during the trial, the judge, pointing to the audience, said: 'No, no, you are mistaken; so you may say of all the people gazing here, they not being legally here, are not here: I tell you, a man being brought by force hither, we may tender him the oath, and if he take it not, he may be committed to prison' (Crook 1791, 165). Crook later remarked: 'Here I was interrupted, but might have said, That the people that were spectators, beholding and hearing the trials, are not to be called gazers, as the judge terms them; because it is their liberty and privilege, as they are Englishmen, and the law of England allows the same; so that they are not to be termed gazers upon this account, but are legally in that place, to hear trials, and see justice done, and might have spoken, if occasion had been, any thing in the prisoner's defence, tending to clear up the matter in difference, and the court must have heard them or him: and this as a stander-by, or *amicus curiae*; so saith Coke' (165-166). See also *Truth Rescued from Imposture*, where William Penn speaks about people present at his own trial at the Old Bailey in 1670 (Penn [1671], 8).

19 On the three different languages used in court – French, Latin, and English – see Baker 2000, ch. 14. French remained, till the seventeenth century, the language of formal pleading in court. As a Frenchman said in 1592 about French legalese: it 'may be worthily compared to some old ruins of some fair building, where so many brambles and thorns are grown that scarcely it appeareth that ever there had been any house [...] almost there is no language more far from the true French than the French of our [meaning, their] laws, there being almost no word which either by intermingling, or adding, or diminishing, or changing of a letter into another, they have not altered or corrupted [and] their pronunciation differeth so much from ours as it is impossible for a Frenchman to understand them' (Baker 2000, 244; on Latin and the dangers of 'false Latin', see 239ff.).

judges. Generally speaking, the 'behaviour and speech of ordinary people was liable to be distorted by the formal and ritualized arenas of court room and gallows' (Gaskill 2000, 24). But there were exceptions; for example, cases such as the trial of John Crook, during which the defendants refused to conform to the prescribed rules and ceremonies. Thus, the presiding Judge saw the need to admonish, from the beginning of the trial, the defendant to follow the rules of the court unconditionally: 'Your tongue is not your own, and you must not have liberty to speak what you list' (Crook 1791, 153). Later on, the Chief Judge warned Crook in similar words that 'we are to tell you what is law, and not you us' (156). The rules of an institutionalised legal discourse prescribe what may be said and what not, in which way and when, and the judges have the authority to enforce these rules.[20]

The accused could not be silenced, however, as he was continuously breaking the rules of discourse and giving his own interpretations as to questions of law-finding and fact-finding. He did so on the assumption that established forms of rhetoric are representative of an old social hierarchy, whereas he himself was seeking to realise free commerce of language, not in a free market, but in a new community of free speech unhampered by any form of market economy (Hazelton 2000, 269). Thus, Crook, to a certain extent, succeeds in transforming the court into a site of the public sphere; he does this through 'speaking boldly', that is, by means of continual discussions with the presiding judge and others, to an extent that the common hangman is called in to enforce the rules by means of gagging the accused. Crook gives a vivid account of what happened after he addressed the Judge:

> therefore we dare not break Christ's commands, who hath said, Swear not at all; and the apostle James said, Above all things, my brethren, swear not – (interrupted) the court calling again to the executioner to stop my mouth; which he did accordingly, with his dirty cloth, as aforesaid, and his gag in his hand. (Crook 1791, 177)[21]

The accused is hindered in continuing with his questioning factual and legal problems and, thus, hindered in converting the court into a freer site of public discourse.

Some of Crook's argument have to do with questions of procedure. At the beginning of the trial, he is asked if he has already taken the Oath of Allegiance.[22] Crook does not agree with this legal procedure, so he does not answer the question, but complains about having been imprisoned for six weeks now, against 'the law of the land' (154).[23] He demands, again and again, 'that my accuser [...] be brought forth to accuse me for

---

20 We should, however, be careful not to draw conclusions from written material that cannot be an exact description of the testimony at court (for linguistic considerations, see Gaskill 2000, 24ff.).

21 For 'gagging' as a technique of literally stopping the Quaker's mouths, see Hazelton 2000, 266. See also Horle 1988, 104.

22 For legislation on refusing to swear the Oath of Supremacy or the Oath of Allegiance or Obedience, see Horle 1988, 49f.

23 He was taken, as he informs the reader, by a 'rude man called Miller', who, 'with a long cane in his hand, [...] laid violent hands on me, with some others, beating some, commanding the constables who came in after him, but having no warrant, were not willing to meddle, but as his threatening prevailed, they being afraid of him, joined with him to carry several of us before Justice Powel' (Crook 1791, 155).

my delinquency, and then I shall answer to my charge, if any I be guilty of' (ibid.). In addition, he argues that the indictment is in Latin, he has not been allowed to read it, and he is without any counsel at all; and that there is no need to swear the oath of allegiance because this Tudor act was directed at the Papists in consequence of the Gunpowder Plot. Crook, in a very learned manner, gives his interpretation of the Act in question, continuously referring to his use of 'reason', thus challenging the 'artificial reason' of the judge.

VIII. Crook's Court-Room Appeal to the Laws of England

Crook continuously invoked 'the laws of England', referring the Judge to the Magna Carta and the Petition of Rights (155), and, in his 'Epistle to all Moderate Readers', he invokes King Alfred's laws, some passages from *The Mirror of Justices*, and Coke's *Institutes*, all these arguments referring the hearer and the reader back to the concept of the 'ancient constitution'. As this 'ancient [unwritten] constitution' was considered to be a safeguard against 'arbitrary power', resting on certain formal guarantees, Crook is telling the judges that '[you] ought to be my counsel, and not my accusers, but to inform me of the benefit of those laws; and wherein I am ignorant, you ought to inform me, that I may not suffer through my own ignorance of those advantages which the laws of England inform as an Englishman' (ibid.). The presiding judge should not be allowed 'to threaten me, neither are those menaces fit for the mouth of a judge'; he should refrain from using words (like 'sirrah' or 'cant') that do not become a judge (156). Crook goes on to assert his 'liberty, as an Englishman', demanding again and again to be judged 'according to law' (ibid.). He asks that a certain statute mentioned 'may be read, for I have consulted it, and do not understand that you [the judge] have power by that statute to tender me the oath' (158). He even demands that the judge proceed 'according to the laws already made, and not to make laws; for you ought to be ministers of the law' (160). By challenging the rules of court, we are made aware of the fact that these rules are indeed institutionalisations in the sense of being more or less binding and permanent; thus, symbolising otherwise perhaps hidden structures of hegemony and power.

IX. The Publication Layer of Publicness

Crook's self-defence and that of his fellow prisoners is in fact a severe criticism not of the English laws, but of the practice of the courts. The publication of the trial account in itself is, therefore, a way of disclosing abuses within the legal system. This is emphasised by a quotation from the Bible on the title page of the book: 'Therefore thus saith the Lord, If thou return, then will I bring thee again, and thou shalt stand before me: and if thou take forth the precious from the vile, thou shalt be as my Mouth' (Jer. 15.19 KJV; Crook 1791).[24]

24 The legal criticism is clear: the title page of the 1791 edition of 'The Cry of the Innocent for Justice' also carries the following remark, as did the original edition: 'Published for no other end but to prevent Mistakes, and to satisfy all Moderate Enquirers, concerning the Dealings and Usages that

In his 'Epistle to all Moderate Readers', a sort of preface to 'The Cry of the Innocent for Justice', Crook refers his audience not only to the Bible, but also to the history of the English legal system and to the 'Law-books' which record 'several acts of justice that were executed upon unjust judges for their not keeping unto the laws and rules of justice, made and appointed both for the peoples safety, and them to act by' (Crook 1791, 149). One of Crook's authorities was the fourteenth-century *Mirror of Justices* that informs its readers about the Anglo-Saxon king Alfred (871-899). Alfred is said to have condemned forty-four unjust judges to death within the space of one year.[25]

For the eminent seventeenth-century legal-expert, Sir Edward Coke, the *Mirror* had the status of 'a very ancient and learned treatise of the laws and usages of this kingdom whereby the commonwealth of our nation was governed about eleven hundred years past'.[26] The *Mirror* (or *Le Mireur a justice*, as the French title was) was printed in England at the beginning of the conflicts between king and parliament in 1642; it was translated in 1648 into English and is said to be a collection of 'bulls and [...] holy usages which we have obtained since the time of King Arthur'.[27] Several times in his *Institutes*, Coke himself alludes to the *Mirror* and its concept of the pre-Norman conquest *ancient constitution*, which critics of the English monarchy and 'arbitrary power' in general saw as a safeguard against political and religious persecution and, thus, as a guarantee of the *rule of law*.[28]

It thus becomes clear that Crook argues within a religious discourse shared, even during the times of the Restoration, by a great number of politicians and political

---

the said J.C. and other met withal, from the beginning of the said Trials to the end.' There follows a quotation from the Bible: 'If thou seest the oppression of the poor, and violent perverting of Judgement and Justice in a province, marvel not at the matter; for he that is higher than the highest, regardeth; and there be higher than they' (Eccles. 5.8 KJV). We should bear in mind that Crook's book was republished immediately following the French Revolution and the reaction which set in during the 1790s. See Houswitschka's study of the 1794 treason trials (2002).

25 See Vaughan's review of Bushell's Case (Vaughan 1707, 135-158), wherein he, too, refers the legal experts to the *Mirror of Justices* (139).

26 Whittaker 1895, ix-x. Coke refers to the *Mirror* in his *Reports*, saying that it was representative of the legal system of king Arthur's times: 'the great antiquity of the said courts of the common law, and in particular of the High Court of Parliament ever since the time of King Arthur, who reigned about the year of our Lord 516' (quoted in Burgess 1993, 76).

27 Whittaker 1895, 3. The book was referred to over and over again till the end of the eighteenth century as a sourcebook for statements about the ancient constitution; see Hill 1986, 103 and Thompson 1987, 53-54.

28 'After that God had abated the nobility of the Britons, who had recourse to force rather than to law, He delivered the kingdom to the humblest and simplest of all the neighbouring nations: to wit, the Saxons, who came to conquer it from the parts of Almaine. Of which folk there were as many as forty sovereigns, who all aided each other as fellows. They first called this land England, which theretofore was called Britannia Major. And they, after great wars and tribulations and pains long time suffered, chose from among themselves a king to reign over them and to govern the people of God and to maintain and defend their persons and goods by the rules of right.

And at his crowning they made him swear that he would maintain the Christian faith with all his power, and would guide his people by law without respect of any person, and would be obedient to holy Church, and would submit to justice and would suffer right like any other of his people. And after this the kingdom became heritable' (Whittaker 1895, 6).

thinkers. Whenever he calls himself 'an Englishman, and by the law of England I ought not to be taken, nor imprisoned, nor disseized of my freehold, nor called in question, nor put to answer, but according to the law of the land' (Crook 1791, 154),[29] he is in fact arguing from the widely shared point of view of the ancient constitution. He even uses the concept of 'legal' reason that Coke and others had defined as something authentic or 'artificial', but which had always been used in defence of Englishmen's rights: 'The law is built upon right reason, or right reason is the law; and whatever is contrary to right reason, is contrary to law; the reason of the law, being the law itself' (166).

In accordance with this, Crook not only provides the entire indictment in both the original Latin and in translation, but he also enters, for the benefit of the reader, into a learned discussion of legal matters, especially of the concept of *premunire*, quoting from Fortescue, *The Mirror of Justices*, Coke and other sources (183ff.). He also discourses upon the laws made against the Catholics after the Gunpowder Plot, 'For the Discovering and repressing of Popish Recusants' (185ff.), and on the problem of when and under what circumstances to take a certain oath (189ff.), not only alluding to a great number of laws and precedents, but also to another important treatise on English law, Christopher St German's *Doctor and Student*, first published in 1523 (Crook 1791, 192 and 199).[30] In this context, Crook again speaks of 'the good old laws of England' (199):

> It hath been said, that the laws of England are like Hercules's pillars, that have a *ne plus ultra* upon them, as well as they are pillars to Hercules: but surely by such pulls as these, in causing mens mouths to be stopped by the executioner when they are at the bar to make their defence, to preserve their liberties and estates, must needs shake those houses which have no other foundations to stand upon. Judges in former times, when there was no law for cases that sometimes fell out, forbore proceedings until a parliament was called to make laws, for it is a higher juridiscion, *dare leges*, to give laws, than to minister, or rule by them. But these judges to shew dislike unto the laws already made, and that lately too, and on purpose against those persons called Quakers, that deny all oaths. [...]. Surely if the law of England be a merciful law, as they said it is, then they must needs be most unmerciful judges, who passed so severe a sentence, drawn from such merciful laws, as they said the laws of England are; and surely in this, the judges make their little finger, as was said, heavier than late parliament's loins. (207-208)

Thus, we are able to discern within the entire text a number of layers and manifestations of publicness, directed at different moments in time to different sections of the public sphere, but always subverting the established and institutionalised rules of official discourse.

---

29 See: 'I am an Englishman, as I have said to you, and challenge the benefit of the laws of England.' He then refers the judge to the Magna Carta and the Petition of Right 'mentioned in the third of Car. I. and in other good laws of England' (Crook 1791, 155). Also: 'I am bold to assert my liberty, as an Englishman' (156); 'I desire justice, according to the laws of England' (160). Later, he quotes form older English laws, speaking of 'the old law of the land' (162).

30 For Saint German, see the introductory material in St German 1974; and Burgess 1993, 30ff.

The power of the authorities, however, proved too strong, so that Crook and his brethren had to suffer the unjust measures of *premunire*, in the words of the presiding judge:

> The jury for the king do find, that John Crook, John Bolton, and Isaac Gray, are guilty of refusing to take the oath of allegiance; for which you do incur a *premunire*, which is the forfeiture of all your real estates during life, and personal estates for ever; and you to be out of the king's protection, and to be imprisoned during his pleasure: and this is your sentence. (177)[31]

Nevertheless, Crook seems to have been released a few weeks later, but was in prison again in 1663 and at various later times throughout the rest of his life (Tibbutt 1947, 117 and 121).

X. Judges and Jurymen Admonished

The second trial to be addressed is that of William Penn and William Mead at the Old Bailey in London. The indictment was for unlawful assembly and disturbance of the peace in August 1670 (Green 1985, 202ff.). During the sixties, the Quakers had narrated and described in a number of tracts the sufferings of members of the sect through the courts; they had received some sort of legal education in order to defend themselves,[32] and, in a way, they developed into legal experts and openly began to admonish jurymen to apply the Conventicles Act 'lawfully', especially with regard to the proof that was required for sedition (203; 203, n.9). This was done in tracts such as *The Jury-men charged; Or; A Letter to a Citizen of London* (London 1664) or the several pamphlets under the title of 'The Cry of the Innocent and Oppressed for Justice' (London 1664 and 1665; see 203, n.9). Jurymen were told again and again that the Friends, on no account, met in 'seditious conventicles', as forbidden in the preface of the respective Act, but met simply in order to worship God. They had criticised the assumptions that:

> proof of a meeting under color of religion and contrary to the allowed liturgy sufficed for conviction; and that proof or mere presence at a Quaker meeting cast upon the defendant the burden of proving either that the meeting had not been for religious worship, or that the worship had been according to Anglican form. (205)

Juries were admonished again and again not to convict Quakers who worshipped God according to the 'true religion'; judges were admonished not to diverge from the 'Magna Charta, the great preserver of our lives, freedoms, and properties', and not to introduce 'arbitrary government' (Pepys; quoted in Green 1985, 219, n.81). There are a

---

31 For the meaning of this curious concept of *premunire* ('to be out of the king's protection') in the context of the older Germanic concepts of the *wargus* or *werewolf* and the man who has been banned from the 'city', see Agamben 1998, §3 and §6. Agamben quotes from Rudolf Jhering's analysis of Roman law: 'That which is considered to be an impossibility for Roman antiquity – the killing of the proscribed outside a judge and law – was an incontestable reality in Germanic antiquity' (Agamben 1998, 104; see Jhering 1981, 19).

32 On Quaker legal defence, see Horle 1988, ch. 5; he focuses more on the eighties than on the earlier period.

number of cases in which juries acquitted Friends, to the displeasure of the judges (Braithwaite 1962).

As meetings were held in silence, Courts were often at a loss how to interpret and use the supposed evidence of witnesses. Thus, the problem for judges and juries was not the oral (supposedly seditious) dissemination of Quaker ideas at the meetings of the Friends, but rather the Friends' altogether silent manifestations of solidarity, which posed problems for the prosecution and the witnesses. Judge Orlando Bridgeman instructed the jury at the Hertford summer assizes of 1664 on this problem:

> [You] are not to expect a plain, punctual evidence [...] for [Quakers] may speak to one another though not by or with auricular sound, but by a cast of the eye, or a motion of the head or foot [...] if you find, or believe in your hearts that they were in the meeting, under colour of religion in their way, though they sat still only, and looked upon each other, seeing they cannot say what they did there: it was an unlawful meeting.[33]

Often, juries followed the lead of the defendants who told them to consider the 'true law', and there were a number of cases when they returned a verdict that did not follow the interpretation of the judges. Thus, they were fined by Lord Chief Justice, John Kelyng, and Chief Justice of King's Bench, Sir Robert Hyde (Green 1985, 205, n.17; 206; 206, n.19; 208-209). But, as Matthew Hale's comments in his *History of the Pleas of the Crown* (1736)[34] show, there were widespread doubts about this kind of 'arbitrary practice', although fining was considered to be legal at the King's Bench (Green 1985, 210). Nevertheless, a committee of the House of Commons concluded that Judge Kelyng had 'used an arbitrary and illegal power, which is of dangerous consequences to the lives and liberties of the people of England' (213). The House of Commons, however, decided after Judge Kelyng's defence that there should be no further proceedings against him, but that a bill should be drafted that fining and imprisonment of juries were illegal – which in the end came to nothing (219; see Pepys quotation, 219, n.81).

XI. The Trial of William Penn and the Rules of Discourse Subverted

When Penn's case came to trial in 1670, the situation had changed in several ways and was different from that at the beginning of the sixties. As the City of London authorities had ordered the meeting places of the Quakers to be locked, the Friends began to gather on the streets. Thus, on 14 August 1670, William Penn and William Mead addressed a crowd of some hundred people on Grace Church Street. They were disturbed after a short while and sent to Newgate for 'preaching seditiously and causing a great tumult of people [...] to be gathered together riotously and routously',[35] being charged under the renewed Conventicles Act. They refused to obtain release

33 Quoted in Green 1985, 205; on the same trial, see also Horle 1988, 105f.

34 Published posthumously; Hale lived from 1609 to 1676.

35 Quoted in Green 1985, 222. Unauthorised religious meetings could be prosecuted as riots; three or more persons gathered, involved in violence or intending to commit a violent act, were said to constitute a riot; see Horle 1988, 47.

through a payment of fines, but demanded jury trial (Green 1985, 222), clearly for reasons of publicity. The were not indicted under the Conventicles Act; rather, they were charged with causing an unlawful assembly and a disturbance of the peace.

The trial accounts were published under the title *The Peoples Ancient and Just Liberties asserted, in the Tryal of William Penn, and William Mead, At the Sessions held at the Old-Baily in London, the first, third, fourth and fifth of Sept. 7⁰. against the most Arbitrary procedure of the Court* (1670).[36] There is neither a publisher nor an author mentioned on the title page. This account is supplemented with an address, 'To the English Reader' (*Peoples Ancient* 1670a, 3-4), with Thomas Rudyard's '*An* Appendix, *by way of* Defence *for the* Prisoners, as what might have been offered against the Indictment, and illegal Proceedings of the Court thereon, had they not violently over-rul'd and stopp'd them' (24-34), and with '*A Rehearsal of the Material Parts of the Great Charter of* England' (35-56) as well as with 'A Postscript: *The Copy of Judge Keeling's Case, taken out of the Parliament Journal*' (60-62).[37] Thus, we again have a text consisting of several layers of publicness, but, again, we do not know under what circumstances the trial itself was recorded.[38]

This trial account was reprinted,[39] with all the Appendices mentioned above, in *Phenix XI*, a sort of periodical publication (in *Peoples Ancient* 1670b, 304-349); in addition, *The Second Part of the People's Antient and Just Liberties asserted, in the Proceedings against, and Tryals of Thomas Rudyard* was printed in *Phenix XII* (in *Peoples Ancient* 1670b, 350-387), supplemented by another legal treatise, an 'Appendix, by way of Dialogue, in a Plain and Friendly Discourse between a Student in the Laws and Liberties of England, and a true Citizen of London' (387-404).

As Penn and Mead challenged the Bench during the trial and in the trial accounts, the Lord Mayor of London, Sir Samuel Starling, who presided at the trial, saw the necessity to publish *An Answer To the Seditious and Scandalous Pamphlet, Entituled, The Tryal of W. Penn and W. Mead* (1671). Starling's answer will be discussed below. The whole case gained another dimension of notoriety through Edward Bushell, the

---

36 According to Bronner and Fraser (1986), the pamphlet went through nine printings in 1670 and several more before the publication of William Penn's *Works* in 1726. The copy used here (1670a) is, according to Bronner and Fraser's descriptive bibliography, the third edition, second issue; 'asserted' an the title page reads 'asssrted' (Bronner and Fraser 1986, 121-122).

37 According to Bronner and Fraser, Penn was not the author of the pamphlet, as he admitted a few months later in his *Truth Rescued from Imposture*. But the material in the second half of the pamphlet may have been by Penn himself (Bronner and Fraser 1986, 118). For evidence of Rudyard's authorship, see Green 1985, 230, n.125; and Bronner and Fraser 1986, 119. For Rudyard, see also Braithwaite 1962.

38 Bronner and Fraser suggest the use of shorthand (1986, 119). See Fraser's reference to *A pen pluckt from an eagles whinge, or the most swift compendious and speedy method of short writing*, published by the Quaker printer John Darby who, after being harassed several times by Roger L'Estrange, began to officially register such titles in 1671 (Fraser 1986, 74-75).

39 This reprint is not mentioned in Bronner and Fraser. It is used here because of its better condition as source of quotations in the text. In addition, see the Lord Mayor of London version (Starling 1671) and the version included in the *State-Trials* series of 1742 ('Trial of William Penn' 1742), which attributes the text incorrectly to Mead and Penn.

jury's foreman, who was imprisoned after the trial and who claimed that he was held without lawful cause. Bushell sued a writ of *habeas corpus* out of the Court of Common Pleas, and Chief Justice Edward Vaughan then ruled that a jury's verdict could not be questioned or nullified by the Bench, thus illustrating the far-reaching repercussions of public opinion as well as of the inner legal culture.

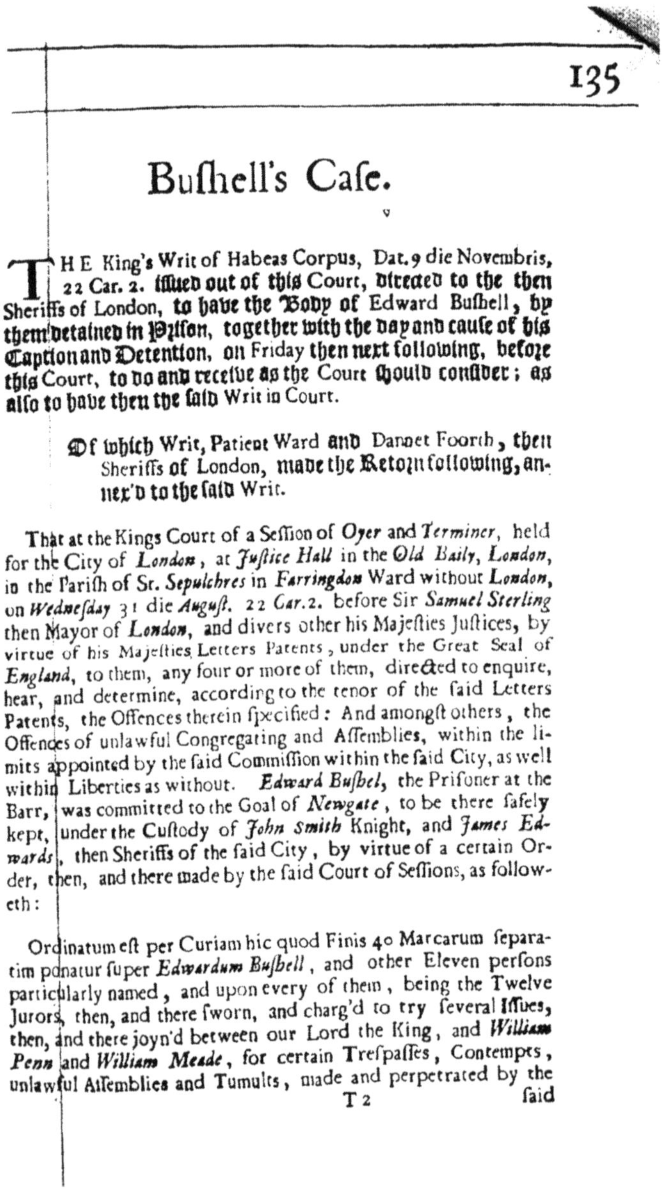
135

Buſhell's Caſe.

THE King's Writ of Habeas Corpus, Dat. 9 die Novembris, 22 Car. 2. iſſued out of this Court, directed to the then Sheriffs of London, to have the Body of Edward Buſhell, by them detained in Priſon, together with the day and cauſe of his Caption and Detention, on Friday then next following, before this Court, to do and receive as the Court ſhould conſider; as alſo to have then the ſaid Writ in Court.

Of which Writ, Patient Ward and Dannet Foorth, then Sheriffs of London, made the Return following, annex'd to the ſaid Writ.

That at the Kings Court of a Seſſion of *Oyer* and *Terminer*, held for the City of *London*, at *Juſtice Hall* in the *Old Baily*, *London*, in the Pariſh of St. *Sepulchres* in *Farringdon* Ward without *London*, on *Wedneſday* 31 die *Auguſt.* 22 *Car.* 2. before Sir *Samuel Sterling* then Mayor of *London*, and divers other his Majeſties Juſtices, by virtue of his Majeſties Letters Patents, under the Great Seal of *England*, to them, any four or more of them, directed to enquire, hear, and determine, according to the tenor of the ſaid Letters Patents, the Offences therein ſpecified: And amongſt others, the Offences of unlawful Congregating and Aſſemblies, within the limits appointed by the ſaid Commiſſion within the ſaid City, as well within Liberties as without. *Edward Buſhel*, the Priſoner at the Barr, was committed to the Goal of *Newgate*, to be there ſafely kept, under the Cuſtody of *John Smith* Knight, and *James Edwards*, then Sheriffs of the ſaid City, by virtue of a certain Order, then, and there made by the ſaid Court of Seſſions, as followeth:

Ordinatum eſt per Curiam hic quod Finis 40 Marcarum ſeparatim ponatur ſuper *Edwardum Buſhell*, and other Eleven perſons particularly named, and upon every of them, being the Twelve Jurors, then, and there ſworn, and charg'd to try ſeveral Iſſues, then, and there joyn'd between our Lord the King, and *William Penn* and *William Meade*, for certain Treſpaſſes, Contempts, unlawful Aſſemblies and Tumults, made and perpetrated by the

T 2 ſaid

From Chief Justice Edward Vaughan's decision on Bushell's Case.

As the legal problems have already been discussed at length by Thomas Andrew Green in his book on the *English Criminal Trial Jury*, there is no need to go into the technical questions again. Instead, I will discuss the trial of Penn and Mead and the several layers of oral and written publicness in the context of the emerging public sphere and its respective sites of discourse. From the beginning, Penn and Mead refused to conform to the rules and the practices of the legal discourse at court. Penn was asked to plead guilty, but he argued that he is unable to remember the twenty-six lines long 'Indictment *verbatim*; and therefore we desire a Copy of it, as is customary in the like occasions' (*Peoples Ancient* 1670b, 307). The Recorder (John Howell) tells him that (according to common practice, that is, institutionalised formal rules) he 'must first plead to the Indictment, before you can have a Copy of it' (ibid.). As the Recorder agrees that no 'Advantage shall be taken against you; you shall have liberty; you shall be heard', Penn pleads not guilty 'in manner and form'. The Court was then adjourned, the defendants being present during the afternoon while different trials were taken up. The unnamed 'observer', whose function was to comment on the proceedings, considered this an 'unkind Practice of the Court to the Prisoners, to make them wait upon the Tryals of Felons and Murderers, thereby designing, in all probability, both to affront and tire them' (308).

When they were brought back into the court room the next day, they were asked why they took off their hats and they were ordered to put them on again. But the moment they were brought before the bar, they were told that they did not pay adequate respect to the Court and were fined forty Marks for contempt of court for not removing their hats (308).[40] One should, however, know that George Fox had repudiated of all formal courtesies and mannered gestures by declaring that 'the Lord [...] forbade me to put off my hat to any, high or low; and I was required to "thee!" and "thou" all men and women, without respect to rich or poor, great or small' (see Keeble 1994). William Penn himself had published a tract in 1669, written during his imprisonment in the Tower, entitled *No Cross, No Crown, Several Sober Reasons against Hat-Honour, Titular Respects, You to a Single Person, with the Apparel and Recreation of the Times* (see Penn 1682).[41]

Apart from the defendants' 'disrespect' in terms of their outward behaviour, they also began to challenge the Judge upon certain legal matters. Penn asked the Judge

40 See the comment in Starling's version of the court report: 'Nota. This is a great Falsehood, for their Hats were put on behind the Barr, before they came into the Court' (1671, 14). See Penn's version of the incident in his subsequent pamphlet (Penn [1671], 39).

41 See the photo (originally from *Life Magazine*, 1944) of the room in the Tower of London where Penn had been imprisoned for blasphemy in December 1668 after the publication of his pamphlet *Sandy Foundation Shaken* (Bronner and Fraser 1986, in front of the title page). Penn wrote the first draft of *No Cross, No Crown*, as well as *Innocency with her Open Face* there (see Bronner and Fraser 1986, 96-99 and 102-104). Regarding *Innocency with her Open Face*: 'The first two chapters of this slender volume were written to denounce customs of the day which denoted deference to others, and to reject inequalities in the social system. The third, and much longer chapter railed against vanity in apparel and the forms of entertainment that engaged the interests and involvement of the upper classes, and to some degree, the lower classes as well' (103). Penn was released in July of 1669.

'upon what Law you ground my Indictment'. When the Recorder refers Penn to the 'Common Law', he asked:

> Where is that Common Law? [...] Shall I plead to an Indictment that hath no Foundation in Law? If it contains that Law you say I have broken, why should you decline to produce the Law, since it will be impossible for the Jury to determine, or agree to bring in their Verdict, who have not the Law produc'd, by which they should measure the Truth of this Indictment, and the Guilt, or contrary of my Fact. (*Peoples Ancient* 1670b, 310-311)

As the Recorder reminds Penn that the Law is *Lex non scripta*, the legally well-educated defendant explains:

> If the Common Law be so hard to be understood, it's far from being very Common: But if the Lord *Cook* [i.e., Edward Coke], in his Institutes, be of any consideration, he tells, That Common Law is Common Right, and that Common Right is the great Charter-Privileges, confirm'd *9 Hen. 3.29 25 Edw. 1.1. 2 Edw. 3.8. Cook Instit. 2 p. 56.* (311)[42]

And 'The question is not, Whether I am guilty of this Indictment, but whether this Indictment be legal' (ibid.). In addition, Penn again and again referred the Bench, and the audience, too, to 'the Rights and Privileges of every Englishman' (*Peoples Ancient* 1670b, 312), to 'the Fundamental Laws of *England*' (ibid.), the 'Antient Fundamental Laws, which relate to Liberty and Property' (ibid.), and to the 'Rights and Privileges of English-men' (314). Penn even accused the Bench of 'Barbarous and Unjust Proceedings', claiming:

> Who can say he hath right to the Coat upon his Back? Certainly our Liberties are openly to be invaded, our Wives to be ravished, our Children slaved, our Families ruined, and our Estates led away in Triumph, by every sturdy Beggar and malicious Informer, as their Trophies, but our (pretended) Forfeits for Conscience sake; the Lord of Heaven and Earth will be Judg between us in this matter. (312)

Horle maintained that this trial:

> quickly degenerated into a ludicrous dispute between Penn, the lord mayor, and the jury, with Penn endeavoring to elevate a misdemeanor accusation into a critical dissection of the entire common-law tradition and a case on which depended the lives, liberties, estates, and families of all Englishmen. As in many Quaker trials, confusion, noise, and a carnival atmosphere prevailed. (Horle 1988, 116)

This remark seems to be rather unfair towards those not in power, but seeking to convert the court room into a site of public discourse and presenting their dissenting arguments to the audience: 'If my noise was *uncivil*, it was because it was Legal, and I expect not a better Character from such, as to proclaim me a broacher of Heresies, *because I honestly demanded the free course of the Fundamental Laws of* England' (Penn [1671], 43).[43] The 'uncivil noise' was rather a symbol of passive disobedience.[44]

42 Starling's own comment: 'Now the Common Law is Common Right, or *Lex Rationis*, imprinted in every man's understanding' (quoted in Green 1985, 223, n.101).

43 Horle, again and again, rather uncritically uses the term 'criminal activity' when speaking about Quaker activities and actions.

44 See 'Assessing Resistance [of all sorts of Nonconformists]: Passive Disobedience or Sedition?' (Greaves 1990, 121ff.).

XII. THE COURT-ROOM AND PRINTED PUBLICNESS: ACTIONS AND REACTIONS

Penn is in no way conforming to the rules of the legal discourse, openly accusing the Bench of arbitrariness. The Bench in turn hits back by means of verbal aggression and 'manacing Language' (*Peoples Ancient* 1670b, 315), calling him a 'sawcy [...] an impertinent [...] a troublesome Fellow' (311): 'You deserve to have your Tongue cut out' (313) and 'Pull that Fellow down, pull him down' (314);[45] and by sending Penn and, subsequently, Mead to the bale dock.[46] In his subsequent pamphlet *Truth Rescued from Imposture* Penn answers to the charges of disturbing the court-room proceedings by shouting and making noise:

> The plain truth was this; that because I endeavoured to inform the Jury of my Case, and to take off the asperity of some mens passions, they turn'd me, and my Companion, into the *Bale-dock*, which though even with the Bar, yet besides the main Court, and so deeply impaled, that we could not see the Court, nor hear the Charge; but upon information, that the *Recorder* was charging the *Jury, I stept up, and my Fellow-Prisoner after me*, and exclaimed aginst the irregularity of such proceedings. And for this plain Reproof, and but necessary demand of the *English* Right, *of Prisoners being present at the giving of the Charge*, commanded us into the *Hole*, a place so noisom and stinking, that the *Mayor himself would have thought it an unfit Sty for his Swine*. (Penn [1671], 43; cf. 47f.)

When, in the end, the jurymen returned a verdict of Penn being just guilty of 'speaking in *Gracious-street*' (*Peoples Ancient* 1670b, 315) and would not go beyond that point, the Bench began to threaten the twelve, calling their foreman, Bushell, 'an impudent canting Fellow' (316).

Penn, in turn, addresses the jury: '*You are* Englishmen, *mind your Priviledge, give not away your Right*' (317). They are told 'not to be dismiss'd till we have a Verdict that the Court will accept; and you shall be lockt up, without Meat, Drink, Fire, and Tobacco; [...] we will have a Verdict, by the help of God, or you shall starve for it' (316). And again, as the Observer remarked, the 'Court swore several Persons, to keep the Jury all night without Meat, Drink, Fire, or any other Accomodation: They had not so much as a Chamber-pot, tho desired' (317); 'bring in another Verdict, or you shall starve; and I will have you carted about the City, as in *Edward* III's time' (319).[47] Penn

---

45 See Starling's version of the trial account, where the Mayor orders the gaoler to 'Stop his mouth; [...] bring Fetters, and stake him to the Ground' (1671, 28). See also his comment: 'Upon this Mr. *Penn* was very silent and quiet, although nothing was done to him' (29). In his answer to Starling, Penn speaks of the judges' 'Billingsgate Rhetorick' (8).

46 See Starling's note: '*Penn* made such an uncivil noise, that the Court could not give the *Jury* the Charge; he was therefore put into the *Bail-Dock*, which stands even with the Bar, and the Prisoners might hear the Charge as well as a Prisoner might hear at the Bar' (1671, 21).

47 The members of the jury were fined 40 marks, the equivalent of $1,000 today (according to Bronner and Fraser 1986, 119). In a later trial, a case of two Nottinghamshire Appeals in 1676, the jury was unable to find a unanimous verdict. As one of the four jurymen, disagreeing with the rest, was taken ill and was in need of some refreshment, Justice Whaley told them: 'If they did not agree, they should be kept there till they died, and as one of them died, the Court would choose another, till they were all dead' (quoted in Braithwaite 1962, 226).

thereby succeeded in converting the court room into a site of rational public discourse by breaking the formal regulations of the institutionalised hegemonic discourse. As the jury foreman, Edward Bushell, in the end, convinced by Penn's arguments, refused to pay his fine, he was jailed, but after two months, the Court of Common Pleas issued a writ of *habeas corpus* to set him and the others free.

In the address 'To the English Reader', the author from the start attacks the Bench for having violated '*the Fundamental Laws of* England', thereby taking 'Liberty of Conscience' as a '*Pretence for Rebellion, and* Religious Assemblies, Routs, *and* Riots; *and the* Defenders *of both, are by them, reputed* Factious *and* Disaffected' (*People's Ancient* 1670b, 304). Referring to the Recorder's emotional outbreak, advocating '*something like unto the Spanish Inquisition [...] in England*' (319), Sir Samuel Starling is ridiculed for his '*publick Panegyrick upon the* Spanish Inquisition, highly admiring the Prudence of the Romish Church' (305)[48] and, in addition, the Canterbury Chaplain is chastised for a '*printed Mercenary Discourse against Toleration*' (ibid.). Thus, the address to the reader is replete with catchwords, stereotypes and invectives.

On the other hand, the Appendices are examples of legal expertise and comments on the trial account proper. Thus, the 'Appendix [...] *what might have been offer'd against the Indictment*' has some remarks about the Common Law of England, the function of judge and jury, religious assemblies and disturbance of the peace, contempt of the King and the laws, as well as the 'fundamental' and the 'superficial' laws. The author is a staunch defender of the ancient English constitution:

> There is no Country, that has more constantly express'd her Care and deep Sollicitude, to the preservation of her fundamental Laws, than the *English* Nation [...] our own Authors are not lacking to inform us, that the Liberties, Properties, and Privileges of the *English* Nation are very antient. (328)

Quotations from the *Mirror of Justices* and the first centuries of English law follow (328-329), and references to West Saxon King Ine's and to King Alfred's legislation as reported in the *Leges Edwardi Confessoris* and in William Lambarde's *Archaionomia sive de priscis anglorum legibus libri* (from 1658 and 1644, respectively; 328-330; for the historical references, see Wormald 2001). Another seventeen pages are devoted to the '*Rehearsal of the Material Parts of the Great Charter of* England', its confirmation under Edward I (*People's Ancient* 1670b, 330-347), including a comment on the fact that:

> there is no Law against the Hat; and where there is no Law, there can be no Transgression, and consequently no legal Amercement or Fine [...]. But how the Prisoners were trepanned into it, is most ridiculous on the side of the Contrivers, that finding their Hats off, would have them put on again by their Officers, to fool the Prisoners, with a trial of putting them off again; which childish Conceit not being gratified, they Fined them the Forty Marks apiece! (338)

In the end the author returns to the accusation of the Recorder being in favour of the Spanish Inquisition:

> If the *Recorder* has spoke for no more than himself, it is well; but certainly he little deserves to be though a *Protestant, and a Lawyer, that put both Reformation and Law into the Inquisition:* There

48 See Starling's corrections and answers to the charge of having said something similar (1671, 9).

> being nothing more destructive of the Fundamental Laws and Liberties of England, and that noble Design of Primitive Reformation, than the Arbitrary Power and Terrifying Racks of the *Spanish* Inquisition [...] doubless the supreme Governors of the Land are highly oblig'd in Honor and Conscience [...] to take thise things into their serious Consideration, as what is expected from them by those who earnestly wish Theirs and the Kingdom's Safety and Prosperity. (347)

Penn's trial was supplemented by several additional texts: Samuel Starling's *Answer To the Seditious and Scandalous Pamphlet, Entituled, The Tryal of W. Penn and W. Mead* and Penn's own *Truth Rescued from Imposture* (1671). Starling's pamphlet of some thirty-eight pages openly attacks the authors of *The People's Ancient and Just Liberties*, which, according to Starling, seems to have been 'composed by *William Penn* the half *Quaker*', and which he calls a 'Blasphemous Treatise'. Penn does not 'blush to villifie and contemn the Kings Court, and falsely scandalize and reproach the Kings Justice' (Starling 1671, 1). Starling is thereby carrying on the debate at a different site of discourse, addressing 'the Gentlemen of the long Robe':

> look to your selves, and your *Westminster-Hall*: If these learned Reformers of Religion shall likewise Reform your Laws and Methods of Proceedings (as doubtless they design it) and make twelve Jury-men, eleven of which it's possible can neither write nor read, to be the sole Judges both of Law and Fact; farewell then to your great Acquisitions, your Year books then will be out of date, and an *Ouster* will be put to your Books of Entries. (Starling 1671, 2)

Starling's appeal to the said Gentlemen is meant to make them aware of the fact that institutionalised rules of court, derived from 'time immemorial', ought to be kept intact and stable. The reference to 'your great Acquisitions' is meant to remind them of the long standing institution of the 'Year Books' (such as Edmund Plowden's famous *Les commentaries, ou les reportes de dyvers cases*, 1571) and, thus, of the control the inns of court and chancery had over reporting and case law (see Baker 2000, ch. 10).[49] In fact, Starling is giving what he calls 'an Eye and Ear witness of all that passed, to give a True and Impartial Relation of that Affair' (Starling 1671, 10).

Different from the court room, the public exchange of legal arguments over the rights of Judges and Juries and the fining of Jurors is much more heated, aggressive and, at times, even scatological. Starling accuses his opponents and especially the 'Youngster' Penn (otherwise 'this wild rambling Colt *William Penn*' [6]) of their glorying so much in the Magna Charta 'for their own Ends, although when it toucheth them in point of observing the Laws of the Holy Church and Gods Worship, they will call it *Magna Fartha*, or something worse' (2-3). In the end, after discussing the question of fining the Jurors, Starling addresses his readers, 'the Honourable Sages of our Law', and he prays 'That in this, and in all other Business of Concernment, that God (the Great Judge of Heaven and Earth) would guide and direct them' (38). Thus, Starling's audience is seemingly not only a restricted one of legal specialists, but also

49 'The principle purpose of the record [of the plea rolls] was to establish what had been decided, so that the decision might be final: what later lawyers would call estoppel by judgment or *res judicata*. Like minutes of meetings at the present day, they were concerned to record the outcome of proceedings rather than the discussions and reaons which explain how the result was arrived at. [...] in the case of trial by jury [...] it noted the process to summon the jurors, the swearing in of the

AN

ANSWER

To the *Seditious* and *Scandalous*

PAMPHLET,

ENTITULED,

The Tryal of *W. Penn* and *W. Mead*, at the Sessions held at the *Old Baily, London*, the 1, 3, 4, 5, of *Sept.* 1670.

CONTAINED

In FOUR SECTIONS.

SECT. I. *The Design of the Libellous Pamphlet discovered.*

II. *The Scandals against the then Lord-Mayor, Sir* Thomas Bludworth, *and Sir* John Hovel *Recorder, Answered.*

III. *The Justice and Honour of that Court Vindicated, by a True and Impartial Relation of that whole* TRYAL.

IV. *The Fining of that Jury that gave two contrary Verdicts justified, to prevent a Failer of Justice in* LONDON.

Jude, Verse 8.

These filthy Dreamers, defile the Flesh, despise Dominions, speak evil of Dignities.

Verse 19.

These be they, who separate themselves, sensual, having not the Spirit.

Written by *S. S.* a Friend to JUSTICE, and Courts of JUSTICE.

LONDON, Printed by *W. G.* 1671.

those in power, asking them to stick to the institutionalised juridical processes and precedents.

Penn, on the other hand, challenging Starling with a pamphlet entitled *Truth Rescued from Imposture; Or, A Brief Reply to a meer Rapsodie of Lies, Folly, and Slander*,[50] includes two epigraphs from the Bible, one of them: '*A Whip for the Horse, a Bridle for the Ass,* and a Rod for the Fools Back' (Prov. 26.3 KJV) – meaning Starling's back. On the title page, Penn calls himself, 'a profest Enemy of Oppression'. Penn's intended audience is less restricted than Starling's. He even asks his readers,

> *first to peruse his* Fardle *of Impostures, and Abuse, before thou read'st me; lest thou shouldst think I have wrong'd him in citation:* So scurrilous, so false, and withal so ridiculous is he in his own whole conceited Enterprize, *that but a little charity would make one think, that no man could be so great an Enemy to* Truth, *and to* Himself. (Penn [1671], 3)

Penn is clearly in favour of an open discussion in public. Without going further into the legal debate, Penn harks back to his earlier arguments: the 'English Priviledge', that is, the Fundamental Laws, is endangered and trials seem to turn 'upon the sole pin of Will and Power' (ibid.). Concerning the legal controversy over the power of juries, Penn, answering Starling, bases his arguments on 'antient Law of the Land, Confirmed by thirty two Parliaments, acknowledged by all *Lawyers*' (30).

XIII. The Court Room, the Public Sphere, and Epistemological Relativity

A few moths later, Lord Chief Justice Vaughan 'finally laid the problem' of the fining of jurors to rest (Green 1985, 237), ruling that a judge was not allowed to punish or threaten a jury that arrived at a different conclusion than the Bench, thereby establishing the principle of noncoercion. Without going into the legal problems of law-finding of fact-finding (see 200ff.); Vaughan was of the opinion that, 'when the King hath constituted any man a Judge under him, his ability, parts, fitness for his place, are not to be reflected on, censured, defamed, or vilified by any other person' (Vaughan 1707, 138). On the other hand, Vaughan is clearly of the opinion that people differ in their conclusions from evidence and in their opinions, thus, establishing a truth that is at the basis of our concept of the public sphere:

> I would know whether any thing be more common, that for two men Students, Barristers, or Judges, to deduce contrary and opposite Conclusions out of the same Case in Law? And is there any difference that two men should inferr distinct conclusions from the same Testimony? Is any

---

jury, and the verdict, but not the evidence adduced by the parties or the submissions of counsel. [...] the judges' reasons and the guiding authorities, if any there were, formed no part of the record' (Baker 2000, 134-135). 'The year books [...] do seem to have been a peculiarly English phenomenon. They reproduce what purports to be a verbatim account, in Anglo-French, of legal discussions in the royal courts, principally in the Common Bench. Doubtless they are not strictly verbatim, in that they are obviously truncated versions of what must in reality have been longer discussions' (136).

50 The title page states 'Printed in the Year, 1670'; but at the end of the pamphlet, Penn admits having written the pamphlet 'From *Newgate* Prison in *London*, the first Moneth, 1671'.

> thing more known than that the same Author, and place in that Author, is forcibly urg'd to maintain contrary conclusions, and the decision hard, which is in the right? Is any thing more frequent in the controversies of Religion, that to press the same Text for opposite Tenents? How then comes it to pass that two persons may not apprehend with reason and honesty, what a witness, or many, say, to prove in the understanding of one plainly one thing, but in the apprehension of the other, clearly the contrary thing? (141-142)

After looking into more of the legal arguments, Vaughan adds another observation about the problem of ascertaining the truth, arising out of the epistemological subjectivity that is the reason for the multiplicity of viewpoints: 'A man cannot see by anothers Eye, nor hear by anothers Ear, no more can a man conclude or inferr the thing to be resolv'd by anothers Understanding or Reasoning' (148; cf. Green 1985, 244). Such an epistemology of relativism and subjectivity underlies the concept of the public sphere as a field of mediation between different points of views.

XIV. Crook, Penn, and the Public Sphere during the 1790s

It is not surprising that trial accounts of Crook and of Penn were reprinted shortly after the French Revolution. The nineties were a time of growing repression and intimidation of the radical supporters of a democratic change of society which had, for some time, met and discussed political problems in a number of debating societies (McCalman 1987; Thale 1989). These societies, in London and elsewhere, attracted all sorts of people, most of them from the lower classes, who wanted to practice speaking in public. Apart from the London Corresponding Society and the debating clubs, the Constitutional Society played an important role in propagating a change of society. Edmund Burke, in his *Reflections on the Revolution in France* (1790), warned his correspondent that he must not be 'reckoned among the approvers of certain proceedings in France, from the solemn public seal of sanction they have received from two clubs of gentlemen in London, called the Constitutional Society and the Revolution Society' (Burke 1969, 85). Burke goes on the praise the English Revolution of 1688 and those:

> who cultivate the memory of our revolution, and those who are attached to the constitution of this kingdom will take good care how they are involved with persons who, under the pretext of zeal toward the Revolution and Constitution, too frequently wander from their true principles. (86)

The London branch of the Constitutional Society (or Society for Constitutional Information):

> appears to be of a charitable, and so far of a laudable, nature: it was intended for the circulation, at the expence of the members, of many books, which few others would be at the expence of buying; and which might lie on the hands of the booksellers, to the great loss of an useful body of men. Whether the books so charitably circulated, were ever as charitably read, is more than I know. Possibly several of them have been exported to France; and, like goods not in request here, may with you have found a market. I have heard much talk of the lights to be drawn from books that are sent from hence. What improvements they have had in their passage (as it is said some liquors are meliorated by crossing the sea) I cannot tell: but I never heard a man of common judgment, or the least degree of information, speak a word in praise of the greater part of the publications circulated

by that society; nor have their proceedings been accounted, except by some of themselves, as of any serious consequence. (87)

As the interest in the French Revolution was growing, the government was alarmed at the proliferation of the public debate of parliamentary reform. Thus, in May 1792, the king issued a proclamation 'for preventing seditious meetings and writings [...] tending to excite tumult and disorder' (quoted in Thale 1989, 64). And after the *Habeas Corpus* Act had been suspended in May 1794, the radical leaders Thomas Hardy, J. Horne Tooke, and John Thelwall were arrested and put to trial. In the end, they were acquitted and released, but the Government renewed the suspension of the *Habeas Corpus* Act for another half a year, while the 'Two Acts' of 1795 and a royal proclamation told magistrates 'to discourage, prevent and suppress all seditious and unlawful assemblies' (Emsley 1985, 811).

Hardy, Tooke and Thelwall used the court room as a site of the public sphere, reasoning about legal and political matters (Houswitschka 2002). Thus, there was a widespread interest amongst the radicals and the lower classes to look back into history and study what radicals more than 120 years earlier had done and written. In particular, the Constitutional Society, or Society for Constitutional Information, founded in 1780, was looking for precedents in Anglo-Saxon, English, and American history (Thompson 1968, 94). Thus, there was a 1791 reprint of Crook's 'The Cry of the Innocent for Justice',[51] and *The People's Ancient and Just Liberties Asserted* was reissued under William Penn's name by the Sheffield Constitutional Society (Penn 1794).[52] The printer, J. Crome, had already published Thomas Paine's *Address and declaration, of the friends of universal peace and liberty* (Paine 1791). The title page of the Penn trials bore a motto taken from James Thomson's poem, 'Liberty' (1735):

Unblest by Virtue, government a League,
Becomes a circling Junto of the Great.
To rob by Law; Religion mild a Yoke
To tame the stooping Soul, and trick of State
To make their Rapine, and to share the Prey.
What are without it Senates, but a Farce
Of consultation deep, and Reason free,
While the determined Voice and Heart are sold?
What boasted Freedom, but a sounding Name?[53]

51 In the 1791 edition of *The Design of Christianity, with other Books, Epistles, and Manuscripts*, 'The Cry of the Innocent ' has its own title page which is actually dated '1790'.

52 The Society for Constitutional Information did not have local branches, but other Constitutional Societies, founded and conducted independently, corresponded with London (see Thompson 1968, 115, n.3).

53 'Liberty', 5.99-107; in Thomson 1961, 395. The speaker throughout the whole poem is goddess of liberty. For 'Liberty' (1735) read as a didactic narrative poem on politics and history, see Müllenbrock 1974, 201ff., wherein it is examined in the context of the 1730s and the opposition of Tory and Whig writers against Robert Walpole, who was accused of undermining the idea of liberty. According to historians since the sixteenth century, the ideas of liberty, mixed monarchy, and balance of powers was associated with the concept of the ancient constitution that, according to this theory, had been developed by early Germanic tribes, especially the Goths, later on taken over

One of the arguments was that the governing elite was robbing the people by misusing the law. As the poet George Dyer frankly remarked in his *Complaints of the Poor People of England* (1793): 'Several poor men are now lingering in prison, when the men who have thrown them in are the criminals. But ignorance was the lot of the poor man, and their prosecutors and lawyers were, in broad English, KNOWING RASCALS' (in Wu 1995, 42). It was no longer just the press that had assumed the function of a public watchdog (Hellmuth 1990), but the radicals themselves took over the job in one way or another. They looked back into history, searching for examples and prominent cases of public prosecution. There were the well-known trials of John Lilburne and Algernon Sidney, but, as far as I have been able to determine, the trial accounts of John Crook and William Penn have never been placed within this tradition of resistance located in public sites where institutionalised norms and forms of discourse had to be subverted.

Primary Literature

Besse, Joseph (1753). *A Collection of the Sufferings of the People Called Quakers, for the Testimony of a Good Conscience*. 2 vols. London: Hinde.

Burke, Edmund (1969). *Reflections on the Revolution in France and on the Proceedings in Certain Societies in London Relative to that Event*. Ed. with an intro. Conor Cruise O'Brien. Harmondsworth: Penguin. Original edition 1790.

Crook, John (1662). *The Cry of the Innocent for Justice: being a Relation of the Tryal of John Crook, and others, at the General Sessions, held in the Old Bayley, London [...] Published for no other end but to prevent Mistakes, and to satisfie all moderate Enquirers, concerning the Dealings and Usages that the said J.C. and others met withal, from the beginning of the said tryals to the end*. In *British Trials, 1660-1900*. Microfiche edition. Cambridge: Chadwyck-Healey, 1993, no. 628.

_______ (1701). 'The Cry of the Innocent for Justice.' In *The Design of Christianity, with other Books, Epistles and Manuscripts, of that Ancient Faithful Servant of Christ Jesus, John Crook, Who departed this Life the 26th Day of the Second Month, 1699. In the Eighty-second Year of his Age*. London: Printed by T. Sowle, 150-207.

_______ (1706). *A Short History of the Life of John Crook. Containing some of his Spiritual Travels and Breathings after God, in his Young and Tender Years: Also an Account of various Temptations wherewith he was Exercised, and the Means by which he came to the Knowledge of the Truth. The Manuscript hereof, Written by his own Hand, was found since his other Works were Published in Print*. London: Printed and sold by T. Sowle.

_______ (1791), 'The Cry of the Innocent for Justice [1790].' In *The Design of Christianity, with other Books, Epistles, and Manuscripts, of that Ancient Faithful Servant of Christ Jesus, John Crook. To which is Prefixed a Short Account of His Life Written by Himself*. London: Printed by James Phillips, 146-211.

Fox, George (1831). *A Collection of many Select and Christian Epistles*. 2 vols. Philadelphia.

---

by the English (240ff.). For an historical analysis of this idea, see Böker 2002. For a commentary on the lines quoted as an epigraph, see Müllenbrock 1974, 282f. Thomson's poem and his ideas on liberty were highly approved of by the republican historian Catherine Macaulay in her *History of England* (8 vols., 1763-1783), but also by the British radicals of the 1790s who emphasised the Germanic origins of time-honoured institutions that had to be defended against the onslaught of governmental repression (see Vernon 1996).

Paine, Thomas (1791). *Address and declaration, of the friends of universal peace and liberty, As Address and declaration, As some gentlemen have industriously laboured to throw an odium on the French Revolution, [...] it is therefore judged advisable, [...] to re-print the following address [...] At a select meeting of the friends of universal peace and liberty, held at the Thatched-House Tavern, August 20th. 1791*. Sheffield: Reprinted by J. Crome.

Penn, William [1671]. *Truth Rescued from Imposture; Or, a Brief Reply to a meer Rapsodie of Lies, Folly, and Slander; But a pretended answer, to the tryal of W. Penn and W. Mead &c. writ and subscrib'd S.S. By a profest Enemy to Oppresion. W.P.* [London].

________ (1682). *No Cross, No Crown, Or Several Sober Reasons Against Hat-Honour, Titular-Respects, You to a Single Person, with the Apparel and Recreation of the Times [...] Printed in the Year, 1669*. 2nd enlarged ed. London: Printed for Mark Swaner. Original edition 1669.

________ (1794). *People's Ancient and Just Liberties Asserted [...]*. Sheffield: Printed for the Constitutional Society by J. Crome.

*Peoples ancient and just liberties asssrted [*sic*], in the Tryal of William Penn, and William Mead, At the Sessions held at the Old-Bailey in London, on the first, third, fourth and fifth of Sept. 7⁰. against the most Arbitrary procedure of that Court* (1670a). [London: Andrew Sowle].

Peoples Ancient and Just Liberties asserted, in the Tryal of William Penn, and William Mead, at the Sessions held at the Old-Bailey in London, the first, third, fourth and fifth of Sept. 1670. against the most Arbitrary Procedure of that Court (1670b). In *British Trials, 1660-1900*. Microfiche edition. Cambridge: Chadwyck-Healey 1993, no. 4 (10/1) and no. 5.

Saint German, Christopher (1974). *St. German's Doctor and Student*. Ed. T.F.T. Plucknett and J.L. Barton. London: Selden Society. Original edition 1523.

S[tarling], [Sir] S[amuel] (1671). *An Answer To the Seditious and Scandalous Pamphlet, Entituled, The Tryal of W. Penn and W. Mead, at the Sessions held at the Old Bailey, London, the 1, 3, 4, 5, of Sept. 1670 [...]. Written by S.S., a Friend to Justice, [...]*. London: Printed by W.G.

Thomson, James (1961). *The Complete Works*. Ed. J. Logie Robertson. London: Oxford University Press.

'Trial of William Penn and William Mead, at the Old-Baily, for a Tumultuous Assembly, the 1st, 3d, 4th, and 5th of September, 1670. 22 Car.II. Wrote by themselves' (1742). In A *Complete Collection of State-Trials, and Proceedings upon High-Treason, and other Crimes and Misdemeanours; from the Reign of King Richard II. to the Reign of King George II*. Vol. 2. 3rd ed. London, 610-616.

Vaughan, Edward, ed. (1707), *The Reports and Arguments of that Learned Judge Sir John Vaughan Kt. Late Chief Justice of His Majesties Court of Common Pleas. Being All of them Special Cases, and many wherein he Pronounced the Resolution of the whole Court of Common Pleas; At the time he was Chief Justice there*. London. Printed by Thomas Roycroft and Richard Marriott.

REFERENCES

Agamben, Giorgio (1998). *Homo Sacer: Sovereign Power and Bare Life*. Trans. Daniel Heller-Roazen. Stanford: Stanford University Press.

Baker, J.H. (2000). *The Common Law Tradition: Lawyers, Books, and the Law*. London: Hambledon Press.

Bell, Ian A. (1991). *Literature and Crime in Augustan England*. London: Routledge.

Böker, Uwe (1996). 'Literatur, Kriminalität und Rechtskultur: Ein Forschungsbericht.' In Uwe Böker and Christoph Houswitschka (eds.), *Literatur, Kriminalität und Rechtskultur im 17. und 18. Jahrhundert: Tagung am 17. und 18. Juni 1994 an der Technischen Universität Dresden*. Essen: Blaue Eule, 11-35.

________ (2001). 'The Institutionalisation of Legal Norms and Values in England (1500-1900).' In Uwe Böker and Julie A. Hibbard (eds.), *Processes of Institutionalisation: Case Studies in Law, Prison and Censorship*. Essen: Blaue Eule, 13- 60.

________ (2002). 'Angelsächsische Geltungsgeschichten der frühen Neuzeit: Die Legitimierung der *Ancient Constitution* und das Prinzip der *Rule of Law*.' In Gert Melville (ed.), *Geltungsgeschichten*. Cologne: Böhlau, forthcoming.

Braithwaite, Alfred W. (1962). 'Early Friends' Experiences with Juries.' *Journal of the Friends' Historical Society* 50, 217-227.

Bronner, Edwin B., and David Fraser (1986). *William Penn's Published Writings, 1660-1726: An Interpretative Bibliography*. Philadelphia: University of Pennsylvania Press.

Burgess, Glenn(1993). *Politics of the Ancient Constitution. An Introduction to English Political Thought, 1603-1642*. University Park: Pennsylvania State University Pres.

Calhoun, Craig, ed. (1992). *Habermas and the Public Sphere*. Cambridge, MA: MIT Press.

Cragg, Gerald R. (1971). *Puritanism in the Period of the Great Persecution, 1660-1688*. New York: Russell and Russell. Original edition 1957.

Dolin, Kieran (1999). *Fiction and the Law: Legal Discourse in Victorian and Modernist Literature*. Cambridge: Cambridge University Press.

Emsley, Clive (1985). 'Repression, "Terror" and the Rule of Law in England during the Decade of the French Revolution.' *English Historical Review* 100, 800-825.

Fraser, David (1986). 'William Penn and the Underground Press.' In Bronner and Fraser, *William Penn's Published Writings, 1660-1726: An Interpretative Bibliography*. Philadelphia: University of Pennsylvania Press, 49-86.

Friedman, Lawrence M. (1971). *Law and Society: An Introduction*. Englewood Cliffs, NJ: Prentice Hall.

________ (1975). *The Legal System: A Social Science Perspective*. New York: Russell Sage.

________ (1990): *The Republic of Choice: Law, Authority, and Culture*. Cambridge, MA: Harvard University Press.

Gaskill, Malcolm (2000). *Crime and Mentalities in Early Modern England*. Cambridge: Cambridge University Press.

Gladfelder, Hal (2001). *Criminality and Narraitve in Eighteenth-Century England: Beyond the Law*. Baltimore: Johns Hopkins University Press.

Greaves, Richard L. (1990). *Enemies under His Feet: Radicals and Nonconformists in Britain, 1664-1677*. Stanford: Stanford University Press.

Green, Thomas Andrew (1985). *Verdict According to Conscience: Perspectives on English Criminal Trial Jury, 1200-1800*. Chicago: University of Chicago Press.

Habermas, Jürgen (1962). *Strukturwandel der Öffentlichkeit: Untersuchungen zu einer Kategorie der bürgerlichen Gesellschaft*. Neuwied: Luchterhand.

________ (1992a). 'Further Reflections on the Public Sphere.' In Craig Calhoun (ed.), *Habermas and the Public Sphere*. Cambridge, MA: MIT Press, 421-461.

________ (1992b). *Faktizität und Geltung: Beiträge zur Diskurstheorie des Rechts und des demokratischen Rechtsstaats*. Frankfurt/Main: Suhrkamp.

Hazelton, Meiling (2000). '"Mony Choaks": The Quaker Critique of the Seventeenth-Century Public Sphere.' *Modern Philology* 98, 251-270.

Hellmuth, Eckhart (1990). '"The Palladium of all other English Liberties": Reflections on the Liberty of the Press in England during the 1760s and 1770s.' In Eckhart Hellmuth (ed.), *The Transformation of Political Culture: England and Germany in the Late Eigtheenth Century*. Oxford: Oxford University Press, 467-501.

Hill, Christopher (1986). *Puritanism and Revolt: Studies in Interpretation of the English Revolution of the Seventeenth Century*. Harmondsworth: Penguin.

Hohendahl, Peter Uwe, ed. (2000). *Öffentlichkeit: Geschichte eines kritischen Begriffs*. With Russell A. Berman, Karen Kenkel, and Arthur Strum. Stuttgart: Metzler.

Horle, Craig. (1988). *The Quakers and the English Legal System 1660-1688*. Philadelphia: University of Philadelphia Press.

Houswitschka, Christoph (2002). *Die Rechtskultur der High Treason Trials von 1794 und die Literatur der Demokratisierung*. [Forthcoming].

Ingle, Homer L. (1994). *First Among Friends: George Fox and the Creation of Quakerism*. Oxford: Oxford University Press.

Jhering, Rudolf von (1981). *Abhandlungen aus dem römischen Recht*. Aalen: Scientia. Original edition Leipzig: Breitkopf und Härtel, 1844.

Keeble, N.H. (1994). 'The Politic and the Polite in Quaker Prose: The Case of William Penn.' In Thomas N. Corns and David Loewenstein (eds.), *The Emergence of Quaker Writing: Dissenting Literature in Seventeenth-Century England*. London: Frank Cass, 112-125.

Knott, John R. (1993). *Discourses of Martyrdom in English Literature, 1563-1694*. Cambridge: Cambridge University Press.

________ (1994). 'Joseph Besse and the Quaker Culture of Suffering.' In Thomas N. Corns and David Loewenstein (eds.), *The Emergence of Quaker Writing: Dissenting Literature in Seventeenth-Century England*. London: Frank Cass, 126-141.

Kraus, W. (2000). *Das erzählte Selbst: Die narrative Konstruktion von Identität in der Spätmoderne*. 2nd ed. Pfaffenweiler: Centaurus Verlag.

Le Goff, Jacques (1974). 'Mentalities: A History of Ambiguities.' In Jacques Le Goff and Pierre Nora (eds.), *Constructing the Past: Essays in Historical Methodology*. Cambridge: Cambridge University Press, 166-180.

Lottes, Günther (1979). *Politische Aufklärung und plebejisches Publikum: Zur Theorie und Praxis des englischen Radikalismus im späten 18. Jahrhundert*. Munich: Oldenbourg.

Lüderssen, Klaus (1996). *Genesis und Geltung in der Jurisprudenz*. Frankfurt/Main: Suhrkamp.

McCalman, Iain (1987). 'Ultra-Radicalism and Convivial Debating-Clubs in London, 1795-1838.' *The English Historical Review* 102, 309-333.

McMullan, John L. (1984). *The Canting Crew: London's Criminal Underworld 1550-1700*. New Brunswick, NJ: Rutgers University Press.

________ (1987). 'Policing the Criminal Underworld: State Power and Decentralised Social Control in London 1550-1700.' In John Lowman, Robert J. Menzies and T.S. Palys (eds.), *Transcarceration: Essays in the Sociology of Social Control*. Cambridge Studies in Criminology 55. Aldershot: Gower, 119-138.

Müllenbrock, Heinz-Joachim (1974). *Whigs kontra Tories: Studien zum Einfluß der Politik auf die englische Literatur des frühen 18. Jahrhunderts*. Heidelberg: Winter.

Negt, Oskar, and Alexander Kluge (1972). *Öffentlichkeit und Erfahrung: Zur Organisationsanalyse von bürgerlicher und proletarischer Öffentlichkeit*. Frankfurt/Main: Suhrkamp.

Nelken, David (1995). 'Disclosing/Invoking Legal Culture: An Introduction.' *Social & Legal Studies* 4, 435-452.

________, ed. (1997). *Comparing Legal Cultures*. Aldershot: Ashgate.

Penney, Norman, ed. (1907). *The First Publishers of Truth: Being early Records (now first printed) of the Introduction of Quakerism into the Counties of England and Wales*. London: Headley Brothers.

Perkin, Harold (1969). *The Origins of Modern English Society 1780-1880*. London: Routledge.

Price, Richard (1999). *British Society 1680-1880: Dynamism, Containment and Change*. Cambridge: Cambridge University Press.

Raiser, Thomas (1987). *Rechtssoziologie: Ein Lehrbuch*. Frankfurt/Main: Metzner.

Rehberg, Karl-Siegbert (1994). 'Institutionen als symbolische Ordnungen: Leitfragen und Grundkategorien zur Theorie und Analyse institutioneller Mechanismen.' In Gerhard Göhler (ed.), *Die Eigenart der Institutionen: Zum Profil politischer Institutionentheorie*. Baden-Baden: Nomos, 47-76.

Rottleuthner, Hubert (1987). *Einführung in die Rechtssoziologie*. Darmstadt: Wissenschaftliche Buchgesellschaft.

Schönert, Jörg, ed. (1983). *Literatur und Kriminalität: Die gesellschaftliche Erfahrung von Verbrechen und Strafverfolgung als Gegenstand des Erzählens – Deutschland, England und Frankreich 1850-1880*. Tübingen: Niemeyer.

________, ed. (1991). *Erzählte Kriminalität: Zur Typologie und Funktion von narrativen Darstellungen in Strafrechtspflege, Publizistik und Literatur zwischen 1770 und 1920*. Tübingen: Niemeyer.

Stallybrass, Peter, and Allon White (1986). *The Politics and Poetics of Transgression*. London: Methuen.

Straub, Jürgen. (1998). 'Geschichten erzählen, Geschichte bilden: Grundzüge einer narrativen Psychologie historischer Sinnbildung.' In J. Straub (ed.), *Erzählung, Identität und historisches Bewußtsein: Die psychologische Konstruktion von Zeit und Geschichte*. Frankfurt/Main: Suhrkamp.

Swan, Beth (1997). *Fictions of Law: An Investigation of the Law in Eighteenth-Century English Fiction*. Frankfurt/Main: Lang.

Thale, Mary (1989). 'London Debating Societies in the 1790s.' *The Historical Journal* 32, 57-86.

Thompson, E.P. (1968). *The Making of the English Working Class*. Harmondsworth: Penguin.

Thompson, Martyn P. (1987). *Ideas of Contract in English Political Thought in the Age of John Locke*. New York: Garland.

Tibbutt, H.G. (1947). 'John Crook, 1617-1699: A Bedfordshire Quaker.' *Publications of the Bedfordshire Historical Record Society* 25, 110-128.

Vernon, James (1996). 'Notes Towards an Introduction.' In James Vernon (ed.), *Re-reading the Constitution: New Narratives in the Political History of England's Long Nineteenth Century*. Cambridge: Cambridge University Press, 1-21.

Weiler, Inge (1998). *Giftmordwissen und Giftmörderinnen*. Tübingen: Niemeyer 1998.

Whittaker, William Joseph, ed. (1895). *Mirror of Justices*. Intro. F.W. Maitland. Publications of the Selden Society 7, London: Quaritch.

Wormald, Patrick (2001). *The Making of the English Law: King Alfred to the Twelfth Century*. Vol. 1: *Legislation and its Limits*. Oxford: Blackwell.

Wu, Duncan, ed. (1995). *Romanticism: An Anthology*. Oxford: Blackwell.

Zaret, David (2000). *Origins of Democratic Culture: Printing, Petitions, and the Public Sphere in Early-Modern England*. Princeton: Princeton University Press.

Juliet H. Wightman

'All the world is but a bear-baiting'[1] – Violence and Popular Culture in the Renaissance

Late sixteenth and early seventeenth-century England was governed by a small elite headed by the monarch. The machinery of state authority was concealed from those subject to its control, and there was no place for critical discussion of state policy. Consequently, there was no question of the public having a formative role in the decision-making processes of government. As David Zaret notes: 'Popular participation in political discourse was limited to the receiving end of symbolic displays of authority' (Zaret 2000, 7). However, during this period, individuals were not only subject to monarchic authority. Protestantism also made stringent demands upon its adherents, exerting its influence on all aspects of public and private life. The spiritual authority of the church was similarly removed from public scrutiny. But although the public were not privy to the internal workings of the church and state, and were therefore unable to comment on policy making, there was widespread cultural debate upon the general nature of authority. Various forms of popular entertainment provided the context for such discussions: frequenters of inns, alehouses, playhouses and bear pits exchanged news, rumours and gossip and negotiated cultural concerns through diverse shows and spectacles. The playhouses and baiting arenas, which were often housed within the same structure, were some of the most popular and important venues.

In Elizabethan and Jacobean England, as Louis Montrose asserts, 'the professional theatre seems to have been perceived by the Crown as potentially if indirectly useful, both as an instrument for the aggrandizement of the dynastic nation-state and for the supervision and governance of its subjects' (Montrose 1996, 29). Supporters of the theatre affirmed its importance as a means of educating and entertaining the public and it was variously presented as an institution committed to providing moral instruction and encouraging civil obedience. In his treatise of 1612, *An Apology for Actors*, Thomas Heywood attempted to provide a systematic account of the positive influence of stage plays. He suggested that their purpose was:

> to teach the subjects obedience to their King, to shew the people the untimely ends of such as have moved tumults, commotions, and insurrections, to present them with the flourishing estate of such as live in obedience, exhorting them to allegeance, dehorting them from all trayterous and fellonious stratagems. (Heywood 1612, F4^{v})

Arguments such as Heywood's were often backed up with 'domesticke' or 'home-borne' examples of the theatre's contribution to the maintenance of civil order, and there are accounts of stage plays prompting spontaneous confessions from members of the

1 From 'Digest of a letter in Latin' by 'Honest William' (1639); quoted in Hotson 1928, 59.

audience for crimes as serious as murder.[2] But attempts to align the theatre with the established authorities were not straightforward. Such examples were countered by suggestions that plays actually incited criminal activity, and that, by their involvement, certain spectators had 'learned the cleanely conveyance of their trechery, and how, in what sort, with what secrecy, and by what means to effect their treason' (Greene 1615, D2^{r}).

In contrast then, there were other groups in society who believed that theatre was the cause of public disorder. Henry Crosse was of this opinion, and suggested that the behaviour found in playhouses was symptomatic of poor government. He believed that they inevitably attracted:

> the leaudest persons in the land, apt of pilferie, perjurie, forgerie, or any rogories, the very scum, rascallitie, and baggage of the people, thieves, cut-purses, shifters, cousoners; briefly an uncleane generation, and spaune of vipers: must not here be good rule, where is such a broode of Hell-bred creatures? for a Play is like a sincke in Towne, whereunto all the filth doth runne: or byle in the body, that draweth all the ill humours unto it. (Crosse 1603, Q1^{r})

Not only was the theatre believed to be instrumental to the spread of disease, and in particular the plague, but it was also conceptually linked to a number of Protestant theological concerns. Anti-theatrical sentiment was reified in a Protestant discourse that linked the perceived psychological dangers of the theatre with the substantive dangers of the plague. As well as being an all-too-real physical threat, the idea of the plague was developed metaphorically to suggest an equally disastrous contagion of doctrinally unsound beliefs and practices.

Whilst there was extensive and continued debate surrounding the legal and moral authority of playhouses, they were an undoubted attraction for a great number of people. As a result of its popularity, the theatre became the socio-cultural space in which conceptions of authority were contested and reformulated. In a parallel movement, demonstrations of state power became increasingly 'theatrical'. From its outset, the Elizabethan state initiated a process of exploiting and appropriating existing dramatic forms and revising their cultural significance for its own political ends. This process continued, and both Elizabeth I and James I carefully and consciously dramatised their power.

---

2 Heywood gives one such example of 'A Strange accident happening at a play' in *An Apology for Actors*: 'At *Lin* in *Norfolke*, the then Earle of *Sussex* players acting the old History of Fryer *Francis*, & presenting a woman, who insatiately doting on a yong gentleman, had (the more securely to enjoy his affection) mischievously and secretly murdered her husband, whose ghost haunted her, and at divers times in her most solitary and private contemplations, in most horrid and fearfull shapes, appeared, and stood before her. As this was acted, a townes-woman (till then of good estimation and report) finding her conscience (at this presentment) extremely troubled; suddenly skritched and cryd out Oh my husband, my husband! I see the ghost of my husband fiercely threatening and menacing me. At which shrill and uexpected [*sic*] out-cry, the people about her, moov'd to a strange amazement, inquired the reason of her clamour, when presently un-urged, she told them that seven yeares ago, she, to be possest of such a Gentleman (meaning him) had poysoned her husband, whose fearfull image personated it selfe in the shape of that ghost: whereupon the murdresse was apprehended' (Heywood 1612, G2^{v-r}).

The playhouse was a unique, communal space and, as a secular institution, was frequently charged with offering explanations for aspects of human experience that were not explicitly addressed by the church. The theatre addressed the function of violence in Renaissance society and tragedy in particular explored paradigms of violence, and was involved in the complexities of their cultural codification. As John Drakakis notes, 'the *staging* of violence in the public theatre is both a displacement and a transference of a violence which existed not very far beneath the surface of Elizabethan society itself' (Drakakis 1992, 15). The aesthetics of Renaissance tragedy developed during a period that was at times devastated by the plague and at others terrified by its dormant threat, and in which austere Protestant theology was accompanied by an acknowledged tendency towards religious despair. The tragic aesthetic cultivated a sense of human agency that was often obfuscated in the strict Calvinist doctrine of double-predestination, and which was effectively removed in the plague-induced periods of crisis. The theatre provided a focus for cultural anxieties and offered a generic cultural template whereby patterns of societal violence and an unusually fraught understanding of mortality were ostensibly circumscribed by the evolving notion of a tragic ideal.

Discussions of the nature of tragedy have traditionally focused upon its agonistic form, that is to say, upon the way in which it negotiates conflicting explanations of human experience. On the one hand, it engages with an understanding of human suffering as the result of a transcendent order which the individual is powerless to counter; on the other, it deals with a conception of individual autonomy and ultimate personal responsibility. Michael Neill has argued that English Renaissance tragedy 'catered for a culture that was in the throes of a peculiar crisis in the accommodation of death – one that reflected the strain of adjusting the psychic economy of an increasingly individualistic society to the stubborn facts of mortality' (Neill 1997, 30). The theatre was consequently an important cultural space, instrumental to the process of mediating between individual and social attitudes towards death. This was of great importance because people's understanding of death has profound implications for the way in which they live. The Renaissance saw an unprecedented development in tragic drama as the concerns of the individual became focused upon notions of personal identity and on the importance of being remembered after death. By 'aestheticising' death in this way, the theatre became involved in the dramatisation of human agency, and, consequently, with a reworking of perceptions of 'reality'. This is significant, for as Stephen Greenblatt reminds us, 'each society is constructed to a significant degree out of *specific* qualities of its language and symbols' (Greenblatt 1990, 32).

But if, as Sir Sidney Lee asserts, 'promoters of public amusement seem to have placed the attractions of bull baiting and bear baiting on much the same level as dramatic performances' (Lee 1950, 2: 426), it is only to be expected that the contiguous, and equally prominent spectacle of bear baiting was also an important factor in the codification and dissemination of paradigms of violence. Therefore, although the theatre was a singularly significant cultural space, the reproduction and reformulation of cultural meanings was not confined to this domain. This parallel form of popular entertainment provided a challenge to this stylised aesthetic ideal of supreme violence. A Jacobean advert notifies the public that:

> Tomorrowe beinge Thursdaie shalbe seen at the Beargardin on the banckside a greate Mach plaid by the gamstirs of Essex who hath chalenged all comers what soever to plaie v dogges at the single beare for v pounds and also to wearie a bull dead at the stake and for your better content shall have plasant sport with the horse and ape and whipping of the blind beare. Vivat Rex (Foakes 1977, 2: 106)

Bear baiting, and also bull, horse and monkey baiting, were extremely popular and constituted a form of state sanctioned violence that was enjoyed by the general public and royalty alike. Both Elizabeth I and James I displayed a particularly keen interest in the sport and, early in her reign, Elizabeth staged a bull baiting for a visiting French ambassador who was greatly impressed by the spectacle and took a number of English mastiffs back to France (see Macdonogh 1999, 212).

A detailed description of London baiting matches is given by the Venetian sailor and merchant, Alessandro Magno, who, in the records of his voyage to England, observes that:

> First [...] they bring in [...] a worthless horse with all its trappings, and a monkey in the saddle, then four to six of the younger dogs, with which they make an attack. Then these are replaced by leading in more experienced ones, in which baiting it is a fine sight to see the horse run, kicking and biting, and the monkey grip the saddle tightly and scream, many times being bitten, in which baiting, after the attendants have intervened for a while, with frequently the death of the horse, and it is removed from the scene, they bring in some bears, either one by one or several together, but this baiting is not very fine to see. Finally they bring in a wild bull, and they tie it with a rope about two paces long to a stake that is fixed in the middle of the enclosure. The baiting is finer to see than the others and is more dangerous for the dogs than the others, many of which are wounded and die, and it lasts until evening. (Quoted in Dawson 1964, 98-99)

As well as being the finest of form of such entertainment, in Magno's view, bull baiting was said to add to the flavour of the bull's meat which would be eaten after the match. Stephen Dickey notes that 'in an efficient symbiosis of sport and sustenance, bulls were obliged to be baited prior to being butchered. The more valuable bears, if they survived, were headed no place other than future bouts in the ring' (Dickey 1991, 256). Although Magno complains that the bear baiting 'is not very fine to see', Lee affirms that it was 'pursued in England with an earnestness which was hardly known elsewhere' (Lee 1950, 2: 426).

Robert Langham's contemporary account of a match at Kenilworth testifies to the great enjoyment derived from these spectacles. He enthuses:

> It waz a sport very pleazaunt of theez beastz: to see the bear with hiz pink nyez leering after hiz enmyez approcj, the nimblness and wayt of the dog too take hiz avauntage, and the fors and experiens of the bear again to avoyd the assauts: if he wear bitten in one place, hoow he woold pynch in an oother too get free: that if he wear taken onez, then what shyft with byting with clawing, with roring tossing and tumbling he woold work too wynde hym self from them: and when he waz lose, to shake hiz earz twyse or thryse with the blud and the slaver about hiz fiznamy, waz a matter of goodly relief. (Langham 1983, 48)

This account foregrounds the intense and relentless violence which characterised such events. In contrast to the teleological thrust of tragic drama, the violence of a bear baiting operated without a demonstrable sense of progression towards an ending. After the death of a 'worthless horse', and the baiting of a bull for food, the action continued with bears as more animals were introduced into the ring. The main casualties were the mastiff dogs, which were often killed by the bear within moments. Members of the public would bring their own dogs to be pitted against the bears, often wagering large sums of money. Indeed, the bear-pit's undeniable popularity with gamblers is testimony to the indeterminacy of the matches. Therefore, despite the inevitable casualties, the outcome of a baiting was always uncertain. Death, in this context, was not an end of the violence.

Bear baiting therefore offers an alternative cultural framework from within which to understand violence in the early seventeenth century. In contrast with the tragic model of violence, the trajectory described by the baiting of a bear was markedly different. As Dickey notes, 'the effective outcome of a bear baiting match was something best expressed as a stalemate' (Dickey 1991, 259). Rather than codifying violence in determinable positive or humanist terms, bear baiting presented an inescapable *experience* of violence that could be qualitatively aligned with a negative providential outlook. The suffering of a bear – tied to the stake and forced to endure continual and unremitting violence – offered the audience an alternative representation of their own subjectivity. Rather than the tragic aesthetic of Cleopatra's 'immortal longings', and heroic challenge, 'Where art thou, Death? / Come hither, come!' (Shakespeare 1995, 5.2.45-46), bear baiting exemplified an understanding of human suffering more akin to Macbeth's conception of his own situation: 'They have tied me to a stake: I cannot fly, / But, bear-like, I must fight the course' (Shakespeare 1951, 5.7.1-2).

The figure of the bear was of considerable symbolic importance during the Renaissance. In addition to the celebrated role of characters such as Harry Hunks, Sackerson, and Tom of Lincoln, the bear made a number of significant symbolic appearances at particular events in the Renaissance calendar. Principally, the bear was linked to the Candlemas celebrations, as François Laroque details in his discussion of Shakespeare's festive world:

> There was a direct link, in popular belief, between the beginning of carnival and the end of the bear's hibernation which was liable to take place on Candlemas Day (February 2). As the beast emerged from its lair, it was thought to look around to see what the weather was like. If it was fine, it went back in, which was a sign that winter would continue for another forty days [...] if, on the other hand, the weather was overcast, the bear emerged for good, thereby marking an early end to winter. (Laroque 1991, 48)

Signifying a period of carnivalesque excess which would continue until the beginning of Lent, Candlemas marked the beginning of the agricultural year, and therefore, the imminent return to work. The recurrent image of the Candlemas bear emphasises what was an essentially cyclical conception of temporality. Indeed, the infamous cameo appearance of the bear in *The Winter's Tale* plays upon this association. One of the most frequently discussed aspects of the play is the striking gap of a vast sixteen years, and its relation to the overall tragic-comic structure. In Act 3, scene 3, the bear appears onstage and promptly pursues Antigonus offstage and to his death. However, the bear does not function solely as a signifier of violence here. Shortly before his demise,

Antigonus comments, 'I never saw / the heavens so dim by day' (Shakespeare 1999, 3.3.56-57), a sign which, in conjunction with the emergence of the bear, would herald the end of winter. Here, the bear mediates between the play's initial tragic form and the forthcoming comic conclusion (see Newman 1988; and Bristol 1991).

This peculiar ambivalence is characteristic of the way in which bears were perceived in the Renaissance popular imagination. Their natural fierceness and aggression was thought to run parallel to their strong nurturing instincts. In Edward Topsell's comprehensive study, *The Historie of Foure-Footed Beastes* (1607), he relates the following story in order to illustrate their 'most venerous and lustfull disposition':

> a Beare carried a young maide into his denne by violence, where in venerous manner he had the carnal use of her body, and while he kept her in his denne, he dailye went foorth and brought her home the best Apples and other fruites he could get, presenting them unto her in very amorous sort; but always when hee went to forage, he rouled a huge great stone upon the mouth of his denne, that the Virgin shoulde not escape away. (Topsell 1607, E1^{r})

This uneasy combination of violence and benevolence illustrates the profound uncertainty with which these creatures were viewed. They were powerful symbols of the end of winter and the beginning of spring and, therefore, of fertility and rejuvenation. But also, their renowned aggression signalled their capacity for great destruction. It is possible to suggest, then, that people's reactions to the figure of the bear in the baiting arena were informed by the cultural meanings ascribed to them in the seasonal calendar and popular folklore.

The idea of bear baiting was often developed metaphorically to suggest a combination of suffering and punishment. In a number of early modern discourses, these ideas are inextricably linked to the condition of selfhood. Various permutations of the metaphor of bear baiting are explored in a series of early seventeenth-century pamphlets that comprise a debate upon the nature of women. John Swetnam uses this metaphor in his controversial misogynist pamphlet, *The Arraignment of Lewde, idle, froward, and unconstant women* (1615). He announces in his opening pages, 'if thou mean to see the Bear-bayting of women, then trudge to this beare-garden apace.' He likens his dogged and lengthy rebuke of women to a bear baiting, and throughout the tract relies heavily upon ambivalent cultural conceptions of the bear; in particular, the perceived contrast between their fierceness and their 'femininity'. He compares the general temperament of women, unfavourably, with the aggression of the bear, asserting that 'the Beare being robbed of her young ones [...] [is] nothing so terrible as the fury of a woman' (Swetnam 1615, 2). He makes explicit reference to the similarities of an angered woman and a bear at the stake, stating that 'a froward woman in hir frantick mood will pull haule, swerve, scratch & teare all that stands in her way' (12). Although seeming to link women firmly with their ursine counterparts, he develops the metaphor of baiting to suggest an experience of acute but continual violence akin to men's experience of marriage. In doing so, he also implicitly allies men with the figure of the bear.

In a lively response, Constantia Munda proposes that Swetnam's objections are a 'strange blasphemy'. Dismissing his argument, and his choice of metaphor, she counters,

> You promise your spectators the Beare-baiting of women, and yet you think it not amisse to drive all women out of your hearing; for that none but your selfe the ill-favoured Hunckes is left in the Beare-garden to make your invited guests merry: whereupon it may very likely be, the eager young men [...] set their doges at you. (Munda 1617, 25)

Overturning his initial formulation, Munda aligns Swetnam himself with a well-known stage bear, the 'ill-favoured Hunkes', thereby suggesting that he is the figure upon whom the reader or spectator's desires for entertainment will converge. She claims that his attempts to articulate his own position have merely worked to single him out for the ridicule he intended for women. As Munda conceives it, then, the bear symbolises a pitiful, ill-tempered and humiliated figure.

In her contribution to the debate, Rachel Speght provides an intelligent and patient response to Swetnam's text, focusing upon his lack of rhetorical sophistication in addition to the flaws in his argument. She declares that in '*the Beare-bayting of Women*, you have plainely displayed your owne disposition to be Cynicall, in that there appeares no other Dogge or Bull, to bayte them, but your selfe' (Speght 1617, B2^{r}). In contrast to Munda's treatment of Swetnam's metaphor, Speght retains the bear-like image of women, figuratively tied to the stake. However, she locates the significance of such a restraint within a theological context, arguing that God created women 'for mans sake [...] as a good yokefellow' (C2^{r}). Women's subjection here is construed as a direct result of their relationship with God and, therefore, as an intrinsic aspect of their subjectivity.

Speght goes on to criticise Swetnam's 'roaring cogitations', equating his poor grammar with an animalistic sense of disorder: 'You,' she accuses, 'being greedie to botch up your mingle mangle invective against Women, have not therein observed, in many places, so much as Grammer sense' (B2^{r}). By labelling Swetnam 'Melastomus', she conflates the tearing and biting that characterise a baiting, and the equally destructive operations of language, into the idea of an 'evil-mouth'. Consequently, language itself, which can be seen to 'setteth a rankling tooth into the sides of truth' (B^{v}), is identified not only as an instrument of baiting but also as that which is baited.

The trope of bear baiting is implicated in all of these texts, but the figure of the bear functions as an ambivalent signifier, unable to be categorically aligned with either the persecuted or persecuting subject. This ambiguity increases baiting's metaphorical currency, however, particularly in its relation to the prevailing Protestant theology of the time. At the level of the corporeal, it is not difficult to discern a certain paradigm of violence and to identify an aesthetic correlation between the experience of the bear, bound to the stake, and the image of the Christ on the cross. Many scholars have suggested that the figure of Jesus crucified was marginalised in Reformation theology, but, as Adrian Streete observes, 'the doctrine of election and reprobation, as it was most commonly understood in early modern England, was a deeply Christological doctrine' (Streete 2001, 146). Christians were exhorted to identify with Christ, and devotional rhetoric forged express corollaries between the suffering of Jesus and the suffering of the elect.

Concentrated upon the crucifixion, this reciprocal relationship reached its crisis as the process of assimilation invoked a dual identification. Not only was the individual encouraged to empathise with the figure of Christ, but also, more radically, with his tormentors. Highlighting the Renaissance fascination with cruelty, Debora Kuller Shuger makes specific reference to Calvinist passion narratives, which she observes, 'while less absorbed by the techniques of cruelty, fix compulsively on its psychology' (Shuger 1994, 91). In these texts, the unusually detailed descriptions of Christ's sufferings take on overtly sadistic and erotic overtones. Indeed, in the vivid portrayal of Christ, 'his face blue and black with buffeting, his eyes swoln, his cheeks beslavered with spittle' (Hall 1863, 2: 654), the graphic focus upon his tortured body is redolent of the enthusiastically grotesque descriptions of the 'blud and the slaver' of the baited bear.[3]

Moreover, the listener or reader of the passions is positioned so that they, too, are implicated in the acts of physical and mental violence. Shuger explains:

> The notion that since Christ died for our sins we are all responsible for the Crucifixion originates early in Christian thought, but the Calvinist passion narratives intensify this complicity by merging the position of the reader with that of the torturer. Our sins become not simply the antecedent cause of Christ's sacrifice; rather we find ourselves sucked into the scene as participants in the act of cruelty. (Shuger 1994, 92-93)

Like the complexities of the baiting metaphor in the pamphlets of Swetnam, Speght and Munda, where the bear's ambiguous position problematised any attempts to consistently align one party with the baited bear and the other with the dogs, the passion narratives hinder the reader's ability to identify him or herself exclusively with Christ. As a central tenet of Protestant doctrine, the literary treatment of the Crucifixion exposes this aporia: subjectivity is constituted in conflict, experienced by the individual as a continual torment.

Various scholars have focused critical attention on the centrality of Protestantism for the development of the Renaissance subject. The metaphor of bear baiting shares with Protestant Christology a concern for the process of externalising the inward experiences of the individual, and rendering them visible to the outside world. Katherine Eisaman Maus explains that in 'early seventeenth-century England the sense of discrepancy between "inward disposition" and "outward appearance" seems unusually urgent and consequential for a very large number of people, who occupy virtually every position on the ideological spectrum' (Maus 1995, 13). Just as the rhetoric of popular piety urged Christians to emulate Christ and, in doing so, to make their outward actions the signifiers of their inward thoughts, the rhetoric of the bear-pit was in a similar manner concerned with the reification of internal conflict.

In an evolving taxonomy of violence, the codification of various forms of 'internal' violence are complicated by their unrepresentability. Notions of internal violence are,

3 Artaud reminds us that 'there can be no spectacle without an element of cruelty at the basis of every show [...] metaphysics must be made to enter the mind through the body' (1993 ,77).

by implication, linked to suffering and, in her study, *The Body in Pain*, Elaine Scarry postulates that 'whatever pain achieves, it achieves it in part through its unsharability, and it ensures this unsharability through its resistance to language' (Scarry 1985, 4). Bear baiting is utilised as a metaphor for the inherent violence of human experience, precisely because the experience cannot be represented in any other way. Scarry goes on to explain that 'physical pain – unlike any other state of consciousness – has no referential content' (5). Indeed, what separates this figurative construction – developed from a form of popular entertainment – from the theological tropes that address the same experience is its attempt to articulate the realities of such internal conflict. In contrast, theological tropes are frequently attributed with the capacity to generate exactly this form of conflict.

The metaphor of bear baiting was derived from the public domain, but the experiences it realised were nevertheless deeply private. Authority, derived from a number of conflicting public discourses, informed the interior life of the Renaissance subject. This process is described by John Stachniewski who argues that,

> The task of dismantling the Calvinist-puritan vocabulary and replacing it with another proves unachievable, even systematically unthinkable, partly because the authority of the first discourse maintains its status as an accurate description, but more fundamentally because the experience is generated by the words themselves, inheres in them, and is not a detachable entity receptive to alternative explanation. (Stachniewski 1991, 8)

The metaphors of the bear-pit are always already infused with established modes of understanding, and therefore, 'even where [...] linguistic reinforcement of negative intuitions is finally overcome, or converted into the positive terms, the trace of the former experience and its linguistic encoding remains influential' (5). The rhetoric of the bear baiting is part of a series of metaphors which mediate between the public and private life of the individual. The dynamics of the Renaissance tragic aesthetic were as much concerned with the way in which habits of discourse structure people's lived experience as with the effects of patterns of actual physical violence. Indeed, tragedy's involvement with the dramatisation of human agency was complicated by the burgeoning vocabulary of ongoing internal violence which the metaphors of the bear-pit addressed.

Coward and Ellis assert that 'because the practices that make up a social totality take place in language, it becomes possible to consider language as the place in which the social individual is constructed [...]. In other words, man can be seen *as language,* as the intersection of the social, historical and individual' (1977, 1). The reworking of pervasive forms of actual violence into linguistic figures and tropes demonstrates the manner in which language mediates and structures the relationship between subjective and social realities. Therefore, it was through an internalisation of the laws embodied in linguistic structures that Renaissance subject achieved entry into the symbolic order. As a popular form of entertainment, bear baiting was involved with the processes of social regulation because it served to displace malignant psychic energies. Moreover, the bear-baiting metaphor linguistically actualises an awareness of the paradoxical conditions of the individual's subjectivity, suggesting that they are metaphorically bound to the stake, both the administrator and sufferer of their condition as subject.

REFERENCES

Artaud, Antonin (1993). *The Theatre and Its Double*. Montreuil: Calder.

Bristol, Michael (1991). 'In Search of the Bear: Spatiotemporal Form and the Heterogeneity of Economies in *The Winter's Tale*.' *Shakespeare Quarterly* 42, 145-167.

Coward, Rosalind, and John Ellis (1977). *Language and Materialism – Developments in Semiology and the Theory of the Subject*. London: Routledge and Kegan Paul.

Crosse, Henry (1603). *Vertues Common-Wealth, or the High-Way to Honour*. London: John Newberry.

Dawson, Giles E. (1964). 'London's Bull-Baiting and Bear-Baiting Arena in 1562.' *Shakespeare Quarterly* 15, 97-101.

Dickey, Stephen (1991). 'Shakespeare's Mastiff Comedy.' *Shakespeare Quarterly* 42, 255-275.

Drakakis, John (1992). *Shakespearean Tragedy*. London: Longman.

Foakes, R.A., ed. (1977). *The Henslowe Papers*. 2 vols. London: Scolar Press.

Greene, John (1615). *A Refutation of the Apology for Actors*. London: W. White.

Greenblatt, Stephen J. (1990). *Learning to Curse – Essays in Early Modern Culture*. New York: Routledge.

Hall, Joseph (1863). *The Works*. Ed. Philip Wynter. 10 vols. Oxford: Oxford University Press.

Heywood, Thomas (1612). *An Apology for Actors*. London: Nicholas Oakes, STC 13309.

Hotson, Leslie (1928). *The Commonwealth and Restoration Stage*. Cambridge, Mass.: Harvard University Press.

Langham, Robert (1983). *Robert Langham: A Letter*. Ed. R.J.P. Kuin. Leiden: Brill.

Laroque, François (1991). *Shakespeare's Festive World – Elizabethan Seasonal Entertainments and the Professional Stage*. Trans. Janet Lloyd. Cambridge: Cambridge University Press.

Lee, Sidney (1950). *Shakespeare's England*. 2 vols. Oxford: Clarendon Press.

MacDonogh, Katherine (1999). *Reigning Cats and Dogs*. London: Fourth Estate.

Maus, Katherine Eisaman (1995). *Inwardness and Theatre in the English Renaissance*. Chicago: University of Chicago Press.

Montrose, Louis (1996). *The Purpose of Playing: Shakespeare and the Cultural Politics of the Elizabethan Theatre*. Chicago: University of Chicago Press.

Munda, Constantia (1617). *The Worming of a Mad Dogge*. London: Lawrence Hayes.

Neill, Michael (1997). *Issues of Death – Mortality and Identity in English Renaissance Tragedy*. Oxford: Clarendon Press.

Newman, Judie (1988). '"Exit, Pursued by a Bear": *The Winter's Tale*.' *Notes and Queries* 233/4, 484.

Scarry, Elaine (1985). *The Body in Pain – The Making and Unmaking of the World*. Oxford: Oxford University Press.

Shakespeare, William (1951). *Macbeth*. Ed. Kenneth Muir. The Arden Shakespeare. London: Methuen.

________ (1995). *Antony and Cleopatra*. Ed. John Wilders. The Arden Shakespeare. London: Routledge.

________ (1999). *The Winter's Tale*. Ed. J.H.P. Pafford. The Arden Shakespeare. London: Thomas Nelson.

Shuger, Debora Kuller (1994). *The Renaissance Bible: Scholarship, Sacrifice, and Subjectivity*. Berkeley: University of California Press.

Speght, Rachel (1617). *A Mouzell For Melastomus, The Cynicall Bayter of, and foule mouthed Barker against Evahs Sex*. London: Nicholas Oakes, STC 23058.

Stachniewski, John (1991). *The Persecutory Imagination*. Oxford: Clarendon Press.

Streete, Adrian (2001). '"*Consummatum Est*": Calvinist Exegesis, Mimesis and *Doctor Faustus*.' *Literature and Theology* 15, 140-158.

Swetnam, John (1615). *The Arraignment of Lewde, idle, froward, and unconstant women*. London: Thomas Archer.

Topsell, Edward (1607). *The Historie of Foure-Footed Beastes*. London: William Jaggard.

Zaret, David (2000). *Origins of Democratic Culture: Printing, Petitions, and the Public Sphere in Early-Modern England*. Princeton: Princeton University Press.

Alastair Mann

Parliaments, Princes, and Presses: Voices of Tradition and Protest in Early Modern Scotland

Early modern European society was, in an age before modern communications and transport, a traditionally more private world where the political public sphere was dominated by small elites, many of whom were not strongly connected to the lives of ordinary folk other than those in their immediate locality. Centres of power and networks of vertical interaction, in Scotland and elsewhere, were often highly localised as mercantile and landed elites interacted with retainers and tenants. Parliaments and legislative assemblies, along with other institutions of secular and religious government, provided opportunities for elite horizontal integration (Whyte 1997; Houston 1994, 18-103). But the early modern period was a time of flux and of crisis over political ideas. Questions were raised over the relationship between institutions of government and the wider public sphere. In Scotland the clash between different philosophies on the nature of kingship and sovereignty coupled with the spread of printing, with its challenges to authority and opportunities for dissent, led to confused political agendas that sought both to control and facilitate an expanding public sphere. When the Crown of Scotland united with that of England in 1603, and king if not Parliament moved from Edinburgh to London, the sense of shifting sovereignty increased the prospects for Anglo-Scottish elite rivalry and popularly expressed discontent. Those who governed Scotland, in Edinburgh and London, became increasingly concerned at the philosophical, typographical and sometimes violent voices of the disenchanted.

When the Scottish King James VI became King of England in 1603 he found himself the imperial guardian of two kingdoms (excluding Ireland), two parliaments and two national churches. James favoured a union between the institutions of church and government, a perfect marriage that would unite the hearts and minds of the English and Scottish. However, within four years, his union scheme collapsed with both Edinburgh and London parliaments unwilling to put at risk ancient rights and privileges. James was left to move by stealth to achieve objectives. Royal prerogative was used to make symbolic changes: the title king of Great Britain was adopted and a union flag created. Royal patronage was used extensively to encourage loyalty to the new imperial crown and dynasty. Anglo-Scottish religious harmony was to be advanced, not by union of the churches of Scotland and England but by the mutual toleration of brotherly Protestants. Scotland, in spite of its Presbyterianism, was to be made more accepting of bishops, though James started the process before 1603, and England's Anglican church was to moderate its criticism of Scotland's Presbyterian system of church courts. James, head of the church in England, carefully slipped into a position of greater authority over the church of Scotland (MacDonald 1998).

But King James was a scholar king and had to explain, in writing, his philosophies and objectives with regard to kingship and religion. Political tracts such as *The True Law of Free Monarchies* (1598) and *Basilikon Doron* (1599 and, in an anglicised edition, 1603), the latter a guide to his son, outlined James's attitude to kingship before 1603. Thereafter, he relied increasingly on other authors to explicate royal policy and to fuel the royalist propaganda machine. Such a case in point was *God and the King* (1616), a small pocket-sized book written by the Englishman Richard Mocket and printed in England and Scotland in large quantities. Referred to by contemporaries as a catechism, it was a Humanist dialogue through which loyalty to the king and to God was promulgated. (Mann 2000a, 21, 51-52) The more radical Presbyterian ideas, as expounded by the academic Andrew Melville (1542-1622) and later by the historian David Calderwood (1575-1651), concerning 'parity', equal status for all clergymen, and the doctrine of two kingdoms, where church and state were separate powers with different jurisdictions leaving the clergy above civil authority, were countered with the simple message: the king sovereign over the church atop a hierarchy of loyal bishops. A hierarchical church structure that mirrored the natural order was essential, 'parity' being the 'mother of confusion, and enemy of unitie'. (James 1944, 1: 76). As James said bluntly in 1604 'No bishops, no king' (Shriver 1982, 60). *God and the King* was distributed throughout the burghs of Scotland and prescribed for all householders. Those appointed to positions of authority had to take publicly an oath of loyalty. Meanwhile, extreme Presbyterians, repulsed by the notion of royal stewardship of church affairs, were condemned as 'phanatick spirits' (James 1944, 1: 79).

James's support for the Episcopal clergy, from a parliamentary point of view, had a straightforward justification: no bishops, less king. Unlike, say, the parliaments of England, Hungary and Poland, Scotland's Parliament was unicameral (single chamber), but, like many European assemblies, it was a gathering of estates (Rait 1924; Bonney 1991; Myers 1975). The Scottish Parliament consisted of three or four estates: clerics appointed by the Crown (absent from 1638 to 1660 and after 1689); nobles who attended by right; representatives of royal burghs, elected by their respective town councils, and representatives of the shires elected from the barons or lesser landowners. In addition, a management committee, the Lords of the Articles, was chosen to draft business before voting by the whole house, a committee whose power has been the subject of much historiographical revision in recent years (Tanner 2000 and 2001; MacDonald 2002). Also, the Scottish Privy Council, usually including clergy, governed between parliaments, a 'cabinet' passing acts on day to day matters.

James, his son and grandson, Charles I and Charles II, each considered themselves to be sovereign over Parliament. James and Charles I, the former, theoretically the latter, more overtly believed sovereign authority rested entirely with the king, the divine right of king's passing on via the hereditary principle. These traditional realities were preserved through Crown selection of clerical members of Parliament, the first estate, and the appointment of officers of state (a fifth estate perhaps) who also had the right to vote in Parliament. Naturally, the granting of titles and lands added to the process of political management and royal policy went to extraordinary lengths to ensure Crown sovereignty was retained.

Whig historians affirm that the British revolutions of 1688/89, which saw the Catholic James VII and II removed, clergy banished from the Scottish Parliament and a 'more' constitutional monarchy put in place, delivered strengthened and more independent parliaments for England and Scotland (Macaulay 1979, 358-432; cf. Firth 1918; Speck 1988). However, Scotland's monarchy, like England's, was already restricted by constitutional limits going back to the fourteenth century. The extent to which the crown was given by the people or taken by the rightful heir was and is open to considerable debate; yet, both the coronation oath taken by the king and the oath to Parliament taken by members provide evidence of a counterbalancing relationship between the Crown and the people. Such public declarations were essential to the maintenance of authority, the rule of law and of social order. Oaths were, like witnessed legal documents, a point of convergence for the public and private spheres.

The significance of Scotland's coronation oath was subjected to varied interpretation by early modern contemporaries. Indeed it was at the core of philosophical and political arguments that raged from the removal of Mary, Queen of Scots, in 1567-8 and into the eighteenth century (see Burns 1996; Mason 1998, 187-241). George Buchanan (1506-1582), the greatest political writer of the period, and the most significant Scottish author of any genre, as well as tutor to James VI, argued in his explosive dialogue *De Jure Regni Apud Scotos* (1579) that:

> When our king's are publicly inaugurated, they give a solemn promise to the entire people that they will observe the laws, customs and ancient practices of our ancestors [...] [We can] see the nature of power which they have received from our ancestors, namely, the same as is held by those who [... ,] chosen by election, swear to observe the laws. (Buchanan 1579, 66)[1]

Buchanan is able to use the public ceremony of the coronation to advance his two central tenets: Scottish kings were elected and also subject to the authority of the law.[2] Thus, sovereignty rests with the people, not the Crown; though, by 'people', Buchanan meant the elite representatives, the Estates in Parliament. Furthermore, the coronation oath was a contract between king and people, such that loyalty of the subject is given up in exchange for the just rule of the monarch. Arbitrary rulers and tyrants could be removed and even killed. Buchanan had extrapolated a resistance theory justifying the removal of Mary, Queen of Scots, in favour of the infant James VI and providing inspiration for the subsequent revolutions against Charles I and James VII and II. Though Buchanan was a secularist, Melville and other radical Presbyterians used his analysis to underpin their ideology. Small wonder than *De Jure*, along with Buchanan's great *Rerum Scoticarum Historia*, which placed 'constitutionalism' in the context of a largely manufactured history of Scottish kings, were repeatedly banned in Scotland from the 1580s to the early eighteenth century.

The coronation oath taken by Charles I in 1633, based closely on the words said in 1567 on behalf of the infant King James VI, does indeed reflect a level of mutuality.

---

1 Buchanan references are from the forthcoming English translation by Roger Mason and Martin Smith. My thanks to Dr Mason of the University of St Andrews for access to this much needed translation.

2 Mason 1982; Mason 1998, 236-237. For sovereignty before 1603, see Goodare 1999, 11-37.

The form of words was outlined by Parliament in 1560. Charles swore to maintain 'the true religion of Jesus Christ, the preaching of his holy word and the due and right ministratione of His sacraments now receaved [to prevent] all false religion', and to rule 'according to the lovabill lawis and constitutionis resavit of this realme' (*RPC* 1877, 542). Even though in 1689 the Estates of Scotland offered the crown conditionally to William and Mary, the words in the oath were exactly those of James VI, Charles I and Charles II, who promised to: 'preserve and keep inviolated the rights and rents, with all just priviledges of the croune of Scotland [... and] forbid and repress in all Estates [...] reife [plunder], oppression, and all kind of wrang And [...] command and procure [...] justice and equity in all judgements' (*APS* 9: 48).

Other earlier oaths, such as James II's oath to Parliament of 1445, suggest a more overt submission to the Estates, where the king promised to 'be leille [loyal] and treu to God and Haliekirk, and to the thre estaitis' with the 'statuts of the realme nother to eike [increase] nor mynisshe [diminish] without the consent of the 3 estaites',[3] but the post-Reformation form of coronation oath nevertheless suggests a bargain with the people and the clear sense of continuity with ancient law. The revolutionary regime of 1688/89 was concerned to underscore its legitimacy and ensured that the traditional coronation oath was applied, as it was to Queen Anne in 1702.

When he assumed personal rule in 1584, James set about banning Buchanan and attacking his 'republican' manifesto. In his *True Law*, James expanded on his ideas of divine right kingship. Princes succeeded by blood and heredity and not by election, the ancient kings taking the land by conquest. So, because of the divine providence of the succession, the promise to God, not that to the people was the most significant element in the coronation oath. Thus, while the king swore to carry out his office 'honourably and truly', only God and not the people could pass judgement if these promises were broken. The oath did emphasise the duties of a good king to 'uphold the religion presently confessed [...] good laws made by [...] predecessors [and] everie state therein, in al their ancient privilges and liberties'; yet, princes were only 'countable to that great God' who had appointed James a 'naturall father to all his leiges at his coronation'. This patriarchal analogy is typical of James's approach, as was his anatomical model of the kingdom with the prince as the head and the people as members. To remove the king would be like trying to cure the body by chopping of the head, an action 'monstrous and unnatural' (James 1982, 78-79, 61-62, 74-75).

James was not alone in Scotland in expounding divine right kingship. A century later, Sir George Mackenzie of Rosehaugh (1636-1691), Scottish jurist, lord advocate and politician, penned his *Jus Regium, Or the Just and Solid Foundation of the Monarchy of Scotland* (1684) largely to counter the constitutionalism of Buchanan, his works being re-published in English editions in the 1680s (Durkan 1994, 215-216, 234). Mackenzie was a royalist, much alarmed at how extreme Presbyterianism in his

3 Lyall 1977, 9-10; Tanner 2001, 112-115; NLS 1488. NLS 1488 is a copy of the form of oaths taken in parliament in 1445. The same oath was recorded in manuscript versions of 'Regiam Majestatem', Scotland's compilation of law, in 1520 (NLS [Adv. Ms 25.5.9 f.132]) and ca.1565 (NLS [Adv. Ms 7.1.9 f.109]), but it is doubtful the oath was used then, especially after 1560.

own time had caused near civil war in parts of Scotland, especially in the southwest. Those who rebelled and Buchanan 'poissoned the nation' with ideas 'that our monarchs derive their rights from them'. Sovereignty could not be with the people. Notions of a contract between the people and their monarch were 'absurd and extravagant'. As for the coronation oath, Mackenzie proclaimed it unnecessary, and it was the duty of all to support the succession of the Catholic Duke of York and Albany, the future James VII, regardless of his religion (Mackenzie 1684, 4, 9, 41-42). James VI would not have gone so far as to devalue the oath, but he did believe a subject's duty was to obey the sovereign and his 'lawfull heires and posteritie' (James 1982, 80), and this 'contract' existed regardless of oaths taken by princes.

Notwithstanding the views of Mackenzie in the difficult succession crisis of the 1680s, constitutionalists and royalists had a common interest in conserving the ceremony of the coronation oath. The oath was taken before God and the representatives of the Estates (the people), though, as it was a religious ceremony, not actually before a full Parliament. Therefore, 'the people', witnessed the promises made by the sovereign before and to God, and before and to the political community. Royalists and absolutists could take comfort from this as it emphasised the divine relationship between king and God and the ultimate legitimisation of royal sovereignty. Equally, constitutionalists could witness what they regarded as the essential participation and presence of the political community with whom sovereignty was either shared or was superior to the will of the monarch. Both parties, who in late seventeenth-century Scotland became roughly drawn along the lines of Tory/Jacobite Episcopalians and Whig Presbyterians, understood that the legitimacy of sovereign government depended on the public expression of loyalty and ancient continuity inherent in the coronation ceremony and oath.

When Buchanan considered sovereignty in the Scottish political system, he stated that the basis of national law, something that sat above kings, was the Estates in Parliament (Burns 1996, 290-291). King's had little or no legislative role to play. James VI, on the other hand, emphasised that Parliament was 'nothing else but the head court of the king and his vassals', and that 'kings in Scotland were before any estates'; thus, 'king's were the authors and makers of the lawes, and not the lawes of the kings.' In any case, no law could pass, indeed, literally, in Scottish parliamentary proceedure, 'without his scepter put to it for giving force of law', either by the king or, after 1603, by the royal commissioner, who sat on the throne as king's representative (James 1982, 70-71). Mackenzie went further, believing that kings protected the people from parliaments:

> it is strange and unsufferable to hear such as appeal to parliaments, cry out against their [king's] power [...] and why should we oppress our kings and raise civil wars, whereby we endanger so much ourselves to procure powers to parliaments, if parliaments be such ridiculous things as we cannot trust when they are empowered by us. (Mackenzie 1684, 8-9)

Nonetheless, Mackenzie and other members of the Scottish Parliament were also required to take their own oath. The parliamentary oath, which existed in the fifteenth century and no doubt before, was taken before the king (or his commissioner), the assembled Estates and, of course, God. It was, like the coronation oath, directed at different audiences. It was essentially both an oath to the Estates and an oath of allegiance to the king with God as a witness to both. Thus, the oath taken in 1661, after the restoration of monarchy, proclaimed 'faithfull obedience to my most gracious and redoubted soverane' as 'supream governour of this kingdome over all persons and in all causes' and to 'defend assist and mantaine his majesties jurisdiction forsaid against all', but also to 'faithfullie give [...] advice and vote in every thing [that] shall be propoundit in parliament as [he] shall answeir to God' (*APS* 7: 7).

The combined promise to king and Parliament (or the people) applied to all members, but had an additional resonance for those elected by the burghs (representing town councils) and shires (representing shire gentry). Burgh members in particular were expected to represent the interests of their specific towns as well as the trade of the nation. Many reported back to their burghs before votes were taken, or gathered within their estate to debate specific measures before voting with the whole house (MacDonald 2002). In fact, from the 1580s, the numbers of elected members and size of the entire Parliamentary increased, rising from under 100 to over 200 members. Some of this resulted from a larger noble estate accounted for by expanding royal patronage; yet, it also arose through the extension of the franchise as more towns were allowed to elect members and shires to elect additional members. By the 1690s the elected members represented over two thirds of the membership (Rait 1924, 232-237, 272-276). Therefore, although the Scottish electorate was small compared to the likes of England and Holland, and family and client networks still proliferated, the greater size of Parliament and its expanding representativeness from the 1580s helped to slowly open Scotland's legislature to more contact with the interests of the nation at large. This was a process that altered the boundaries between the elite world of politics and the wider public sphere. Also, it provided extra fuel for the development of party politics from the 1670s. As Buchanan put it, 'as a general rule, a multitude of people is a better judge of all affairs than an individual', even a king (Buchanan 1579, 33). 'Participation in the institutions of the political realm' came long before Habermas' eighteenth-century transformation of the public sphere (Habermas 1989, 231-235; 1996, 28-31).

Printed public and political public developed simultaneously. The Revolution of 1688/89 saw the final defeat of court Catholicism, and therefore we would expect the last seventeen years of the Scottish Parliament, before it merged with that of England in 1707, to have been a relatively quiet period in the long campaign against seditious press activity. In fact, the government was very anxious to control the press, seeking to censor subversive and disruptive material on the one hand, and to produce official propaganda on the other (Mann 2000a, 163-191). Parliament, however, had a dual responsibility to facilitate the policing of the press, yet also, to retain the context of debate essential in a period of complex and heated party politics (Brown 1992; Riley 1979). Controlling the spread of information to the wider public sphere was a dilemma for members of Parliament, although there is evidence that some resolved this by banning books in public and distributing them in private. There was much to protest about and, particularly, the growing economic crisis.

Law is the foundation of censorship. The legal basis for censorship in Scotland, as in England, rested on two long-standing traditions. The first of these was the law of heresy, the preoccupation of canon or church law before the sixteenth century. Scotland's first anti-heresy law was passed in 1425 and it continued into the sixteenth century with the banning of the works of Luther in 1525. By 1560 canon and secular law had united against undesirable religious ideas. The second essential strand of censorship law was the law against 'leasing-making', comparable to the English crime of *scandalum magnatum.* 'Leasing-making' was the spreading of harmful ideas and untruths fomenting discord between the king and government and the people. The statutory crime dates back to 1318 and from 1424 became treason and, later, from the 1550s became synonymous with slander – spoken, written or printed – of the Crown and government and not merely of the king himself. Thereafter, throughout the early modern period, different Scottish governments took it upon themselves to interpret the law against printing or selling undesirable books with varied severity. The ultimate sanction of execution was rare in Scotland and was only ever applied to authors, not book traders; even then, almost all cases required the lifting of a sword as well as a pen, as in the cases of the extreme Presbyterians William Harvey (1682) and James Renwick (1688). There was no immediate or technical change in the law with the 1689 revolution, but demands for freedom of speech in Parliament, enshrined in the Articles of Grievance delivered by the Estates to William of Orange, helped encourage government moderation (Mann 2000a, 163-166, 170, 182)

The Privy Council was the key executive body responsible for the day-to-day administration of book policy – this applied to serious trade disputes and copyright patents as well as actions over censorship (Mann 2000b, and 1998). Nonetheless, the Privy Council always operated within a context created by parliamentary legislation. The censors understood that an act of parliament provided the most effective means of universal legitimacy. Using these laws, at least seventy titles were officially banned in Scotland from the 1570s to 1708, the year of the demise of the Scottish Privy Council. Of these, the vast majority were after the Restoration of monarchy in 1660. The intensity then built up from the 1680s. In fact, twenty were banned in the 1680s, nine in the 1690s, and fifteen in the years 1700 to 1708. However, whereas 60% of banned books were about church politics in the 1680s (in previous decades, church politics was the main target for censorship); in the 1690s, the majority were related to secular politics; and, in the 1700s, 90% were secular in nature (Mann 2000a, 178-180). The defeat of Catholicism in 1689-1690 is certainly reflected here, but so, also, is the feverish debate over secular policy. Equally, as those out of power criticised ministers, there was a growing government sensitivity to criticism during times of crisis.

Government prosecutions for illegal authorship, printing, and book selling were carried out mostly before the Privy Council or its committees, although, occasionally Parliament, as in the 1661 case of Christopher Higgins, the royal printer, for printing *The Causes of God's Wrath* (1653), a book which blamed the woes of the nation on the immorality of the king! Of the fifty prosecutions that took place from the 1540s to 1708, twenty-nine took place from 1680 to 1708. From 1690 to 1708, seventeen cases arose involving three authors, six private individuals (who possessed the wrong books), and eight book traders (Mann 2000a, 186-191). Never before in the early modern period had the government of Scotland been so successful in prosecuting printers.

Considering the context of this censorship activity, it is obvious to say that all aspects of the book trade were greater in scale in the 1690s than in previous decades: numbers of printers and booksellers and general distribution of stock both domestic and imported. Printing doubled in activity from the 1640s to 1690s (there were, on average, a dozen presses and thirty printers active in Scotland from 1690 to 1710) and the scale of book selling increased three times, with about sixty known booksellers throughout Scotland by the 1690s (Mann 2000a, 214-224; and Mann 2001). Thus, it was essential towards the end of the seventeenth century to abandon notions of licensing the entire press, and to concentrate on specific targets in terms of censorship.

At the end of the seventeenth century, the Scottish censor was faced with an increasingly varied press output (Emerson 1995), much of it controversial. Part of government propaganda was, of course, to print proclamations and open letters between king and Council in order to explain official policy. Indeed, the greatest government print effusion of the period was reserved for 1689 and the Revolution. Declarations and proclamations spread and letters flew between two alternative monarchies and the Estates and Privy Council. For the next two years, the Jacobite question – that is, whether James VII and II would return with the help of a French army – continued to dominate press output. Government measures against supporters of James ensured a large output of printed proclamations in 1690, along with news books of the conflict in Ireland, culminating in Jacobite defeat at the Battle of the Boyne that July. Strangely, while government returned to something like normality in 1691, the appetite for books giving news from Ireland or the minute details of some judicial trial of a notable Jacobite was even greater (Mann 2000a, 217).

The apex of government printing after 1689 was the year 1695, which witnessed one of the most hectic parliamentary sessions in the history of the Scottish Parliament. Measures were passed such as the foundation of the Bank of Scotland and the formation of a great trading company, the Company of Scotland, which vainly attempted to set up a trading post at Darien in Panama. Indeed, the issue that gripped Scotland from 1695 to 1700 was the Darien scheme. Some 15% of the press output of 1696 related to the subscription, recruitment, and financing for the doomed project. In 1699, when the scheme began to collapse, a similar proportion of output, some anonymous, expressed resentment with the king, English Parliament, and East India Company, who were accused of cutting off financial, naval, and colonial support (Mann 2000a, 218; Aldis 1970). The *Edinburgh Gazette,* which started in 1699 and was Scotland's first regular newspaper, stepped into the Darien controversy a few times. The government had trouble controlling the content of this newspaper, but it was no longer practical to suspend publication in the manner of the 1660s. Newssheets and journals were now too commonplace, and a news blackout was beyond the means of the authorities. In any case, an educated Scot was now expected to be familiar with the affairs and politics of the day. Information was a necessity for polite society and indicative of an expandingly literate and sophisticated public sphere.

The main targets of government censorship between 1690-1707 were undesirable information or 'false news' that reflected badly on the government, specifically the Darien affair, Jacobite pieces, Catholic books, blasphemy, and books that speculated too heatedly on the union of the parliaments and fuelled nationalism. The government employed two methods to tackle undesirable pamphlets and tracts in the late 1690s: firstly, in October 1696, the Privy Council formed a 'committee for searching for erroneous books' which arranged the searching of book traders premises and the approval of catalogues. Secondly, a new licensing act of council was agree in 1697, which confirmed the sanctions of confiscation and banishment for offenders. However, these measures did not stem the censoriousness of the press. In June 1699, weeks after James Donaldson was granted the patent to publish the *Edinburgh Gazette,* he was arrested for printing 'untruthful' and unauthorised news. The next month, the Edinburgh printer William Jaffrey was arrested by the Privy Council for printing a pamphlet protesting the Darien fiasco (PCR).

The following year, Parliament entered the fray. The MP William Seton of Pitmedden, an enthusiastic advocate for the benefits of union with England, was imprisoned for writing the pamphlet *Memorial to the MPs of the Court Party*, which questioned the status of the independent church and state of Scotland. Seton was released after a fulsome apology to Parliament. The same month, the Privy Council sought the arrest of Walter Herries, author of various controversial pro-Darien tracts blending Jacobite sympathies which were banned by the government. Parliament set the huge reward of £6000 Scots for information leading to his arrest (*APS* 10: 210, 214).

Another weapon against Jacobitism was more government propaganda. Whig anti-Jacobite propaganda was overwhelmingly printed in London, which signifies the attempt at centralised information control by English ministers (Steele 1981). Authors such as William Fuller were used by King William to write spurious accounts of the birth of King James VII and II and to develop the traditional 'warming-pan' slur, suggesting he was not the true heir but was spirited into his mother's delivery room. In Scotland the revival of 'moderate' Jacobitism, as seen in the Parliamentary election of 1702 which produced a hung parliament, made partisan Scottish printing too divisive.

In spite of the victory against court Catholicism in 1689, censorship of Catholic books returned to the agenda. The international context was the Nine Years War (1689-1697) which, until the late months of 1695, was going the way of France and Louis XIV. Matters deteriorated markedly in 1696, especially in Edinburgh and the burgh of Aberdeen. In early 1696, the Council forbade commerce and communication with France, and enforced the seizure of horses and arms belonging to known Catholics. In March a warrant was given to the magistrates of Aberdeen to arrest a 'Dr. John Jamesone [...] and master John Abercrombie papist priests', and three weeks later, the lord advocate informed the council that three particular Catholic books had been discovered in Edinburgh. The provost of the burgh was instructed to have them burnt. Two years later, the problem still festered in both burghs. A new Catholic cell had been discovered in Aberdeen along with 'a great many popish books', and a further cell was located in the capital, a group consisting mainly of merchants (PCR). In

November 1700, Parliament felt it necessary to produce a new statute 'for preventing the growth of popery' and the spread of mass books, which, in legal precedent, traced its ancestry back to 1579 and a hundred and twenty years of anti-Catholic censorship legislation (*APS* 10: 453-454, 463-464, 572-573). The clergy were not, of course, silent on the question of press censorship whether or not they were present in Parliament (Mann 2000a, 52-62). Bishops or no bishops, the clergy sought parliamentary ratification for initiatives from the educational to the moralistic. Clerical alarm in the 1690s at the rise of blasphemy and the new heresy of Deism, belief in God but not in revealed religion, forced Parliament to revise the law of blasphemy in June 1695. Thomas Aikenhead, an Edinburgh student, was the only individual to suffer stage three of the code, death by hanging (*APS* 9: 386). Nonetheless, the heresy of Deism continued in Scotland well beyond the 1690s, though never so extensively as in France and Germany.

In the four years before the union of 1707, Parliament itself became obsessed with a strange two-headed book policy consisting of national propaganda on the one hand, and the suppression of extremist views on Anglo-Scottish union on the other. In the reign of King William, a culture of lively political pamphleteering – pro-Jacobite, anti-English interference, aggrieved at the Darien fiasco and generally critical of the executive – soured the debate over parliamentary union. By 1702 Parliament was attuned to some raw emotions of popular 'nationalism'. Private tracts on the merits of union had been published before 1703, but that year was crucial to the collapse of Anglo-Scottish relations and Queen Anne's first abortive attempt to unite her parliaments. By 1705 matters deteriorated further. Firstly, England passed the Alien Act which, unless negotiations over union commenced, threatened the Scots with alien status in England and banned their exports. This was the year of the 'Worcester affair', where the Edinburgh government stood by as hysteria and popular resentment led to the seizure of the English ship 'The Worcester' and the judicial murder of the captain. This event of public revenge for Darien produced a stream of printed pamphlets with titles such as *Captain Thomas Green's Last Farewell to the Ocean and All the World, who was executed with Two More of his Crew [...] for Piracie and Murder.* Most condoned the harsh treatment of the English seamen. Anglo-Scottish relations were at their lowest point since the Cromwellian occupation.

That summer, Parliament was also outraged at the publication of two offensive anti-Scottish tracts written by the Englishman William Atwood: *The Superiority and Direct Dominion of the Imperial Crown of England, over the Crown and Kingdom of Scotland* and *The Scots Patriot unmasked.* Both pamphlets were ordered to be burnt, but in the same month the Edinburgh government set about financing a 'nationalist' publishing campaign. Firstly, James Hodges, who had written tracts questioning the union on economic grounds, was awarded £4800 Scots for producing works supportive of the prestige of the ancient kingdom of Scotland, including his *First Treatise on the Rights and Interests of the Two British Monarchies* (1705). Also, Parliament awarded the solicitor James Anderson £4800 Scots for composing his *Ane Historicall Essay shewing that the Crown and Kingdom of Scotland is imperial and independent* (1705). And a special ale tax was set for Glasgow to raise £3600 Scots to enable Anderson to prepare an account of the ancient charters and seals of Scotland (*APS* 11: 221, 244-245, 299, 306).

Although, in autumn 1705, the Scottish Parliament agreed to send commissioners to negotiate the union treaty, the 'nationalist' press persevered. In November, Parliament set up a committee to monitor progress on Anderson's great work. This committee included the jurists Sir John Lauder of Fountainhall and Andrew Fletcher of Saltoun, the latter, the most respected opponent of union with England. This committee of lawyers and union sceptics reflected the desire of many MPs to produce a symbolic record of the sovereign state and nation of Scotland as well as the conflicting objectives and emotions of the Parliament. As the articles of union were voted on one by one, and troops were stationed to suppress rioting, anti-union tracts were suppressed and destroyed, yet, so also was a pamphlet that claimed the subordination to England of the Crown and kingdom of Scotland. With Parliament entering its final weeks, the 'Anderson committee' reported on the need to supply Anderson with additional funds, and a further ale tax was set, this time on the lucky drinkers of Dundee (*APS* 11: 319, 344, 355, 357, 427, 429, 479). Government commitment to publish this final volume of national iconography is one of the enigmas of Scottish print history, but it nonetheless reflects most clearly the interweaving of propaganda and censorship priorities. The Scottish Parliament from 1702 to 1707 had to balance its duty to prevent dissent with an instinctive desire to protect ancient rights.

It would be convenient to suggest that levels of Scottish censorship declined as the size of the book trade increased and governments, Parliament and monarchs became more enlightened, or, conversely, that it increased as the target became easier to hit. In fact, the level of Scottish censorship did not so much get greater throughout the period as change in character. As the supply of books expanded, optimistic, early efforts to license the entire press were replaced by the targeting of seditious literature dealing with specific topics. At the end of the seventeenth century, this policy switch achieved a more effective administrative outcome which increased the number of prosecutions. Meanwhile, penalties for breaches were generally more moderate for, after 1689, the vitality of party politics and basic parliamentary arithmetic made it more difficult to banish all but the most extreme points of view. Nonetheless, if a few infamous executions are set aside with the misleading notoriety of some early and pre-1685 cases, censorship under William and Mary and Queen Anne was the most strident in early modern Scotland. It was an odd high point in the history of the Scottish book as the eighteenth century commenced: the government getting tougher and more efficient in censorship when, simultaneously, the press explosion was about to make the printed word entirely irrepressible. It was, however, a typical reaction of European institutions of government at the turn to the eighteenth century. All attempted to draw a new line in the sand that limited the scope for the public sphere at the very time that the language of dissent was more respectable and widespread. The philosophical interpretations of kingship and sovereignty and of the dialogues of public oath and published print were part of this complex social and political process.

PRIMARY SOURCES

APS = *Acts of the Parliaments of Scotland* (1814-1875). Ed. Thomas Thomson and Cosmo Innes. Vols. 7, 9, 10, and 11. Edinburgh.

NLS = National Library of Scotland [Edinburgh]. Advocates Manuscripts (1488) [Adv. Ms 25.5.6 f. 203v]; (1520) [Adv. Ms 25.5.9 f.132]; (ca.1565) [Adv. Ms 7.1.9 f.109].

PCR = Privy Council Records. Manuscript Registers of the Privy Council, National Archives of Scotland, Edinburgh. PC.1. 51, 20 and 28; PC.1.27, 202; PC.1.51, 576 and 583; PC.1.52, 14.

RPC = *Register of the Privy Council, 1545-1567* (1877). Edinburgh.

REFERENCES

Aldis, Harry G. (1970). *A List of the Books Printed in Scotland before 1700: Including those Printed furth of the Realm for Scottish Booksellers*. Edinburgh: National Library of Scotland.

Bonney, Robert (1991). *The European Dynastic States 1494-1660*. Oxford: Oxford University Press.

Brown, Keith M. (1992). *Kingdom or Province? Scotland and the Regal Union, 1603-1715*. Basingstoke: Macmillan.

Buchanan, George (1579). *De Jure Regni Apud Scotos*. Trans. Roger Mason and Martin Smith. Edinburgh: Charteris.

Burns, James H. (1996). *The True Law of Kingship: Concepts of Monarchy in Early Modern Scotland*. Oxford: Oxford University Press.

Durkan, John (1994). *Bibliography of George Buchanan*. Glasgow: University of Glasgow [Library].

Emerson, Roger L. (1995). 'Scottish Cultural Change 1660-1710 and the Union of 1707'. In John Robertson (ed.), *A Union for Empire*. Cambridge: Cambridge University Press, 122-144.

Firth, C.H. (1918). 'Macaulay's Treatment of Scottish History.' *Scottish Historical Review* 15, 273-291.

Goodare, Julian (1999). *State and Society in Early Modern Scotland*. Oxford: Oxford University Press.

Habermas, Jürgen (1989). *The Structural Transformation of the Public Sphere: An Inquiry into a Category of Bourgeois Society*. Trans. Thomas Burger. Cambridge: Polity Press. Original German edition 1962.

_______ (1996). *The Habermas Reader*. Ed. William Outhwaite. Cambridge: Polity Press.

Houston, Robert A. (1994). *Social Change in the Age of Enlightenment, Edinburgh 1660-1760*. Oxford: Oxford University Press.

James [King of Scotland] (1982). *The True Lawe of Free Monarchies*. In *Minor Prose Works of King James VI and I [...]*. Ed. James Craigie. Edinburgh: Scottish Text Society. Original edition, Edinburgh: Waldegrave, 1598.

_______ (1944). *The Basilicon Doron of King James VI*. Ed. James Craigie. 2 vols. Edinburgh: Scottish Text Society. Original editions, Edinburgh: Waldegrave, 1599 and 1603.

Lyall, Roderick (1977). 'The Medieval Scottish Coronation Service: Some Seventeenth-Century Evidence.' *Innes Review* 28, 3-21.

Macaulay, T.B. (1979). *The History of England*. Ed. and abridged with an intro. Hugh Trevor-Roper. Harmondsworth: Penguin. Original edition 1848-1861.

MacDonald, Alan R. (1998). *The Jacobean Kirk, 1567-1625: Sovereignty, Polity and Liturgy*. Aldershot: Ashgate.

_______ (2002). 'Deliberative Processes in the Scottish Parliament before 1639: Multi-Cameralism and the Lords of the Articles.' *Scottish Historical Review* 81/1, no.211, forthcoming.

Mackenzie, Sir George (1684). *Jus Regium, Or the Just and Solid Foundation of the Monarchy of Scotland*. Edinburgh: 'Anderson' nee Campbell.

Mann, Alastair J. (1998). 'Book Commerce, Litigation and the Art of Monopoly: The Case of Agnes Campbell, Royal Printer 1676-1712.' *Scottish Economic and Social History* 18/2, 132-156.

________ (2000a). *The Scottish Book Trade 1500 to 1720: Print Commerce and Print Control in Early Modern Scotland.* East Linton: Tuckwell Press.

________ (2000b). 'Scottish Copyright before the Statute of 1710.' *The Juridical Review* 2000/1, 11-25.

________ (2001). 'The Anatomy of the Printed Book in Early Modern Scotland.' *Scottish Historical Review* 80/2, no.210, 181-200.

Mason, Roger A. (1982). '*Rex Stoicus*: George Buchanan, James VI and the Scottish Polity.' In John Dwyer et al. (eds.), *New Perspectives on the Politics and Culture of Early Modern Scotland.* Edinburgh: John Donald, 9-33.

________ (1998). *Kingship and Commonweal: Political Thought in Renaissance and Reformation Scotland.* East Linton: Tuckwell Press.

Myers, Alex R. (1975). *Parliaments and Estates in Europe to 1789.* London: Thames and Hudson.

Rait, Robert S. (1924). *The Parliaments of Scotland.* Glasgow: MacLehose.

Riley, Patrick W.J. (1979). *King William and the Scottish Politicians.* Edinburgh: John Donald.

Shriver, Frederick (1982). 'Hampton Court Revisited: James I and the Puritans.' *Journal of Ecclesiastical History* 33, 48-71.

Speck, William A. (1988). *Reluctant Revolutionaries: Englishmen and the Revolution of 1688.* Oxford: Oxford University Press.

Steele, Margaret (1981). 'Anti-Jacobite Pamphleteering, 1701-1720.' *Scottish Historical Review* 60/2, no.170, 140-155.

Tanner, Roland J. (2000). 'The Lords of the Articles before 1540: A Reassessment.' *Scottish Historical Review* 79/2, no.208, 189-212.

________ (2001). *The Late Medieval Scottish Parliament.* East Linton: Tuckwell Press.

Whyte, Ian D. (1997). *Scotland's Society and Economy in Transition, c.1500 to c.1760.* Basingstoke: Macmillan.

Annette Pankratz

Over the King's Bodies: The Emerging Public Sphere in Seventeenth-Century England

The transition from representative publicness to the bourgeois public sphere in Early Modern England[1] happened in leaps and bounds. The times of the Civil Wars (1642-1649), the Interregnum (1649-1660), the Exclusion Crisis (1679-1681) and the 'Glorious' Revolution (1688) witnessed the emergence of the public sphere in Habermasian terms, 'the public of *private* individuals who join in debate of issues bearing on state authority' (Calhoun 1992, 7; cf. Zaret 1992, 216; Norbrook 1994, 7); while during the Restoration period proper (1660-1662) and the early 1680s the traditional model of representative publicness – strongly identifying country, ruler and the ruler's body (Habermas 1990, 60-67) – prevailed.

The characteristics of an emergent public sphere, the gradual separation of ruler and country, society and state (Calhoun 1992, 7), tie in with a shift towards secularisation and capitalism and a change in political theories – from divine-right ideology to contract theories (Zaret 1992; Price 1999, 192-194). All of these processes very often went 'over the king's body' and affected the traditional 'mystic fiction' (Kantorowicz 1997, 3) of the 'King's Two Bodies' – the union of sacred body politic and mortal body natural (4, 7, 13).

This paper will correlate images of royalty with political discourses and the emergent public sphere in three ways: first, the Civil War and Commonwealth is correlated with the separation of body natural and body politic and the formation of multiple public spheres; second, the early Restoration is correlated with the attempted reunion of the two bodies and the suppression of the public spheres; and, third, periods of crisis, especially the Exclusion Crisis, are correlated with the formation of a third royal body and a resurfacing of the public sphere.

I.

Around the middle of the seventeenth century, political discourse enhanced a gradual separation of society and ruler (Calhoun 1992, 7-8).[2] The unitarian idea of a sacred monarch who embodied the entire country and did not need the consensus of his subjects

---

1 Habermas dates the beginnings of the public sphere in the early eighteenth century (Habermas 1990, 91-92); a position which was revised by, among others, Zaret (1992), Norbrook (1994), McDowell (1998) and Price (1999), who propose the emergence of the public sphere from the 1620s onward.

2 This may in part be due to the change of dynasties from the Tudors to the originally Scottish Stuarts. The mystic fiction of the king's two bodies did not apply to Scottish monarchs. I am grateful to Alastair Mann for this information.

(Mendle 1993, 105) gave way to the idea of a 'mixed monarchy', the assumption that both king and parliament represented the body politic proper. In 1640 John Pym (in his 'Speech on Grievances') promoted this idea with the words: 'A parliament is that to the Commonwealth which the soul is to the body' (quoted in Kenyon 1986, 184). In 1642 the 'Nineteen Propositions' likewise claimed that 'matters of state' could not be settled without the consent of parliament (see Kenyon 1986, 222-226).[3]

During the Civil War, parliament asserted that it was opposing the king – the body physical – to defend the King – the sacred body (Kantorowicz 1997, 21). The trials against the monarch in 1648/1649 fully isolated the private opinion of 'Charles Stuart' from public reason[4] and found him guilty of 'levying war against the [...] Parliament and people' (quoted in Lagomarsino and Wood 1989, 2).

His public execution put the textual annihilation into practice (Condren 1994, 37). It not only demonstrated that a king's body could indeed be violated without immediate punishment from God, it also triggered off critical debates in the public sphere(s). Various texts tried to invest the death of the king with divergent meanings: whereas the apologetic *Eikon Basilike* (1649) insists on the suffering of a royal martyr more sinned against than sinning, Milton's *Eikonoklastes* (1649) demystifies the king and sets the mechanisms of representative publicness against the genuinely reasonable and consensual public opinion. Resistance against Charles Stuart originated from the 'general voice of the people', which was 'almost hissing him and his ill-acted regality off the Stage' (Milton 1962, 355; see also 361, 364).[5] The consensus of the people, truth, reason, law and freedom necessitated the separation of the body politic, as legitimated by public consensus, from the body of a ham actor in the role of king:

> for if the Parlament represent the whole Kingdom [...] then doth the King represent onely himself; and if a King without his Kingdom be in a civil sense nothing, then without or against the Representative of his whole Kingdom he himself represents nothing, and by consequence his judgement and his negative is as good as nothing; and though we should allow him to be something, yet not equivalent, or comparable to the whole Kingdom, and so neither to them who represent it. (Milton 1962, 410; see also 458, 592-593)

The dialogue between *Eikon Basilike* and *Eikonoklastes* formed part of the debate which erupted during the Civil War over the most rational and appropriate forms of government, a debate which raged from 'the defined battleground of official statements to the street warfare of often-anonymous pamphlets' (Mendle 1993, 116; cf. Zaret 1992, 217). Patriarchal rule and divine-right ideology were contested by contract theories; others

---

3 See also Henry Parker's claim that the king had 'deserted' the 'whole body of the State' (*Observations upon Some of His Majesties Late Answers and Expresses* [1642]; quoted in Mendle 1993, 117).

4 'Law in a Free Nation hath bin ever public reason, the enacted reason of a Parlament; which he [Charles] denying to enact, denies to govern us by that which ought to be our Law; interposing his own privat reason, which to us is no Law' (Milton 1962, 360).

5 For the topos of the 'monarch as actor' as used by Elizabeth I and James I, see Backscheider 1993, 3-4 and Kantorowicz 1997, 41.

proposed a return to the liberties and rights pre-dating the 'Norman yoke'.[6] The Hobbesian 'Leviathan' embodied absolute government created among equals according to the rules of reason (Sommerville 1992; Kamm 1998). Unlike Hobbes, whose subjects turned into private individuals without means of participation after their initial agreement, Diggers, Levellers, Ranters and other religious dissidents envisioned a Christian world upside down – either a republic of property owners or a pre-communist commonwealth – and vented their ideas in the plebeian public sphere. The body politic was not to be restricted to parliament or to the army; it was to be transfused to everybody. Inspired by divine revelation, the Digger Gerald Winstanley called a spade a spade, and the 'present powers of England' not much better than Charles I: 'you call up all the powers of darkness to come forth and help to set the crown upon the head of self, which is that kingly power you have oathed and vowed against, and yet uphold it in your hands' (*A New-Yeers Gift* [1650]; quoted in Wootton 1986, 321; see also 326-327). The only rescue from the devilish and tyrannical entrapment by power, he advised, was the abolishment of property and the 'levelling' of all hierarchies (328).

The governing elites set the concept of public reason modelled on the principles of natural philosophy (Zaret 1992, 227-229) against these instances of an unruly 'revolt in the Revolution' (Hill 1972, 15). The debates in the bourgeois public sphere homed in on the Restoration of the monarchy to secure the social and economic status quo (Zaret 1992, 224). Hence, General Monck was able to fill the power vacuum after Cromwell's death in 1658, and parliament invited the monarch back to England (Haan and Niedhart 1993, 93).

II.

The Restoration in 1660 tried to re-establish the institutions and the ideology of monarchy (Backscheider 1993, 5). The king's two bodies were nominally reunited (Kantorowicz 1997, 7, 13) and pageants, prologues, plays and panegyrics reverted to the strategies of representative publicness and divine-right ideology.[7] 'Rituals of royalty' (to use the term coined by David Cannadine) signalled a detoxification of the kingdom from eighteen years of Civil War and eleven years of republican rule, and juxtaposed rebellion and anarchy with the divinely ordained monarchical order. Clarendon's *The Continuation of the Life* (1759) mentions the hidden agenda of the coronation ceremonies and how it was effected:

---

6 I would like to thank Uwe Böker for pointing this out to me. For a detailed analysis of this governmental theory, see his forthcoming article (Böker 2002).

7 See, e.g., 'Yea princes, sirs, are gods, as they're above, / Though as men in a mortal sphere they move' ('The Answer of Mr. Waller's Painter to His Many New Advisers'; Lord 1963, 1: 154). This echoed James I, who had postulated in 1610 that 'kings are not only God's lieutenants upon earth, and sit upon God's throne, but even by God himself they are called gods' ('Speech to Parliament', 21 March 1610; quoted in Kenyon 1986, 11).

> the Novelties and new Inventions, with which the Kingdom had been so much intoxicated for so many Years altogether, might be discountenanced and discredited in the Eyes of the People, for the Folly and Want of State thereof; his Majesty had directed the Records and old Formularies should be examined, and thereupon all Things should be prepared, and all Forms accustomed be used, that might add Lustre and Splendour to the Solemnity. (Quoted in Knowles 1988, 14)

Although the diversity of opinions which threatened property rights and social hierarchies had supposedly been converted into national unity (Dykstal 1992, 309-310), and although the negotiations in the public sphere had been brought under control by the state apparatus, the king could not and did not entirely ignore public opinion (Harris 2001, 128). 'Lustre and Splendour' necessitated the participation of Charles' subjects. The king acted as 'both our *Triumph* and *Spectator*'[8] – as symbol of the country's reconciliation and its main spectator. Audiences and performers felt themselves to be a representative general public (Backscheider 1993; Löther 1998, 459) and constructed a consensual model of past, present and future. In order to explain and excuse the violent separation of king and country, the texts recurred to a dualistic strategy. They differentiated between the outrageous anarchy of the misguided multitude and the almost inevitable ramifications of the elite conflicts. Regicides, rebellion and the threatening anarchy of the plebeian counter-culture were externalised, while the discourses of the former liberal public sphere were troped as natural phenomena.

Those of the fifty-nine men who had signed the death warrant of Charles I and were still living in 1660 were publicly 'hanged, drawn, and quartered';[9] the bodies of Cromwell, Bradshaw and Ireton were exhumed and ritually executed on 30 January (Backscheider 1993, 7). More celebratory public rituals used biblical iconography to symbolise this externalisation. In the cavalcade through London on 22 April 1661, one day before the coronation,[10] Charles II encountered a Triumphal Arch, with 'Usurpation [...] a Figure with many ill-favoured Heads, some bigger, some lesser, and one particularly shooting out of his Shoulder, like CROMWEL'S' (Ogilby 1988, 28). The apocalyptic beast was also held responsible for instigating mass uprisings and chaos. Rebellion features as allegorical figure in the coronation pageant and characterises herself as 'Hell's Daughter' who makes 'the Vulgar in Fanatique Swarms / Court Civil War, and dote on Horrid Arms' (47).[11]

What about those who belonged neither to the 'rabble' nor to the compromised inner circle of Cromwell's regime? The contesting discourses of the public sphere and the power

---

8 John Tatham, *London's Triumph Celebrated the Twenty-ninth of October 1664*; quoted in Backscheider 1993, 49. This resembled the situation in the public theatres. The king acted both as spectacle for the audience and as central spectator of the performance on stage (Jose 1984, 129).

9 Pepys 'went out to Charing Cross to see Major-Generall Harrison hanged, drawn, and quartered – which was done there – he looking as cheerfully as any man could do in that condition. [...] Thus it was my chance to see the King beheaded at Whitehall and to see the first blood shed in revenge for the blood of the King at Charing Cross' (13 October 1660; Pepys 1970-71, 1: 265).

10 For the likewise highly symbolical entry of the king into London on 29 May 1660, Charles' birthday, see Backscheider 1993, 8; Knowles 1988, 13-14.

11 Cf. Dryden's 'Astraea Redux': 'the vulgar gull'd into Rebellion' (Dryden 1956-89, 1: 23).

struggles between the elites and the king were described as part of nature – unpleasant, but unavoidable. Dryden's 'Astraea Redux' employs the extended metaphor of a thunderstorm, 'A Panegyrick on his Coronation' refers to 'that wild Deluge where the world was drownd' (Dryden 1956-89, 1: 33). In Ogilby's pageant, Plenty greets the monarch:

> Great Sir, the Star, which at Your Happy Birth
> Joy'd with his Beams (at Noon) the wond'ring earth,
> Did with auspicious lustre, then, presage
> The glitt'ring Plenty of this Golden Age;
> The Clouds blown o're, which long our joys o'recast,
> And the sad Winter of Your absence past,
> See! the three smiling Seasons of the Year
> Agree at once to bid You Welcome here. (Ogilby 1988, 165)

The king was celebrated as father of his people, bridegroom of his country, and royal healer whose return secured stability, health, and fertility of the country.[12] The integration of the Civil War into a seasonal and cyclical pattern in turn re-enforced Christological topoi which linked Charles with the Messiah.[13] This tied in with images of the Phoenix as emblem of immortal royalty (Ogilby 1988, 30; Kantorowicz 1997, 388) and with expectations of a Virgilian Golden Age in the near future.[14]

III.

Although Charles did perform in rituals of representative publicness emphasising his sacred royalty,[15] he could not turn back the clocks to the times of his grandfather, James I.[16] The universalising theory of divine right could not accommodate the processes of

---

12 'Whom Our first Flames and Virgin Love did wed. For his long absence Church and State did groan' ('Astraea'; Dryden 1956-89, 1: 22). In the dedication of 'Annus Mirabilis' and, later, in *Albion and Albanius*, Charles was still the groom, but the bride or the lover had changed to the capital city of London: 'Never had a Prince or People more mutual reason to love each other, if suffering for each other can indear affection' (1: 48).

13 From a star shining at his birth ('Astraea'; Dryden 1956-89, 1: 30), his patient suffering during exile (1: 23) until his glorious restoration by divine providence.

14 In 'Astraea', 'Times whiter series' (Dryden 1956-89, 1: 30) and in Ogilby's pageant: 'Comes not here our King of Peace, / Who the Stars so long foretold, / From all Woes should us release / Converting Iron-times to gold?' (Ogilby 1988, 135).

15 Especially the healing ceremonies; see Weber 1995, 50-87; Wagner 1992, 262; and Hammond 1991, 37-38.

16 Even during the coronation festivities, faultlines appeared. Some symbolic meanings needed further explanation; they were not ideologically safe or naturalised ('a company of men all like Turkes; but I know not yet what they are for', 22 April 1661; Pepys 1970-71, 2: 82). The planned static hierarchical order was undermined by the participants themselves. A fight broke out between the king's footmen and the barons of the cinque ports over a ceremonial canopy (2: 86; Ogilby 1988, 186). Besides, Ogilby's

'functional specialisation between the political, cultural and economic sectors' (Price 1999, 192), neither could the stylised staging of the supra-personal dignity of the monarch (Habermas 1992, 426) by means of the traditional forms of status-based, static representative publicness prevent a re-emergence of critical public debates. As Charles had been restored to the same stalemate situation between king and parliament which triggered off the Civil War in the 1640s, he furthermore could not fulfil the expectations of his subjects.

Especially during periods of crisis – the Great Fire, defeat in the Dutch Wars, the Exclusion Crisis – the faultlines resurfaced. Discontent with the present government and discussions of viable alternatives led to the re-formation of a liberal public sphere. Rumours, gossip and debates in coffee houses, alehouses, or clubs spread diverse interpretations of the king's conduct and his policies (Pincus 1995; Harris 2001; Allen 1976); pamphlets, newspapers, newsbooks, sermons or proclamations implicitly or explicitly negotiated different theories of government (Harris 2001).

The controversies during the Exclusion Crisis lent themselves to be grafted onto the king's bodies. Ironically, Charles, who had fathered a host of illegitimate children with various mistresses, did not have a legitimate heir. Thus, the crown was supposed to pass on to his brother James, a Catholic. Due to anti-Catholic hysteria in the wake of the 'Popish Plot', the opposition tried to exclude James from the succession to the throne, thereby undermining traditional notions of dynastic continuity and the automatic passing on of the sacred royal body to the next in line. Similar to the situation at the eve of the Civil War, the newly formed Whig party tried to separate the body natural of the king from the body politic. The second Exclusion Bill shortcuts the customs of hereditary monarchy by assuming James to be legally dead:

> in case the said James, duke of York, shall survive his now Majesty and the heirs of his Majesty's body, the said imperial crown shall descend to and be enjoyed by such person and persons successively during the lifetime of the said James, duke of York, as should have inherited and enjoyed the same in case the said James, duke of York, were naturally dead. ('Exclusion Bill', November 1680; quoted in Kenyon 1986, 387)

The struggle between Tories and Whigs and between king and parliament incidentally led to the lapse of the Licensing Act in 1679 and this in turn led to a pamphlet war and the politicisation of the whole country (Jones 1961, 117). What had before been the subject of secret diary entries and private discussions now became part of the public religio-political discourse. Although Charles II acted more intelligently and carefully than Charles I (see Jones 1987; Hutton 1989), he still had to cope with the institutional faultlines and a series of political and military defeats which were directly blamed on his deficiencies – most prominently on his scandalous sexual life.[17] 'Fixing the political in explicitly sexual

---

celebration of Loyalty and Royalty had been co-designed by Sir Balthazar Gerbier, a former Republican (Knowles 1988, 12).

17 As early as 1662, Pepys notes his discontent about the interference of the king's private life with his public duties: 'my Lady Castlemaine is fallen from Court [...] and yet if the King do it to leave off not

terms' (Zwicker 1993, 108), the texts operated from patriarchal premises and constructed the king's private life as a reflection of his politics.

Tory apologists attempted to deflate criticism by re-writing private vices into public virtues which were natural, commonsensical and, all in all, conducive to the health of the country. Dryden's 'Absalom and Achitophel' (1681) links divine-right and patriarchal ideology with the king's promiscuity: the *pater patriae* quite literally is the father of his subjects, rightly so and attractively so:

> When Nature prompted and no Law deni'd
> Promiscuous Use of Concubine and Bride;
> Then Israel's Monarch, after Heavens own heart,
> His vigorous warmth did, variously impart
> To Wives and Slaves: And, wide as his Command,
> Scatter'd his Maker's Image through the Land
> (Dryden 1956-89, 2: 5; see also Weber 1995, 89; Zwicker 1993, 132-135)

Whig critics appropriated the panegyrists' textual strategies (Weber 1995, 48) in order to demonstrate its disadvantageous effects:

> The royal evil so malignant grows,
> Nothing the dire contagion can oppose.
> In our wel-public scarce one thing succeeds
> For one man's weakness a whole nation bleeds
> ('An Historical Poem'; Lord 1963, 2: 161).[18]

Satires imbued the standard epithets of monarchical grandeur with deep irony: 'A god incarnate England's throne does grace, / Chaste in his pleasures, in devotion grave, / To his friends constant to his foes he's brave;' ('An Ironical Satire'; Lord 1963, 2: 200).[19] References to classical divinity likewise stress the king's irresponsibility and the blatant clash between the claims to sacredness and to the divine right of kings and the deficient present representations of it by the monarch. Charles metamorphoses into 'poor Priapus King' ('Historical Poem'; Lord 1963, 2: 158)[20] or 'amorous Jove' who spends his 'lightning and thunder' on Nell Gwynn and a great number of other mistresses ('A Ballad Called the Haymarket Hectors'; Lord 1963, 1: 169).[21]

Making use of the Bakhtinian potential of sexualised bodies (Bakhtin 1985; Knowles 1988, 15) and merging them with the charged terms of rebellion which had earlier denoted the upheavals of the Civil War, the Whig satires refashioned Charles as a monarch upside down and inside out, situated at the intersection of conflicting discourses of power, gender and property. Instead of explicitly separating the body natural of the king from the body

---

only her but all other mistresses, I should be heartily glad of it, that he may fall to look after business' (3 July 1663; Pepys 1970-71, 4: 213).

18 See also 'Fourth Advice to a Painter' (Lord 1963, 1: 142, l. 36); and Weber 1995, 48.

19 Cf. John Freke, 'The History of Insipids' (Lord 1963, 1: 243-244);'The Earl of Rochester's Verses for Which he was Banished' (1: 424); and Hammond 1991, 17.

20 See also 'Hodge' (Lord 1963, 2: 147).

21 Cf. 'The Royal Buss' (Lord 1963, 1: 263).

politic, as the Commonwealth writers had done, texts created a third, unofficial royal body, which violated the boundaries between public and private, male and female, and emotional and reasonable. Going beyond a mere vilification of the king's body natural, satires transposed the assaults on the king to a realm of mythically bestial and subhuman sexuality.[22]

Anxieties about the succession of James, threats of absolutism and foreign (especially French) influence are linked with or expressed as royal promiscuity or impotence. Misdemeanours in the private sphere violated seemingly natural hierarchies: the king was neither able to rule his passions nor his mistresses, not to mention his country:

> howe'er weak and slender be the string,
> Bait it with whore and it will hold a King.
> Almighty pow'r of women! Oh, how vain
> Are Salic laws, for you will ever reign [...]
> To command pow'r and to enslave a King.
> ('Flatfoot the Gudgeon Taker'; Lord 1963, 2: 191)[23]

The feminisation of the king denoted the threat of the country by Catholicism and absolutism. The king was either troped as tyrannical rapist of his country, or as impotent victim of foreign (female) powers. Britannia complains in John Ayloffe's 'Oceana and Britannia' (1681): 'Shall I ne'er rest for this lewd ravisher? / Rapes, burning, murders are his royal sport; / These modish monsters haunt his perjur'd Court' (Lord 1963, 2: 396). Catholic mistresses of the king, such as Louise de Kéroualle, Duchess of Portsmouth, personified the ubiquitous danger of 'popery and slavery':

> This French hag's pocky bum
> So powerful is of late,
> Although it's both blind and dumb,
> It rules both Church and State.
> ('A Satire'; Lord 1963, 2: 291)[24]

The reversal of gender roles often corresponded to a reversal of social rank[25] and eventually to the degradation of the king to a completely 'senseless thing' ('A New Ballad'; Lord 1963, 2: 176) or a 'monstrous foul beast' (Stephen College, 'A Raree Show'; Lord 1963, 2: 427). In the satires by Marvell, Ayloffe, College and other Whig writers Charles metamorphosed into a 'goat, fox, timorous French ape' (Ayloffe, 'Oceana and Britannia';

---

22 For a more detailed analysis of the king's three bodies, see Pankratz 2001.

23 See also Ayloffe, 'Britannia and Raleigh' (Lord 1963, 1: 233); 'Satyr Unmuzzled' (2: 213); 'A Panegyric' (2: 243); and 'A Satire' (2: 291).

24 Cf. 'Britannia and Raleigh' (Lord 1963, 1: 232); Hammond 1991, 39; Weber 1995, 93; and Marvell, 'Last Instructions to a Painter' (Lord 1963, 1: 136); Zwicker 1993, 116; Riebling 1995; 'Flatfoot the Gudgeon Taker' (Lord 1963, 2: 190-191); and 'Satyr Unmuzzled' (2: 213).

25 Marvell, 'Upon his Majesty's being made Free of the City' (Lord 1963, 1: 237-242); 'The Statue at Charing Cross' (1: 270-273); 'A Dialogue between the Two Horses' (1: 275-283); Hammond 1991, 26.

Lord 1963, 2: 396)[26] or into 'Old Rowley', 'An old ill-favor'd stallion' ('Satire on Old Rowley'; Lord 1963, 2: 185).[27]

The depiction of a grotesque and carnivalesque world upside down, in which hierarchies are fluid and unstable serves as critique of political failures, and as warning of turmoil to come. Both Tory and Whig pamphlets abound with references to 'forty-two' or 'forty-eight', the Civil War and the trial against Charles I. Tory texts evoke the past as a time when the king, property and security were threatened by an anarchic 'rebel rout' ('A New Ballad of London's Loyalty'; Lord 1963, 2: 432);[28] Whigs remind the king of the implicit power of the people and warn him not to make the same mistakes as his father and to rule without parliament.[29]

The portraits of Charles II as rapist of his country re-enact the legal procedures against his father within the private sphere. By denying the monarch both divinity and humanity, texts make a dethroning – metaphorical or real – imaginable: 'What can there be in kings divine? / The most are wolves, goats, sheep, or swine' (John Freke, 'The History of Insipids'; Lord 1963, 1: 251).[30] A republic seems to lurk between these lines, but, on the whole, most texts could not or dared not write outside of the monarchical system.[31]

Instead, they redefined the boundaries between private and public. Charles should get rid of his mistresses ('rise' and 'banish [...] Delilah'), divorce his Catholic wife (the 'barren' 'Portuguese') and propagate a legitimate male heir ('Satire on Old Rowley'; Lord 1963, 2: 186); thus, conforming to the naturalised role model of male dominance. At the same time, the satires recommend that 'Life, liberty and property' have to be preserved by 'mixed monarchy', a consensus between monarch, parliament and people:

> Statesmen, who his true interest would improve,
> Compute his greatness by his people's love:
> That may assist our friends, and foes o'ercome;
> So much he will be fear'd abroad as lov'd at home
> [...] Heaven preserve our legal monarchy

26 Cf. 'Hodge' (Lord 1963, 2: 147); 'A Dialogue between the two Horses' (1: 280).

27 Cf. 'Colin' (Lord 1963, 2: 171); 'Song. Old Rowley the King' (3: 478-483). Rowley was the name of the favourite horse of the king (Coote 1999, 247). 'The King's Answer [to Monmouth's Letter]' even mentions the option of the king's fornication with animals (Lord 1963, 2: 255).

28 Cf. 'Queries' (Lord 1963, 2: 293-297); 'The Wiltshire Ballad' (2: 313-318); 'The Whigs' Exaltation: A Pleasant New Song of 82 to an Old Tune of 41' (3: 10-14).

29 ''tis forty to one, if he play the old game, / He'll reduce us ere long to forty and eight' (Marvell, 'The Statue at Charing Cross'; Lord 1963, 1: 271); 'they who conquered the father won't be slaves to the son' ('Two Horses'; 1: 283); 'Satire on Old Rowley' (2: 186); 'A Bill on the House of Commons' Door' (2: 344-345); cf. Burnet's admonitions to Charles at the day of his father's execution (Burnet 1969 2: 294-295).

30 See in the same poem: 'If such kings be by God appointed, / The Devil is then the Lord's anointed' (Lord 1963, 1:251); see 'Hodge' (Lord 1963, 2: 152).

31 Besides, censorship still punished too-obvious attacks on the king (Hammond 1991, 24). Stephen College was tried and executed for 'The Raree Show' (headnote Lord 1963, 2: 425; Weber 1995, 172-205).

And all those laws that keep the people free.
(Thomas Shadwell, 'The Medal of John Bayes';
Lord 1963, 3: 94; see Lessenich 2001, 248).[32]

Although the project of Exclusion failed, its textual strategies were re-employed after the 'Glorious' Revolution. The tactics of deposing of a monarch's first body without killing off his second recur in the debates of the Revolution Parliament and in Locke's *Two Treatises of Government* (see Locke 1967, 149).

IV.

The critique of the monarch, the undermining of traditional legitimatory ideologies of government concomitant with the advocacy of two discrete spheres, a liberal public and a patriarchal private sphere, are not restricted to Whig satires. Although Restoration drama, in general, betrays a certain conservative and elite bias, it nevertheless proffers comparable textual strategies. Nahum Tate's *A Duke and No Duke* (1684) draws a farcical portrait of the discussions about legitimate and illegitimate rule during the Exclusion Crisis. With the help of a magician, the servant Trappolin assumes the shape of the legitimate ruler, Lavinio, and undermines all traditional claims to authority:

TRAPPOLIN: [...] before I treat with your Master, I must know by what Title he holds.
1 EMBASSADOR: By Native and Legitimate Claim.
TRAPPOLIN: That is as much to say, I am an Usurper.
2 EMBASSADOR: By most unquestion'd and immediate Right from Heav'n.
TRAPPOLIN: As who should say, my Preferment came from the Devil. (Tate 1685, 33)

In his opinion, it all boils down to the maxim that 'for ought I know, it is Dress that makes a Duke' (10). While the trickster wreaks havoc in the state, he secures the happiness of the two lovers, Brunetto and Prudentia. Duke Lavinio had forbidden his sister the marriage with her valiant paramour in order to save the dynasty from 'base born taint' (5); 'duke' Trappolin orders them to marry. Strict patriarchy stands opposed to witty materialist hedonism; the subjects are constantly confused both by the hysterical ranting of the legitimate duke and by the pranks of the clever trickster. They do not know whose commands to follow and interpret both as 'madness'. Only the intervention of the magician can solve the impasse and restore the legitimate ruler – Lavinio. Prudentia and Brunetto, however, marry and validate Trappolin's private arrangements. The doubling of rulers[33] highlights the over-determination of political power – by heredity, 'dress', custom, law or divine right – the possibility of a separation between public and private; thus, implicitly questioning patriarchal norms and the ideology of non-resistance.

---

32 Cf. 'The Dream of the Cabal' (Lord 1963, 1: 202).

33 The doubling of rulers is a standard dramatic conflict to be found in the prototypical and proverbial *A King and No King* (1613), by John Fletcher (the pretext of *A Duke and No Duke*), in Aston Cokayne's *Trappolin Creduto Principe* (1657), Dryden's *Marriage a la Mode* (1671) and Buckingham's *The Rehearsal* (1672); see Maguire 2000, 101.

Vanbrugh's *The Provoked Wife* (1697) reverses this balance between public and private: the liberalised political situation does not extend to the private sphere. At the beginning of the play, Lady Brute muses about her marital state:

> I think I promised to be true to my husband. Well; and he promised to be kind to me. But he han't kept his word. Why then I'm absolved from mine. Aye, that seems clear to me. The argument's good between the king and the people, why not between the husband and the wife? (Vanbrugh 1982, 59).[34]

Why not? The plays imply that leaving their safe homes and their families would endanger women. Even if the patriarch proves deficient, the norms of patriarchy have to be internalised and naturalised. Female characters are threatened by rape and murder once they try to transgress domestic boundaries. Lady Brute and her sister Belinda venture forth to a rendezvous with their admirers Constant and Heartfree in Spring Garden. The two women appear 'masked, and poorly dressed' (129) and are consequently taken for prostitutes. The gallants keep their distance, while Lady Brute's husband, Sir John, plans to make the most of the chance encounter, by force if necessary: 'I'll devil you, you jade you. I'll demolish your ugly face. [...] I'll swoon her' (131). Again, as in the satires against the king, the patriarch turns into a rapist, but with the consent of the other two men. Constant and Heartfree decline to save the anonymous women from the advances of Sir John ('CONSTANT: Adieu, ladies; make much of the gentleman. [...] HEARTFREE: Ay, ay, you are in good hands. Adieu, adieu' [ibid.]) and only come to their rescue once they find out their 'true' identity.

Women need to be fixed within the parameters of class and family; the rules of chivalry do not extend to public and/or poor women or women without the protection of male family members.[35] The only liberties female protagonists dare ask before they 'dwindle into wives' is the granting of privacy. Millamant in Congreve's *The Way of the World* (1700) demands in the proviso 'to pay and receive visits' and to be 'sole empress of [the] tea-table' (Congreve 1982, 375). But it remains the prerogative of the future husband to define the boundaries: no confidants, non-alcoholic drinks served and 'genuine and authorised tea-table talk' (376).

The same exclusionary tactics hold true for members of the lower classes. Although servants are endowed with 'the same Whoreson Appetites' (*Love for Love* [1695]; Congreve 1982, 229) as their masters, they cannot be granted the right to satisfy them. A violation of social hierarchies would spell anarchy and, especially, the loss of property. Trappolin may pose as Duke, but only for a short time. Afterwards he has to face banishment and severe admonitions from his betters. Shadwell's *Squire of Alsatia* (1688) juxtaposes the legitimate amorous adventures of protagonist Ned Belfond with the

34 There are similar cases in Southerne, *The Wives' Excuse* (1691) and in Farquhar, *The Beaux' Stratagem* (1707).

35 Another example of this is Sedley's *Bellamira* (1687). The protagonist Lionel feels no qualms about raping Isabella. Although he professes to love her, her insecure status as orphan and 'fellow Servant' (Sedley 1928, 85) suspends moral standards. Only the discovery that Lionel's best friend happens to be Isabella's brother and that Isabella herself is a wealthy heiress initiates the conventional happy ending.

escapades of his elder brother, Tim, in 'Alsatia', a criminal state-within-a-state. The three Alsatians, Cheatly, Shamwell and Hackum, successfully cheat the wealthy heir of his money and, in addition, try to marry him off to the former mistress of his younger brother Ned. Although Belfond junior also sows his wild oats, in the happy ending, he proves a 'Compleat Gentleman, fit to serve his Country in any Capacity' (Shadwell 1927, 232). Not only does he get rid of two mistresses – by force and by the payment of money – and marry the rich, virginal heiress (279), he also defeats the rabble of Alsatia and thereby secures order in both family and society (see Breuer 1996, 196; Wheatley 1993, 33-57).

V.

The various experiments connected with the emergence of the public sphere tried to separate body politic from body natural and ranged from (textual and actual) execution to vilification. The topos of the king's bodies was appropriated to redefine boundaries between private and public and to destabilise traditional ideas of government. The ideal of a public sphere of equals engaged in rational discourse invited the participation or at least the consensus of all English subjects. Nevertheless, texts relegating women to the domestic realm still controlled by patriarchal norms. The separation between patriarchal rule in the families and seemingly consensual rule of parliament and king secured patrilinear inheritance, the submission of women and the transfer of wealth and power (see Calhoun 1992, 10). The emphasis on property as a basis for power furthermore secured the position of the traditional elite with the possibility to co-opt rich and conforming newcomers. This excluded people of the lower classes from the public sphere (see Habermas 1992, 425) without explicitly denying them access to power or political discourse.

Within the framework of two discrete spheres and the tactics of inclusion and exclusion, though, the texts contain vestiges of subversion. Discourses from other 'competing publics' (McDowell 1998, 8) undercut any attempts at prescribing a definitive set of norms and values. The critique of Charles's politics via an attack of his libertinism operated from exclusionary patriarchal premises, but employed tactics from the plebeian counter-culture (see Bakhtin 1985). Uncontrolled sexuality denoted both the vitality of popular resistance[36] and the deficiencies which led to the creation of the unofficial third body bestial. Although errant wives such as Lady Brute, servants such as Trappolin, or the Alsatian rogues are eventually put into their supposedly rightful places and made to conform to social norms, farces and comedies draw attention to the 'performability of social behavior' (Holland 2000, 109) and the inherent instability of hierarchies of class and gender. Sex and crime not only appeared dangerously attractive, they also proved

36 Potentially, also echoing the sexual licentiousness of dissident Commonwealth sects (Hill 1972, 161 and 172).

lucrative.[37] Guarded by the rhetoric of tradition and/or usefulness, taboo topics were to develop into commodities in the literary marketplace of the eighteenth century, establishing their own sub-genres and textual strategies.

To some extent, this development also holds true for the images of royal bodies. Although the topoi of royalty had been desacralised, and although contract theories and the dominant model of 'mixed monarchy' no longer presented politics as *arcanum imperii* (Jose 1984; Hammond 1991, 13) but as result of a consensus between subjects and rulers open to 'rational-critical discourse' (Calhoun 1992, 9), they did not completely replace traditional notions of government. As individuals refrained from taking up the 'devilish crown', they needed the monarch (or monarchs in the case of William and Mary) as icons of institutionalised power, with its symbols and rituals (see Melville 1998, ix) and as focus for discussions in the public sphere – be it in satires, debates or reports of the yellow press.

REFERENCES

Allen, David (1976). 'Political Clubs in Restoration London.' *Historical Journal* 19, 561-580.

Backscheider, Paula R. (1993). *Spectacular Politics: Theatrical Power and Mass Culture in Early Modern England.* Baltimore: Johns Hopkins University Press.

Bakhtin, Michail (1985). *Literatur und Karneval: Zur Romantheorie und Lachkultur.* Frankfurt/Main: Ullstein.

Böker, Uwe (2002). 'Angelsächsische Geltungsgeschichten der frühen Neuzeit: Die Legitimierung der *Ancient Constitution* und das Prinzip der *Rule of Law*.' In Gert Melville (ed.), *Geltungsgeschichten.* Cologne: Böhlau, forthcoming.

Breuer, Horst (1996). 'Literarische Reflexe des englischen Freistättenrechts.' In Uwe Böker and Christoph Houswitschka (eds.), *Literatur, Kriminalität und Rechtskultur im 17. und 18. Jahrhundert: Tagung am 17. und 18. Juni 1994 an der Technischen Universität Dresden.* Essen: Blaue Eule, 184-198.

Burnet, Gilbert (1969). *History of His Own Time.* Ed. Martin Joseph Routh. 6 vols. Hildesheim: Georg Olms. Original edition 1724-36 .

Calhoun, Craig (1992). 'Introduction: Habermas and the Public Sphere.' In Craig Calhoun (ed.), *Habermas and the Public Sphere.* Cambridge, MA: MIT Press, 1-48.

Condren, Conal (1994). *The Language of Politics in Seventeenth-Century England.* New York: St Martin's.

Congreve, William (1982). *The Comedies of William Congreve.* Ed. Anthony G. Henderson. Cambridge: Cambridge University Press.

Coote, Stephen (1999). *Royal Survivor: A Life of Charles II.* London: Hodder and Stoughton.

Dryden, John (1956-89). *The Works of John Dryden.* General ed. H.T. Swedenberg, Jr. 20 vols. Berkeley: University of California Press.

Dykstal, Timothy (1992). 'Conversation and Political Controversy.' In Kevin Cope (ed.), *Compendious Conversations.* Frankfurt/Main: Peter Lang, 306-320.

Haan, Heiner, and Gottfried Niedhart (1993). *Geschichte Englands vom 16. bis zum 18. Jahrhundert.* Munich: Beck.

---

37 E.g., the success of *The Squire of Alsatia* was probably not due to its smug bourgeois ethics, but to its detailed portrayal of the underworld (cf. 'Preface' in Shadwell 1927).

Habermas, Jürgen (1990). *Strukturwandel der Öffentlichkeit: Untersuchungen zu einer Kategorie der bürgerlichen Gesellschaft*. Frankfurt/Main: Suhrkamp. Original edition 1962.

________ (1992). 'Further Reflections on the Public Sphere.' In Craig Calhoun (ed.), *Habermas and the Public Sphere*. Cambridge: MIT Press, 421-461.

Hammond, Paul (1991). 'The King's Two Bodies: Representations of Charles II.' In Jeremy Black and Jeremy Gregory (eds.), *Culture, Politics and Society in Britain: 1660-1800*. Manchester: Manchester University Press, 13-48.

Harris, Tim (2001). 'Understanding Popular Politics in Restoration Britain.' In Alan Houston and Steve Pincus (eds.), *A Nation Transformed: England after the Restoration*. Cambridge: Cambridge University Press, 125-153.

Hill, Christopher (1972). *The World Turned Upside Down: Radical Ideas during the English Revolution*. London: Temple Smith.

Holland, Peter (2000). 'Farce.' In Deborah Payne Fisk (ed.), *The Cambridge Companion to English Restoration Theatre*. Cambridge: Cambridge University Press, 107-126.

Hutton, Ronald (1989). *Charles the Second: King of England, Scotland, and Ireland*. Oxford: Clarendon Press.

Jones, J.R. (1961). *The First Whigs*. Oxford: Clarendon Press.

________ (1987). *Charles II: Royal Politician*. London: Allen and Unwin.

Jose, Nicolas (1984). *Ideas of the Restoration in English Literature: 1660-1671*. Cambridge, MA: Harvard University Press.

Kamm, Jürgen (1998). 'The Government of the Tongue: Der Diskurs um Herrschaft und Sprache im England des 17. Jahrhunderts.' In Barbara Bauer and Wolfgang G. Müller (eds.), *Staatstheoretische Diskurse im Spiegel der Nationalliteraturen von 1500 bis 1800*. Wiesbaden: Harrassowitz, 427-444.

Kantorowicz, Ernst (1997). *The King's Two Bodies: A Study in Mediaeval Political Theology*. Princeton: Princeton University Press. Original edition 1957.

Kenyon, J.P., ed. (1986). *The Stuart Constitution 1603-1688: Documents and Commentary*. Cambridge: Cambridge University Press.

Knowles, Ronald (1988). 'Introduction.' In John Ogilby, *The Entertainment of His Most Excellent Majestie Charles II in His Passage through the City of London to His Coronation*. Ed. Ronald Knowles. Binghamton, NY: Medieval and Renaissance Texts and Studies, 9-51.

Lagomarsino, David, and Charles Wood, eds. (1989). *The Trial of Charles I: A Documentary History*. Hanover: University Press of New England.

Lessenich, Rolf (2001). 'Tory versus Whig: John Dryden's Mythical Concept of Kingship.' In Wolfgang Görtschacher and Holger Klein (eds.), *Dryden and the World of Neoclassicism*. Tübingen: Stauffenburg, 243-256.

Locke, John (1967). *Two Treatises of Government*. Ed. Peter Laslett. Cambridge: Cambridge University Press.

Lord, George deForest, ed. (1963). *Poems on Affairs of State: Augustan Satirical Verse, 1660-1714*. 7 vols. New Haven: Yale University Press.

Löther, Andrea (1998). 'Städtische Prozessionen zwischen repräsentativer Öffentlichkeit, Teilhabe und Publikum.' In Gert Melville and Peter von Moos (eds.), *Das Öffentliche und Private in der Vormoderne*. Cologne: Böhlau, 435-459.

Maguire, Nancy Klein (2000). 'Tragicomedy.' In Deborah Payne Fisk (ed.), *The Cambridge Companion to English Restoration Theatre*. Cambridge: Cambridge University Press, 86-106.

McDowell, Paula (1998). *The Women of Grub Street: Press, Politics, and Gender in the London Literary Marketplace 1678-1730*. Oxford: Clarendon Press.

Melville, Gert (1998). 'Geleitwort.' In Gert Melville and Peter von Moos (eds.), *Das Öffentliche und Private in der Vormoderne*. Cologne: Böhlau, iv-xi.

Mendle, Michael (1993). 'Parliamentary Sovereignty: A very English Absolutism.' In Nicholas Phillipson and Quentin Skinner (eds.), *Political Discourse in Early Modern Britain*. Cambridge: Cambridge University Press, 97-119.

Milton, John (1962). *Complete Prose Works of John Milton*. Vol. 3: *1648-1649*. New Haven: Yale University Press.

Norbrook, David (1994). '*Areopagitica*, Censorship, and the Early Modern Public Sphere.' In Richard Burt (ed.), *The Administration of Aesthetics: Censorship, Political Criticism, and the Public Sphere*. Minneapolis: University of Minnesota Press, 3-33.

Ogilby, John (1988). *The Entertainment of His Most Excellent Majestie Charles II in His Passage through the City of London to His Coronation*. Ed. Ronald Knowles. Binghamton, NY: Mediaeval and Renaissance Texts and Studies.

Pankratz, Annette (2001). 'The Culture of the King's Three Bodies.' In Wolfgang Görtschacher and Holger Klein (eds.), *Dryden and the World of Neoclassicism*. Tübingen: Stauffenburg, 257-272.

Pepys, Samuel (1970-71). *The Diary: A New and Complete Transcription*. Vol. 1: *1660*. Vol. 2: *1661*. Vol. 4: *1663*. Ed. Robert Latham and William Matthews. London: Bell.

Pincus, Steve (1995). '"Coffee Politicians Does Create": Coffeehouses and Restoration Political Culture.' *The Journal of Modern History* 67, 807-834.

Price, Richard (1999). *British Society 1680-1880: Dynamism, Containment and Change*. Cambridge: Cambridge University Press.

Riebling, Barbara (1995). 'England Deflowered and Unmanned: The Sexual Image of Politics in Marvell's 'Last Instructions."' *SEL* 35, 137-157.

Sedley, Charles (1969). *Bellamira, or The Mistress*. In *The Poetical and Dramatic Works of Sir Charles Sedley*. Ed. Vivian da Sola Pinto. Vol. 2. New York: AMS. Original edition 1928.

Shadwell, Thomas (1927). *The Squire of Alsatia*. In *The Complete Works of Thomas Shadwell*. Ed. Montague Summers. Vol. 4. London: Fortune Press.

Sommerville, Johann P. (1992). *Thomas Hobbes: Political Ideas in Historical Context*. New York: St Martin's.

Tate, Nahum (1685). *A Duke and no Duke: A Farce*. London: Printed for Henry Bonwicke.

Vanbrugh, John (1982). *The Provoked Wife*. Ed. Antony Coleman. Manchester: Manchester University Press.

Wagner, Michael (1992). 'Ein englischer Weg zum Absolutismus? Die Tories und die Monarchie 1678-1688.' In Rolf Gundlach and Hermann Weber (eds.), *Legitimation und Funktion des Herrschers: Vom ägyptischen Pharao zum neuzeitlichen Diktator*. Stuttgart: Franz Steiner, 259-284.

Weber, Harold (1995). *Paper Bullets: Print and Kingship under Charles II*. Lexington: University Press of Kentucky.

Wheatley, Christopher J. (1993). *Without God or Reason: The Plays of Thomas Shadwell and Secular Ethics in the Restoration*. Lewisburg: Bucknell University Press.

Wootton, David, ed. (1986). *Divine Right and Democracy: An Anthology of Political Writing in Stuart England*. Harmondsworth: Penguin.

Zaret, David (1992). 'Religion, Science, and Printing in the Public Spheres in Seventeenth-Century England.' In Craig Calhoun (ed.), *Habermas and the Public Sphere*. Cambridge: MIT Press, 212-235.

Zwicker, Steven N. (1993). *Lines of Authority: Politics and English Literary Culture, 1649-1689*. Ithaca: Cornell University Press.

Heinz-Joachim Müllenbrock

PUBLIC OPINION IN EIGHTEENTH-CENTURY ENGLAND

I.

In 1726 an intellectually proud but by then politically disgruntled Swift put the following statement into Gulliver's mouth:

> it was with extreme difficulty that I could bring my master to understand the meaning of the word *opinion*, or how a point could be disputable; because *reason* taught us to affirm or deny, only where we are certain; and beyond our knowledge, we cannot do either. So that controversies, wranglings, disputes, and positiveness in false or dubious propositions, are evils unknown among the Houyhnhnms. (Swift 1962, 286)

Ironically, Swift's satirical denigration of English conditions referred to the very aspect which eventually became England's most conspicuous claim to fame in the eyes of bewildered but admiring observers from the European Continent: the cultivation of public opinion. By the time *Gulliver's Travels* appeared, the newly developed culture of contention was well under way; Swift himself, of course, had substantially contributed to its launching as the leading journalist of the Harley government during the closing years of Queen Anne's reign, to which I shall return a little later. The optimistic expectations raised by the gradual expansion of public opinion may be seen in the enthusiastic utterance of the radical essayist William Hazlitt almost a century after the appearance of Swift's masterpiece: 'The sincere expression of the feelings of the people must be true; the full and free development of the public opinion must lead to the truth, to the gradual discovery and diffusion of knowledge in this, as in all other departments of human inquiry' (Hazlitt 1932, 7: 272). This was a far cry from Gulliver's belittlement of public dispute.

The important status and specific quality achieved by public opinion in English self-recognition may further be gauged by a comparative look at other European countries. When in 1798 C.M. Wieland published his essay 'Über die öffentliche Meinung' (contained in *Gespräche unter vier Augen*), summarising the German situation, he assumed that millions of people might be classified as '*unmündig*', adding, 'aber sie haben den allgemeinen Menschenverstand zum Vormund, und man darf darauf rechnen, daß in Sachen, die das Wohl oder Weh der unendlich grösseren Mehrheit unmittelbar betreffen, der Ausspruch dieses Vormunds auch die öffentliche Meinung ist' (Wieland 1984, 345). Here the very language – epitomised by the twice-used noun '*Vormund*' (guardian) – indicates a thinking in old-fashioned categories which smacks of authoritarian or at least paternalistic posturing. In Spain the first occurrence of the expression '*opinión pública*' is recorded in the year 1797,[1] but in this as well as in the

1 According to the Real Academia Española's *Banco de datos del Español*.

immediately following cases, the term does not mean more than widely shared convictions, with no implications of public wrangling or intellectual altercation.

Although Hazlitt's statement correctly voiced the optimism spread in the wake of the development of a public political culture, linguistic usage is by no means a wholly dependable instrument for measuring what was being accomplished in eighteenth-century England. Thus, for example, only in the course of the 1780s did references to public opinion become more frequent, and only then was the modern form of the expression, that is, without the definite article, more commonly used (Gunn 1983, 281) – you may have noticed that even in the quotation from Hazlitt, who still uses both forms indiscriminately, the older practice has not been discarded. But though linguistic usage is not a good indicator of far-advanced conditions prevailing in England, it is a fairly reliable gauge for the fact that the theoretical assessment of public opinion was lagging well behind its actual development; in France, by the way, where the formation of public opinion was far less advanced than in England, theorising about the new phenomenon was more marked (Gunn 1989, 247-265). And though the collective singular public opinion gained in prominence compared with older terms such as 'public interest' or 'public spirit', the press became known rather late as a 'fourth estate' in comparison with the equally eligible candidates 'opposition' and 'people' (Gunn 1983, 88).

II.

In spite of the fact that the theoretical elevation of public opinion to the rank of a distinct element in politics was a rather slow process, the thing itself existed early on. In point of fact, public opinion was firmly entrenched in British political life right from the beginning of the eighteenth century; its impact on national politics can be dated precisely from the reign of Queen Anne. Printing and publishing, which had experienced a tremendous boom after the expiry of the Licensing Act in 1695, reached their climax in the public controversy over the ending of the War of the Spanish Succession from 1710 to 1713, the first example of a public debate of a great national issue with full media participation (Müllenbrock 1997). This public dispute was conducted on a bipartisan basis characterised by the antagonism between Whigs and Tories and – even more importantly – directed by government and opposition alike, both of which, led by members of the ruling elite, generously handed out political literature in order to improve their standing in the eyes of the public. It is this competitive, agonistic pattern of mobilising public opinion which makes Jürgen Habermas' notion of *bürgerliche Öffentlichkeit* irrelevant to the conditions prevailing in England; he sees the public and the state as diametrically opposed, and his central assumption is that the sole or, at least, predominant rationale of the process of cultivating public opinion instigated by the middle classes was to undermine the position of the ruling aristocracy. As I have already explicated in my book *The Culture of Contention* (1997) why Habermas' class-based concept is not applicable to England, where the public comprised most, if not all, social groups, especially the gentry and the nobility, I shall not go into further detail here (Müllenbrock 1997, 23-28).[2]

It was of the essence that the government was an active agent and even took the initiative in appealing to the public; 'when the organisation of government propaganda matched, and then surpassed, the output and efficiency of opposition propaganda' (Downie 1982, 50) under Harley's auspices, the cultivation of public opinion stood a chance of being divested of any taints of subversiveness which might otherwise be attached to it. In England, significantly, the expansion of political literature did not become an underground phenomenon as in pre-Revolutionary France. The impetus given to public opinion through the protracted struggle over the conclusion of the Peace of Utrecht proved to be of lasting impact; with the benefit of hindsight, one can even designate this controversy, though it still took place in the twilight of uncertain and often disputed legitimacy, as the decisive break-through in the long-term establishment of public opinion as an indispensable component of political life – its virtual institutionalisation, especially in the Latin sense of starting a project or assigning oneself a task. By institutionalisation, I do not mean instituting by enactment – the legal framework remained very much the same for a long time – or through administrative measures, but becoming part of the intellectual equipment of the nation, i.e., the process of public consent rather than statutory approbation.

When I suggest that the die was thus cast early as far as the hold of public opinion on the national consciousness is concerned, I am not, of course, denying that it was an arduous path form its inception to its unhampered practice. Thus, the 'law of seditious libel', frequently invoked by political bodies, still hung like the sword of Damocles over the heads of wayward writers, and the principle of the desirability of a free press was not as loudly proclaimed during the first half of the century as during the second, though the liberty of the press was increasingly seen as part of the traditional rights and liberties of the English (Barker 2000, 13, 28). The full institutionalisation of public opinion was a protracted affair, and the English privilege was not to be gained without a struggle. But this struggle cannot be described in terms of clear-cut clashes between advocates of freedom or tyranny, the heroes and villains so dear to the practitioners of the Whig interpretation of history. Rather, it was a gradual process with chequered party-political responsibilities in the course of which ever more precedents in favour of once suspect but now established behaviour accumulated. In retrospect, it seems quite typical of English conditions that plans to curb the press never materialised. As early as the closing years of Queen Anne's reign, when Bolingbroke and the High Church wing of the Tory party flirted with the idea of again applying restraining measures, such plans – despite the introduction of the Stamp Act in 1712 – proved abortive, with prominent authors such as Addison and Defoe vigorously defending the right of free expression of opinion. On this occasion, it became manifest that the development of public opinion was intimately bound up with the bipartisan structure of British politics;

2 For a critical assessment of Habermas' approach, see also Barker 1998, 179-180. Habermas' thesis that the political sphere issued more or less directly from the literary sphere is flatly denied by Winkler 1997, 216, 220, 222. But see Hohendahl in this volume.

accordingly, both writers stressed the symbiotic relationship between a free press and political parties (Müllenbrock 1997, 22-23). In early Hanoverian England, things remained on the same footing. Even Walpole, who faced a veritable literary *fronde* (see Goldgar 1976) and closed the theatres except those with royal patents, shied away from legal measures to cope with the widespread printed criticism of his regime and tolerated most aspects of the press (Downie 1982, 58). It is not without irony, by the way, that the term 'public opinion' made its first appearance in the Walpole era. Of course, the longer non-intervention on the part of the government lasted, the more probable it became that the concept of the printed word as a means of wooing public opinion was bound to stay and take root in intellectual habits, while the rival concept of licensed printing was gradually falling into disuse. The ambivalent symbol of the expansion of the press and public opinion was, by the way, the much-derided coffee-house politician, against whom complaints increased considerably over the course of time.

The subsequent course of events confirmed that institutionalisation through habituation[3] without any formal blessing proved to be the English way to the final establishment of public opinion – a method less brilliant than effective in the production of long-term results. The Seven Years' War was the next stage in the assertion of an unattested right. As Leslie Stephen correctly remarked, 'War naturally generates journalism' (1910, 68); the popularity of Pitt the Elder, fostered through his appeal to the patriot image, was promoted by press support (see Peters 1980), and the fierce dispute over the ending of the war further entrenched the cultivation of public opinion as an integral part of political life. In this respect, the Peace of Paris proved as gratifying as the Peace of Utrecht. The spectacular confrontations between the government and Parliament on the one side and the public on the other, which took place from 1763 on and centred on the flamboyant personality of John Wilkes, the pugnacious champion of liberty, were also conducive to the self-assurance of the press, which played a prominent part in extra-parliamentary campaigns and was less and less disposed to eat humble pie. Surely it was no mere coincidence but, rather, corresponded to the logic of contextual determinants that in 1771 the House of Commons tacitly relinquished its right to prohibit parliamentary reporting – an important step in the emancipation of public opinion from the traditional confines (Aspinall 1956, 227). The growing self-confidence of public opinion was confirmed by the general election of 1784, when Pitt the Younger, in his struggle with the House of Commons, gained a landslide victory through his appeal to the new appellate authority, preparing the way for the modern assumption that public opinion, expressing the will of the people, must be the final arbiter of the right course to be steered in politics (Kelly 1972, 84, 88) – under Charles II, it had been taken for granted that the Commons did represent public opinion (Miller 1995, 376). In 1787 – my last date before the outbreak of the French Revolution – the *English Review* stated categorically, 'The press has almost swallowed up the political consequences of the

3 The use of this term justifies, of course, recourse to Bourdieu's concept of *habitus*, although it is by no means obligatory to make such a connection. See Rehberg 2001, 17.

pulpit, and awes and controls even members of parliament and ministers of state' (Anon. 1787, 315); public opinion had at last gained constitutional relevance.

Towards the end of the eighteenth century, the German anglophile publicist Johann Wilhelm von Archenholz paid effusive tribute to the '*Nationalfreiheit*' (Archenholz 1785, 1: 7-8), which left its imprint on all fields of English life; public opinion was part and parcel of this secular achievement.

III.

What more general conclusions may be drawn from my outline of the main stages in the development of public opinion, adding some observations to link up with the frame-concept of institutionalisation? Altogether, the label 'gradualism', used in both a temporal and a structural sense, can fittingly be attached to the process I have been describing.

Although the discontinuation – significantly: lapse – of the Licensing Act in 1695 was a revolutionary event and, in point of fact, ushered in a new epoch in the history of free expression, its innovative potential was not realised at the time and, thus, the long-term development of public opinion was smoothly put on its way. And though the subsequent expansion of a political culture of contention under Queen Anne constituted a quantitative and qualitative leap as far as freedom of expression is concerned – a new dimension manifest in the extensiveness of public exchanges and the sophisticated interaction of print and politics (see Müllenbrock, 1997, 111-114) – no break with legal precedent seemed to be involved. As I remarked earlier, the fact that the government itself played a major, even decisive role in the journalistic underpinning of politics did much to ward off the taint of subversiveness or hostility to the state from the wooing of public opinion. Thus, the new and – to many contemporary observers – disturbing phenomenon of a battle of opinions did not meet with real resistance from official quarters despite incessant complaints about the licentiousness of the press (see Hellmuth 1990) and stood a fair chance of eventual acceptance, of being integrated into the British political system, at least in the long term.

From this point on, public opinion can be viewed as an unattested institutional mechanism, an unacknowledged legislator so to speak, making its impact felt within the framework of a political system nominally still circumscribed by the traditional confines of Court and Parliament. Sometimes officially disregarded or even ignored as long as deemed opportune, public opinion became a catalyst of ever increasing effectiveness, a force whose continually growing influence gave it a share in the debate on all important political matters and, thereby, something like institutional validity. On a representational or symbolic level, the increasing presence of public opinion in national political life can be gathered from the growing output of caricatures dealing with the so-called coffee-house politician, with comments upon which I shall conclude my paper.

Thus, we can observe the progressive participation of public opinion in the political process long before the relinquishment of the ban on parliamentary reporting – the first important outward acknowledgement of the new component in British politics. When at last the formation of a government in the traditional manner had to be corrected, owing to public pressure, this event spectacularly set the seal on the steady permeation of the British political system by the power of public opinion, which had unmistakably gained constitutional relevance – an irreversible achievement. Gradualism had won the day.

IV.

Let me – as promised – draw to a close by taking a short look at the representation of the spread of public opinion in literature and graphic art. The quintessential symbol of the novel and alarming phenomenon of a culture of contention was the so-called coffee-house politician, who loomed large in the consciousness of contemporary observers of the public scene. The representations of this emblematic figure can be said to be of a Janus-faced character. A particularly instructive example is provided by the fourth part of Edward Ward's *Vulgus Britannicus: or, the British Hudibras*, published in 1710, which also illustrates intermedial orchestration. While a frontispiece entitled 'The Coffeehous Mob'[4] pictorialises the spectacle observed, cantos eleven and twelve describe with graphic vividness the noisy political altercations taking place in a by-no-means convivial atmosphere. The two media operate like communicating tubes. While the satirical print visualises the intense debates caused by the Sacheverell affair and features newspapers and pamphlets, the Hudibrastic description expatiates upon the pictorial version and gives a detailed, highly topical account of the fierce arguments thrown at each other's ears. The reader is given to understand that 'The *Coffee Tables* now were spread, / With all the worst that could be said' (Ward 1710, 120), and such a coffee house is even likened to 'Bedlam' (122). The interpretative insight gained by these representations is twofold: on the one hand, they convey the traditional bewilderment at the opening of the public sphere to the lower strata of society, perhaps comparable to a certain degree to the – in part – persistent official disdain of this phenomenon; on the other hand, they testify to the entrenchment of public opinion in British political life through the very vividness of their accounts, through their realistic view of the circumstances described.

The same observations may be drawn from other representations of the coffee-house politician who occupies a prominent position, for example, in the periodical essays, the new and popular communications media written by Addison and Steele, which are particularly informative as regards contemporary conditions. For instance, Addison devoted an entire number of the *Spectator* periodical (no. 403, 12 June 1712) to the reception of the news of the day in the various coffee houses of London. Time and again, the coffee-house politician is depicted as somebody who neglects his daily business in order to meddle with politics which, as it is often suggested, are beyond his grasp – an issue of *Tatler* (19 November 1709) sardonically states that 'an upper Lip covered with Snuff, denotes a Coffee-house Statesman' (*Tatler* 1987, 2: 97). The

4 Reproduced in Brewer 1986, 127.

disruptive consequences of such politicising became a topos in public discourse and are well illustrated in a print of 1 April 1772 entitled 'The Coffee-house Politicians',[5] where political debate leads the coffee boy to spill the contents of his tray and an informally dressed figure on the right to spill his coffee. Though these representations of coffee-house politics express criticism, the satire is mostly aimed at extravagances and excesses rather than vile offences. In Addison's and Steele's papers, especially, the mildness of the criticism implies that it is a question of easily corrigible vices which are held up to ridicule.[6] Over and above adverse commentary, literature and graphic art provide impressive evidence of the vitality of public opinion and the extension of the political nation; in its own way the ambivalent symbol of the coffee-house politician reflects, as in a burning mirror, the naturalisation of the culture of contention in eighteenth-century England.

References

Anon. (1787). 'National Affairs for April, 1787.' *The English Review; or, an Abstract of English and Foreign Literature* 9, 313-320.

Archenholz, Johann Wilhelm von (1785). *England und Italien.* 2 vols. Leipzig: Dyk.

Aspinall, A. (1956). 'The Reporting and Publishing of the House of Commons' Debates 1771-1834.' In Richard Pares and A.J.P. Taylor (eds.), *Essays Presented to Sir Lewis Namier.* London: Macmillan, 227-257.

Barker, Hannah (1998). *Newspapers, Politics, and Public Opinion in Late Eighteenth-Century England.* Oxford: Clarendon Press.

________ (2000). *Newspapers, Politics and English Society, 1695-1855.* Harlow: Longman.

Brewer, John (1986). *The Common People and Politics 1750-1790s.* Cambridge: Chadwyck-Healey.

Downie, Alan (1982). 'The Growth of Government Tolerance of the Press to 1790.' In Robin Myers and Michael Harris (eds.), *Development of the English Book Trade, 1700-1899.* Oxford: Polytechnic Press, 36-65.

Goldgar, Bertrand A. (1976). *Walpole and the Wits: The Relation of Politics to Literature, 1722-1742.* Lincoln: University of Nebraska Press.

Gunn, J.A.W. (1983). *Beyond Liberty and Property: The Process of Self-Recognition in Eighteenth-Century Political Thought.* Kingston: McGill-Queen's University Press.

________ (1989). 'Public Opinion.' In Terence Ball, James Farr, and Russell L. Hanson (eds.), Political Innovation and Conceptual Change. Cambridge: Cambridge University Press, 247-265.

Hazlitt, William (1932). *The Complete Works of William Hazlitt.* Ed. P.P. Howe. 21 vols. London: Dent.

Hellmuth, Eckhart (1990). *'Liberty' und 'Licentiousnes': Der Diskurs über Pressefeiheit im frühneuzeitlichen England (ca. 1660- ca. 1800).* Unpublished Habilitationsschrift. University of Trier.

Kelly, Paul (1972). 'Radicalism and Public Opinion in the General Election of 1784.' *Bulletin of the Institute of Historical Research* 45, 73-88.

Klein, Lawrence E. (1996). 'Coffeehouse Civility, 1660-1714: An Aspect of Post-Courtly Culture in England.' *Huntington Library Quarterly* 59, 45-51.

5 Reproduced in Brewer 1986, 129.

6 Klein even stresses the fact that Whig cultural ideologists such as Addison and Steele, while they did not ignore its problematic aspects, regarded the coffee house as a welcome arena in their struggle for politeness and urbanity (1996, 45-51).

Miller, John (1995). 'Public Opinion in Charles II's England.' *History* 80, 359-381.

Müllenbrock, Heinz-Joachim (1997). *The Culture of Contention: A Rhetorical Analysis of the Public Controversy about the Ending of the War of the Spanish Succession, 1711-1713.* Munich: Fink.

Peters, Marie (1980). *Pitt and Popularity: The Patriot Minister and London Opinion during the Seven Years' War.* Oxford: Clarendon Press.

Rehberg, Karl-Siegbert (2001). 'Weltrepräsentanz und Verkörperung: Institutionelle Analyse und Symboltheorien – Eine Einführung in systematischer Absicht.' In Gert Melville (ed.), *Institutionalität und Symbolisierung: Verstetigungen kultureller Ordnungsmuster in Vergangenheit und Gegenwart.* Cologne: Böhlau, 3-49.

Stephen, Leslie (1910). *English Literature and Society in the Eighteenth Century.* London: Duckworth.

Swift, Jonathan (1962). *Gulliver's Travels.* London: Dent. Original edition 1726.

[Ward, Edward] (1710). *The Fourth Part of Vulgus Britannicus: or, the British Hudibras; In two Cantos: [...] Written by the Author of the London Spy.* London: James Woodward and John Morphew.

Tatler, The (1987). Ed. with an introduction and notes by Donald F. Bond. 3 vols. Oxford: Clarendon Press.

Wieland, Christoph Martin (1984). *Sämmtliche Werke.* Vol. 10. Hamburg: Hamburger Stiftung zur Förderung von Wissenschaft und Kultur.

Winkler, Karl Tilman (1997). 'Publikum und Tagesschrifttum am Beispiel Englands im 18. Jahrhundert.' In Hans-Wolf Jäger (ed.), *'Öffentlichkeit' im 18. Jahrhundert.* Göttingen: Wallstein, 203-228.

Ian A. Bell

LITERATURE, CRIME, AND SOCIETY IN EIGHTEENTH-CENTURY ENGLAND[1]

TALKING ABOUT THE LAW

In 1758, Sir William Blackstone delivered for the first time the series of lectures later published as his *Commentaries on the Laws of England*. Speaking at the University of Oxford, he was addressing an audience drawn exclusively from the privileged and propertied male elite of his society. For their benefit and instruction, Blackstone presented a systematic and easily comprehensible unfolding of the benign principles which, he argued, upheld the whole elaborate fabric of the English legislature. His stated aims could not be simpler, or more obviously partisan – 'I think it is an undeniable position, that a competent knowledge of that society, in which we live, is the proper accomplishment of every gentleman and scholar; an highly useful, I had almost said essential part of liberal and polite education' (Blackstone 1979, 1: 5-6). With a tone of sustained complacency, Blackstone sought to demonstrate the manifest and manifold felicities of his native constitution. Although it might appear bafflingly complex and incomprehensible to the uninitiated, the body of statute was in fact covertly unified by its concern for the liberty of the propertied oligarchy. Without apology or embarrassment, Blackstone proudly and rhetorically underlined the ways in which the law entitled his listeners to lead lives of unimpeded security and comfort:

> these rights consist, primarily in the free enjoyment of personal security, of personal liberty, and of private property [...]. And all of these rights and liberties it is our birthright to enjoy entire; unless where the laws of our country have laid them under necessary restraints. Restraints in themselves so gentle and moderate, as will appear upon farther enquiry, that no man of sense or probity would wish to see them slackened. (1: 140)

This robustly conservative version of the body of law ('*our* birthright ... *our* country'), which so outraged Bentham and the later reformers, combines a reverence for the law with a class-based ideology of Englishness. The overall impression that the speaker was trying to convey is that the landed or propertied Englishman may live more or less unrestrained in a world organised for his benefit. Of course, to advance such an argument, however intelligently or fastidiously, Blackstone had to maintain a discreet silence on the subject of those less generously treated by the laws – the poor, slaves, women, children – and there could be no place whatsoever in his rhetoric for thoughts of agitation or dissent.

Reading his words now, we can hear the voice of mid-eighteenth-century privileged confidence at its most assured and triumphant. Blackstone seems remarkably

---

1 This paper is an extract from Ian A. Bell (1991), *Literature and Crime in Augustan England* (London: Routledge), 6-28 and 231-233. The editors would like to thank Mr Bell for permission to reprint his work here.

untroubled by anxiety or apprehension, and encourages his prosperous listeners to have faith in the law, which is designed to support and maintain their cultural dominance. In doing so, he demonstrates the ideological centrality of legislation and enforceable contracts in bourgeois society, which he saw as necessary and wholly desirable. The authoritative chapter and verse which could regulate conduct and arbitrate in the disputes of his audience were not to be found in Holy Scripture, as they might still have been for less comfortable Augustans, but in the statute book.

This was by no means an eccentric or idiosyncratic position. As Adam Smith recognised in *The Wealth of Nations* (1776), an unquestioning belief in the reliability and justice of the laws of contract had been (and still was) the ideological cement which held post-agrarian society together:

> Commerce and manufactures can seldom flourish long in any state which does not enjoy a regular administration of justice, in which the people do not feel themselves secure in the possession of property, in which the faith of contracts is not supported by law, and in which the authority of the state is not supposed to be regularly employed in enforcing the payment of debts from all those who are able to pay. Commerce and manufactures, in short, can seldom flourish in any state in which there is not a certain degree of confidence in the justice of the government. (Smith 1976, 2: 910)

Smith is here talking about the ways in which the maintenance of the law permits and supports the activities of a mercantile culture, but his language shows a very interesting reliance on ideology rather than on reality. The members of this commercial civilisation must have 'faith' and 'a certain degree of confidence' in things. That is to say, they have to *believe* in the efficacy of the law for their society to function. Whether or not that confidence was entirely justified is a separate, perhaps unnecessary, question, for the belief was sufficiently instrumental to make the law work.

Blackstone's *Commentaries* can be seen as part of the ideological machinery by which this system of belief and confidence is created. His exposition is an elegant, seemingly effortless attempt to bolster belief, to disseminate confidence, to reassure his audience that the laws of England had their best interests at heart. He was demonstrating to them their right to conduct business unhindered, and at the same time instructing them in their future duties as administrators, magistrates and even members of parliament. Furthermore, he was offering the promise that, while the laws of conveyancing, for example, might justly regulate the transaction of property, they would in no way address the fundamental inequities in the prevailing distribution of that property. As well as holding symbolic and ideological importance, the civil law might, on acquaintance, serve certain useful practical purposes in the day-to-day life and business of his listeners – 'the understanding of a few leading principles, relating to estates and conveyancing, may form some check and guard upon a gentleman's inferior agents, and preserve him at least from very gross and notorious imposition' (Blackstone 1979, 1: 7).

Some knowledge of the civil law, and attendant confidence in its authority, is thus made to seem like a useful part of a gentleman's social equipment. The statutes could be relied upon to articulate bourgeois hegemony, and to reify the values of the landed classes, and keep 'inferior agents' on their guard. And that, for Blackstone (and his listeners) was the way things should be. However, it is most interesting to notice that even Blackstone becomes much more hesitant in his treatment of contemporary criminal law. Far from demonstrating the felicities of the English constitution, and enabling a gentleman to conduct his business smoothly and legitimately, the criminal statutes seemed to Blackstone to be rather rough and ready:

> The criminal law is in every country of Europe more rude and imperfect than the civil [...]. Even with us in England, where our crown-law is with justice supposed to be more nearly advanced to perfection; where crimes are more accurately defined, and penalties less uncertain and arbitrary; where all our accusations are public, and our trials in the face of the world; where torture is unknown, and every delinquent is judged by such of his equals, against whom he can form no exception nor even a personal dislike; – even here we shall occasionally find room to remark some particulars, that seem to want revision and amendment. (4: 3)

Blackstone here includes all the features which were regularly cited by patriotic commentators to demonstrate the superiority of English criminal legislation over its continental counterparts – the virtual absence of torture and the alleged impartiality of jurors being two of the most potent and regularly flaunted items. However, after this flag-waving defence of English legislation, Blackstone is required to pause and to acknowledge the visible imperfections in the criminal law, and to question the necessity for the savage restraints it could impose.

Whereas the earlier, more relaxed and informal system of judge-made law seemed to Blackstone to be well-nigh perfect, the newly developed criminal statute, created by a distant and occasionally ill-informed or partisan Parliament, gave him cause for concern. Blackstone's preferred system was one where magistrates would be local men, well-informed of the particular circumstances of cases, and sufficiently acquainted with the niceties of the law through works such as Richard Burn's *The Justice of the Peace and Parish Officer*, Giles Jacob's *The Statute-Law Common-plac'd*, John Mallory's *The Attorney's Pocket Companion*, Michael Dalton's *The Country Justice*, Theodore Barlow's *The Justice of the Peace*, or any of the other digests available in the mid-century. By this method, a magistrate could make appropriate judgements – in keeping with the broad principles set down by Coke, Hale, Stamford and Hawkins, yet responsive to local requirements, and without excessive or pedantic legalistic quibbling.

But as Blackstone saw it, the sensitive and flexible methods so established were being swept away by the growth of rather clumsier centralised legislation. When introducing a discussion of the 'Bloody Code', as it came to be known, his earlier urbanity and confidence begin to disappear. He has to recognise that English criminal law could and did perpetrate grotesque outrages – he mentions that the death sentence could be passed on someone found 'to break down (however maliciously) the mound of a fishpond, whereby any fish shall escape; or cut down a cherry tree in an orchard' (4: 3) – but he tries to play these down by attributing such severity to a minor bureaucratic inefficiency in supervising and articulating the law.[2] His solution, of course, is to seek

2 The statutes referred to by Blackstone are 9 Geo. I c.22, and 31 Geo. II c.42.

for intelligent procedures of 'revision and amendment' rather than to demand any more radical or challenging reforms.

Blackstone's unease here is most interesting. It looks as though he is having to confront a discourse which violates those ideals of gentlemanly conduct which the civil law enshrined and which the tone of his lectures tried to reproduce. Whereas the civil code seemed to weave a fabric of cultured civilisation, the criminal codes could look like the flagrant exercise of power and violence to secure rights and property for a few. Of course, that was not the only function of the criminal law, nor the one that was most widely recognised. The ideological significance of the law was that it managed for much of the time to create the illusion of impartiality and fairness, and it was seen by many as an acceptable tribunal for arbitrating disputes. In most of its operations, the law was not a direct and unmediated articulation of power, but an ideological transfiguration of class values, shrouded in ritual, mystery and ceremony, continually protesting its disinterest. And, as J.M. Beattie puts it, 'to be seen to be serving the interests of the broader community in a fair manner it had indeed to be doing so' (Beattie 1986, 622; see also Hay 1975). Perhaps it often was doing so, discouraging violence and fraudulent practice by the most drastic of means, and even, now and then, defending the weak against the strong. But yet, to the modern commentator, there seem to be far too many occasions when the mask of impartiality slipped, and the criminal law seemed to be acting aggressively 'to sustain and legitimize the established social and economic and political arrangements of the society' (Beattie 1986, 621).

The traditional view of eighteenth-century English criminal legislation is that it represents a kind of Dark Age, lying in wait for the battalion of enlightened reformers such as Cesare Beccaria, Jeremy Bentham, John Howard, Sir Samuel Romilly, William Eden, Sir Thomas Fowell Buxton, Sir James Mackintosh and Elizabeth Fry – names almost as well known to the general reader as the names of famous criminals. As Sir Leon Radzinowicz, at his most apologetic and progressivist, famously put it, 'Lord Macaulay's generalisation that the history of England is the history of progress is as true of the criminal law of this country as of the other social institutions of which it is a part' (Radzinowicz 1948, ix).[3] Such Whiggish confidence in the perfectibility of law has not been borne out by the various more recent studies of the period. Whereas Radzinowicz seems assured that 'the criminal law of England has always been sensitive to the needs and aspirations of the English people' (ibid.), more recent commentators have seen the evolution of the criminal code as reflecting the needs and aspirations more exclusively of certain groups and classes (like those which made up Blackstone's audience) than of some happily amorphous mass called 'the English people'. Although there are very significant differences of emphasis among the most recent commentaries, to which we shall return, they share the perception that, throughout the Augustan period, many traditional and previously acceptable practices were being criminalised by the introduction of new laws, and that the very rapid growth in statutes (especially in capital statutes) at the time is indicative of 'the aggrandizement of the property rights of the gentry at the expense of common right and customs'.[4] Although

3 A very different version of the developments in penal behaviour will be found in Ignatieff 1985.

4 Ignatieff 1978, 17; see the discussion of this argument in Philips 1985.

the law represented class interests in a mediated and disguised form, shrouded in the majesty of ceremony and the performance of ritual, those class interests were still its central generative force.

It is important to recognise that this version of the ideological function of criminal legislation had a place in the widespread discussion of the law in the eighteenth century itself. There was, as we might expect, intense and sustained discussion of the legal system, even if most of it looked primarily at the practicalities rather than the politics of law. The feature which attracted most attention was that the criminal code in England, while in some respects less atavistic than others to be found in Europe, still relied on a mixture of ceremony and savagery in the form of ritualised executions, transportation, and various violent corporal punishments. Throughout the century, more and more offences, including apparently trivial ones, could be punished by death, although a certain amount of discretion could be exercised in sentencing. The most notorious piece of legislation was the 'Waltham Black Act' (9 Geo. I c.22), which introduced around fifty new capital offences virtually overnight, including the fish-mound example raised by Blackstone. This act has been seen as 'the onset of the flood-tide of eighteenth-century retributive justice', and it served as a focus for discussions of the status of the legal system (Thompson 1975, 23). For Blackstone, even the discretion which could be employed in the courts did not prevent this act from seeming excessive – 'it is true, that these outrageous penalties, being seldom or never inflicted, are hardly known to be law by the public: but that rather aggravates the mischief, by laying a snare for the unwary' (Blackstone 1979, 4: 4). So although Blackstone is scrupulous in not pointing the finger at anyone for this cruelty, he cannot remain unaware of the potential savagery of at least part of the English constitution.

The problem that the Black Act dramatised and intensified could be seen as a tension within the discourse of law itself. In trying to regularise and legitimise the whole procedure, Blackstone inevitably ran up against the problems of the apparent injustices perpetrated by the legal system itself. He could not help but see that a system for preserving life and property which depended on the sanctions of destroying life and confiscating property was morally complex and might not always be capable of a benign interpretation. Blackstone acknowledged these problems but did not investigate them thoroughly. Other commentators, of a more aggressively ironic temper, could see the paradoxes much more clearly. David Hume, for example, in his *Treatise of Human Nature* (1739), isolated the institutional complexity of the law, and sought to make sense of it:

> When I relieve persons in distress, my natural humanity is my motive; and so far as my succour extends, so far have I promoted the happiness of my fellow-creatures. But if we examine all the questions, that come before any tribunal of justice, we shall find, that, considering each case apart, it wou'd as often be an instance of humanity to decide contrary to the laws of justice as conformable to them. Judges take from a poor man to give to a rich; they bestow on the dissolute the labour of the industrious; and put into the hands of the vicious the means of harming both themselves and others. The whole scheme, however, of law and justice is advantageous to the society; and 'twas with a view to this advantage, that men, by their voluntary conventions, established it. (Hume 1976, 579)

Hume's argument draws attention to those paradoxes in the operation and purpose of law which many eighteenth-century commentators exploited. On the one hand, it looks as though it was possible to present the institution of law as the public formalisation of a gentlemanly code of good practice, motivated largely by 'natural humanity', as Blackstone does. On the other hand, and with more persuasive support, it could be seen as a powerful, virtually self-regulating institution, very remote from questions of individual conscience, unable to dwell on the minute particulars of individual cases, requiring to act by broad and imprecise principles of social utility as part of a maintained state apparatus of coercion and compulsion. Although the law obviously perpetrated cruelties and defended existing inequalities, it might still be sanctioned as a necessary component in the 'whole scheme' of civilisation. According to many contemporary commentators, the law in practice might inevitably be imperfect, but at the very least it had to be better than the anarchic possibilities of total lawlessness.

Broader questions of the morality of punishment, the role of the state, and the relationship between the law and ethics were widely and frequently discussed throughout the Augustan period, attracting the attention of theologians, philosophers, pamphleteers, poets, politicians, dramatists, novelists, and virtually everyone else with access to print. The legal system and the courts acted as stimuli to discussions of the nature of humanity, the principles of civic organisation, and the possibilities of a rational, just society. In this chorus of commentary, cries for reform vie with cries for consolidation, pleas for mercy alternate with demands for increased severity, respectful praise sits alongside disrespectful hostility, and reverence jostles with contempt. Sir William Blackstone's voice may have been one of the most authoritative and persuasive, but it was by no means the only one talking about the law.

TALKING ABOUT CRIME

The cultural and ideological importance of law in eighteenth-century England ensured that it remained at the centre of public discussion throughout the period. Contemporary commentaries were multi-vocal, and it is hard to provide a consistent or even a fully coherent version of them. With the enviable benefits of hindsight, we might wish to emphasise the rising chorus of cries for reform, as Michael Ignatieff and Sir Leon Radzinowicz do in their different ways, or we might, as Michel Foucault does, try to record a change in the patterns of penal behaviour. In a very stimulating and influential analysis, Foucault compares the grotesquely lingering execution of a French regicide in 1757 with a regimented prison timetable from eighty years later. From these documents, he constructs an elaborate and fascinating argument about changes in 'penal style' and 'the disappearance of torture as a public spectacle' (Foucault 1977, 7). I have no wish to quarrel with this version of events – indeed, I am much indebted to it – but I feel that both Ignatieff and Foucault (and, from a different perspective, Radzinowicz) overrate the availability of unanimity and coherence. As I hope to show, it is possible to use documents as selectively as Foucault does to present a very different version of the period.

All commentaries on the law, of course, have to be commentaries on crime, and criminal activities in themselves attracted a great deal of intense discussion. From the very beginning of the century, it is possible to find many commentators strenuously declaring that crime was growing all the time. In 1701 an anonymous pamphlet called *Hanging Not Punishment Enough For Murtherers, Highway-men and Housebreakers* made an impassioned plea for aggravated forms of the death penalty, such as breaking upon the wheel. Mere hanging, it claimed, was too lenient and insufficiently fearsome for the hardened criminals of the day, and, as a result, it was no longer safe to walk the streets:

> Were it not so, our Roads would not be so pester'd with that wicked Generation of Men, nor our Sessions-Paper Monthly, and the Publick News daily full of so many Relations of Robberies and Murthers, and all the Pleasure and Satisfaction of Travelling destroyed, as it is now, by being so dangerous and unsafe [...]. If some Remedy be not found to stop this growing Evil, we will shortly not dare to travel in England, unless, as in the Desarts of Arabia, it be in large Companies, and Arm'd. (Quoted in Beattie 1972, 299-300)

This rather hysterical outburst, pointing to the imminence of social collapse and suggesting a very recent deterioration in manners, adopts a rhetorical stance that can be found throughout the eighteenth century and beyond. In fact, as has been pointed out by a number of writers, the bizarre myth of a golden age of law-abiding citizens lurking just within the reaches of memory in the recent past is an essential component of a perennially potent conservative ideology (see esp. Pearson 1983, 183-202; and Williams 1973, passim). This particular early eighteenth-century pamphlet is only one of many on similar themes, calling for increased severity in punishment to combat what the writer believes to be a flagrant unchecked growth in crime and lawlessness. Like the similarly intense calls for the introduction of even more elaborate methods of execution in George Ollyffe's *An Essay Humbly Offer'd* (1731), this piece may well have confirmed some temporary anxieties, and reproduced a particular structure of feeling which can still regularly be heard. However, despite the writers' failures to offer persuasive supporting evidence for their claims, their attitudes were so much part of the ideological fabric of their age that virtually no one questioned or challenged such highly contentious assumptions.

Throughout the century such anxieties about the growth of crime and the dangers it presented to the public appear frequently, and the insistent repetitions can at first sight make the case look persuasive. In 1718 Charles Hitchen, the City Marshal of London, announced:

> Now it is the general complaint of the taverns, the coffee-houses, the shop-keepers and others, that their customers are afraid when it is dark to come to their houses and shops for fear that their hats and wigs should be snitched from their heads or their swords taken from their sides, or that they may be blinded, knocked down, cut or stabbed; nay, the coaches cannot secure them, but they are likewise cut and robbed in the public streets, &c. By which means the traffic of the City is much interrupted. (Quoted in George 1925, 10-11)

These fears of the universality and imminence of theft or violence seem to have been strongly felt by many, and they are articulated again and again by contemporary commentators, often involving the anxieties created by the large number of discharged service personnel drifting about after the Peace of Aix-la-Chapelle. In 1751 Henry Fielding's pamphlet, *An Enquiry into the Causes of the Late Increase of Robbers*, opened with a very bleak picture of city life:

> The great Increase of Robberies within these few Years, is an Evil which to me appears to deserve some attention; and the rather as it seems (tho' already become so flagrant) not yet to have arrived to that Height of which it is capable, and which it is likely to attain: For Diseases in the Political, as in the Natural Body, seldom fail going on to their Crisis, especially when nourished and encouraged by Faults in the Constitution. In fact, I make no Doubt, but that the Streets of this Town, and the Roads leading to it, will shortly be impassable without the utmost Hazard; nor are we threatned with seeing less dangerous Gangs of Rogues among us, than those which the *Italians* call the Banditi.[5]

It is tempting to see this eloquence as merely a hyperbolic flight of rhetoric, but as the century progressed, the need for a more effective system of policing was made very prominent, and public debate was still provoked by a general feeling that the streets were terrifyingly lawless. In 1775 Jonas Hanway wrote,

> I sup with my friend; I cannot return to my home, not even in my chariot, without danger of a pistol being clapt to my breast. I build an elegant villa, ten or twenty miles distant from the capital: I am obliged to provide an armed force to convey me thither, lest I should be attacked on the road with fire and ball. (Hanway 1775, 224; quoted in Tobias 1967, 24)

The most egregiously systematic of these tirades actually appeared as late as 1796. Patrick Colquhoun, a stipendiary magistrate, wrote a *Treatise on the Police of Metropolitan London* in which he claimed that as many as 115,000 people in the city – probably representing something like one in eight of the total population – were 'regularly engaged in criminal pursuits'. He broke these startling figures down into separate categories, the coolness of his statistical procedure contrasting sharply with the sensationalist pitch of his argument. There were, he claimed, at least 8,000 'thieves, pilferers and embezzlers', and 2,000 'Professional Thieves, Burglars, Highway Robbers, Pickpockets and River Pirates'. These are very dramatic figures, made much starker and somehow more authoritative in tone by the remarkable lack of supporting evidence or substantiation offered.[6]

The notion of a widespread criminal class stealthily at work throughout the land, a furtive and nefarious mirror-image of the frightened hard-working citizen, was a very potent idea in the eighteenth-century popular imagination. It can be seen in all these examples I have quoted, and in many others as well. Unfortunately, some influential historians have taken such statements out of their ideological context, and simply reproduced them as incontestable fact. Basil Williams, for instance, in the original *Oxford History of England*, talks blithely of 'a large idle or criminal class who earned a

5 Fielding 1988, 75; for a discussion of the importance of Fielding's argument, see Amory 1971, 189-190.

6 Colquhoun1796, vii-xi, 5, 230; for a discussion of these figures, see Rudé 1985, 123. An accessible account of them, as well as a detailed table of the figures, will be found in Low 1982, 23-32. Rudé attributes the sensationalism of Colquhoun's demonstration to his 'Gaelic imagination' (1985, 123). The researches of the present writer have been unable to confirm that this fervour is an intrinsic part of the psychological make-up of the inhabitants of Dumbarton.

precarious subsistence by their misdirected wits, and whose existence was fostered by the absence of an efficient police-system, the ill-lighted streets, and the horrible rookeries full of brothels' (Williams 1962, 132-133). This very lurid picture seems to hold a peculiar appeal for historians, who mostly lead sheltered and bookish lives, but there is very little to support it other than the iterations of axe-grinding pamphleteers. Of course, it might be tempting to think that something said as often as that has to have some truth in it, but the case for identifying a peculiarly virulent 'crime wave' in the Augustan period would be much more persuasive if there was some more substantial corroboration available to support it. As E.P. Thompson puts it, 'eighteenth-century class prejudice unites here with the anachronistic employment of the (inadequate) terminology of some twentieth-century criminology' (Thompson 1975, 4). Indeed, on closer examination, the whole notion of 'crime' and attendant groups of organised perpetrators of illegal activity becomes very uncertain.

It is very important to see that these questions about crime lie in the realm of ideological fantasy rather than demonstrable reality. In Adam Smith's model of a mercantile society, the integrity of commerce was maintained by a belief in the reliability and enforceability of contracts. In David Hume's argument, the sporadic inequities of the legal system were eventually excused, as far as possible, by the belief in the necessity of law. So, in many other contemporary arguments, the whole state apparatus of punishment and restraint is supported and legitimised by the creation of an elaborate scare about growing criminality and an organised criminal class. To put it bluntly, laws would more easily be brought in, and receive more widespread public assent, if they were thought to be in defence of the rights of honest citizens, under threat from the lawless and violent criminal class.

The moral panic about crime which was orchestrated and sustained throughout the eighteenth century seems to have been very effective in maintaining belief in the necessity of the 'Bloody Code'. But was it in any way justified? Despite its obviousness, any such question is remarkably difficult to answer. Alongside the prurient perception of Basil Williams, it is salutary to place the calmer comments of J.A. Sharpe:

> We must therefore conclude that there was little professional crime in our period and, equally, few traces of a 'criminal class' or a 'criminal subculture', at least outside the capital [...]. For the most part, whatever the damage to their individual victims, it would seem more sensible to regard the criminal as an irritant to honest people rather than a menace. (Sharpe 1984, 119-120)

This historian's version of events is unlike anything we have encountered so far, and it needs some consideration. If there were no real menaces to society, only irritants, why does the number of offences and executions seem to increase so much? Part of the answer, at least, lies not in the activities of so-called criminals, but in the behaviour of the legislature. It is obvious that the greater the number of laws, and the greater the severity with which they are enforced, the more crimes will seem to have been committed. But to say that without qualification begs the all-important question of whether these new crimes are discovered or created. Does a rise in the number of recorded prosecutions indicate a change in the behaviour of the accusers or the accused, or even both? The traditional view seems to be that criminality was increasing. However, many prominent recent historians, most notably E.P. Thompson and George Rudé, are in broad agreement with Sharpe's view, and have persuasively expressed scepticism about the existence of an active criminal network.

A full discussion and resolution of this issue would require some reliable and incontestable data, and, alas, these cannot be found. The earliest collections of criminal statistics which are of any use (although even these must be treated with caution) are the work of the Statistical Society of London, and date from 1834. In the absence of full documentary information, it might be possible, as J.M. Beattie has shown, to compile lists of actual court cases in given districts at given times, and to use these to speculate on trends. Even this tentative procedure, however, does not avoid important problems. For one thing, it only provides the possibility of seeing crime in its contemporary categories – that is to say, taking the statute as the final arbiter, and unquestioningly accepting the ways it categorises behaviour. More importantly, there is the problem of the so-called 'dark figure' – the number of potential offences which go undetected and unrecorded. Since crime is by its nature furtive, and since criminals understandably invest a great deal of their energy and ingenuity in avoiding capture, the 'dark figure' must always disable the accurate computation of illegal behaviour. A recent study suggests that, even today, only around 20% of criminal behaviour is discovered and reported, and there is no reason to imagine that eighteenth-century procedures of detection were any more successful.[7]

Any attempts to produce accurate or reliable figures about criminal or illegal activities at any time are thus extremely difficult. For the period in question, some very tentative guesses have been made. Many commentators seem to think that a particular combination of factors in the first half of the century made it seem, at least, as though criminal activity was on the increase. As E.P. Thompson puts it, 'if that unsatisfactory term "crime wave" could ever be used with conviction, it might possibly be applied to the early 1720s' (Thompson 1975, 196). Thompson's hesitations and uncertainties are unavoidable, and show the precarious, provisional nature of the whole exercise. Although some other writers have been confident enough to talk of a decline in crime after the 1760s, any such estimate must be of necessity unreliable.[8] The paradoxes involved in the venture are clearly illustrated by J.M. Beattie, who quotes the preamble to the 'Murder Act' of 1752 (25 Geo. II c.37). This statute tried to increase the severity of the penalty for homicide, on the grounds that it had been 'more frequently perpetrated than formerly and particularly in and near the metropolis.' Despite this stern warning, the available evidence seems to suggest, according to Beattie, that 'the number if anything declined over the century' (Beattie 1986, 78). What we seem to be confronted with, then, is a sustained chorus of anxiety about crime, about the dangers of living in the metropolis, and about the threat to personal safety, which seems to exist more or less independently of any facts which can be identified.

Of course, even to talk of 'facts' here is misleading. In this area, more obviously than in almost any other one, there can be little possibility of objective data. There can be,

7 Hough and Mayhew 1983. For discussions of the 'dark figure', see Samaha 1974, 13-24; Sharpe 1984, 46-48; Tobias 1967, 10-21; Zehr 1976, 14-19.

8 See George 1925, 16-18; for an exactly opposite view, see Rudé 1985, 96-98.

for good or ill, no facts, only interpretations, always open to scrutiny and revision. Since positivist historical study is a matter of pragmatism and probability, it is possible to exert pressure on whatever documentary evidence might be available, to squeeze out of it as much information as possible, and thereby to construct more or less plausible hypotheses. But even the most optimistic and erudite historians are invariably circumspect when attempting to identify the rate of crime in England in the eighteenth century.

The acknowledged expert in this field is J.M. Beattie, who places what trust he has in records of indictments. He is sensitive to the recognised limitations of archival research, but eventually comes to a surprisingly positive account of the possibilities of quantification. His argument, put very simply, is as follows. Although precise and exact figures even of prosecutions in Britain at this time are unavailable – prosecutions were privately instigated and might not always be scrupulously recorded – there are assize records from specific parishes which can be used to reconstruct a sufficiently complete picture. Fluctuations in the number of indictments can certainly provide a picture of how the legal process operated, and that might well be useful for comparative purposes. However, Beattie argues further that these fluctuations reflect changes in the patterns of crime, and that they can be used to provide reliable evidence for increases and decreases in the number of offences. Beattie, here, follows Douglas Hay, who investigated the records of the Staffordshire assize for the later part of the century, and tried to correlate the number of offences with identifiable extra-legal factors. Hay's confidence in these figures comes from their accidental nature – they were not recorded for historical purposes – and their proximity to the events. Although Hay recognises that 'control waves' and 'moral panics' cannot be ignored, he sees the private nature of prosecutions as, to some extent, mitigating the degree of control that could be enforced. Although duly cautious, he concludes that some kind of measurement of fluctuation is possible, even if the base figure of offences committed must always remain elusive.[9]

The confidence exhibited by Beattie and Hay is exhilarating, even if the eventual results seem less exciting. At the very least, though, it can be argued that archival sources can be informative about the mechanics and procedures of the legal system, about how courts conducted themselves, about what punishments were meted out, about what proportion of those indicted were acquitted, and on what grounds. These sources might also yield valuable information about who prosecuted whom, and with what success, and could, at least in theory, offer comparison of trends in indictments and such extra-legal factors as war, or famine. All such information is valuable, and gives us some purchase on the slippery slopes of historical reconstruction. However, what this archival work cannot reveal is the contemporary climate of opinion surrounding the legal system, the pressures it was under to rectify or ignore social abuse, and all the perceptions of legality and illegality that were disseminated and contested throughout the period. To find out what the accusers and the accused thought

9 Beattie 1986, 199-200; Hay 1982; for a summary of this discussion, see Sharpe 1984, 41-48.

of the law, and in what standing it was publicly held, we have to leave the historians scrimmaging in the book stacks and rifling the record offices, and move elsewhere.

Reading about Crime

The statistical or quantitative approach to crime confidently advocated by many recent historians has thus revealed only a limited amount of information, and it has inevitably turned into a kind of administrative history, revealing much about the way legal institutions have operated but comparatively little about popular perceptions of, or attitudes towards, illegal behaviour. This apparent failure has led one writer to describe the pursuit of reliable statistics in this field as 'something of a dead end', but that does seem unduly harsh (Styles 1988, 39). However, if we are to move away from the archives and record offices in search of more enlightening information, where should we look? At the risk of provoking hoots of scornful mirth from certain historians, I wish to suggest that suitable sources for the study of crime during this period might be found in the contemporary press. Whatever else may be said of them individually, the law and the press together can be seen as the two central generators of ideology in early eighteenth-century England, twin bodies of commentary on human behaviour, sometimes overlapping, sometimes competing, progressively overtaking the church as the most widely-heeded guides to conduct. The body of statute can be seen as a sustained and elaborate commentary on human activity, which is of necessity categorical, explicit, univocal. The press, on the other hand, provides a body of commentary which can be multi-vocal, inexplicit, suggestive and ambiguous, exploiting the possibilities of human absurdity and the inability to be exactly precise. And we must remember that both the press and the law, of course, can be equally misleading and unreliable guides to the actual behaviour of contemporary people.

Throughout this period the press was instrumental in creating a repository of ways of thinking about social issues, including crime and the law, and, even if the views it presented were inevitably contested and various, it still set the agenda for public discussion. According to some recent critics, the press alternately took on a 'static' and a 'dynamic' role in early eighteenth-century culture:

> The newspaper continued to help define and integrate communities around the dominant social and economic groups and in this respect emphasized the primarily 'static' position of the press [...]. Paradoxically, this integrative role was combined with a more 'dynamic', even a potentially more radical, approach developed through the consistent involvement of sections of the English press in the workings of the political system [...]. Throughout the eighteenth century sections of the English press offered readers a torrent of abuse and criticism leveled at those in authority. (Harris and Lee 1986, 21)

Such a vociferous press, variously supportive and subversive of established authority, did much to create and disseminate ideas of and attitudes to crime and legality in early eighteenth-century England. Since crime was one of the pressure points of ideology, if I may put it that way, the press can give us access to both the conservative and the more radical arguments at their most fully developed and articulate. And, although contemporary newspapers and journals are perhaps the most immediate forms of commentary, attention should also be paid to more ruminative and reflective styles, such as diaries, biographies, pamphlets, poems, novels and plays.

Although this seems an eminently sensible position to me, the merest mention of 'literary sources' is enough to set the archivists roaring and falling about. J.A. Sharpe, for instance, puts the case against the use of literature in historical research as forcefully as anyone:

> we are confronted with a refusal to take social history seriously, and the limitations of what might be termed the *Belles-Lettres* approach to the study of the subject are all too apparent. It is indicative of the priorities of English historical writing that historians who would otherwise have prided themselves on their scholarship, intellectual rigour, and talent for source-criticism should become slack, lazy, and uncritical when using literary sources to discuss historical subjects, crime included [...]. Unfortunately, the familiarity, the vividness, and accessibility of literary sources makes them very attractive, and a number of writers, professional English scholars among them, have thrown these sources together to form easily palatable if hopelessly inadequate books. (Sharpe 1984, 8-9)

It seems that when faced with the blowsy charms of literature, dignified historians go all to pieces, and start behaving like Professor Unrat in *The Blue Angel*. Professional English scholars, on the other hand, a less scrupulous bunch to begin with, see the same material as an opportunity for a kind of smash-and-grab exercise, acting like what the Right Villainous John Hall would call 'running-smoblers'.

There may be something in what Sharpe says, for there are certainly some pretty feeble books on Shakespeare's England and the Elizabethan underworld and Dickens' London and so on, written as though the literary text was a direct and uncontroversial source of reliable information. Similarly, there are plenty of examples of historians being bamboozled by 'imaginative' writing, blithely lifting citations from plays and novels to illustrate the issues they are researching. James Heath, for example, makes surprisingly casual use of *Bartholomew Fair*, *Tom Jones* and *Measure for Measure* in discussing the theories of punishment in eighteenth-century England (Heath 1963, 27, 39, 52). Previous generations of historians were even less inhibited in their reliance on such sources, following Macaulay's famous discussion of the eighteenth-century country gentleman in his *History of England*, which he admitted was derived entirely from 'the lighter literature of that age'.[10] It would be startling to come across anything as sweeping as that today, but, surprisingly enough, it is still possible to find one of the most dogged of modern archivists referring to that load of preposterous tomfoolery known as *The English Rogue*, by Richard Head and Francis Kirkman, as 'descriptive' (Macfarlane 1981, 24).

The attractiveness of literary sources is obvious, but so are the dangers. What seems to get in the way of serious study here is a persistent uncertainty about the cognitive functions of literature. The traditional Aristotelian idea that literature is somehow *more* true than history still lingers on despite all the efforts of modern literary theorists to dislodge it. For some traditionalist and high-minded literary critics, historians may make agreeable colleagues, but they can at best provide backgrounds to help us understand the more important transcendent activities of the great imaginative writers.

10 Macaulay 1913, 1: 310-313; see also the discussion of this point in Speck 1983, 3-13.

If there is any basis for the belief that literature somehow encapsulates the essential truth, the *real* truth about things, as Shelley argued, then history can only be a shabby second-hand thing in comparison. But surely literary and historical study need not be forced into such a hierarchical relationship, nor need they be inscribed in such an impasse. It is perfectly possible to re-insert literature in its social and historical context, and talk about the written word as something other than the unsullied product of a singular imagination, without behaving in the way that Sharpe caricatures. Literary works are quite obviously informed by history, and the problem for historically-oriented critics is finding a language adequate to express the very complex relationship between texts and their various contexts without being reductive or over-emphatic.

Since history surrounds and infiltrates literature, and literature intervenes in history, how is their mutual relationship to be described? The first and most naïve assumption is that they are inseparable, that literature is a kind of window on the past, offering reliable access to lost worlds. Such an attitude lies silently behind the crudest historical uses of literature, like Macaulay's, and is clearly misguided. The notion that literature can be impartial, non-partisan, or even simply referential cannot be sustained beyond the simplest inspection. Anyone who used, say, the eighteenth-century novel as a source of unproblematic information about eighteenth-century society could only end up with a bizarre caricature of the individuals and institutions concerned, since literature so often dramatises the exceptional in preference to the mundane, the remarkable in preference to the ordinary. And the whole system of selection, omission and deliberate or inadvertent distortion that goes into the construction of any piece of writing (including this one, of course) means that an unproblematic access to truth and reliability can never be found. Many examples could be offered to substantiate this argument – to assume that, say, Smollett's picture of naval life in *Roderick Random* is in any way accurate or representative is clearly misguided, and can lead to great misconceptions, as recent scholarship has shown.[11]

A more subtle suggestion is that literature reflects society, with a greater or lesser degree of distortion perhaps, but with sufficient accuracy for the skilled viewer to discover the true picture. The theory of reflection has a long history, and in the eighteenth century it surfaced most powerfully in Dr Johnson's defence of Shakespeare as 'the poet that holds up to his readers a faithful mirror of manners and of life' (Johnson 1984, 421). In discussion of the novel in particular, the image of the mirror has repeatedly been used in the service of the idea of 'realism'. Any notion of verisimilitude must have, somewhere behind it, the enabling belief that literature can accurately portray life or reality or whatever. As is well known, these arguments were most strongly put in the nineteenth century by George Eliot in Britain, and by Balzac, Flaubert and Zola in France, and they are still occasionally heard today. If this belief in the accuracy and reliability of literature were true, fortunate historians would be able to use imaginative texts as unproblematic source material. Unfortunately, of course, it is not.

11 For a persuasive sceptical assessment of Smollett's version of the navy, see Rodger 1986, 14.

The problem is always the inevitable partisanship and tendentiousness of literature, be it conscious or unconscious. After all, even what you see when you look in a mirror is a kind of construction, and the notion of writing being a special sort of mirror is full of hidden problems and complexities. For one thing, this way of thinking makes literature seem very passive, simply receiving and transmitting (to change the metaphor) the signals which society puts out. But all writing is by its very nature interventionist and partial, involving the selection of details, the relative positioning and prioritising of individual elements, and the omission of features thought to be irrelevant or accidental. Literature, that is to say, is always a construction, not just a revelation, a more or less deliberate act of shaping and forming, which is under no compulsion to give the whole picture, or even an accurate part of it. Writers do not invariably act as faithful *amanuenses*, but as ardent reactionaries or *agents provocateurs*, their works being relatively nostalgic or progressive as they articulate disappearing or emergent structures of feeling. In the early eighteenth century, when the scratching of pens so often coincided with the grinding of axes, any protestation of disinterest by an author should be treated with the utmost suspicion. Our knowledge of the political role of the Augustan press shows that it was inherently ideological, both in its 'static' and its 'dynamic' roles, disseminating false consciousness and illusion, offering allegiances to different constructions of the past, present or future, rather than determining truth in a disinterested way. Perhaps that is always the way writing works in societies, and, if so, the historian's job in interpreting it is made no easier.

Given that writing is so inherently ideological, might it offer a way for us to gain privileged access to important eighteenth-century ideologies? Or at least, might reading imaginative literature allow us to retrieve those particular issues to which the eighteenth century gave special priority? R.W. Malcolmson attempts to use literature in this way in his discussion of foundlings:

> In England they have appeared periodically in the annals of the poor law, and more memorably, in works of the literary imagination: Fielding's *Tom Jones*, Eppie in George Eliot's *Silas Marner*, and the central character in Oscar Wilde's *The Importance of Being Earnest*. Such recognition attests, perhaps, to the prominence of abandoned infants in everyday experience, but details of those fictional careers should not be accepted too literally. (Malcolmson 1977, 188)

No, indeed not. It is a sad fact that the plays of Oscar Wilde cannot be taken as wholly reliable historical documents, unless we wish to argue that nineteenth-century railway stations functioned as surrogate maternity wards. But even on a more serious level, the casual use of imaginative writing here weakens rather than strengthens Malcolmson's case. Can the appearance of foundlings in only *three* books, written between 1749 and 1895, really attest to 'the prominence of abandoned infants in everyday experience'? The case would be more convincing if Malcolmson produced whole torrents of novels, plays and poems with foundlings in them (*Oedipus Rex*? *The Winter's Tale*? *The Bundle*?). But to produce only three, from such different periods, looks mightily unimpressive. By a similar argument, the selective deployment of *Evelina*, *The Murders in the Rue Morgue* and *King Kong* would allow the interested historian to remark on the frequent appearance of variously-sized rampaging apes in everyday bourgeois social experience.

A different and more useful perspective on literature is adopted by W.A. Speck, who has a more flexible version of its historical functions. While acknowledging that 'if [...] we use it to try to document social realities, we shall be seriously misled', Speck remains confident that 'it can become a prime source for the ideologies of the period 1700-60' (Speck 1983, 12). Throughout his study of literature in society, Speck takes it as axiomatic that the written word documents or records or reflects ideologies. Although this is broadly incontestable, and provides him with a very fruitful way of contextualising literature, Speck concentrates almost exclusively on the 'static' role of the press. However, as we shall see, literature was a forum in which ideologies were contested as well as disseminated, and it is this ability to challenge and subvert which is particularly interesting when dealing with legislation and crime.

Many of the 'criminal' texts which I shall go on to discuss do not simply reproduce in a more decorative way an ideological position which can be isolated and identified elsewhere. Rather, they disrupt the protestations of ideologies to be something other than themselves. Most ideological writing adopts a disguise, disowning its ideological status, and pretending to be something else, objective or impartial: the voice of moderation, the space beyond ideology. What a great many eighteenth-century texts do is contest the authority of other texts, to show that finality and fixity must be sought but cannot be found. I will go into this in more detail later, but for the moment we need to ask if a study of literature can ever be anything other than the exploration of disappointingly uninformative fantasies and rhetoric. To put it another way, can literature ever inform its readers of anything, other than the principles of its own construction?

To reverse the usual terms of discussion, the question is: how can we turn the base metals of literary works into the pure gold of historical information? In alchemy, this magical transformation is achieved by the philosopher's stone. In recent historiography, it is just as magically achieved by Lawrence Stone. Professor Stone's remarkable work on popular attitudes and behaviour draws heavily on literary sources, and shows all the challenging and attractive possibilities and impediments of this method. At times, he is at pains to sound even-handed and judicious, using selected literary examples to indicate only areas of uncertainty and controversy:

> This literary evidence shows that there was a prolonged public argument during the late seventeenth and eighteenth centuries about a child's freedom of choice of a marriage partner, with more liberal views becoming more common among authors catering both to the middling ranks of commercial and professional people, and also to the wealthy landed classes. (Stone 1977, 280-281)

It is hard to argue with Stone's conclusion: if there is indeed a body of literature in which such a question is prominent, then it is reasonable to assume that many people were concerned by it. If the focus of the discussion changes, then it is reasonable to assume that the audience's interests similarly change (though it remains a matter of debate whether the writing responds to a re-orientation or helps to initiate one). Elsewhere, Stone presses his information a little harder, and tries to get more evidence from it. In his discussion of conventional marriage practices, he quotes a passage from George Crabbe, which suggests that successful marriage partners need not be romantic lovers. Stone concludes:

> The urban tradesmen and artisans and the rural smallholders of the late eighteenth century were *thus* probably largely unaffected by the new demands of love, generated among their betters by the romantic movement of the age. (Stone 1977, 366; italics mine)

Although Stone supports his conclusion with a few contemporary diary entries as well, the burden of proof is still almost exclusively carried by the isolated and possibly unrepresentative Crabbe passage.

Perhaps, in a rough and ready sort of way, the lack of rigour in Stone's procedure is acceptable. In this context, Crabbe is probably a reliable enough witness, but it would be reassuring to see some more tangible support for his isolated remarks. Where Stone goes completely to pieces, however, is when he starts seeing not only his various authors as reliable informants, but their characters as well. And what characters! In his lengthy discussion of mating arrangements, an area of obvious difficulty, Stone calls upon some pretty unlikely witnesses:

> In lower middle-class circles, where capital was a critical factor in getting a start in life by buying a shop or starting a business, it was inevitable that financial considerations should continue to play a very large part in marriage plans [...]. Defoe's Moll Flanders, who moved in these circles, soon came to the sad conclusion that 'marriages here are the consequence of politic schemes, for forming interests, carrying on business', and that love had no share or very little in the matter. After a bitter experience she decided that 'money only made a woman agreeable ... the money was the thing'. In other words, in terms of marriage, a woman in the late seventeenth and eighteenth centuries was still regarded in these circles less as a companion or a sex object than as property, and to some extent also as a status object.[12]

To suggest that financial arrangements are central to Moll's wedding plans is a perfectly plausible and orthodox reading of Defoe's fictional narrative. But to what extent can the behaviour of this character, however meticulously imagined, fairly be seen as typical? After all, Moll does not really move 'in these circles' at all, but inhabits instead the shady and mendacious realm of a work of prose fiction. If her views on money and marriage are to be taken as typical, which features of her experience are to be seen as idiosyncratic, and by what criteria are they distinguishable? Stone seems impelled by the logic of his argument to accept all of Moll's experiences as representative, and a glance at the book's title-page, with its hectic promise of the most extraordinary adventures, makes this look rather unlikely.

In this instance, Stone seems seduced by the plain style of the narrative into accepting it as a factual record, a genuine confession acceptable in a court of law. A similar and even more unlikely reading involves his search for evidence of preferred styles of love-making in different social groups. The clinching evidence appears when he argues that sexual modesty was peculiar to the lower-middle classes: 'James [*sic*] Cleland's Fanny Hill, a respectable country girl, was genuinely shocked to discover that some men and women took all their clothes off in daylight to make love.'[13] While it is hard to avoid the suspicion that any case supported by Moll Flanders and Fanny Hill is struggling to persuade, this particular example is especially interesting in the way it raises all the problems of irony. What if this point was introduced by Cleland to reveal

---

12 Stone 1977, 294; the passage quoted is from *Moll Flanders* (1991), 57-58, 52.

13 Stone 1977, 522; the author of *Fanny Hill* was, of course, *John* Cleland, not James Cleland.

Fanny's entertaining and incongruous innocence? After all, there is no intrinsic reason to assume that the story-teller has to represent the voice of authority within the tale. As anyone familiar with *Gulliver's Travels* or *Tristram Shandy* can testify, unreliable narrators are not exactly unknown in eighteenth-century fiction. If Cleland expected his audience to be amused by Fanny's surprise, we could read the episode as evidence of the prevalence of daytime sexual disrobing. Maybe everybody *except* Fanny Hill knew all about it.

Areas of well-trodden difficulty are coming into view here, and need not be further explored at the moment. The single point to make now is that it can only be a high-risk strategy to rely on the evidential authority of literary characters. Any individual episode within a work of fiction might be an idiosyncratic feature of the character's personality, or there might be some overall ironic structure controlled by the author which could make isolated extracts unrepresentative. One promising way of trying to avoid this problem, and to arrive at a compromise between the requirements of literary and historical study, is to move beyond individualised or idiosyncratic characters and to concentrate on the representative character. If it is possible to read across a range of texts and find similar figures presented in similar ways, it might be possible to identify a stereotype, which might be evidence of a widely-shared perception of some group or profession.

This is another method employed by W.A. Speck, following the work done by John Loftis on dramatic characters (Speck 1983, ch. 2; Loftis 1959, passim). In a more recent work, Lawrence Stone, too, deals with 'the stereotypes of fiction, the theatre, and popular imagination' (Stone and Stone 1986, 19). I have argued elsewhere that this kind of supervised, typological reading, where the meaning of specific texts accrues from similarities to, and differences from, acknowledged generic forms, is particularly appropriate for the popular writing of this period (see Bell 1985, esp. ch. 3). And it is clearly possible to find suitable stereotypes permeating the presentation of legal affairs in eighteenth-century writing, which may be taken as symptomatic of widely-held attitudes. In particular, the character of the lawyer is treated with almost universal contempt by writers who might disagree about virtually everything else. In a host of graphic representations, lawyers are figured as avaricious leeches, unscrupulous and unprincipled, much more concerned with fees than with verdicts. In narratives as diverse as the *Memoirs of Martinus Scriblerus*, *The Whore's Rhetorick* and *Tom Jones*, lawyers may he represented with differing emphases, but to much the same vitriolic end. And not only lawyers were treated this way. As Speck puts it, 'the subjects of Queen Anne seem to have pretty well agreed that all lawyers were pettifoggers who deliberately bamboozled their clients, all doctors were ignorant quacks who bilked their patients, and all clergymen were timeserving careerists bent on ascending the ladder of preferment at all costs (Speck 1980, 127). I shall deal more fully with this later, but, for the moment, it is only necessary to point out that as lawyers became more prominent in legal proceedings throughout the century, their popularity seems to have remained consistently low, despite their strenuous efforts to adopt the legitimising mantle of professionalisation. If, that is, this kind of literary evidence can be trusted.

The treatment of lawyers and other professions is unusually unanimous, and it is hard to present a repertoire of other images of equal stability and consistency. Although it might be possible to identify at least a few other obvious stereotypes – cuckolded husbands are more frequently presented as figures of scorn rather than sympathy, for example – most representations are contested and polarised. And there remains the vexing question of how many repetitions it takes to create a stereotype. In fact, analysis of the literary evidence almost invariably reveals doubts and uncertainties instead of unanimity and confidence. Literature seems to draw attention to the pressure points in ideology, those places where a culture is less confident of itself, where the greatest contestation of images can occur. To say this is partly to repeat the traditional view, scarcely unfamiliar in late twentieth-century Britain, that the press in all its forms encourages controversy while playing on shared prejudices, but it is also to say that literature both disseminates and resists ideology. In the case of crime, for instance, the representations of the criminal are fascinatingly diverse rather than unanimous. Criminals are sometimes presented as menaces to society, sometimes as mere irritants, sometimes as a social problem to be solved, and even sometimes as romantic brigands and outlaws. Images of demonic cruelty alternate with images of heroic banditry. Opprobrium alternates with admiration, admonition with panegyric, until it becomes virtually impossible to find any consensus which might allow easy speculation about a general or universal attitude towards crime.

This diversity of response is apparent not only in the literary incarnation of criminals, but, as far as we can tell, in their public appearances as well. When criminals were put on display in the pillory or at Tyburn, they could receive cheers or jeers. Fernand Braudel claims that 'the crowd that milled around scaffolds and gibbets out of morbid curiosity was never on the side of the victim' (Braudel 1982, 516). There is certainly some evidence to support this view in the records of the very violent and abusive treatment of condemned homosexuals, or other especially unpopular individuals, who were sometimes stoned to death or very badly injured in the pillory (see Jarrett 1974, 51-52). However, alongside these there are well-known counter-examples where the crowd refused to endorse the sentence passed on the victim, and responded much more positively, as most famously in the triumphant appearance of Daniel Defoe in the pillory and the popular success of Jack Sheppard.[14]

By looking at the whole body of writing concerned with crime, it is possible to see parallels to this unpredictable public response, which, we must remember, is in itself only available to us through mediated written accounts. The literary testimony is exceptionally various, and shows that the conceptual structure surrounding the ideological notion of crime was volatile and unstable. A number of recent writers, particularly those associated with *Albion's Fatal Tree*, have discussed those cases where the criminalisation of previously acceptable practices met with concerted resistance. I want to range more widely than that, and look at the ways in which literature intermittently explored the mismatching of law and morality, isolating and exploiting paradoxes and ironies which the univocal body of statute sought to ignore or

14 For the most recent account of this incident, see Backscheider 1988. Interesting examples of the approval and occasional violent disapproval of pilloried felons are given in Beattie 1986, 464-468.

suppress. By looking at the different ways that criminals were treated in the parallel discourses of law and letters, it may be possible to identify some of the ideological tensions of early eighteenth-century English culture. It is unlikely that such examination will result in the identification of anything as unanimous as an attitude to crime shared by many, or a fugitive alternative system of ideology. The law, by its ideological centrality, provided the focus for a whole range of expressions, both supportive and adversary, static and dynamic, and it is these which will be explored, in the hope of clarifying the social function of literature and revealing the contested status of legislation.[15]

15 For further development of these ideas, please see Bell 1991.

REFERENCES

Amory, Hugh (1971). 'Henry Fielding and the Criminal Legislation of 1751-2.' *Philological Quarterly* 50, 189-190.

Backscheider, Paula R. (1988) 'No Defense: Defoe in 1703.' *PMLA*, 274-284.

Beattie, J.M. (1972). 'Towards a Study of Crime in Eighteenth Century England: A Note on Indictments.' In Paul Fritz and David Williams (eds.), *The Triumph of Culture: Eighteenth-Century Perspectives*, 219-313. Toronto: A.M. Hakkert.

________ (1986). *Crime and the Courts in England 1660-1800*. Oxford: Clarendon Press.

Bell, Ian A. (1985). *Defoe's Fiction*. London: Croom Helm.

________ (1991). *Literature and Crime in Augustan England*. London: Routledge.

Blackstone, William (1979). *Commentaries on the Laws of England: A Facsimile of the First Edition of 1765-1769*. 4 vols. Chicago: University of Chicago Press. Original edition London,1765-1769.

Braudel, Fernand (1982). *The Wheels of Commerce*. Trans. S. Reynolds. Civilization and Capital, 15th-18th Century 2. London: Collins.

Colquhoun, Patrick (1796). *A Treatise on the Police of the Metropolis*. London: Printed for C. Dilly.

Defoe, Daniel (1991). *Moll Flanders*. Everyman Library 32. New York: Knopf. Original edition 1722.

Fielding, Henry (1988). *An Enquiry into the Causes of the Late Increase of Robbers and Related Writings*. Ed. Malvin R. Zirker. Oxford: Clarendon Press. Original edition Dublin, 1751.

Foucault, Michel (1977). *Discipline and Punish: The Birth of the Prison*. Trans. Alan Sheridan. London: Allen Lane. Original edition 1975.

George, M. Dorothy (1925). *London Life in the Eighteenth Century*. London: K. Paul, Trench, Trubner.

Hanway, Jonas (1775). *The Defects of Police, the Cause of Immorality, and the Continual Robberies committed, particularly in and about the Metropolis [...]*. London: Printed for J. Dodsley.

Harris, Michael, and Alan Lee, eds. (1986). *The Press in English Society from the Seventeenth to Nineteenth Centuries*. London: Associated University Press.

Hay, Douglas (1975). 'Property, Authority and the Criminal Law.' In D. Hay, P. Linebaugh, J.G. Rule, E.P. Thompson and C. Winslow (eds.), *Albion's Fatal Tree: Crime and Society in Eighteenth-Century England*. London: Allen Lane, 17-63.

________ (1982). 'War, Dearth and Theft in the Eighteenth Century: The Record of the English Courts.' *Past and Present* 95, 117-160.

Heath, James (1963). *Eighteenth Century Penal Theory*. Oxford: Oxford University Press.

Hough, Mike, and Pat Mayhew (1983). *The British Crime Survey: First Report*. Home Office Research Study 76. London: H.M.S.O.

Hume, David (1976). *A Treatise of Human Nature*. Ed. L.A. Selby Bigge. 2nd ed. rev. P.H. Nidditch. Oxford: Clarendon Press. Original edition 1739.

Ignatieff, Michael (1978). *A Just Measure of Pain: The Penitentiary in the Industrial Revolution, 1750-1850*. London: Macmillan.

________(1985). 'State, Civil Society and Total Institutions: A Critique of Recent Social Histories of Punishment.' In Stanley Cohen and Andrew Scull (eds.), *Social Control and the State*. Oxford: Basil Blackwell, 75-105.

J.R. (1701). *Hanging Not Punishment Enough For Murtherers, Highway-men, and House-breakers: offered to the consideration of the two houses of Parliament*. London: Printed for A. Baldwin (1701).

Jarrett, Derek (1974). *England in the Age of Hogarth*. London: Hart-Davis MacGibbon.

Johnson, Samuel (1984). '"Preface" to *The Plays of William Shakespeare*.' In *Samuel Johnson*. Ed. Donald Greene. Oxford: Oxford University Press, 419-456. Original edition 1765.

Loftis, John (1959). *Comedy and Society from Congreve to Fielding*. Stanford Studies in Language and Literature 19. Stanford: Stanford University Press.

Low, Donald A. (1982). *Thieves' Kitchen: The Regency Underworld.* London: Dent.

Macaulay, T.B. (1913). *The History of England: From the Accession of James the Second.* Ed. Sir Charles Firth. 6 vols. London: Macmillan. Original edition 1848-1861.

Macfarlane, Alan (1981). *The Justice and the Mare's Ale: Law and Disorder in Seventeenth-Century England.* Oxford: Basil Blackwell.

Malcolmson, R.W. (1977). 'Infanticide in the Eighteenth Century.' In J.S. Cockburn (ed.), *Crime in England 1550-1800.* London: Methuen, 187-210.

Pearson, Geoffrey (1983). *Hooligan: A History of Respectable Fears.* London: Macmillan.

Philips, David (1985). '"A Just Measure of Crime, Authority, Hunters and Blue Locusts": The "Revisionist" Social History of Crime and the Law in Britain, 1780-1850.' In Stanley Cohen and Andrew Scull (eds.), *Social Control and the State: Historical and Comparative Essays.* Oxford: Basil Blackwell, 50-74.

Radzinowicz, Leon (1948). *A History of English Criminal Law and Its Administration from 1750.* Vol. 1: *The Movement For Reform.* London: Stevens and Sons.

Rodger, N.A.M. (1986). *The Wooden World: An Anatomy of the Georgian Navy.* London: Collins.

Rudé, George (1985). *Criminal and Victim: Crime and Society in Early Nineteenth-Century England.* Oxford: Clarendon Press.

________ (1971). *Hanoverian London, 1714-1808.* London: Secker and Warburg.

Samaha, Joel (1974). *Law and Order in Historical Perspective: The Case of Elizabethan Essex.* New York: Academic Press.

Sharpe, J.A. (1984). *Crime in Early Modern England 1550-1750.* London: Longman.

Smith, Adam (1976). *An Inquiry into the Nature and Causes of the Wealth of Nations.* Ed. R.H. Campbell, A.S. Skinner and W.B. Todd. 2 vols. Oxford: Clarendon Press. Original edition 1776.

Speck, W.A. (1980). 'The Harlot's Progress in Eighteenth-Century England.' *British Journal for Eighteenth-Century Studies* 3, 127-130.

________ (1983). *Society and Literature in England 1700-1760.* Dublin: Gill and Macmillan.

Stone, Lawrence (1977). *The Family, Sex and Marriage in England 1500-1800.* London: Weidenfeld and Nicholson.

Stone, Lawrence, and Jeanne C. Fawtier Stone (1986). *An Open Elite? England 1540-1880.* Abridged ed. Oxford: Oxford University Press.

Styles, John (1988). 'The Criminal Past: Crime in Eighteenth-Century England.' *History Today* 38/3 (March), 36-42.

Thompson, E.P. (1975). *Whigs and Hunters: The Origin of the Black Act.* London: Allen Lane.

Tobias, J.J. (1967). *Crime and Industrial Society in the Nineteenth Century.* London: Batsford.

Williams, Basil (1962). *The Whig Supremacy 1714-1760.* 2nd ed. rev. C.H. Stuart. Oxford: Clarendon Press. Original edition 1939.

Williams, Raymond (1973). *The Country and the City.* London: Chatto and Windus.

Zehr, Howard (1976). *Crime and the Development of Modern Society: Patterns of Criminality in Nineteenth-Century Germany and France.* London: Croom Helm.

Beth Swan

DEFOE AND THE CRIMINAL LAWYER: EIGHTEENTH-CENTURY IDEOLOGIES OF JUSTICE

'Scripture bids us not despise [...] a Thief, who steals to satisfie his Hunger; not that the Man is less a Thief, but despise him not, you that know not what Hunger is' (Secord 1938, 543-544). Defoe in his *Review*, here, on 8 February 1709, is articulating a moral view, but one which is rooted firmly in contemporary juridica l discourse concerning crime and justice. Defoe responded to contemporary fear and fascination with crime with popular criminal biographies[1] such as the *History of John Sheppard*, promising: 'His History will astonish! And is not compos'd of Fiction [...] but Facts done at your Doors, Facts unheard of, altogether new, Incredible, and yet Uncontestable' (Defoe 1968, 234-235).[2] *Moll Flanders* lacks this journalistic hype but it clearly owes much to this tradition.

McLynn notes, 'Breaking and entering private property with felonious intent was the most commonly encountered capital crime of the eighteenth century' (McLynn 1989, 87). Rawlings points out that the term 'crime' evoked 'physical danger [...] gangs and a whole criminal underworld, of moral collapse and anarchy' (Rawlings 1992, 17). Such fears are embodied in Moll Flanders. As a felon, Moll is by definition also her own defence lawyer since felons usually defended themselves in court.[3] The figure of the criminal lawyer is doubly significant here, as part of both the criminal body and the legal process. In the course of his editorial work for Applebee's *Journal* in the 1720s, Defoe would have seen numerous examples of the criminal as lawyer. This experience informs much of the writing of *Moll Flanders*.

In theory, the eighteenth-century legal system embodied ideals of justice to which the accused could appeal in the form of Judges and juries. Yet justice inevitably lies in the eye of the beholder: the criminal lawyer is concerned not with justice but with winning his case.[4] Part of the drama of the eighteenth-century courtroom lay in the figure of the criminal lawyer, effectively pleading for his or her life, trying to manipulate and, indeed, subvert the system. Through the figure of Moll Flanders as criminal lawyer, Defoe encourages the reader to engage imaginatively in the difficult process of balancing the interests of the individual with those of society.

---

1 For discussions of crime literature, see Faller 1993, 4-31; and 1987, 203-208; Foucault 1977, 65-69; Rawlings 1992, 1-27; Richetti 1992, 23-59.

2 For the question of Defoe's authorship, see Furbank and Owens 1997.

3 Blackstone, arguably the foremost legal commentator of the age, explains: 'no counsel shall be allowed a prisoner [...] in any capital crime, unless some point of law shall arise proper to be debated' (1979, 349-350). Felons did not have the right to a defence lawyer until 1836.

4 Swift famously defined lawyers as 'a society of men' skilled 'in the art of proving by words multiplied for the purpose, that white is black, and black is white' (1988, 296).

Defoe opens his address 'To the Citizens of London and Westminster', which introduces John Sheppard's narrative, with an appeal to the readers' collective understanding of crime: 'Experience has confirm'd you in that everlasting Maxim, that there is no other way to protect the Innocent, but by Punishing the Guilty.' Exploiting the popularity of the criminal biography, he articulates – and arguably feeds – public fear of crime: 'At this time the most flagrant Offenses, as Burning of Dwellings; Burglaries, and Highway Robberies abound,' promising, 'here's a Criminal bids Defiance to your Laws'. The 'your' is significant here, implying collective ownership of the law, depicted as a protective force, 'providing necessary and wholesome Laws against these evils' (Defoe 1968, 234-235). Defoe here reflects contemporary juridical discourse: James Mountagu charged the jury: 'the Law is the Safeguard [...] the Custody of all private Interest' (Lamoine 1992, 141).

This collective social interest is traditionally embodied in the jury. The magistrate Henry Jodrell identified the importance of this public role in justice: 'you may be able, collectively, to redress what, in your private capacities, you have had occasion, individually, to complain of' (Lamoine 1992, 78). The public also played a role in the legal system as spectators: Hay notes that 'Tradesmen and labourers journeyed in to enjoy the spectacle, meet friends, attend the court and watch executions' (Hay 1975, 27). Fielding criticised this practice as 'mak[ing] a holiday for, and [...] entertain[ing] the mob', acknowledging that 'Foreigners have found fault with the cruelty of the English drama, in representing frequent murders upon the stage' (Fielding 1967, 123).

Beccaria problematised the spectacle of justice: 'The penalty of death becomes for most men a spectacle, and for a few an object of compassion mingled with indignation, one or other of these sentiments occupying the spectator's mind to the exclusion of that salutory dread which the law pretends to inspire' (Beccaria 1996, 55). Fielding objected similarly that the sight of 'a poor wretch, bound in a cart, just on the verge of eternity, all pale and trembling' (Fielding 1967, 123) will raise compassion, not disgust, in the heart of the spectator.[5] The legal rationale for public executions lay largely in their function as a deterrent from crime; it was therefore crucial that they had the right impact on the audience. Fielding acknowledged, 'No man indeed of common humanity or common sense can think of a man and a few shillings to be of an equal consideration,' but argued that the terror of the example of execution is an effective deterrent; hence, 'one man is sacrificed to the preservation of thousands' (120-121).

Spectators debated issues of justice both at the Sessions and subsequently in coffee houses and taverns, providing an informal verdict of their own.[6] We see the significance of such informal trials in many Charges to the Jury, which, delivered in public, addressed both formal and informal juries and sought not only to explain the

---

5 He also objected to the possible glorification of the criminal: 'His procession [...] attended with the compassion of the meek and tender-hearted, and with the applause, admiration, and envy, of all the bold and hardened' (Fielding 1967, 122).

6 Beccaria argues that 'Proceedings and proofs of guilt alike should be public' (1996, 25). Linebaugh suggests that this 'counter-theatre of the Old Bailey' provided more considered verdicts than 'the hurried agreements of jurors who couldn't avoid a Shylock reasoning' (1991, 87-88).

law but to encourage belief in the universality of justice, collective ownership of the system: 'We All', declared a Guilford magistrate, 'in our Several Stations, Partake of its supposed Virtue and Effects' (Lamoine 1992, 298).[7] Prisoners were able to watch the proceedings at the Sessions House from where they stood fettered, paralleling the role of the public as spectators but with a particular professional interest, often informed by studying legal books in prison, sometimes with the help of law students (see Linebaugh 1991, 75-77; Sheehan 1977, 237).

Defoe exploits public interest in trials in *Moll Flanders,* presenting every step of the judicial process, encouraging the reader to enter imaginatively into its various stages; as Zomchick notes of contemporary collections of trial narratives, 'readers become [...] unofficial magistrates' (Zomchick 1989, 540).

Moll is indicted on two counts: larceny and burglary. She insists, 'I had neither broken any thing to get in, nor carried any thing out,' echoing the legal definition of larceny: Blackstone notes that 'there must not only be a taking, but a *carrying away*' (Blackstone 1979, 231). She is clearly guilty, admitting to the reader, 'certain it was, that I had taken the Goods, and that I was bringing them away', but she also faces a charge of burglary. Wood notes in his *Institute*, 'there must be an *Entry*' such as 'Draw[ing] the Latch' or 'Setting the Foot over the Threshold after the Door is Broke open' (Wood 1728, 3: 377). Moll insists in full cognisance of the legal implications, 'they stop'd me before I had set my Foot clear of the Threshold' (Defoe 1989, 348, 362, 361).[8]

Moll is found 'Guilty of Felony, but' is 'acquitted of the Burglary', presumably because the incident took place in the daytime and theft was only deemed burglary if it occurred at night.[9] She realises that the distinction is somewhat academic: they are both capital crimes. She is temporarily speechless when she is brought before the Judges to be sentenced, but an anonymous voice, presumably that of a clerk of the court, prompts her to plead with the Judges, who have the power to recommend a reprieve or a pardon. Moll is asked, 'What I had to say, why Sentence should not pass', referring to the *allocutus.*[10] She knows that she is on tenuous ground, 'I had nothing to say to stop the Sentence' (362); she cannot plead benefit of clergy because, as Blackstone explains, it was denied 'in all larcinies to the value of 40 *s.* from a dwelling-house' even 'without breaking in' (Blackstone 1979, 240). Yet as a graduate of the Newgate school of law, Moll recognises that she has other options: the death sentence did not necessarily mean death.

---

7 Georges Lamoine notes in his introduction to *Charges to the Grand Jury*: 'Considering the publicity given to the sessions, the importance of the magistrate's speech to the crowd, always restless and ready to riot, could be considerable' (1992, 8).

8 For a more detailed account of the legal context to Moll's trial, see Swan 1998.

9 Wood explains, 'If the like Offence is Committed by Day, It is call'd *House-breaking*' (1728, 3: 376).

10 The accused was given the opportunity to speak not to argue in mitigation but to present anything which would prevent the court from pronouncing judgement: presentation of a pardon already granted, a plea for benefit of clergy, or a plea of pregnancy, which entitled women to a respite from judgement until the birth of the baby.

Moll's plea is calculated according to specific legal criteria. She stresses 'the Circumstances' of the case: 'I had broken no Doors, and carried nothing off' (Defoe 1989, 362), presenting it as minor and as a 'first Offence' (363), exploiting the law which determined ironically that, in spite of the 'prevailing [...] fatal Report of being an old Offender [...] I was not in the Sense of the Law an old Offender' because 'I had never been before [the Judges] in a judicial way before' (371).

Moll is confident in her performance as lawyer, 'I spoke [...] in such a moving Tone [...] that I cou'd see it mov'd others to Tears' (363), but her rhetoric fails to convince the court and the Judges, who, seemingly omnipotent, pronounce the death sentence. Defoe evokes the powerful atmosphere of the courtroom, the process of judgement and the dramatic ceremony which surrounds it, designed to create awe in the 'spectators'. Fielding argued, 'It is not the essence of the thing itself, but the dress and apparatus of it which makes an impression on the mind' (Fielding 1967, 124). Dramatic and sombre robes reinforced the image of authority and, in an eighteenth-century context, the power of life and death, symbolised by the black cap worn when pronouncing the death penalty and the white gloves worn at the end of a 'maiden assize' when no prisoners had been condemned to death (see Hay 1975, 27-29).

Beccaria criticised 'the solemn priests of justice, who with tranquil indifference have a criminal dragged with slow ceremony to his death' (Beccaria 1996, 59), the word 'priests' reflecting the popular association of religion and law but also the authority over life and death, which many believed was usurped. Beccaria argued: 'men [...] have always believed that life should be at the mercy of none save that Necessity which rules the universe' (ibid.).

Defoe reflects accurately the reality of court procedure and language, a language which deliberately alienates itself from everyday life, highly formalised and symbolically powerful, with hidden meanings of life and death. As Swift's Gulliver comments: 'this society hath a peculiar cant and jargon of their own, that no other mortal can understand' (Swift 1988, 297).

It is tempting to assume that because the eighteenth-century criminal law system was 'one of the bloodiest criminal codes in Europe', as Douglas Hay assessment it (1975, 19), it was always inequitable. Beccaria's description eighteenth-century criminal punishment lends weight to Hay's thesis:

> the groans of the weak, sacrificed to cruel indifference and to wealthy idleness, the barbarous tortures that have been elaborated with prodigal and useless severity, to punish crimes unproven or illusory, the horrors of prison, compounded by that cruellest tormentor of the wretched, uncertainty, ought to have shaken into action that rank of magistrates who guide the opinions and minds of men. (Beccaria 1996, 8-9)

Fielding acknowledged, 'that many cart-loads of our fellow-creatures are once in six weeks carried to slaughter is a dreadful consideration' (Fielding 1967, 127).

However, legal theorists such as Blackstone and Beccaria testify the concern for justice from within the system itself, concern which is reflected in Charges given by individual magistrates. The Norfolk charges in 1767 indicate a tradition of genuine concern for the accused: 'the most tender Regard has always been had on the Tryal of [capital crimes] so as to preserve the Life of the Criminal where other Circumstances do not render him an Object unfitt for mercy' (Lamoine 1992, 378).

Zimmerman acknowledges that 'Justice is done at Moll's trial', but argues that it is achieved 'despite the legal system' (Zimmerman 1975, 103), citing the malice of the witnesses as an example. His cynicism is understandable but, in this case, it is misplaced. Moll receives a fair trial precisely because of the law, not in spite of it. The malice of the witness is irrelevant: Moll is guilty and it is the evidence which convicts, not private malice.

Courts were concerned not only with the nature of the crime but its motive. Moll pleads 'necessity', a common and often genuine excuse for crime, used in court to present the accused as a person of fundamentally good character and deserving of a pardon. Defoe's narrative reflects contemporary legal debate: Blackstone argues, 'theft, in case of hunger, is far more worthy of compassion, then when committed through avarice, or to supply one in luxurious excesses' (Blackstone 1979, 15). Beccaria argued, 'Who made these laws? Men of wealth and power who have never [...] had to share out a mouldy loaf of bread, to the innocent out-cry of their starving children,' declaring that theft 'is generally the crime of the wretched and the desperate' (Beccaria 1996, 57, 88).

Chief Justice Aston argued that theft could be motivated by 'a mere Spirit of Malice and Mischief', in which case 'nothing can be urged in the Mitigation of such Crimes, and they deservedly receive the utmost Severity in Punishment' (Lamoine 1992, 403). Moll comes closer to this kind of felon than to the thief who steals through poverty. She admits, 'as I was not at a loss to handle my Needle, it was very probable [...] I might have got my Bread honestly enough' (Defoe 1989, 267).

The debate concerning the bearing motive should have on punishment is reflected in literary criticism, with most scholars providing a very sympathetic jury. Starr argues, 'We are asked to distinguish between act and agent – between what Moll does and what she essentially is,' apparently falling victim to Moll's persuasive rhetoric (Starr 1970, 79).[11] He cites Defoe in support of this moral relativism: 'there are very few things in the world that are simply evil, but things are made circumstantially evil when they are not so in themselves' (ibid.). Yet, clearly much of Moll's criminal career is 'simply evil' rather than 'circumstantially evil', perhaps the most obvious example being preying on a young child. Starr argues that Moll 'distinguishes her essential self from her admittedly reprehensible doings' (80). Indeed, she does but we should not.

Hay notes, 'The grounds for mercy were ostensibly that the offence was minor, or that the convict was of good character, or that the crime [...] was not common enough [...] to require an exemplary hanging' (Hay 1975, 43) none of which apply to Moll. Not only do such popularly accepted extenuations for crime not apply to Moll, but aggravations do: Chief Justice Aston declared 'The principal Aggravations of Larceny are, where the felonious taking is from the Person, or from the House, and where it is

11 For other sympathetic readings of Moll and her crimes, see Watt 1967, 113-114 and 131; and Mitchell, who argues, 'Moll steals because she is poor and leads a moral life because she is prosperous' (1978, 17).

accompanied with the Circumstance of [...] putting in Fear' (Lamoine 1992, 403). The reader knows, although the court does not, that Moll is guilty of all of the above.

Nonetheless, her apparent penitence impresses the Ordinary, the Newgate prison chaplain, who gains her a reprieve, and she requests transportation.[12] Hay notes that 'Roughly half of those condemned to death during the eighteenth century did not go to the gallows, but were transported to the colonies or imprisoned' (Hay 1975, 43).[13] He cites transportation in a context of powerful ideologies of mercy, arguing that the courts were 'a selective instrument of class justice' (45), serving the ruling classes and their interests, 'yet simultaneously proclaim[ing] the law's incorruptible impartiality' (48) by occasionally sparing the lives of the poor, with pardons 'presented as acts of grace' (47). Swift highlights the potential injustice of the system through Gulliver, who explains: the 'method is short and commendable': 'the judge first sends to sound the disposition of those in power, after which he can easily hang or save the criminal, strictly preserving all the forms of law' (Swift 1988, 297).

While we need to allow for court rhetoric, many Charges to the Jury demonstrate genuine concern for justice, a concern which Hay acknowledges in parenthesis[14] but whose implications he does not address. A Guilford magistrate declared 'Those Forms of Government are the mildest and best that So temper their Justice and Mercy [...] Where Justice is not loose to range at large in an arbitrary cruell manner and carry its avenging Sword without control' (Lamoine 1992, 293).

Blackstone commented, 'juries, through compassion, will sometimes forget their oaths, and either acquit the guilty or mitigate the nature of the offence: and judges, through compassion, will respite one half of the convicts' (Blackstone 1979, 19). He declared the proper principles of law to be 'conformable to the dictates of truth and justice, the feelings of humanity, and the indelible rights of mankind' (3).

I would not want to echo Blackstone's at times disturbing confidence in eighteenth-century law, nor his assurance that 'the thorough and attentive contemplation of [the system] will furnish its best panegyric' (436). Nonetheless, this arch defender of English law argued: 'Where the evil to be prevented is not adequate to the violence of the preventive, a sovereign that thinks seriously can never justify such a law to the dictates of conscience and humanity' (10-11). Beccaria warned, 'let the laws be inexorable [...] but let the lawmaker be gentle, lenient, and humane [...] and let the public interest be the outcome of the interests of every individual' (Beccaria 1996, 69-70). Defoe anticipates such arguments in *Moll Flanders*.

---

12 Transportation was a form of pardon, when the sentence was commuted to a period of exile in the colonies. Baker notes that it 'was in regular use by 1615' and was so widespread in the eighteenth century 'that trial judges automatically prepared and returned to the secretary of state calendars of those convicted [...] marking those recommended for transportation, or for free pardons' (1977, 44).

13 Baker gives similar statistics (1977, 43).

14 Hay cites the case of a Chief Justice who expressed deep concern for a young girl he had sentenced to death for infanticide (1975, 29), and acknowledges that 'Visitors remarked on the extreme solicitude of judges for the rights of the accused, a sharp distinction from the usual practice of continental benches' (32).

Faller identifies the wider sociological significance of the system: 'The capture, trial, and punishment of criminals can [...] contribute to social solidarity, giving all good people occasion to reaffirm [...] the orthodoxies that bind them together' (Faller 1993, 91). Such ideological constructs form the backdrop to *Moll Flanders*, which represents Moll's experience as a kind of experiment in juridical mercy. Blackstone articulates the difficulties of judicature: 'It is, it must be owned, much *easier* to extirpate than to amend mankind' (Blackstone 1979, 17). Human justice is inevitably flawed, but Defoe considers ways in which it can be used equitably to balance the needs of society with those of the individual.

Backscheider argues pertinently that *Moll Flanders* 'include[s] powerful propaganda for the' Transportation Act of 1718 (1989, 485), which enabled courts to transport felons if they believed the death penalty to be too harsh and whipping too lenient.[15] Transportation was hardly an easy option, but as Moll admits, 'we shall all choose any thing rather than Death' (Defoe 1989, 371). Moll faces her juridical fate squarely, arguing, 'we should live as new People in a new World' (383). Her optimism reflects Defoe's belief in transportation as a means of rehabilitating felons, giving them the opportunity to break the pattern of crime, which for Moll has become something of an addiction and make a new life for themselves within society as opposed to in conflict with it.[16]

Foucault identifies two types of felon: '"monsters", moral or political, who have fallen outside the social pact', and 'the juridical subject rehabilitated by punishment' (Foucault 1977, 256). Defoe's representation of Moll is less clear-cut: the ideological focus of the text is not on Moll's repentance *per se*, but on the way in which the law can best deal with her. Repentance is significant not spiritually but insofar as it may indicate the likelihood of her re-offending. The fact that Moll does not re-offend testifies to the positive potential of transportation, although the cynical reader may counter that she has become wealthy and therefore has no need to return to crime.

Defoe has to balance the sympathetic aspects of his criminal's character and the ideological concerns which underpin the narrative. The reader may enjoy Moll's roguery, participating vicariously in her exploits. Yet Moll must be punished because she has consistently transgressed moral and social values (she has committed theft, bigamy and even contemplated murdering a child). By having the court find Moll guilty, Defoe gives the law its due and maintains respect for the system. However, if the death penalty were exacted, the reader would be likely to revolt against the very system Defoe is seeking to defend; as Blackstone explains, 'when the punishment surpasses all measure, the public will frequently out of humanity prefer impunity to it' (Blackstone 1979, 17). Beccaria argued that 'extreme severity of punishments' would 'contradict justice and the nature of the social contract itself' (Beccaria 1996, 15), declaring that unnecessarily severe punishment is actually contrary to the justice it

15 Prior to the Transportation Act, grand larceny (theft of goods worth more than twelve pence) was often punished by death. Convicted felons could not be sentenced to exile, although they could be pardoned on condition that they transport themselves voluntarily.

16 It is perhaps worth noting that, as a merchant, Defoe himself profited from transporting people. See Backscheider 1989, 485.

purports to serve. Defoe's representation of judicial clemency is vital in encouraging the reader to support the legal system. In this instance, at least, transportation serves the ideals of justice more effectively than the death penalty would. As Blackstone phrases it, the 'hope of transportation' prevents 'frequent [judicial] assassination and slaughter' (Blackstone 1979, 18).

However, Beccaria objected, 'by a long and almost wholly pointless slavery [transported felons] may set an example to nations they have never offended' (Beccaria 1996, 67), criticising 'the disorder of a penal system in which pardon and mercy are necessarily proportioned to the absurdity of laws and the appalling severity of sentences' (69). Blackstone identifies problems with the system of pardons which provide an effective context for reading Moll:

> Among so many chances of escaping, the needy or hardened offender overlooks the multiple that suffer [...] and, if unexpectedly the hand of justice overtakes him, he deems himself peculiarly unfortunate, in falling at last a sacrifice to those laws, which long impunity has taught him to contemn. (Blackstone 1979, 19)

Fielding argued that the hope of a pardon 'inspires men to face the danger' of law and, thus, 'the design of the law [to deter and thus prevent crime] is rendered totally ineffectual' (Fielding 1967, 120, 121). Defoe counters such objections by demonstrating that even a calculating criminal like Moll can change, at least in terms of behaviour, and no longer be a threat to society. In encouraging the reader to acknowledge the justice of transportation rather than execution in the case of Moll, guilty of grand larceny, the text invites us to support such mercy for people who have committed lesser crimes.

While in Newgate, Moll experiences what Bender refers to as 'A redemptive hell for the wayward soul, a reformative regime for the felonious mind.' He goes further than I would wish to do in arguing that Moll's 'secular rehabilitation is complete' (Bender 1987, 150, 47).[17] I am not convinced that Moll internalises the values of the juridical system, but she does learn to co-operate with it. More significantly, her apparent penitence makes her an appropriate candidate for clemency. Her willingness to accept her punishment suggests some form of rehabilitation in social if not spiritual terms.

The issue of penitence derives much of its significance in eighteenth-century terms from the parallel between human and divine judgement.[18] Eighteenth-century spectators assumed that those facing execution were going to face the ultimate court of Judgement Day, where truth would become apparent. Mr Baron Lovell charged the jury, 'If [God] has ordained eternal punishment to such as disobey his omnipotence, what insect will dare take the place of divine justice' (Lamoine 1992, 77-78).

Defoe's narrative shares with criminal biographies an interest in the circumstances and motivation for crime but also a religious context. *The Newgate Calendar,* one of the most popular collections of 'criminal lives', recounts criminal exploits (from minor

17 Faller discusses the significance of felons' repentance (1987, 98-109).

18 See Hay 1975, 29-30. The link between religion and law was further underlined by the assize sermon, preached by the sheriff's chaplain.

theft to a cannibal living in a cave in Scotland, who murdered and ate tourists).[19] It combines graphic detail of violent crime with a degree of moral earnestness in a manner which would make all but tabloid journalists blush, insisting not only on the horrors of the crime but the significance of the spiritual state of the criminal.

Joseph Blake, alias Blueskin, was indicted, like Moll, for theft. In spite of ingeniously cutting the famous Jonathan Wild's throat to prevent him from testifying, he was found guilty and was executed. However, unlike Moll, he 'did not shew a concern proportioned to his calamitous situation' and turned not to religion but to alcohol, 'observed to be intoxicated even while he was under the gallows' (Wilkinson 1991, 134-135).

Charges to the Jury regularly use religious language to exhort the audience; Sir John Gonson declared: 'the Fear of God, so manifestly tends to preserve the Peace of Society [...]. Take away Religion, and you take away with it mutual Faith and human Society, and the most Excellent of Virtues, Justice' (Lamoine 1992, 259). The law derives authority and majesty from Heaven itself, encouraging confidence in its workings. Beccaria declares, 'Divine justice and natural justice are of their essence constant and unchangeable,' but he acknowledges that human courts are but a pale reflection of divine justice: 'human justice, or rather political justice [...] can vary in proportion as [...] actions become useful or necessary to society' (Beccaria 1996, 5).

Human justice is further problematised by relying on fallible beings to interpret evidence. Beccaria argues: 'The gravity of sin depends upon the inscrutable wickedness of the heart. No finite being can know it without revelation' (78). 'Truth' in a human court is not an absolute but a probable, dependent on the interpretation of rhetorical figures. As Robert Frost famously commented, 'A Jury consists of twelve persons chosen to decide who has the best lawyer.'

It is these difficulties in interpreting the evidence, the 'truth', that Defoe explores in *Moll Flanders*, leaving the reader with what Posner refers to as 'the problematics of interpretation.'[20] His text grapples with issues of justice which have yet to be resolved, difficulties in reconciling practice and principle in a system struggling with the contradiction of principles of justice and the common good sitting alongside what Beccaria referred to as 'cold, legalized barbarity' (Beccaria 1996, 8). Many Charges to the Jury stress the importance of equitable application of the law: a Guilford magistrate declared 'All Laws [...] are no more than a dead letter, except they are enliven'd and actuated by a fair and due Execution' (Lamoine 1992, 294). We will find much in the eighteenth-century legal system to exercise our cynicism, but this should not blind us to its genuine engagement with ideals of justice. Defoe reflects the discourse of magistrates who sought to apply the law humanely and consistently, inviting the public's confidence in law as a protective force against Hobbesian 'wildness of ungoverned Multitude' (283). Defoe articulates the ideal, if not always the

---

19 For the character of Sawny Beane, see Smith 1973, 138.

20 Posner provides a useful introduction to the theoretical issues raised by the study of literature and law, noting the 'parallel concern with the problematics of interpretation' and discussing the ways in which 'Judges and other lawyers resemble literary artists in the close attention they pay to the choice of words' (1988, 11).

practice, of eighteenth-century law, charging his jury as a Guilford magistrate exhorted his: 'Our laws are neither writ in Sand nor with Blood' (ibid.).

REFERENCES

Baker, J.H. (1977). 'Criminal Courts and Procedure at Common Law 1550-1800.' In J.S. Cockburn (ed.), *Crime in England 1550-1800*. London: Methuen, 15-48.

Backscheider, Paula R. (1989). *Daniel Defoe: His Life*. London: Johns Hopkins Press.

Beccaria, Cesare (1996). *On Crimes and Punishments*. New York: Marsilio Publishers. Original edition 1764.

Bender, John (1987). *Imagining the Penitentiary: Fiction and the Architecture of Mind in Eighteenth-Century England*. London: University of Chicago Press.

Blackstone, William (1979). *Commentaries on the Laws of England: A Facsimile of the First Edition of 1765-1769*. Vol. 4: *Of Public Wrongs*. Chicago: University of Chicago Press. Original edition London, 1769.

Defoe, Daniel (1968). *The History of John Sheppard*. In *Selected Poetry and Prose of Daniel Defoe*. Ed. M.F. Shugrue. London: Holt, Rinehart and Winston. Original edition 1724.

________ (1989). *Moll Flanders*. Ed. David Blewett. London: Penguin. Original edition 1722.

Faller, Lincoln B. (1987). *Turned to Account: The Forms and Functions of Criminal Biography in Late Seventeenth- and Early Eighteenth-Century England*. Cambridge: Cambridge University Press.

________ (1993). *Crime and Defoe: A New Kind of Writing*. Cambridge: Cambridge University Press.

Fielding, Henry (1967). *An Enquiry Into the Causes of the Late Increase of Robbers*. In *The Complete Works of Henry Fielding*. Vol. 7: *Legal Writings*. London: Cass. Original edition 1751.

Foucault, Michel (1977). *Discipline and Punish: The Birth of the Prison*. Trans. Alan Sheridan. London: Penguin. Orignal edition 1975.

Furbank, P.N., and W.R. Owens (1997). 'The Myth of Defoe as "Applebee's Man."' *Review of English Studies* NS 48, 198-204.

Hay, Douglas (1975). 'Property, Authority and the Criminal Law.' In D. Hay, P. Linebaugh, J.G. Rule, E.P. Thompson, and C. Winslow (eds.), *Albion's Fatal Tree: Crime and Society in Eighteenth-Century England*. London: Allen Lane, 17-63.

Linebaugh, Peter (1991). *The London Hanged: Crime and Civil Society in the Eighteenth Century*. London: Penguin.

Lamoine, Georges, ed. (1992). *Charges to the Grand Jury 1689-1803*. London: Royal Historical Society.

McLynn, Frank (1989). *Crime and Punishment in Eighteenth-Century England*. London: Routledge.

Mitchell, Juliet (1978). 'Introduction.' In Daniel Defoe, *The Fortunes and Misfortunes of the Famous Moll Flanders*. Ed. J. Mitchell. Harmondsworth: Penguin.

Posner, Richard (1988). *Law and Literature: A Misunderstood Relation*. London: Harvard University Press.

Rawlings, Philip, ed. (1992). *Drunks, Whores and Idle Apprentices: Criminal Biographies of the Eighteenth Century*. London: Routledge.

Richetti, John J. (1992). *Popular Fiction Before Richardson: Narrative Patterns, 1700-1739*. Oxford: Clarendon Press.

Secord, Arthur W., ed. (1938). *Defoe's Review*. Reproduced from the orig. ed., with an intro. and bibliographical notes. New York: Columbia University Press. Original edition London, 1704-1713.

Sheehan, W.J. (1977). 'Finding Solace in Eighteenth-Century Newgate.' In J.S. Cockburn (ed.), *Crime in England 1550-1800*. London: Methuen, 229-245.

Smith, Capt. Alexander (1973). *Memoirs of the Life and Times of the Famous Jonathan Wilde, Together with the History and Lives of Modern Rogues [...]*. Facsimile edition with an introduction by Malcolm J. Bosse. New York: Garland Publishing. Original edition London, 1726.

Starr, George A. (1970). *'Moll Flanders.'* In R.C. Elliott (ed.), *Twentieth-Century Interpretations of* Moll Flanders. Englewood Cliffs, NJ: Prentice Hall, 78-94.

Swan, Beth (1998). 'Moll Flanders: The Felon as Lawyer.' *Eighteenth-Century Fiction* 11, 33-48.

Swift, Jonathan (1988). *Gulliver's Travels*. Ed. Peter Dixon and John Chalker. London: Penguin. Original edition 1726.

Watt, Ian (1967). *The Rise of the Novel: Studies in Defoe, Richardson and Fielding*. London: Chatto and Windus.

Wilkinson, G.T., ed. (1991). *The Newgate Calendar*. London: Sphere Books.

Wood, Thomas (1728). *An Institute of the Laws of England.* 4 Vols. 4th ed. London: Lintot and Williamson.

Zimmerman, Everett (1975). *Defoe and the Novel*. London: University of California Press.

Zomchick, John P. (1989). 'A Penetration which Nothing Can Deceive.' *Studies in English Literature* 29, 535-561.

Greta Olson

KEYHOLES IN EIGHTEENTH-CENTURY NOVELS AS LIMINAL SPACES BETWEEN THE PUBLIC AND PRIVATE SPHERES

The height of embarrassment is when two sets of eyes meet through a keyhole. (Unknown)

Creating the space in which this conference becomes possible is Habermas' seminal thesis that a public sphere of literate private individuals arose in the eighteenth century that provided a buffer between the intimate sphere of the conjugal family and the domain of institutionalised authority (Habermas 1962). Coffee houses and voluntary organisations described this public sphere, and a print culture featuring pamphlets, periodicals, and newspapers grew up to feed its needs. Ian Watt's *The Rise of the Novel* (1957) tells another story about the time in question. Watt suggests that the rise of the mercantile middle class in England led to a preoccupation with the detailed life stories of non-aristocratic individuals: Daniel Defoe's *Robinson Crusoe* (1719) tells of a rebellious middle-class son who leaves his family to seek his fortune and remakes the world on an island, and his *Moll Flanders* (1722) describes a highly sympathetic prison-born thief and occasional prostitute's rise to respectability and prosperity in the new world. Through perseverance, energy, and self-confidence, the middle and lower-class protagonists create themselves anew in a literal and representational new world order (Watt 1987).

Both the stories that Watt and Habermas tell have undergone revision in recent years. Habermas has been criticised for his neglect of all those who were excluded in the public domain: the underclass and women.[1] Watt's portrait of the development of the novel as a result of the emergence of an educated, ambitious middle class has likewise been challenged for being too monolithic in design and negligent of questions of gender.[2]

Into the space created by the breaks in these stories appears the figure of the keyhole, a recurrent image in literature in general, and an important trope in the eighteenth-century novel. Specifically, this paper addresses the keyholes in one text. Having taught Samuel Richardson's epistolary novel *Clarissa* (1747-1748), and having witnessed students' dumbfounded reactions to a book that describes in over sixteen-hundred pages how a libertine gentleman devises plots to seduce a meticulously virginal young lady, I found it necessary as an instructor to try to provide a key to the seemingly formidable lock of this text. Students asked, 'Didn't he, Lovelace, have

---

1 Habermas himself has revised his initial argument to admit that his original conception of the bourgeois public sphere was too homogenous and overly idealised in that it ignored some of the exclusionary practices and patriarchal aspects of the sphere it described. See his 'Further Reflections' (Habermas 1992).

2 On Watt's neglect of questions of gender and sexuality, see Armstrong 1987, 7, 268; for a summary of criticism on Watt's account of the novel's development as being too simplistic in his descriptions of genre, realism, and class, see McKeon 1987, 1-4.

anything else to do with his time other than to write letters and drive this lady crazy?' Lovelace writes approximately 14,000 words on 10 June, the same day on which he masterminds several complicated plots in order to trick Clarissa into returning to London with him. Revealing our own middle-class ethos, the students asked, 'Why doesn't he get a job?' Or, they commented that Clarissa frankly got on their nerves with her endless stress on virtue and decorum. 'Why,' students asked, 'doesn't she ever have fun? If she's so feisty to Solmes – the slimy guy her family wants her to marry (she refuses to be near him and likens him to a frog) – why can't she be more forceful towards Lovelace?'

While the main text I wish to address is *Clarissa*, I hope to offer a keyhole view onto other prose texts of the time and the cultural field out of which they arose and into which they were received. Keyholes in literature represent liminal spaces between the emerging and interdependent public and private spheres during the long eighteenth century. The development of a predominantly masculinised public sphere and realm of public opinion led by definition to the simultaneous emergence and delineation of a privatised feminine sphere of domesticity and decorum. Fictional keyholes provide a glimpse at the interrelation between the two.

Keyholes make practices of privacy manifest. The *Lexikon des Mittelalters* describes the development of individual cells in monasteries as reflecting a new awareness of monks' differing reading habits as well as reflecting the perception of an increased need for privacy. Spaces separated originally only by fabric were increasingly closed in with wood or walls. Doors were installed with openings – originally to look through – which became consistently smaller, until they were replaced by keyholes. Each monk possessed the key to his own cell (Lentes 1998, 520-521). Historically, then, keyholes function both as visual frames and as modes of ensuring privacy.

Prior to the seventeenth century, keyholes to living spaces were usually only to be found on the outside of buildings. Shakespeare's *Richard III* offers literary documentation of this. With the following words, Lady Anne laments over the hearse of Henry VI: 'poor key-cold figure of a holy king, [...] stabbed by the selfsame hands that made these holes' (Shakespeare 2000, 158: 1.2.5-11). The image of the stiff cadaver of Anne's father-in-law as a 'key-cold' king would have been clear to contemporary audiences because keys were kept in or near doors leading to the outside at the time. Furthermore, they would have stayed cold, because of their large size (158, n.5).

Architecturally, the move from cold keys to exterior doors to warm keys hidden in the bosoms of letter-writing protagonists was marked by a move to smaller rooms. 'Special rooms for the individual family members' replaced great halls and family rooms (Trevelyn, quoted in Habermas 1989, 45). Increasingly, homes contained spaces for the individual to be alone rather than to spend time with others. Furthermore, locks on interior doors became commonplace (Watt 1987, 188-199).

The newly perceived need for privacy as translated into interior architecture has been understood as a shift to an individualism in which the self was defined through the degree to which one could control how much one was seen (Gillis 1984, 6-7).

Clarissa's personal space in the Harlowe home consists of her parlour, her chamber, and a smaller writing closet with a windowed door and a curtain which she closes for further privacy. During the first third of the novel, she increasingly retreats into the inner recesses of this space in order to write.

In their most obvious function, keyholes and keys demarcate private property and claims to property in *Clarissa*. While still the privileged and most-beloved daughter of the Harlowe home, Clarissa carries all the keys to the manor. Substituting for her mother – due to her excellent qualities as a homemaker – she has the power to open all the stores in the house. This highlights Clarissa's value as an overseer of property – the idealised gender role at the time[3] – and her relatively high level of authority in the paternalistic Harlowe home. When Clarissa is punished by her family for her suspected romantic attachment to Lovelace and her refusal to marry the hideous Solmes, her keys are taken from her and she is discharged of 'mistressly management' (Richardson 1985, 183 [Letter 40]).[4] As she writes to her best friend Anna, 'This moment the keys of everything are taken from me' (116 [L 21]). Later, the family confiscates the keys to her 'cabinet, library, and drawers' (313 [L 78]). Divested of authority, Clarissa is made a prisoner in her family home; her private things are searched for incriminating evidence of correspondence with Lovelace.

The Harlowes keep Clarissa under lock and key because they regard her as a piece of property – a potentially highly profit-bringing one: if she married Solmes, the total liquid value of the Harlowes would substantially increase through the addition of his lands. By contrast, Lovelace's claim through marriage to Clarissa's inheritance from her grandfather represents a clear liability to the family. As Nancy Armstrong points out, girls of propertied families represented potential forms of capital for their husbands' families, and possible liabilities for their families of origin: husbands gained access to the capital of their wives' families and could potentially make their in-laws liable for their acquired debts (Armstrong 1999, 27-29).

The Harlowes' locking up Clarissa and, conversely, her locking herself away from her family and then from Lovelace in order to stay safe provide manifestations of opinions about the degree to which a young woman had the right to take possession of herself. Neither her family nor Lovelace take Clarissa's repeated wish to remain single seriously. As James writes in an incensed letter to Clarissa:

---

3 Nancy Armstrong argues, in her study *Desire and Domestic Fiction*, that domestic fiction of the eighteenth century and conduct books inaugurated a change from celebrating the surface values and shine of aristocratic women to valuing the inner qualities of the domesticated middle-class woman. Fiction encouraged women to supervise conduct and maintain objects and household ledgers in the private household after the model of Pamela (Armstrong 1987, 277-278). Puritan values were propagated: men should acquire wealth, women should oversee and tend it; men should transverse the public world, women should guard their virtue by controlling whom they saw and who saw them. Both sexes should carefully use and guard their time (18-19, 110-134).

4 Because each text contains different material, three editions of *Clarissa* were used in this paper. Most frequently, quotations are taken from the 1985 Penguin *Clarissa*, which is a complete text of the first edition. Later changes to the text made by Richardson in response to criticism, including didactic footnotes and disparaging images of Lovelace, can be found in the later editions of *Clarissa*.

> [Lovelace] says you are *his*, and *shall* be *his*, and he will be the death of any man who robs him of his PROPERTY. So, miss, we have a mind to try this point with him. My father supposing he has the right of a father in his child is absolutely determined not to be bullied out of that right. (Richardson 1985, 223 [L 52])

Clarissa's painful incarceration and the struggle to control point to the central theme of the novel. As the subtitle claims, this story '*comprehend*[*s*] THE MOST IMPORTANT CONCERNS OF PRIVATE LIFE *And particularly showing* THE DISTRESSES THAT MAY ATTEND THE MISCONDUCT BOTH OF PARENTS AND CHILDREN; IN RELATION TO MARRIAGE.'

The novel explores how parents should handle maturing daughters, husbands their wives, and how daughters should respond appropriately to their parents' and husbands' claims upon them as property and subservient members of the family group. In letters to mostly-female correspondents, Richardson repeatedly underlines the moral of the tale: 'One great Design of this Piece, was to enforce the Duty of Children to Parents, whether Parents did theirs or not; and to hold out a Warning to parents in the Punishment worse than that of Death, of the Harlowe-Parents for their Defects in theirs' (Richardson 1964, 199-200). The misuse of patriarchal and filial power may be documented in the first names of Clarissa's father and brother. James Senior and James Junior may refer to James I and II, and James Jr's absurd and ugly grasping for power in his family may relate to James II's belief in his divine authority as king.

The issue of property in *Clarissa* relates closely to that of rape. As has been documented in secondary literature on Clarissa, in the eighteenth century, 'rape' was punished more for the loss of private property it represented than for the violence done to an individual. Had James Harlowe Sr sued Lovelace for the crime of 'seduction' (speak 'rape'), it would have been on the basis of his entitlement to damages for the loss of his daughter's services to him (Schwarz 1999, 272). Had he taken Lovelace to court for abduction – Clarissa is abducted twice: once, with some degree of free will, from her father's house; once, wholly against her will, from the boarding house she has run away to in Hampstead – it would have been on the basis of the loss of property. Both methods of legal address would have required Clarissa to act as a 'prosecutorix' of Lovelace in court, and providing detailed evidence against him.

Lovelace shows how unlikely it was for him to have been prosecuted when he writes to his friend:

> For a rape, thou knowest, to us rakes is far from being an undesirable thing. Nothing but the law stands in our way, upon that account; and the opinion of what a modest woman will suffer rather than become a *vive voce* accuser, lessens much an honest fellow's apprehensions on that score (Richardson 1985, 896-897 [L 261.1])

Lovelace's most callous plot to rape Clarissa's best friend and her best friend's mother displays Richardson's knowledge of criminal procedure at the time. Added to later editions of the novel in response to many readers' wishes that Clarissa marry Lovelace, this episode describes Lovelace's plan to rape Anna, her mother, and her maid while they are underway to the Isle of Wight. After the fact, he pictures how he will proceed from the prison to the sessions house with a bevy of young ladies to accompany him, all dressed in white and begging for mercy in sentencing. Blame, Lovelace judges, will fall on the women for prosecuting at all and not on handsome Lovelace. And Lovelace's family will make sure he doesn't hang (Richardson 1833c, 190 [L 34]).

Clarissa confirms Lovelace's view when she writes to her spiritual mentor, Rev Lewen, in response to his insistence that she prosecute her abuser: 'It would no doubt have been a ready retort from *every* mouth, that I ought not to have thrown myself into the power of such a man, and that I ought to take for my pains what had befallen me' (Richardson 1985, 1253 [L 428]). Clarissa accurately lists all the ambiguities of her case: she left willingly with Lovelace the first time. To prove the trickery involved in this is well nigh impossible. She lived with him – apparently willingly – under one roof for several weeks, without her complaining of his having violated her. Finally, Lovelace's family is simply too powerful to allow the full measure of the law to be taken. And what would have been required of Clarissa in terms of testimony against Lovelace is inconceivable to her. As a review of abduction and seduction cases shows, 'for a woman to prevail within the legal system was an excruciating ordeal, even when she did win' (Schwarz 1999, 299).

Keyholes also find metaphorical usage in *Clarissa*. Just after her rape under drugs, when Clarissa becomes cognisant of what has happened to her, she writes:

> Oh! Lovelace! if you could be sorry for yourself, I would be sorry too – but when all my doors are fast, and nothing but the key-hole open, and the key of late put into that, to be where you are, in a manner without opening any of them – Oh wretched, wretched Clarissa Harlowe!
> (Richardson 1985, 894 [L 261.1])

Here, the keyhole has a double meaning. On the one hand, the forcing of the lock represents Lovelace's physical violation of Clarissa. On the other hand, however, Clarissa's personhood has not been penetrated by him at all. Lovelace has not opened 'any' of 'her doors'. Having fought fiercely to escape her rapist and having been violated while doped, Clarissa retains a sense of her deepest self as being unimpeachable. In the last third of *Clarissa*, the protagonist appears ever more saintly before she dies and her complete story is made public by her friends. Just after her rape, she tears her clothes and writes fragmented pieces of text. Yet she gradually rebuilds her sense of self as she succeeds in getting away from Lovelace and in controlling her own space and thoughts again. On her journey from the scene of her rape to her coffin, she transforms the violation of her body into a form of transcendence over materiality. Her coffin, her final resting place, resembles a keyhole or liminal space in that it marks the site of her passage into the hereafter.

The notion of the secrets of selfhood as being figuratively represented by a locked keyhole is reiterated by Richardson in his last novel, *Sir Charles Grandison* (1751). Here, Harriet Bryon, who loves the eponymous hero, writes about what his sister says of his sense of privacy regarding his emotions: he has 'double-locked the door of his heart, and left open not so much as the key-hole uncovered by which I might have peeped into it' (Richardson 1833d, 221). Again, the deepest self is signified as residing behind a locked door. Personhood is understood in terms of ownership of hidden valuables.

Keyholes, locks, and keys function as metaphors for sexuality in *Clarissa*. The amatory promise of these images was not new to Richardson, however. Henry Fielding reminds us of Pyramus and Thisbe, the lovers from Greek mythology who communicated through a hole in the wall between their homes (Fielding 1996, 48). And as early as Gottfried von Straßburg's *Tristan* (1210), one may find the simile for sexual love in the form of a locked door. This text describes a locked door in the cave of love where Tristan and Isolde run away to. If this door is opened by 'Deceit or Force' rather than willingly from within, this 'betokens Treachery' (Gottfried von Straßburg 1960, 265).[5]

Most particularly, keyholes relate to voyeuristic sexual pleasure in *Clarissa*, both Lovelace's and the reader's. As Ian Watt writes,

> Richardson's impersonal and anonymous role allowed him to project his own secret fantasies into a mysterious next room; and the privacy and anonymity of print placed the reader behind a keyhole where he, too, could peep in unobserved and witness rape being prepared, attempted, and eventually carried out. (Watt 1987, 199)

Peeping is the theme of Laura Mulvey's analysis of scopophilia in which she takes up Freud's theory of sexual perversion to isolate the objectifying gaze of desire in the context of film. For Mulvey, the eye of the movie producer and viewer is a male one, possessing agency, whereas the female is represented in fragmented body parts as passive. This dichotomy between gaze and object, activity and passivity, has deep roots in Western culture:

> In a world ordered by sexual imbalance, pleasure in looking has been split between active/male and passive/female. The determining male gaze projects its fantasy onto the female figure, which is styled accordingly. In their traditional exhibitionist role, women are simultaneously looked at and displayed, with their appearance coded for strong visual and erotic impact so that they can be said to connote *to-be-looked-at-ness*. (Mulvey 1989, 19)

In a later formulation of her original thesis, Mulvey cites the image of a prone and chained Andromeda of Greek myth being saved by Perseus, who literally flies in and slays the monster that threatens her (32). Similarly, we find the phenomenon of scopism in eighteenth-century texts in which sex and visual desire often provide the impulse to move the plot along.

The reader experiences scopic pleasure with Lovelace in proxy. Lovelace's will to dominate over Clarissa and revenge himself on her family translates into his visual desire for her. In three separate scenes, Lovelace or his underling, Dorcas, peep through the keyhole into Clarissa's chamber to observe her. Lovelace's fantasies are cinematic:

---

5 'On the inside, across the door of bronze, there ran two bars. Inside, too, there was a latch most ingeniously let through the wall, where Tristan, indeed, had found it. This latch was governed by a lever, which passed from the outside to the inside and guided it this way and that. There was neither lock nor key to it, and I will tell you why. There was no lock for this reason – that any device which one applies to a door (I mean on the outside) for the purpose of opening and shutting it, betokens Treachery. For when anyone enters at Love's door who has not been admitted from within, it cannot be accounted Love, since it is either Deceit or Force. Love's gate is there to prevent it, the door of bronze bars the way [...]' (Gottfried von Straßburg 1960, 264-265).

> And now imagine (the charmer overcome) thou seest me sitting supinely cross-kneed, reclining on my sofa, the god of love dancing in my eyes and rejoicing in every mantling feature; the sweet rogue, late such a proud rogue, wholly in my power, moving up slowly to me at my beck, with heaving sighs, half-pronounced upbraidings from murmuring lips, her finger in her eye, and quickening her pace at my *Come hither, dearest!* (Richardson 1962, 211)

As the rape draws closer to being committed, Lovelace's visual encroachments on Clarissa's body increase. Against her will, he removes the handkerchiefs over Clarissa's breasts in order to kiss 'the beauty of beauties' (Richardson 1985, 705 [L 220]) and complains to Belford that she is 'ashamed to communicate to her adorer's sight' such visual delights. Similarly, after Lovelace has set a fire in Sinclair's house at night so as to gain access to Clarissa's rooms, he relishes the sight of her in her under-petticoat with bared arms and half-uncovered bosom. Although Richardson condemns Lovelace's actions and sentences him to a dramatic death, he nonetheless invites his reader to identify with the rapist and enjoy the sight of Clarissa's revealed flesh and the fantasy of her sexual subjugation.

Key and keyhole provide a metaphorical synecdoche for the male and female body during coitus. That Clarissa is treated as a piece of property to be locked up and unlocked at the will of her owner makes this meaning of the keyhole all the more vivid. When Clarissa agrees to 'unbolt' the garden house door to meet Lovelace at her family home, he is 'sure of her' (399 [L 99]). Indeed, with this action Clarissa does open herself to being abducted by Lovelace and to being seen – in the world's eye – as culpable for this abduction. When she attempts to leave Lovelace by opening the door to the garden with a key, he takes it from her, gives it back to her, and takes it again as if to double lock the door. The imagery of opening the closed hymen is clear. Similarly, Lovelace narrates how he hears Clarissa's door 'unbar, unbolt, unlock, and open' (723 [L 225]) as he anticipates seeing her in her nightdress.

Clarissa is not the only novel of the period in which keyholes are infused with sexual connotations. In Richardson's first novel, *Pamela; or, Virtue Rewarded* (1740), the keyhole provides a means for Mr B's spying on the object of his desire, his servant Pamela. In a scene that is emblematic of much of the action of the novel, Pamela resists Mr B's attempts to put her on his knee, kiss her neck and lips, and put his hand in her bosom. She runs into another room and locks the door behind her. Mr B, the force of whose passion makes him resemble more a rabid dog than anything else, rips off a piece of her gown that was caught in the door. Pamela faints – as she will do often in the novel – and awakens: 'for I fell into a fit with my terror, and there I lay, till he, as I suppose, looking through the key-hole, spyed me upon the floor, stretched out at length, on my face' (Richardson 1833a, 26). This image is classically erotic: the partially dressed prone body of the woman lies supine and not entirely conscious. Think of Heinrich von Kleist's *Marquise von O*, or any number of scenes in which the view of the supine female body is described as inflaming male desire. The checking agent on Mr B is, of course, the locked door – a door which he has symbolically tried to rip open, just as he rips off part of Pamela's dress, and just as he will later try to rip the flesh of her hymen. Throughout the first part of *Pamela* – which ends in the marriage and domestication of Mr B's seemingly unchecked desire, and with the elevation of Pamela from servant and potential rape victim to honoured wife and mistress of the household – Pamela uses keys and doors to effect her escapes from Mr B's persecutions. Often, to find peace of mind, she locks herself into her closet to write to her parents or other sympathetic individuals. Kept prisoner at Mr B's house in Lincolnshire, she sleeps with her hands on the keys and double locks the doors to her bedroom.

Accepting the 'domesticity thesis' that British conduct books and fiction in the manner of Richardson led to the construction of female subjectivity as domesticated, emotional, and essentially private (Armstrong 1987, 14-15), we find *Pamela* to be a didactic piece on how girls and boys of the period should behave. With a clever mix of ostentatious modesty and almost aggressive virtuousness, and relying upon an ample use of locks and doors, Pamela transforms Mr B's libertine assumption that he has the right to possess her body into a wish to have access to her mind. By taking control of the phallic key and pen, and in displaying her control of these implements to be good and virtuous, Pamela rewrites Mr B into a doting husband and transforms the place where she resides: in Richardson's own words, 'now her prison has become her palace' (1833a, lxxii).

The sexual significance of the keyhole scene in *Pamela* was not lost on those who satirically rewrote her Cinderella story and who questioned how much her virtuousness was, in fact, a strategy to acquire money and power. The title of Eliza Haywood's text speaks for itself: *Anti-Pamela: or Feign'd Innocence Detected; In a series of Syrena's Adventures. A Narrative which has really its Foundation in Truth and Nature; and at the same time that it entertains, by a vast variety of suprizing Incidents, arms against a partial Credulity, by shewing the Mischiefs that frequently arise from a too sudden Admiration. Publish'd as a necessary Caution to all Young Gentleman* (1741). This text, portraying Syrena Tricksy's efforts to marry her master, points out the calculated nature of Pamela's virtuousness. Knowing that Syrena is willing to meet him clandestinely, Mr L. uses the keyhole to make sure he is meeting the right person (Haywood 1741, 70). The heroine's frequently 'mewing herself up' (71), or locking herself in, is accurately perceived by the other servants as part of a larger plan for Miss Tricksy's enlarging herself socially.

Similarly, Henry Fielding's satire of *Pamela* pokes fun at Richardson's lock and key motif. Entitled *An Apology for the Life of Mrs. Shamela Andrews. In which, the many notorious Falshoods and Misrepresentations of a Book called* Pamela, *Are exposed and refuted; and all the matchless Arts of that young Politician, set in a true and just Light* (1741; see Fielding 1987a), *Shamela* features a staged near-rape scene in which Mrs Jervis consciously leaves the bedroom door open so that Squire Booby can have perfect access to 'Sham'. Feigning sleep while her lover lies hidden in bed beside her, Shamela screams and then pretends to faint when Squire Booby (rather than Mr B) puts his hands on her breasts. This scene draws him one step closer to proposing marriage. In these critical rewritings of Richardson's story of how goodness can beget riches and respectability, keyholes and unlocked doors function as literal booby traps.

In Haywood's *Love in Excess* (1725), the keyhole provides a pathway – sometimes a thorny one – to the beloved. Haywood's novel features the desirous gaze of a *woman* through a keyhole.[6] Alovysa, Count D'elmont's [*sic*] wife, spies on her husband after learning that he has received a letter from his former lover (Haywood 2000, 94). The desire for her husband – which leads her later to chase him around at night and fall on his sword – is reduced here to her longing gaze through the keyhole into his chamber. She mistakes the reason for his preoccupied state and his disinterest in her: the Count has fallen in love with Melliora, his ward, and is not pining for his old lover.[7]

In Smollett's *The Adventures of Peregrine Pickle* (1751), the narrator refers to the keyhole as a visual frame for the discovery of illicit sex. Having arrived in Bath, the popular Peregrine causes strife between the older and younger ladies. Members of the older group, called 'Platonists' because of their hypocritical moralising about vanity, spread rumours about younger girls with whom Peregrine dances, saying,

> if girls are determined to behave with such indiscretion, they must lay their accounts with incurring the censure of the world [...]. As for the servant's peeping through the key-hole, to be sure it was an unlucky accident; but people ought to be upon their guard against such curiosity, and give their domestics no cause to employ their penetration. (Smollett 1964, 372)

Here, Smollett pokes fun both at the older women's obvious desire for Peregrine's attention and their hypocritical bragging that they would not be so foolish as to be caught by their servants while cavorting with a man in bed.

Although the image occurs only once in *Clarissa*, the servant or curious woman at the door represents the most frequent motif connected with keyholes in eighteenth-century novels. For the most part, these scenes have comic qualities. In Fielding's *The History and Adventures of Joseph Andrews* (1742; see Fielding 1987b) – another parody of *Pamela* – Mrs. Slipslop listens at the keyhole to how Lady Booby tries to seduce Joseph for the second time, and then fires him for not responding. Slipslop uses this information to blackmail Lady Booby, and both she and her mistress appear as self-serving, greedy, and comically lustful. In *Tom Jones* (1749), the seemingly exceedingly proper Miss Bridget uses the keyhole to listen in on the conversation between her brother, Mr Allworthy, and the servant, Jenny Jones, about Jenny's supposedly illegitimate child (Fielding 1996, 49-50). This child, Tom Jones, of course turns out to be Miss Bridget's own son. The narrator makes fun of Miss Bridget's frustration at not being able to hear better through the keyhole. In light of her supposed virginity and delicacy, Miss Bridget's hunger for livid details about her brother's dealings as justice of peace appears ludicrous. Later in the novel, Sophia's waiting-woman comments, 'I wish some people would trouble themselves only with what belongs to them' (253) just after she has finished listening to a conversation between her mistress and Mrs Western about Sophia having to marry the detested Blifil.

---

6 Toni O'Shaughnessy Bowers documents several other cases of active female desire in Augustan amatory fiction. However, these scenes, involving desirous women and gender reversals, are mostly comic in tone and serve to support the status quo of male sexual primacy and female passivity (Bowers 1994, 55-58).

7 In a symbolisation of strained virtue, Melliora rips up her handkerchief and stuffs it into the keyhole to a door leading to her room to keep the Count from getting to her. Yet when she hears him at the door she is torn between opening it and leaving it closed (Haywood 2000, 129-130).

In *Tristram Shandy* (1768), Mrs Shandy applies her eye to the keyhole in order to satisfy her curiosity about the progress of Uncle Toby's love life (Sterne 1978, 729). Dorcas spies on Clarissa through the keyhole at Lovelace's behest in *Clarissa*, just as Mrs Jewkes finds out where Pamela has hidden her letters for Mr B in *Pamela*. Concerned male servants also spy on their masters. For instance, Roderick Random's faithful Strap peaks in at his master through the keyhole because he fears he will be involved in a duel (Smollett 1979, 293). Significantly, women and servants are portrayed as peeping in at men and masters or listening to their conversations. Such scenes are intended to reveal the weakness and hypocrisy of human nature and the ugliness of human behaviour when no one can observe it.

Tobias Smollett takes the keyhole out of the domestic setting in which we have seen it thus far in *The History and Adventures of an Atom* (1769). For the contentious and satirical Smollett, the keyhole represents a tool for portraying the ineffective monarch George II in an embarrassingly private posture, as being manipulated by the rhetorical virtuosity of William Pitt. Painting a thinly-disguised portrait of contemporary England in the era of the Newcastle and Pitt administrations under the guise of a history of Japan, Smollett gives the reader George II as a monarch who lacks wholly in the qualities of authority and leadership:

> He was rapacious, shallow, hot-headed, and perverse; in point of understanding, just sufficient to appear in public without a slavering bib; imbued with no knowledge, illumed by no sentiment, and warmed with no affection; except a blind attachment to the worship of Fakku-basi, which seemed indeed to be a disease in his constitution. His heart was meanly selfish, and his disposition altogether unprincely. (Smollett 1989, 10)

'Fakku-basi' represents a religion based on supporting the interests of the House of Hanover, particularly through financial means. The excesses of Fakku-basi at the cost of the English motivate this political allegory in large part. For example, because he supported a European balance of powers, the first minister Thomas Pelham-Holles, first duke of Newcastle, is christened 'Fika-kaka' by the narrator, a name suggesting 'cunt-shit' in Italian (Day 1989, 254).

The keyhole scene occurs in *Atom* after the English have suffered significant losses to the French while attempting to defend Hanover during the summer of 1757. Since George II lives only for the possibility of eating Hanover's 'brown bread' and 'delicate porkers' and drinking its 'brown beer' (Smollett 1989, 51), he reacts to news of the losses by locking himself in his 'cabinet'. A trio of politicians then attempt to draw him out. First Newcastle, or Fika-kaka, 'attempted to comfort him through the key-hole. He soothed, and whined, and wheedled, and laughed and wept all in a breath' (52).

When this does not succeed, the 'mob-driver', alias William Pitt, is called in to 'kneel [...] upon a cushion, with his mouth applied to the key-hole' (52-53). In mock-heroic elevated prose, Pitt compares the king to the sun and promises to do anything, including impoverish the English completely, for the sake of recovering Hanover's lands.

Here, the keyhole represents a frame through which the reader may look in at the private person of the – in Smollett's eyes – weak and politically-misguided George II. In terms of political theory, we may look through the keyhole to see the demolition of the picture of a public monarch on the frontispiece of Thomas Hobbes' *Leviathan; or the Matter, Forme, and Power of a Commonwealth Ecclesiasticall and Civil* (1651). In this picture, the monarch's enormous public body represents the unity of his country, as it is comprised of the individual persons and interests who fill his form and whom he unifies. Instead of a public monarch without a private body, we find a furiously private George II in Smollett's text.

George II's authority has been undermined just as his body has become his private domain. When he goes into his bedroom to sulk and fume, he relinquishes the prerogatives of absolute power to a band of ministers who are all depicted as being just as self-interested and self-serving as the egotistical individuals that Hobbes describes.[8]

In summary my review of keyholes in eighteenth-century novels reveals the following patterns:

1) Keyholes signify selfhood as conceived of as a form of private property. For Clarissa after her rape and for Sir Grandison, the keyhole functions as an image of individual ownership of self. Keyholes express a notion of identity as having depth and as being hidden from the eyes of others. They may also represent places of transformation. Locking herself in increasingly small spaces, Clarissa creates her Self.

2) Keyholes serve to frame desire. For Lovelace in *Clarissa*, for Mr B in *Pamela* and his caricature, Squire Booby, in *Shamela*, and for Alovysa in *Love in Excess*, keyholes provide visual images of the desired object and serve as metaphors for the desire to break open the lock or batten down the door and possess the other. Conversely, the object of desire, like Melliora in *Love in Excess*, may fill the keyhole to her chamber to subvert the desiring gaze.

3) Keyholes can also act as instruments of publicity. In *Peregrine Pickle* as well as in the second part of *Pamela*, when the eponymous protagonist has been transformed Cinderella-style from Mr B's servant into his wife, keyholes serve the public eye: they are used to discover and condemn private licentious acts. Catching her servant Polly cavorting with Mr H by peering through a keyhole, Pamela chides her maid for encouraging the gentleman's attentions and says – with no little calculation – that she would not have got where she is if she had let Mr B take liberties with her (Richardson 1833b, 469). A review of *Select Trials, for Murders, Robberies, Rapes, Sodomy, Coining, Frauds, and other Offences: at the Sessions-House in the Old Bailey* (1734-1735) unearths an instance of the keyhole being literally used to document deviant sexuality. Charles Hitchen, the Under City-Marshal of London who had worked towards the conviction of many sodomites or 'Mollies', was himself accused of the same crime. His witness attested,

> the Prisoner frequently came to my Master's House with Soldiers, and other scandalous Fellows, and call'd for a private Room, which made me suspect him for a Sodomite. And so when he came with the Prosecutor, I peep'd through the Key-hole, and saw him – and – and –
> (*Select Trials* 2: 244, as quoted in Gladfelder 2001, 30)

---

8 For a description of Smollett's political views, see Robert Adams Day's introduction to *The History and Adventures of an Atom* (Smollett 1989, 32-38).

Note the collocation of the enactment of sexuality with the documentation of the same by means of the keyhole. While historically the keyhole provided the means by which privacy was achieved, it also proves sometimes to be the avenue by which private acts are documented and punished publicly.

4) Most often, scenes at keyholes involve servants or women who want to observe their masters' behaviour or overhear their conversations. Intended as humorous, such vignettes portray the alleged weakness of less powerful members of society. The implications of these scenes are disturbing.

5) Keyholes are used to spread rumours from inside the house to the public and to make people visible. Such is the case in *Tristram Shandy*, in which the tale of Mr and Mrs Shandy's altercation 'got vent through the key-hole of a street door' (Sterne 1978, 277). Roderick learns how to see Narcissa again by begging to his elderly friend, Mrs Sagely, through the keyhole to her house (Smollett 1979, 405). Finally, the childlike king who pouts in his chamber is mollified and flattered by his ministers through a keyhole in *The History and Adventures of an Atom.*

Keyhole scenarios reveal the emerging architecture of mind in eighteenth-century England.[9] These scenes demonstrate separate models of private human behaviour for men and women, for those who hold power and those who do not. That curious servants and women figure so predominantly in them holds significance. Socially subservient, these individuals are portrayed as comic when they display curiosity or desire. The culture out of which they arise and which they inform treats a woman's and servant's wish to control their environments as ludicrous or reprehensible. Furthermore, George II's sulking behind the locked door of his room appears to represent a form of effeminacy in the eyes of his author. His being drawn out of his room by beguiling voices resembles a typical seduction scene in eighteenth-century fiction in which the desirous male uses the keyhole to gain access to the enclosed female.

Eighteenth-century authors depict Lovelace's, Mr B's, and Roderick Ransom's scopic desire and will to possess women as an inevitable natural force, if a regrettable one, when it leads to the ruin of women such as Clarissa. However, women who desire men in these texts are treated, at best, with pity like Alovysa and, at worst, with outright derision like Lady Booby or Mrs. Slipslop.

Significantly, the 'angelic' and 'divine' Clarissa Harlowe never looks nor speaks through a keyhole. Yet her sisterly predecessor in fiction, the lower-class Pamela, does, even after she has become a lady. Those who, like Clarissa and Sir Grandison, treat their inmost selves as private property that is to be protected from probing eyes represent a positive ideal of gentile, educated and feminised behaviour. These figures do not act reproachable even when they have locked themselves into their closets.

Increasingly, historians tell the story of post-1688 England in terms of profound instability and change. For example, Richard Price's history of the age portrays

9 For a different reading of private space in the eighteenth century, see Jürgen Schlaeger's paper in this volume.

tensions arising from the events of 1688 regarding the degree to which non-nobility should be represented politically and the public sphere should intrude in the private lives of families, women, and children. The Marriage Act of 1753 gave families 'a legal definition' and formally invested parents with the right to decide questions of marriage until a child was twenty-one, intending to protect property by deterring elopement. Yet the act was hotly contested (Price 1999, 203). Moreover, the separation of the genders that was being entrenched after 1688 was occasioned both by a rise in women's literacy and a plethora of conduct books, sermons, and didactic literature on why their place was in the home. And the public sphere was regarded as being endangered by filth, sex, and incivility (196).

Such contradictions led to the need to treat private behaviour in the public forum of fiction. The multitude of keyhole views in eighteenth-century novels attests to a preoccupation with how people should behave behind the closed doors of the home.[10] Via the keyhole and the larger-seeing eye of fiction, images of private characters become subject to commentary in the public world. Thus, keyholes satisfy the good private citizen's voyeuristic urge to look into the private lives of others, and they fix the preoccupations and worries of the culture. Visions of the dangers of sex in novels such as *Love in Excess*, *Pamela*, and *Clarissa* teach the disciplines of privacy. Locked bedroom doors should not be opened in the night, just as clandestine meetings in garden houses must be avoided. Keyholes serve to enforce an ideology whereby women, like Clarissa, are 'desirous [...] of sliding through life to the end of it unnoted; and [...] not wishing to be observed' (Richardson 1985, 40 [L 1]). The ideal woman of eighteenth-century fiction avoids publicity. She behaves unobtrusively even behind closed doors and attempts to never give reason for someone to peek in at her. As Clarissa writes to her spiritual mentor, Dr Lewen, 'it is certain that creatures who cannot stand the shock of *public shame* should be doubly careful how they expose themselves to the danger of incurring *private guilt*, which may possibly bring them to it' (1253 [L 428]).

Keyholes signify liminality in that they are neither full nor empty spaces. The eye, key, or voice that fills them does not alter their nature as frames and containers and transitional spaces. As sites of permutation, keyholes represent the uneasy shifts and balances in eighteenth-century culture between public areas of discourse and private domains of conduct, between the masculine and feminine spheres, and the emerging social classes. These scenes seek to inscribe differences in gender and power in an unsteady world.

---

10 As Spencer remarks, 'What is new about eighteenth-century experience, it has recently been argued, is not the confinement of women to the home but the new value placed on that home' (Spencer 1996, 217).

REFERENCES

Armstrong, Nancy (1987). *Desire and Domestic Fiction: A Political History of the Novel.* Oxford: Oxford University Press.

_______ (1999). 'Reclassifying Clarissa: Fiction and the Making of the Modern Middle Class.' In C.H. Flynn and G. Copeland (eds.), *Clarissa and Her Readers.* New York: AMS Press, 19-43.

Bowers, Toni O'Shaughnessy (1994). 'Sex, Lies, and Invisibility: Amatory Fiction from the Restoration to Mid-Century.' In John Richetti (ed.), *The Columbia History of the Novel.* New York: Columbia University Press, 50-73.

Day, Robert Adams (1989). 'Key.' In Tobias Smollett, *The History and Adventures of an Atom.* Ed. O.M. Brack, Jr. Athens: Georgia University Press, 249-268.

Fielding, Henry (1987a). *An Apology for the Life of Mrs. Shamela Andrews.* In *Joseph Andrews with Shamela and Related Writings: Authoritative Texts, Backgrounds and Sources, Criticism.* Ed. Homer Goldberg. Norton Critical Editions. New York: Norton. Original edition 1741.

_______ (1987b) *The History of Joseph Andrews, and of his Friend Mr Abraham Adams.* In *Joseph Andrews with Shamela and Related Writings: Authoritative Texts, Backgrounds and Sources, Criticism.* Ed. Homer Goldberg. Norton Critical Editions. New York: Norton. Original edition 1742.

_______ (1996) *The History of Tom Jones, a Foundling.* Oxford: Oxford University Press. Original edition 1749.

Gillis, Christina Marsden (1984). *The Paradox of Privacy: Epistolary Form in* Clarissa. Gainesville: Florida University Press.

Gladfelder, Hal (2001). *Criminality and Narrative in Eighteenth-Century England: Beyond the Law.* Baltimore: Johns Hopkins University Press.

Gottfried von Straßburg (1960). *Tristan.* Trans. A.T. Hatto. Harmondsworth: Penguin.

Habermas, Jürgen (1962). *Strukturwandel der Öffentlichkeit: Untersuchungen zu einer Kategorie der bürgerlichen Gesellschaft.* Neuwied: Luchterhand.

_______ (1989). *The Structural Transformation of the Public Sphere: An Inquiry into a Category of Bourgeois Society.* Trans. Thomas Burger. Cambridge, MA: MIT Press. Original German edition 1962.

_______ (1992). 'Further Reflections on the Public Sphere.' In Craig Calhoun (ed.), *Habermas and the Public Sphere.* Cambridge, MA: MIT Press, 421-461.

Haywood, Eliza (1741). *Anti-Pamela: or, Feign'd Innocence detected; In a series of Syrena's Adventures. A Narrative which has really its Foundation in Truth and Nature; and at the same time that it entertains, by a vast variety of surprizing Incidents, arms against a partial Credulity, by shewing the Mischiefs that frequently arise from a too sudden Admiration. Publish'd as a necessary Caution to all Young Gentlemen.* London: Huggonson. Online. 5 November 2001. Internet: Eighteenth Century Fiction Database.

_______ (2000). *Love in Excess; or, the Fatal Enquiry.* Ed. David Oakleaf. 2nd ed. Ontario: Broadview Press. Original edition 1725.

Lentes, Thomas (1998). 'Zelle.' *Lexikon des Mittelalters.* Ed. Charlotte Bretscher-Gisiger. Vol. 9. Stuttgart: Metzler, 520-521.

McKeon, Michael (1987). *The Origins of the English Novel 1600-1740.* Baltimore: Johns Hopkins University Press.

Mulvey, Laura (1989). *Visual and Other Pleasures.* Bloomington: Indiana University Press. Original edition 1975.

Price, Richard (1999). *British Society, 1680-1880: Dynamism, Containment and Change.* Cambridge. Cambridge University Press.

Richardson, Samuel (1833a). *The Works of Samuel Richardson.* Ed. Leslie Stephen. Vol. 1: *Pamela; or, Virtue Rewarded.* London: Henry Sotheran. Original edition 1740.

________ (1833b). *The Works of Samuel Richardson*. Ed. Leslie Stephen. Vol. 2: *Pamela; or, Virtue Rewarded*. London: Henry Sotheran. Original edition 1740.

________ (1833c). *The Works of Samuel Richardson*. Ed. Leslie Stephen. Vol. 3: *The History of Clarissa Harlowe*. London: Henry Sotheran. Original edition 1751.

________ (1833d). *The Works of Samuel Richardson*. Ed. Leslie Stephen. Vol. 9: *The History of Sir Charles Grandison*. London: Henry Sotheran. Original edition 1754.

________ (1962). *Clarissa or, The History of a Young Lady*. Ed. George Sherburn. Abr. ed. Boston: Houghton Mifflin. Original edition 1759.

________ (1964). *Selected Letters of Samuel Richardson*. Ed. John Carroll. Oxford: Clarendon Press.

________ (1985). *Clarissa or, The History of a Young Lady: Comprehending The Most Important Concerns of Private Life. And particularly shewing, The distresses that may attend the Misconduct Both of Parents and Children, In Relation to Marriage*. Ed. Angus Ross. London: Penguin. Original edition 1747-1748.

Schwarz, Joan I. (1999). 'Eighteenth-Century Abduction Law and *Clarissa*.' In C.H. Flynn and G. Copeland (eds.), Clarissa *and her Readers*. New York: AMS Press, 269-308.

Select Trials, for Murders, Robberies, Rapes, Sodomy, Coining, Frauds, and other Offences: at the Sessions-House in the Old Bailey (1734-1735). 2 vols. London: Printed for J. Wilford.

Shakespeare, William (2000), *Richard III* [1592?]. Ed. John Jowett. Oxford: Oxford University Press.

Smollett, Tobias (1964). *The Adventures of Peregrine Pickle in which are included Memoirs of a Lady of Quality*. Ed. James L. Clifford. London: Oxford University Press. Original edition 1751.

________ (1979) *The Adventures of Roderick Random*. Ed. Paul-Gabriel Boucé. Oxford: Oxford University Press. Original edition 1748.

________ (1989) *The History and Adventures of an Atom*. Ed. O.M. Brack. Athens: Georgia University Press. Original edition 1769.

Spencer, Jane (1996). 'Women Writers and the Eighteenth-Century Novel.' In John Richetti (ed.), *The Cambridge Companion to the Eighteenth-Century Novel*. Cambridge: Cambridge University Press, 212-235.

Sterne, Laurence (1978). *The Life and Opinions of Tristram Shandy, Gentleman*. Ed. Mervyn New and Joan New. 3 vols. Florida: Florida University Press. Original edition 1768.

Watt, Ian (1987). *The Rise of the Novel: Studies in Defoe, Richardson and Fielding*. London: Hogarth. Original edition 1957.

Christoph Houswitschka

FAMILY, CRIME, AND THE PUBLIC SPHERE: 'INCEST' IN EIGHTEENTH-CENTURY ENGLAND

In the *Trial of Job Wells of Redburn in the County of Hertford, for a Rape committed on the Body of his own Daughter, Maria Wells*, which was held at the Assizes on Monday the thirteenth and Tuesday the fourteenth of August 1753, the widowed father of eight children was sentenced to death and executed. The account of the trial was published in the same year by Sir Charles Corbett in London.[1] This is unusual for the eighteenth century according to the studies of Anna Clark and Louise Jackson, who do not mention a single trial of such a nature and who claim that they were more or less non-existent. The question is, why was Job Wells brought to justice? Is there a hidden agenda – that is, are there any ideological reasons which made it more likely for this case to be prosecuted? In other words, to use John P. Zomchick's terminology, why was Job Wells regarded as a 'juridical subject'[2] and eventually hanged, and what was Corbett's interest in publishing this trial?

My paper is divided into four parts: first, I will provide some historical information on child abuse (or incest, as it was called) and the likelihood of the intervention of the state into the private sphere of perpetrators such as Job Wells. Second, I shall examine the specific kinds of incest as documented in eighteenth-century novels.[3] Third, I shall give some details on the account of the trial of Job Wells. And fourth, I will bring together the three issues of family, crime and the public sphere in order to answer the question as to why Wells was singled out to be prosecuted for child abuse.

---

1 Corbett's print shop was situated at Addison's Head, opposite St Dunstan's Church, Fleet Street. Corbett ran his business from 1752 to about 1771, at which time he had to give it up due to bankruptcy.

2 Zomchick defines 'the juridical subject' as 'a representation of the individual identified with the principles and the aims of the law (especially its respect for property) and motivated by an inherent need for affectation and human community fulfilled by the family, which offers a motive for internalizing the law' (Zomchick 1993, i). Zomchick argues 'that the mature juridical subject is both an object of visible and invisible forces of power as well as a subject empowered by her or his internalization of that same law' (xv).

3 As one knows from Hamlet, who denounces his mother for having married his uncle, 'O, most wicked speed, to post / With such dexterity to incestuous sheets!' (1.2), incest has not always been defined in the same manner (see Boehrer 1992, 62-77). It's definition is mainly a legal one, which is usually based on political interests: 'incest prohibition serves as a highly flexible, extremely powerful political tool – authorizing particular alliances, prohibiting others, reinforcing nationalist or internationalist sentiment as the case may require, and in the process literally remaking the identities of specific individuals' (3). In 1603 several forbidden and permitted matches, based on rules devised in 1563, were revised by Elizabeth I. The new rules were made public in the *Book of Common Prayer* in 1662. In 1669 marriage between cousins was legalised. These rules 'pertained only to marriage; people within forbidden degrees who had sexual relations but did not marry one another were guilty simply of adultery or fornication' (Shaffer 1999, n.p.).

I. Incest and Child Abuse in History

There is an inscription above the main entrance to the Central Criminal Court at the Old Bailey: 'Defend the Children of the Poor and Punish the Wrong-Doer.' For Louise Jackson, who begins her recent study on *Child Sexual Abuse in Victorian England* with this quotation, this inscription is representative of the ideals of the late Victorian and early Edwardian paternalistic state, and it gives 'an insight on attitudes to criminality and victimology in this period' (Jackson 2000, 1). Jackson interprets its cultural relevance and points out that, by the turn of the century, 'the figure of the (female) child had become an important symbol of the innocent victim of crime' (2), and that 'the presentation and punishment of child abuse was deployed as a paradigm for the ideals of the English criminal justice system' (ibid.).

According to Jackson and others, child abuse had been neglected by the criminal justice system for a long time.[4] There must have been public awareness of this type of crime – a crime which occurred in the spheres designated by society as private and which was relatively safe from state intervention well into the nineteenth century. It was only in the 1880s that the state tried to control that sexual behaviour it believed to be indecent. Regarding the second section of the *Criminal Law Amendment Act* of 1885, which made it possible to prosecute and sentence Oscar Wilde for 'Gross Indecency with male persons' (Böker 2001, 47-53), we have again changed our values, attitudes and laws in the second half of the twentieth century. But according to Price, the changes in the Late Victorian Period had made it 'possible for the state to invade the most private of private spheres in the name of the public moral interests. Acts committed in the privacy of the home were now made liable to criminal prosecution' (Price 1999, 232). Since the *Prevention of Cruelty to Children Act* of 1889, which made it much easier to prosecute child abuse by allowing the mother to give evidence against the father, our sensibilities have grown even stronger.[5] The attack against the bourgeois family in the 1970s motivated a strong public interest in the protection of children. In other words, interest in the protection of children grows in periods when the ideological meaning of the family as a social institution which stabilises a concept of the private sphere is re-interpreted.

In the Victorian period, the cultural agenda against aristocratic immorality made it possible to prosecute master/servant abuse. Literature played an essential part in articulating these concerns. The stereotype of aristocratic seduction, for instance, which originated in the middle-class novel of the eighteenth century, can also be found in the radical writings of Godwin and Wollstonecraft. According to Anna Clark, this topic finally emerged in the political rhetoric of the anti-Poor Law and the Chartist movements of the 1830s and 1840s. Jackson, following Clark, concludes that 'the seduced maiden and the libertine became a "class metaphor" which represented

4 Mendelson and Crawford point out that, within a patriarchal world, 'women found it difficult to articulate their own perceptions and concerns. In specific terms, it was not easy for women to find a framework in which they could voice criticisms of the excesses and abuses of patriarchy, such as domestic violence, incest, and rape' (1998, 72).

5 The public discourse in some cases even went so far as to suspect that the institution of the family had too often been a sanctuary for sexual criminals rather than a safe heaven for children.

working class against capitalist, as well as bourgeoisie against aristocracy' (Clark 1987, 46). Since most abused women and children were abused by men of their own class and of their own family, however, this class agenda 'falsified reality' as it obscured issues of gender (ibid.). But this deficiency of public awareness had an ideological reason, because 'family was the quintessential unit of the private sphere' and 'family autonomy [...] was in most respects supreme,' as Price explains (1999, 202-203). Therefore, incest became – according to Jackson – one of the most under-reported forms of sexual abuse. Robert Roberts writes about the Manchester slums in his memoirs: 'I don't recall a single prosecution: strict public silence saved miscreants from the rigours of the law' (Jackson 2000, 46).

I do not want to argue against Clark's and Jackson's overall conclusion that, indeed, most cases of child abuse were not reported in the eighteenth and nineteenth centuries, and that it was only in the last century that some progress was made. On the other hand, I cannot imagine that this process of uncovering the hidden cruelties of life in the private sphere of families is one of exclusively linear progress from bad to better. The awareness of sexual deviancies grows with the public's and the central authority's willingness to intervene and to enforce law. However, this is not determined by a gradual process of civilisation, but rather by periods of growing tension between facticity and validity (to use Habermas' terminology) – or social reality (objectivist approach) and ideal (normative approach). Since the idea of free contract and 'voluntary association denoted the primacy of the private sphere in the shaping of civil society' (Price 1999, 195),[6] it was tacitly assumed that this tension was rarely significant enough to justify intervention in the private sphere.[7] In specific cases, however, the social reality of the family no longer reflected the validity of the law. In these cases, the state would intervene in order to reaffirm its overall ideological assumptions.

6 See Habermas: 'Seit Hobbes gelten die Regeln des auf Vertragsfreiheit und Eigentum basierenden bürgerlichen Privatrechts als Prototyp für Recht überhaupt' (1992, 45).

7 Habermas calls this *Hintergrundwissen*, which remains astonishingly stable as long as it is not made an issue of public controversy: 'Was ihm seine eigentümliche Stabilität verleiht und es gegen den Druck kontingenzerzeugender Erfahrungen zunächst immunisiert, ist die eigenartige *Einebnung der Spannung zwischen Faktizität und Geltung*: In der Geltungsdimension selbst wird jenes kontrafaktische Moment einer über das jeweils Gegebene hinausschießenden Idealisierung, das eine enttäuschende Konfrontation mit der Wirklichkeit erst möglich macht, ausgelöscht; zugleich bleibt die Dimension als solche, aus der implizites Wissen die Kraft von Überzeugungen bezieht, intakt' (1992, 39).

II. INCEST[8] AS A TOPIC IN NOVELS

In her pseudo-historical novels, Jane Barker (1675-1743) describes the feelings of her protagonist, who is pursued by her brother Valerius: 'all which I refus'd with equal Aversion, as being inconsistent with Virtue, by Reason of our Consanguity; otherwise his Addresses were honourable, and his Person agreeable' (Barker 1719, 40-41). Her reason does not want to acknowledge the many instances that:

> might justify the Legality of his Pretensions; as indeed, there are but too many Examples of that Kind amongst the Gods and Heroes. Even the present King and Queen of Egypt live in the Same State which our laws call Incest. How the Men of the robe disguise, alter, and transform, what they say is the Law of the Gods, I know not; but we often find they make Vice and Virtue to differ according to Time, Place, and Person; and make that a Crime in one Person, which is none in another; and that a Virtue in one Place, which is a Vice in another. (41)[9]

Incest is used to criticise the legal system and some of its ideological assumptions and legitimations. The fact that even the status of incest as a taboo is questioned here makes this published attack against the divine status of law the more poignant. Here, incest is used as a rhetorical device to intervene from the position of a female counter-culture of sensibility that questions the reasoning of a male-dominated, arbitrary law.[10]

This use is not the rule and is, for instance, markedly different from the sensational 'horrid Sound of Incest' against which Eliza Fowler Haywood (1693?-1756) wants to shriek out in her *Secret Histories, Novels and Poems* (1725). Mary de la Rivière Manley (ca. 1674-1724),[11] however, also uses the motif of incest as a narrative device

---

8 Certainly, legal definitions of incest apply whenever incest is debated in the public. However, it is likely that there is a different category by which incest is defined in the private sphere by those who are not believed to have commited a crime. Samuel Johnson's definition of incest in his 1755 *Dictionary of the English Language* is particularly helpful here; incest is defined as 'unnatural and criminal conjunction of persons within degrees prohibited'. According to this definition, incest was defined not only according to the law, but also according to whether a certain behaviour was thought to be natural or not. Before the eighteenth century, this category was still very dependent on the dominant religious morals. In W.C.'s *Aduentures of Ladie Egeria* (1585), Holy Thomas (otherwise, Pallasus) compares incest with the worst of sins. He presents the example of Lampanus, who not only hanged 'Pantipar his owne sonne,' but also desired 'to commit incest with his owne daughter.' Consequently, Lampanus was 'chaunged to a filthy snake' for his sins – an obvious biblical reference.

9 'These serve to distract the Ignorant, amuse the Curious and Speculative, and is an inexhaustible Source of everlasting Disputes. Wherefore I avoided these Casuistical By-ways, and kept to the open common Road of Virtue, taught me by my Mother, which oblig'd me to oppose the Love of Valerius as incestuous, and contrary to the present known laws of our Country' (Barker 1719, 41).

10 For the question of why Jane Barker is less familiar to the reader of eighteenth-century literature than Richardson and Fielding in spite of her (and Penelope Albino's) coherent ethical design of novels, see Warner 1998, 49. Richetti points out that 'Pious female writers like Jane Barker, Penelope Auburn, and Elizabeth Rowe produced stories that shifted the thematic emphasis of the novella toward virtuous and ultimately victorious resistance to the power of love, providing most of the thrills of watching beleaguered virtue but avoiding the violence and lubricity that usually supplemented them' (1998, 95). For the authorial concerns of Barker, see Straub 1994, 203.

11 McDowell regards Manley 'as a key transitional figure in the history of middling women's political activism through print, mediating between the female political culture of the seventeenth century and the "new wave" of women's writing and self-representation in the eighteenth century' (1998, 220).

to criticise the institutions of law and family in an aristocratic society in her books, *The Power of Love: In Seven Novels* (1720). In the seventh tale, *The Perjur'd Beauty*, Romeo falls in love with a nun who happens to be his sister – a fact which is hidden from the two lovers until it is too late. Romeo discovers 'the nearness of their Relation; which being soon known to the Lady Abbess, increased her Detestation of the incestuous Pair' (Manley 1720, 362). Both lovers are sentenced to death. Romeo is:

> condemned by the Pope and Conclave [...] to lose his Head six Days after, for violating the Nunnery, in stealing away Victoria and then commiting Incest with her; tho' it was urged that his Crime could not be so esteemed, because the Relation between them was unknown to him. But those pious Judges rarely or never pardon any Thing done gainst their Religion, or forgive what brings Scandal upon their holy Order and the Church. (ibid.)

Victoria is sentenced to be immured and to be starved to death. In a letter to her father, Count Rossano, she reproaches him for not having informed her about her origins. Planning her suicide, she hopes that her 'Blood may wash away' her father's guilt and that 'it may be a Warning for others, how they breed up their Offspring in Ignorance of their real Parents, lest more may fall into the same unsuspected Crime, as have the innocent Romeo, and miserable Victoria!' (363). She regrets that she has 'never known the Sweets of being caress'd by a dear Mother! Or to be blest with the Cares and Fondness of a Father!' (364).

What Victoria demands from all those who might learn from her father's wrongdoing belongs to the larger complex of familialisation. Victoria's case is a strong argument for propagating the public significance of the family as a social institution of the private sphere on which stability and order are based. Victoria remains victorious because she makes herself not only a victim, but a martyr of a middle-class public conscience which associates the role of the family with the validity of the law in the private sphere.

The Catholic feudal tyranny of the pope is associated with instability and the arbitrariness of a system of terror and retribution. This system is represented by the aristocratic family in which incest seems to be inevitable because of the alleged absence of marital fidelity. In such a society, law does not provide a matrix of a design for living (as defined by Zomchick 1993), because the family as a middle-class institution is absent. The immuration of Victoria symbolises the techniques of a brutal social order that holds the individual responsible for its malfunctions. Victoria, on the other hand, demands a legal order that has the individual's rights monitored and protected by the institution of the family. The law could not connect the private lives and the social order as long as the private conscience was not supported by a social institution such as the family. The family was believed to supply a microcosm that was organised according to the same principles as the public order of the law; thus, legitimising both the existence of the legislators and their tradition of non-intervention.[12]

---

12 Dr Primrose in Oliver Goldsmith's *The Vicar of Wakefield* believes that the family, 'The little republic to which I gave laws' (1965, 28), is a microcosm of the state, and that the validity of the law is ensured the same way in both realms.

In contrast to such a desired state of affairs, Victoria and Romeo follow their natural sentiments, thus re-organising a legitimate bond, however, unconsciously, in the wrong manner. It is a wrong concept of family that causes the tragedy. The order of the feudal family collides with nature in a manner that degrades law and its legitimisation to give order to society, as Victoria suggests in a farewell letter to her brother shortly before she takes her own life:

> No, my new-found Brother, [...] Are not the Laws of Nature Prior to any other? What has she to do with Kindred or Enclosure? [...] Beat not our Hearts as high, were not our Kisses as sweet, our Delights as perfect, whilst we remained in the State of Ignorance, as if you had never been the Son of Count Rossano, or the innocent Victoria his Daughter? Ah! Must we die? Ah! Must we be separated, the most painful Death, because the Pride of Man, which he calls Reason, has refined upon, or abolished the Law of Nature? (Manley 1720, 365)

Romeo's and Victoria's natural belief that 'humankind's innate benevolence and sympathy lead to community building' (ibid.), is a typical feature of the era's novel of sensibility, as Shaffer (1999) explains. Constructing familialised support usually helps sentimental protagonists to move about and to survive in a hostile world. In the case of the two lovers in Baker's novel, this desire precipitates a deathly error, because they were not brought up within a family. In both novels, however, incest occurs between sister and brother like in most other eighteenth-century novels. Love is destroyed because of its incestuous character which represents disorder in the private sphere due to deficient concepts of family and law.

Most incidents of incest described in literary texts occur among sisters and brothers and are not rape. Child abuse in literature is similarly 'underreported' as in real life.[13] In those novels in which the motif of incest is combined with that of rape, the significance of the crime changes significantly, but not its social interpretation. In these cases, it is more likely that the perpetrator is not the brother but the father who rapes his daughter.[14] In Charles Johnstone's (1719?-1800) satirical roman à clef *Chrysal; or the Adventures of a Guinea* (1760),[15] a father rapes his daughter and kills her in order to hide the incestuous crime. He is a kind of gothic villain, whose crimes

13 According to the historical statistics as put together by Anna Clark, out of 138 cases of sexual assault of girls under the age of thirteen, as reported in her 'sample of London newspapers between 1800 and 1845, eighteen involved incest. Thirteen more incest cases were reported involving girls over twelve, the age of consent' (1987, 101). These figures are for the nineteenth century; in the eighteenth century, sexual assault was hardly believed to be a public issue at all, as Clark concludes from her examination of eighteenth-century newspapers, which 'rarely reported rapes, and when they did, provided little useful detail' (16). Clark 'examined depositions from 165 rape cases from 1770 to 1829 in the assize records of the North-east circuit (Yorkshire, Cumberland, Westmoreland, Northumberland, and Newcastle) in the Public Record Office, Chancers Lane' (16).

14 *The Newgate Calendar* lists many more cases of rape than child abuse. James Wilson was indicted of having attempted to commit incest with his daughter in September 1823 and was sentenced to twelve months of imprisonment (Knapp and Baldwin 1826, 4: 350). Alice Gray was accused of having assisted in the rape of a ten-year-old girl in 1707 (*Bloody Register* 1999, 1: 117). For cases of rape, see Knapp and Baldwin 1825, 2: 385 and 479; 1825, 3: 285; 1826, 4: 6, 233, 347, and 392.

15 Charles Johnstone's *Chrysal* is a satire on important political issues in the troubled early years of George III. Baugh calls *Chrysal* one of 'the most notable, or even notorious' satires of his time, 'with its glimpses of corruption in high places, its scandals about the Medmenham "monks," and its relations to the career of John Wilkes' (1948, 1031).

are covered up by the church.[16] Incest does not just indicate an individual deviance, but the breakdown of the legal status of the family as a social institution. The purpose of the family is to control and to discipline the minds of its members in such a manner as to guarantee the validity of the law in the private sphere. In the absence of this control, the evil in the male perpetrator cuts himself off from his own social nature. Usually, one would assume that the church might have been attributed the social function of controlling people's minds, similar to the family. In Johnstone's novel, however, this expectation seems to have been abandoned altogether. A man of the church tries to excuse the murderous father in the following words:

> For though adultery is a great sin, and, in this case, aggravated by rape and incest, yet, as you say, it was not because she was the wife of another man, and especially your brother, that you desired her, but merely as she was a beautiful woman, therefore the adultery and incest come in but by accident; and then, as you ravished her only because she would not comply, the sin of rape is certainly her's, as I said before; for, if I force a man to commit a crime, I am guilty of that crime, and not he: And again, though murder is a most heinous sin, yet as you killed her, not merely to indulge a murderous intent, but to prevent her discovering you having forced her, and so ruining you, the intention quite alters the nature of the fact, and makes it but self-preservation, which is the first law of nature. And lastly, as you took the jewels, not with a design to rob her, but to offer them to the church, and accordingly have brought them, that conclusion sanctifies the whole action, and makes your peace with heaven. (Johnstone 1760, 58-59)

This rationale satirises a corrupt, male attitude which might have been regarded typical of decisions taken by public authorities who ridiculed the 'rule of law'. It is this blatant irrationality which removes any separation of the public and private spheres. According to Turkel, the separation of public and private elements is waning when the public and private is inconsistent with a rational type of social action. A rational type of action is 'universally understandable on the basis of calculation independent of personal and local knowledge, commitments, and understandings' (Turkel 1992, 131). In Johnstone's novel, the public authority of the church demonstrate a lack of rationality. In the case of the incest committed by Job Wells on his daughter, it is the rationality of the law that has no validity in the institution of the family any longer.

III. The Trial of Job Wells

The year in which Wells was indicted is the same year in which Hardwicke's *Marriage Act* was passed, an act by which, for the first time, the state gave the institution of the family a legal definition. It is not very likely that this alone convincingly explains why the case of Job Wells received the public's and the law's attention, because the reasons for introducing this new law had nothing to do with the families of the poor, but with the interests of the landowners. The legal context for Victoria's literary complaint (that there is no legal definition and protection of the family) and Johnstone's criticism of

16 Elizabeth MacAndrew argues in *The Gothic Tradition in Fiction* that incest is persistently associated with violence because of 'a continual psychomachia' of the evil character: 'Just as the quasi-incestuous relationship of the sentimental characters was a reflecting device, so real incest, an assault against a daughter or sister, seems to epitomize the self-destructive struggle within the evil mind' (1979, 84-85).

the irrationality of the authorities' dealing with the crime of rape and incest, had been revised by the legislators, thus, acknowledging the family as an important institution which defines and supports specific social interests. Let me give you some more information on the *Trial of Job Wells* in order to determine the public interest in an intervention by the central authorities. Job Wells was:

> indicted for that he, not having the Fear of God before his Eyes, but being moved and seduced by the Instigation of the Devil, with Force and Arms [...] on *Maria Wells*, his own Daughter, did make an Assault, and her the said *Maria*, by Violence and against her Consent, did carnally know, against the Peace of our Lord the King his Crown and Dignity. (*Trial* 1753, 3-4).

The sixteen-year-old Maria was questioned in court under oath. She told all the details of her rape[17] and how she was threatened by her father with a knife. Maria had not dared to tell any of her sisters or brothers. But when she was raped a second time, she was asked the next day by a neighbour, Mary Hitchcock, why she was crying. Maria 'told her, my Father wanted to make a Whore of me; and she said, I hope he has not; but I said, he has, indeed' (5). Mary Hitchcock confirms Maria's report and tells how she 'went to the Overseers to tell them of it, for I thought it ought to be looked into; and the Overseers sent for Dr. Law to examine her' (ibid.). Joseph Law, the physician, confirms that his examination of Maria Wells had proved that 'Violence had been used to her' and that she had told the truth (6).[18] After the examination, the 'Overseers of the Poor' retained a warrant and had Mr Wells taken to Justice Carpenter and sent the girl to St Alban's Workhouse. The father tried to defend himself by claiming that he could not remember anything because he had been drunk that night, but maintained that 'his Daughter came to Bed to him willingly' (ibid.). His sister, Patience Ivory, seems to have tried to protect her brother: 'I saw Maria the Day my Brother was taken up, and she did not complain to me, and seemed to walk as well as at any other Time' (ibid.).

The minutes of the interrogations are followed by 'An Account of Job Wells, his Behaviour, Confession, etc.' From this anonymous account we learn how Job Wells came to repent his crime. In the report of 'The Day of Execution', both the sermon of the preacher and the last dying speech of the prisoner are summarised. The preacher admonished the crowd 'to strive with all their Might to get the Mastery of their corrupt Affections'. In addressing 'the unhappy Prisoner', he expressed that 'he hoped his Distress and Punishment would deter every one from giving a loose to their unruly Appetites' (13). Job Wells concluded his last dying speech thusly: '*I desire all People to take Warning by me; I heartily forgive my Daughter, and hope she does me; but she must repent, as well as I, or her Soul will never be saved. Pray for me good People*' (13-14).

---

17 '*Wells*. My Father pulled open my Legs, and got between them; then I cried out, and he threatened to kill me if I did not lie quiet; then he did so and so to me. – *Q*. The law requires in this Case that you should speak out plain, you must therefore say what he did to you in plain express Words. – *Wells*. After he had got between my Legs, he put his **** into me by Force, and hurt me very much. – *Q*. What happened after this; you must speak out. – *Wells*. I felt something warm come from him into me' (*Trial* 1753, 4-5).

18 'for her private Parts were much swelled; and that there had been a Penetration' (*Trial* 1753, 6).

There is no indication that this statement would have met the public's rejection. Maria Wells might have been regarded as a victim, but – being well beyond the age of consent – people seem to have thought her to be a sinner, too. The trial is a warning against the case of both Wellses. What was the situation in this family that motivated the central authority's intervention? The section which might help in understanding why Wells was prosecuted in the first place presents information about his family life. At the age of nineteen, Wells 'married a poor, but honest industrious Woman, by whom he had a great many Children, eight of whom are now alive' (7). We learn that he also used to be an honest and industrious man, 'with respect to his Employment, but much given to Women, especially when he had been drinking, and then he was a down-right Brute' c The crucial change in his life occurred when his wife died 'in child-bed' one year before the crime. 'There is a Report, that he was the Occasion, by forcibly going to Bed to her the next Day after she was delivered, for she died on the third Day'[19] (ibid.). The author of the account ensures his readers that Job Wells 'was a very profligate and abandoned Wretch,' because he is told to have said, '*There is ne'er a Man in* Redburn *dare go through Hell besides myself*' (ibid.).

Job Wells' was a brutal man with a considerable alcohol problem, conditions which likely both caused the crime as well as, considering his bad reputation, its prosecution. But why was Wells crime reported and why was it prosecuted? In other words, what is different in the case of Wells as compared to the hundreds or thousands of cases which were not reported and not prosecuted?

IV. Conclusion

In the novels discussed above, women sacrifice themselves for two reasons: either they want to propagate the family as a social institution defined by law, thus avoiding accidental incest among brothers and sisters; or they criticise the paternalistic deformation of the law as it is associated with an aristocratic concept of family which they believe lacks the rationality of the law. Therefore, the law does not have validity in the latter type of family and, therefore, irrational tyranny and arbitrariness prevail. In the new middle-class institution of the family, coercive justice is replaced by the rationality of the law, notions of which are circulated between the private sphere and the central authority through public media such as novels.

According to Carole Pateman, 'the categories of public and private have been interpreted as equivalent to those of male and female and understood in terms of an ideology of separate spheres' (Eger et al. 2001, 1). In *Women, Writing and the Public Sphere*, it is remarked that:

> Historicized accounts of the emergence of clearly differentiated private and public realms locate the eighteenth century as a period of transition, moving from a time of comparative freedom for women into a world of separate spheres, in which men occupied the public sphere of work while women became increasingly restricted to the private sphere of the family (Eger et al. 2001, 1).

---

19 'He did not care to answer directly to the Question asked him concerning this Report, but only said, *There are more Things said of me than are true*; so that by not denying it, there is too much Reason to fear it was true' (*Trial* 1753, 7).

These findings are also confirmed by Richard Price: 'At its simplest level, the public and private spheres were a binary formation; the public sphere was male and the private sphere was female' (1999, 205). This separation, however, should not be misunderstood as one which excluded women from defining this private sphere from outside. Women authors themselves helped to define the private sphere of families as one which is permeated by the law. The doctrine of the separate spheres has therefore been challenged in recent feminist criticism.

Anne K. Mellor, for instance, argues that 'women writers had an enormous – and hitherto largely uncredited – impact on the formation of public opinion in England between 1780 and 1830' (2000, 11).[20] Mellor questions John Brewer's thesis of the public sphere invading the private sphere, and claims that 'the values of the private sphere associated primarily with women [...] infiltrated and finally dominated the discursive public sphere' (ibid.). McDowell also shows that Manley self-consciously devoted herself to propaganda, and 'created a space for her innovative political fictions [...] by representing herself as a female alternative intelligence agent of the private sphere' (1998, 20)

The thesis of the separate spheres seems to work best on the assumption of a circulation of values and attitudes which reaffirm each other in a reciprocal manner. Whenever an act of communication occurs in which the imagined border of the two spheres is transgressed, social meaning is (re)created with regard to both domesticity and productivity – the private and the public.

This might also help to explain why Job Wells was taken to court. The 1753 account of the trial, which explains that Wells had a good reputation as a worker, but was a brute at home, suggests the same separation of family and public sphere. In contrast to the novels, the account of the trial of Job Wells does not raise the question of the validity of the law, but the facticity (that is, the social reality) of the family. The tension between fact and norm (or facticity and validity) provokes the intervention of the central authority when it becomes clear that the social institution of the family, in the case of the Wells, no longer exists. It is not the domestic violence which makes the authority react to Job Wells, but the fact that, following his wife's death, the family ceased to exist according to the ideological understanding of the time. There was no woman left in the Wells family who was believed to have been sufficiently equipped for domesticity by her moral purity. There was no one who could have either domesticated Job Wells' 'unruly sexuality' (Price 1999, 205) or protected his daughter from committing a sin. When the crime was reported, the legal system intervened because there was no woman who could play the role of a representative of the validity of the law in the private sphere.

20 See also Guest (2000), who breaks down the opposition between domestic and public, arguing that opinions on highly debated political questions were communicated within the 'domestic sphere', e.g., by writing letters among woman. The establishment of female correspondences was a form of resistance to marriage and 'explains why novels of women's correspondence are so little domestic compared to contemporary fiction of the mid to late eighteenth century. They resist the domestic sphere as the new site for the enshrinement and reproduction of patronym and patriline kinship relations' (Alliston 1996, 26).

The fact that Job Wells looked after his children presents to the public the same notion of patriarchal tyranny and lawlessness which is also criticised in the novels. By proving that Mr Job Wells committed a crime against 'the order of King and Country,' a specific concept of family is re-affirmed in the public's view. The message to the public is not that the state will prosecute any rape of a daughter by her father – obviously this was not the case – but that a family without a woman fails to be a social institution which stabilises the private sphere. Without a woman, the validity of the law across the fictitious borderline between the private and the public spheres collapses. The irrationality of the family situation clashes with the alleged rationality of the law. The separation of the two spheres ceases to be acknowledged by the public and the state intervenes.

The members of the Wells family were re-located into other social institutions – the prison and the workhouse – thus, enforcing the law and confirming its contribution in securing a rational order. As soon as the self-description of the individual in the private sphere is regarded to be deficient, the central authority intervenes, assuming that facticity and validity do not merge any longer or, in other words, that the free social contract was broken. It is only then that the rape of his wife 'in child-bed' and the abuse of his daughter legitimise sanctions of the central authority against a man such as Job Wells. Consequently, the publication of the account of the trial and of the moralising narrative pertain to the public approval of this unusual intervention of the state into the private sphere.

PRIMARY LITERATURE

Barker, Jane (1719). *The Entertaining Novels of Mrs. Jane Barker*. Vol. 1: *Exilius; or, The Banish'd Roman; Written (after the Manner of Telemachus) for the Instruction of some Young Ladies of Quality*. Vol. 2: *Celia and Marcellus; or, The constant Lovers [...]*. 2nd ed. London: Printed for A. Bettesworth and E. Curll.

Bloody Register (1999). Ed. with an introduction by Nick Groom. 4 vols. London: Routledge.

Goldsmith, Oliver (1965). *The Vicar of Wakefield*. Chicago: Fountain Press.

Haywood, Eliza (1725). *Secret Histories, Novels and Poems*. 4 vols. 2nd ed. London: Printed for Dan. Browne, Jun. [...] and S. Chapman.

Johnstone, Charles (1760). *Chrysal; or the Adventures of a Guinea*. London: Printed for T. Beckett.

Knapp, Andrew, and William Baldwin, eds. (1824-1826). *The Newgate Calendar; Comprising Interesting Memoirs of the Most Notorious Characters Who Have Been Convicted of Outrages on the Laws of England since the Commencement of the Eighteenth Century; with Occasional Anecdotes and Observations, Speeches, Confessions, and Last Exclamations of Sufferers*. 4 vols. London: J. Robbins.

Manley, Mary de la Rivière (1720). *The Power of Love: In Seven Novels*. Vol. 7: *The Perjur'd Beauty; Never before Published*. London: Printed for John Barber [...] and John Morphew.

Trial of Job Wells of Redburn in the County of Hertford, for a Rape committed on the Body of his own Daughter, Maria Wells (1753). London: Corbett. In *British Trials, 1660-1900*. Microfiche edition. Cambridge: Chadwyck-Healey, 1993, no.394.

W.C. (1585). *The Aduentures of Ladie Egeria, Containing her miserable banishment by Duke Lampanus her husbande*. London: Robert Walde-graue.

REFERENCES

Alliston, April (1996). *Virtue's Faults: Correspondences in Eighteenth-Century British and French Women's Fiction*. Stanford: Stanford University Press.

Baugh, Albert C. (1948). *A Literary History of England*. New York: Appleton-Century-Crofts.

Boehrer, Bruce Thomas (1992). *Monarchy and Incest in Renaissance England: Literature, Culture, Kinship, and Kingship*. Philadelphia: University of Pennsylvania Press.

Böker, Uwe (2001). 'The Institutionalisation of Legal Norms and Values in England (1500-1900).' In Uwe Böker and Julie A. Hibbard (eds.), *Processes of Institutionalisation: Case Studies in Law, Prison and Censorship*. Essen: Blaue Eule 2001, 13-60.

Clark, Anna (1987). *Women's Silence, Men's Violence: Sexual Assault in England 1770-1845*. London: Pandora.

Eger, Elizabeth, Charlotte Grant, Clíona Ó Gallchoir, and Penny Warburton, eds. (2001). *Women, Writing and the Public Sphere, 1700-1830*. Cambridge: Cambridge University Press.

Guest, Harriet (2000). *Small Change: Women, Learning, Patriotism, 1750-1810*. Chicago: University of Chicago Press.

Habermas, Jürgen (1992). *Faktizität und Geltung: Beiträge zur Diskurstheorie des Rechts und des demokratischen Rechtsstaates*. Frankfurt/Main: Suhrkamp.

Jackson, Louise A. (2000). *Child Sexual Abuse in Victorian England*. London: Routledge.

MacAndrew, Elizabeth (1979). *The Gothic Tradition in Fiction*. New York: Columbia University Press.

McDowell, Paula (1998). *The Women of Grub Street: Press, Politics, and Gender in the London Literary Marketplace 1678-1730*. Oxford: Oxford University Press.

Mellor, Anne (2000). *Mothers of the Nation: Women's Political Writing in England, 1780-1830*. Bloomington: Indiana University Press.

Mendelson, Sara Heller, and Patricia Crawford (1998). *Women in Early Modern England, 1550-1720*. Oxford: Oxford University Press.

Price, Richard (1999). *British Society 1680-1880: Dynamism, Containment and Change*. Cambridge: Cambridge University Press.

Richetti, John J. (1998). 'Popular Narrative in the Early Eighteenth Century: Formats and Formulas.' In Richard Kroll (ed.), *The English Novel: 1700 to Fielding*. London: Longman, 70-106.

Shaffer, J. (1999). 'Familial Love and Female Desire in Late Eighteenth and Early Nineteenth-Century Women's Novels.' *Criticism* 41, 67-100.

Straub, Kristina (1994). 'Frances Burney and the Rise of the Woman Novelist.' In John Richetti (ed.), *The Columbia History of the British Novel*. New York: Columbia University Press, 199-219.

Turkel, Gerald (1992). *Dividing Public and Private: Law, Politics, and Social Theory*. Westport, CT: Praeger Publishers.

Warner, William (1998). 'The Elevation of the Novel in England: Hegemony and Literary History.' In Richard Kroll (ed.), *The English Novel: 1700 to Fielding*. London: Longman, 49-69.

Zomchick, John P. (1993). *Family and the Law in Eighteenth-Century Fiction: The Public Conscience in the Private Sphere*. Cambridge: Cambridge University Press.

Anna-Christina Giovanopoulos

Alsatian Eccentricities: An Initial Appraisal of a Nineteenth-Century Collection of Eighteenth-Century News on Crime

> The Bodies of Guyant and Allpress, lately hung in Chains on Finchley Common for robbing the Mail, on Complaint of a Gentleman, were taken down on Tuesday was Se'nnight last, and removed a Mile nearer Town, when another Gentleman, representing they were a greater Nuisance to him, they were on Friday last fixed up again at their first Place of Situation. (*AE* 1274: 17 July 1772)[1]

This is a quotation from the *Alsatian Eccentricities*, a collection of eighteenth-century newspaper clippings focussing on crime.[2] As far as I have been able to determine, no research has yet been done on the compilation. In this paper, I will first characterise and introduce *Alsatian Eccentricities*; second, I will discuss crime and the press; and third, I will show the relevance of the *Alsatian Eccentricities* as a source that reflects the efforts of Henry Fielding and especially of John Fielding to reform detection and prosecution.

I will use the newspaper, i.e., the traditional medium associated with the public sphere (Habermas 1994, 87-88; Weber 1996, 10), in order to investigate developments in the fight against crime during a thirty-year period from about 1750 onwards. At that time, the principles of 'secrecy and privilege' (Zaret 2000, 11; see Weber 1996, 6-7) had been replaced by a public sphere which 'became the culturally mediating and legitimising institutional field in which the role of state power and the rights and obligations of the private individual were discussed' (Böker 2001, 16). As far as the executive power of the state is concerned, England did not have a centralised system of policing (see Hay and Snyder 1989; Wall 1998). Instead, the public was asked to join in the process of regulating crime (Price 1999, 196). Combating crime involved active participation in the process of detection and was propagated by organisations with a preventive reform impetus, such as societies for the reformation of manners (196-197; see also Curtis and Speck 1976) or John Fielding's Marine Society (*AE* below 886).

1 The *Alsatian Eccentricities* entries are numbered; thus, my citations provide the entry number followed by the year (including the date when available). The numbering of the entries is mostly correct (the sequences 560-579 and 1965-1974 were allocated twice); excerpts from chapbooks and illustrations are not numbered; the order in which a case appears may be achronological (see the case involving Joseph Kello, the chronological order of which would be *AE* 489, 486, 483). Joseph Guyant and Joseph Allpress received the death sentence for stopping the Post-Boy driving the North Mail near Edmonton, and 'robbing the same of divers Bags of Letters' (*AE* 1265: 1 July 1772). It was later reported that the two criminals 'will be hung in Chains near Houndsfield, the Place where the Robbery was committed' (1266: 9 July 1772). The original spelling and punctuation has been preserved in quotations from contemporary sources.

2 Uwe Böker brought the source to my attention.

I. T. PURLAND AND THE *ALSATIAN ECCENTRICITIES*

In this section, I will introduce the most salient characteristics of the *Alsatian Eccentricities*. As the term 'Alsatia' (i.e., a sanctuary for criminals)[3] suggests, the source is concerned with crime. The collection[4] comprises about 2,500 newspaper clippings published between 1702 and 1782. However, most of the clippings date from the years 1750 to 1781.[5] Apparently, not much more information on the source exists other than that provided in the following entry from the British Library online catalogue: 'Alsatian Eccentricities, 1700-1782, collected by T. Purland.[6] Being a collection of cuttings from newspapers, containing relations of murders and robberies, reports of trials, dying speeches, together with portraits of celebrated criminals, views, etc.'[7]

As a detailed investigation of the collection proves, this description is misleading. For example, murders do not represent the largest category of crime. Reflecting developments in society, crimes against property account for the largest group of offences. Further, the description might suggest a contemporary collector, but the collection originated in the nineteenth century[8] as confirmed by the British Library, which acquired the source in January 1853.[9] Information on T. Purland is scarce; however, searching the internet and using Frederic Boase's *Modern English Biography* (1897),[10] I have constructed the following (tentative) biography.[11]

---

3 The religious sanctuaries of the Middle Ages were (almost all) abolished in 1624 (Breuer 1996, 186), but 'bastard sanctuaries' or 'pretended privileged places' survived until the early eighteenth century. The most famous of the pseudo-sanctuaries was located in Whitefriars, between Fleet Street, Bridewell Prison, the Thames and Temple Bar; the area was called 'Alsatia', possibly in reference to the contended area between Germany and France. London's Alsatia was an area where debtors, escaped offenders, prostitutes and other criminals were relatively safe from prosecution (187). By the late seventeenth and early eighteenth centuries, Alsatia had become deserted while sanctuaries such the Old Mint in Southwark remained in operation until the mid-1720s (189).

4 The British Library has kindly reproduced the original scrapbook on microfilm (two reels).

5 There is a gap in the collection between 1753 and 1756, nothing for 1771, and hardly any clippings from 1773 and 1779. Further, John Fielding's activities are rarely mentioned in 1781 and 1782.

6 On the flyleaf, the hand-written name 'T. Purland' appears.

7 The entry continues: '2 vols. 4o. (Shelfmark 1243.k.2-3).' The British Library also holds a collection designated '*A collection of cuttings, chiefly from eighteenth century newspapers, made by T. Purland*, [ca. 1850]. Pages not numbered. Shelfmark Cup.408.m.48.' I have not yet been able to see that collection, which was acquired by the British Library in March 1981 (information from Adrian Edwards, Deputy Manager, Rare Books & Reading Room, e-mail from 21 February 2002).

8 Boase (1897) gives the date of Purland's collection as 1847.

9 Information from Adrian Edwards, Deputy Manager, Rare Books & Reading Room (e-mail from 21 February 2002).

10 I would like to thank Dr Richard Virr (Head of the Rare Books Department, McGill University, Canada), who directed my attention to Boase's *Modern English Biography* (1897), of which originally only 250 copies were printed for the author.

11 I have found various references to T. Purland, Theodosius Purland and Thomas (Theodosius) Purland, all of whom seem to be the same person.

Theodosius Purland, PhD, MA, lived from 1805 to 1881; whether he was born in London as was suggested by Alfred Gatty (1882) or whether he was the son of a chemist in Norwich where he went to school and where he met George Borrow (1803-1881) has not yet been established beyond reasonable doubt.[12] Theodosius Purland practised as a surgeon dentist in London and showed a particular aptitude in treating children (Boase 1897; Calcuttensis 1882); he published a treatise on children's teeth in 1831. Purland was concerned with proper procedures and included in his treatise 'strictures upon the practice of pretenders to dental surgery' (Purland 1831). While pursuing a career in dentistry, Purland also became a prolific 'literary collector and antiquary' (J.R.D. 1882). He embarked on the massive task of compiling the popular illustrated collection of Charles Knight's *London* in twenty volumes, published 1841-1844.[13] Charles Knight (1791-1873) was an influential publisher and the most important printer of cheap books in the nineteenth century (Feather 1988, 253; see Knight's autobiography [1864-1865]).

Theodosius Purland was also occupied with mesmerism and collected materials on mesmerism (1842-1854), including correspondence, pamphlets, broadsides, reports from institutions, newspaper clippings, advertisements and portraits.[14] Further, there is the correspondence of Thomas (Theodosius) Purland concerning the early years of the British Archaeological Society, the Royal Antiquarian, and the Numismatic and Syro-Egyptian Societies.[15] In all, my findings suggest that Purland was an enterprising and avid collector and editor.

To characterise the source itself, the *Alsatian Eccentricities* contains newspaper clippings providing information on news of crime.[16] The form of reporting crime had become standardised by an early stage; typically, readers would be informed in one

---

12 Borrow formed a gang of four with his younger schoolmates Theodosius and Francis Purland, and John Dalrymple. As children, they devised a scheme to run away and to become pirates; thus, Borrow's ballad, 'The Wandering Children and the Benevolent Gentleman' (Jenkins 1912). The attraction of George Borrow and his friends to daring schemes with criminal overtones seems to have lasted into adulthood: Borrow assisted in compiling the enlarged edition of the *Newgate Calendar* (Knapp and Baldwin 1824-1826; original edition, 1809-1810).

13 T. Purland's name is mentioned in the Archives Centre Guide of Westminster City Council: Internet, 16 Nov. 2001, available http://www.westminster.gov.uk/archives/guide/guide09.cfm.

14 The signature of Purland appears on the flyleaf of volume 4 of the collection, which is also referred to as the Purland scrapbook. It is held by the US National Library of Medicine, Internet, 16 Nov. 2001, available http://www.press.uchicago.edu/Misc/Chicago/902196.html. See US National Library of Medicine's CATLINE Database, Internet, 16 Nov. 2001, available http://www.anes.uab.edu/aneshist/mesmer2.htm.

15 Thomas (Theodosius) Purland's original correspondence (1846-1849) is held in the Rare Book Department, Archives of McGill University, Montreal, Canada. Internet, 16 Nov. 2001, available http://www.archives.mcgill.ca/guide/volume2/gen8.htm#PURLAND, THOMAS.

16 Before the lapse of the Licensing Act in 1695, a reader's curiosity as to trials was satisfied by the *Old Bailey Proceedings* and by the *Ordinary of Newgate's Accounts* (Harris 1982). But as the *Proceedings* began to serve a specialised readership, different forms reporting from the Old Bailey developed: newspapers took over the task of informing and entertaining readers by describing crime-related events (Harris 1982; Langbein 1978, 268-269).

sentence about the victim, the place, the type of crime and, if known, the offender (e.g., *AE* 1360-1363: 1774).

> A few Days ago Mrs. Banks of Conduit Street, near Hanover Square, was set upon on Rutney Common, coming for London, in her Coach, by two Highwaymen, and robbed of about 20 l. in Money and Rings. One Lady in the Coach that was with her, dropt a Ring of great value in the Bottom of the Coach and saved it. (*AE* 70: 1721)

More shocking types of crime were also committed; for example, a twelve-year-old boy attempted to murder his master three times during one night (1369: 1774). Sometimes, the editor would use the incident to comment on the offence. Crime used for the sake of entertainment sometimes centred around 'polite highwaymen' who chivalrously refused to rob women or to take more than five guineas 'though more was offered' (278: Oct. 1751; see 296: 1751; and 414: 1758).

Pre-trial information accounts for a large group of the clippings. This group includes pre-trial hearings (e.g., 390: 1777; see Langbein 1983 and 1978), comprising the examination of cases, the gathering of evidence (with the help of the public and of private prosecutors), and information on the outcome of the hearing.

Another category of newspaper clippings includes news of Assizes – relatively little information on sessions held outside of London (see *AE* 79: 1729; 208: 1751; 263: 1751; 348: 1752) – and announcements of the beginning and the end of sessions at the Old Bailey. Readers were informed that offenders had been conveyed from various prisons in London to Newgate (669: April 1776); sentences were reported through statements such as 'on Thursday ten Prisoners were tried at the Old Baily [*sic*], one whereof was capitally convicted' (204: 1751).[17] Reports became more detailed from about 1757 on; thus, typical reports stated: 'On Saturday the Sessions ended at the Old Bailey, when twelve Prisoners were tried, five of whom were cast for transportation, and seven acquitted' (604: 1765). Overall, during this sessions, 'one prisoner received Sentence of Death; two to be transported for fourteen years, and twenty-four for seven; and one branded' (ibid.).

Reprieves were routinely mentioned: 'Yesterday the Recorder made his Report to his Majesty of the six Convicts under Sentence of Death to Newgate' (1802: 1775); two were respited 'during his Majesty's pleasure' (ibid.), the rest would be executed. Readers were also routinely informed about executions and about the behaviour of prisoners. The approved behaviour – penitent and confessing – was noted throughout the period, presumably rather as an exhortation at a time when executions had ceased to function as a deterrent (1433: 1775; 1757: 1775); sometimes the journalist claimed that the display of penitence moved the audience (1427: 10 Jan. 1775; 1755: 15 Feb. 1775). From the 1770s on, causes of crime and the effectiveness of capital punishment were discussed by journalists and readers,[18] and executions came to be occasions for calls for reform – not through the abolition of the death sentence, but through removal

17 Further examples may be found in *AE* 68: 1721; 82: 1728; 84: 1728; 228: 1751; 526: 1762; 1113: 1770; 1115: 1770; 1394: 1774; 1400: 1774; 1801: 1775; 1973: 1777; 2150: 1777.

18 Letters from readers were summarised and commented upon by editors.

of the assumed causes of crime. Reform discourse also included the discussion of prisons and of mental institutions.[19]

Information on proactive measures concerned notices to the public on how to prevent crime by being watchful, locking windows and securing luggage.[20] Advertisements afforded newspaper owners with an income (due to the editorship of Purland, only a few advertisements can be found). Session Papers and trials were also advertised.[21] Purland also inserted illustrations, such as views of public buildings and portraits of criminals, e.g., of Stephen McDaniel, the notorious thief-catcher (below 369: 1752; see Paley 1989). Some extracts from chapbooks were also inserted by Purland, including famous cases such as the one of William Hawke, the Flying Highwayman (*AE* 1418: 1774).[22]

Purland was diligent in providing dates of publication; unfortunately, he neglected to name the original sources. I assume that many clippings came either from the *Public Advertiser* or from the *Gazetteer* (see 755: 1767) and, later, from the *London Packet or New Lloyd's Evening Post.*

II. Crime and the Press: The Function of Newspapers

Throughout the time covered by the *Alsatian Eccentricities*, complaints about the (often alleged) rise of crime can be found. In 1718 Charles Hitchen, a corrupt marshal in London, claimed that the streets were not safe at night (Hitchen 1718, 6) – due to the machinations of the (in)famous Jonathan Wild: 'O *London* [...] that thou art become a Receptacle for a Den of *Thieves* and Robbers, and all sorts of villainous Persons and Practices' (5). Hitchen's complaint was typical of the eighteenth century. But was there really a crime wave? Contemporaries certainly thought so (Fielding 1988; Colquhoun 1796),[23] and regardless of later analyses, the perception of

19 See *AE* 1787: 1775; 2119: Sept. 1777; 2121: 1777; 814: 1769; 925: 1769; 1370: 1774.

20 See *AE* 794: 26 Nov. 1767; 608: 27 Sept. 1765; 1196: 1772 (perhaps not meant to be taken quite seriously); 2159: 28 Nov. 1776; 2220: 20 Dec. 1779.

21 See e.g., *AE* 205: 1751; 218: 1751; 369: 1752; 556: 1762. Another example is afforded by entry 1176, where it was announced that the Sessions Paper would be published (i.e., the first part of the last sessions), and that the second part would be available in a few days. The price was 6d, and the material would be sold by J. Cooke, no. 17, Pater-noster Row (1770). Many printers had established businesses in that street.

22 In this case, the excerpt was taken from *An Account of the Life, Trials and Robberies of William Hawke; An Genuine Account of the Life, Robberies, Trial and Execution, of William Hawke, Call'd the Flying Highwayman, Who was Executed at Tyburn, July the First, 1774* (*AE* 1418: 1774).

23 Lack of data and different ideological outlooks and interpretations lead to very different assessments by modern historians. Beattie, who analyses indictments in Surrey and Sussex between 1662 and 1802 (1974, 52), points out the weakness of this method when it comes to shedding light on criminality: only those crimes that an individual reported and prosecuted appear in official records (53-54). Patrick Colquhoun believed that only 10% of crimes committed were reported (Beattie 1974, 54). Also, Beattie finds an unwillingness to prosecute offences as punishments became harsher (54). In time of crisis, more pressure would be put on the authorities to deal with

contemporaries is of singular importance: their construction of society as being under attack influenced attitudes towards crime. For example, note was made in the *Alsatian Eccentricities* in 1765 that 164 felons in New Prison and in Clerkenwell Bridewell were awaiting trial at the next Sessions at the Old Bailey, which would be the 'Largest Session of Gaol-Delivery that has been known in the Memory of the oldest Man living' (*AE* 571: 1765). For the April sessions of 1770, 338 offenders were to be tried; this figure was compared to the 272 offenders tried in 1737[24] and the editor concluded that such a rise was 'in some Measure attributed to the Increase of common Prostitutes, who nightly infest our Streets' (1086: 25 April 1770). In 1775 the rise of crime was not considered to be the result of 'any peculiar Degeneracy in the Minds of the present Generation,' but to be caused by the absence of an 'able Hand' who should 'lay a Plan that might go to the Root of the Evil' – 'daring Violations of the Law' were 'certainly more frequent than they used to be' (1883: 5 Sept. 1775). 'Contemporaries were convinced that they were living in particularly violent times, and that they were surrounded by a world of crime' (Hellmuth 1996, 45; see Beattie 1974, 45).[25] This perception was also encouraged by the growth of the press: as today, crime sells (see Black 2001, 54-57), and newspapers were predominantly an economic enterprise.[26] However, newspapers did not only try to entertain readers, they also played an important part in the institutionalisation (Rehberg 1994, 1995 and 2001) of a professional and centralised law enforcement organisation. I will concentrate on this function of the press, which does not imply that the detection of crime could not be used for purposes of entertainment as well.

In the eighteenth century, prosecution lay in the hands of private individuals.[27] Unless an offender was caught in the act of stealing, for example, one way to retrieve lost property was to advertise the loss in newspapers. Crime advertisements can be found regularly since 1665 in the *London Gazette,* the 'only officially authorized newspaper for most of the period 1665-1695' (Styles 1989, 58). Victims of theft could also approach thief-takers (see Paley 1989), and Jonathan Wild (Howson 1970), who regarded crime as a business and who diligently kept an account of transactions,

---

crimes (55). Another noteworthy development is the understatement of the nature of crime (83); see Innes and Styles 1986.

24 The source mentions the Mayoralty of Sir John Barnard during the reign of George I, which would be 1737.

25 Ruth Paley suggests that the pronounced rise in crime in 1748 (at end of the war) might be linked to the 'activities of a small band of professional criminals' and to the activities of 'thief-takers and other knowledgeable prosecutors [who] may have exerted a quasi-institutional pressure on the legal system by producing a larger proportion of malicious or vexatious prosecutions at times of public disquiet' (1989, 339). Also, the *Alsatian Eccentricities* contains reports of a possible plot by thief-takers who put up advertisements concerning non-existent crimes in order to encourage clients to employ thief-takers (*AE* 1963: 1777).

26 Hannah Barker claims that there were some different (radical) papers for which commercial considerations did not play the chief role (2000, 108, see ch. 8); but Jeremy Black believes that such radical newspapers constituted a minority (2001, 11); see Black's reluctance to follow the argument of the press as a democratising institution (58).

27 See Langbein 1978. For a study of the social position of prosecutors in Essex, see King 1984.

affords an early example of the professionalisation of thief-taking (see Giovanopoulos 2002). Thus, Wild's 'Lost Property Office' can be considered as a forerunner of the public offices such as the one in Bow Street, Covent Garden, run by Henry Fielding and later by John Fielding.[28] The main difference between Wilde and the Fielding brothers was that the Fieldings served as magistrates and did not instigate crime as Wild had done.

Often faced with professional gangs of criminals (Paley 1989, 339), the state institutions had to acknowledge their lack of success. To detect, to apprehend, to prosecute and to convict offenders, it became necessary to create a system that transcended space and time: the 'ability to distribute, marshal, and retrieve information about offences and offenders is essential to the process of criminal investigation' (Styles 1989, 55).[29] John Styles argues 'that the proliferation of printed detective advertisements during the eighteenth century resulted in a real enhancement of the capacity to enforce the criminal law' (88). Implicitly referring to Foucault's concept, Styles maintains that the 'intensification of surveillance' (ibid.; see Foucault 1992) played a central role in controlling criminal activities. Control was not primarily linked to state activity but to the involvement of the public; the crime advertisement depended 'on a form of general access broadcasting of information' (Styles 1989, 88) and on the willingness of the public to participate in the process of detection (91).[30]

In order to determine whether the newspaper could be an adequate medium through which to reach the public, it becomes essential to consider newspapers in terms of circulation figures as well as of readership. After the lapse of the Licensing Act in 1695, which, according to Hannah Barker, removed restrictions rather than secured any rights (Barker 2000, 14-15), newspapers proliferated – especially outside of London (29).[31] Barker estimates that by 1712, twelve papers were produced in the capital. By the mid-eighteenth century there were six weekly, six tri-weekly and six daily newspapers (ibid.). For 1783 Barker finds nine dailies and ten bi- or tri-weeklies,

28 Gerald Howson (1970) follows this view; but not all scholars would agree with the comparison of Wild and the Fielding brothers (Paley 1989, 302-303).

29 John Styles investigates the effect of advertisements in provincial newspapers on the apprehension of offenders. The emergence of the crime advertisement led to new methods of detection, even though Styles does not consider this development as a planned and controlled activity within the reform process after 1750 (1989, 57). However, crime advertisements in newspapers were closely connected to the reform of policing, and were especially supported and used by the Fieldings, as well as by Patrick Colquhoun and by Edwin Chadwick in the nineteenth century (57).

30 The importance of participatory assumptions is stressed by Brewer and Styles 1980, e.g., 16-17.

31 Barker considers the political function of newspapers as a place where public administration could be discussed (2000, 13). She stresses the view that the liberty of the press was an essential prerequisite in a free state by referring, for example, to William Blackstone and to Jeremy (13-14). Through newspapers, the individual (no longer the passive subject) could show a legitimate interest in politics and participate in debates outside of parliament (22). Feather maintains that 'newspapers were [...] becoming the principal vehicles for both fact and opinion' (1988, 85). But historians argue as to when the newspaper was accepted as part of the political system. While Michael Harris (1987) suggests the age of Walpole, John Brewer places the development in the 1760s (Brewer 1976, 24). For the physical appearance of newspapers, see Barker 2000, 43-44; Black 2001, 9.

and by the 1790s the numbers had risen to fourteen dailies, seven tri-weeklies and two weeklies – in all, twenty-three newspapers (30). As far as circulation is concerned, Michael Harris estimates that in the 1720s and 1740s, each newspaper sold on average between 1,000 and 2,000 copies per issue (Barker 1987, 55-57); that figure rose for some papers to 5,000 copies per issue. In 1750 the total weekly circulation was about 100,000 (190). The overall circulation increased from 2.5 million in 1713, to 7.3 million in 1750, 9.4 million in 1760, 9.7 million in 1765, 12.6 million in 1775, 14.0 million in 1780, and 31.0 million in 1835 (Black 2001, 73). Yet the individual circulation remained stable at around 2,000 to 5,000 copies per issue until the early nineteenth century (Barker 2000, 32).[32] Urban growth encouraged the consumption of newspapers; public places of circulation were, for example, inns, shops, book clubs, coffee houses, and other urban spaces where a political culture emerged (36).

As far as ownership is concerned, many London newspapers were in the hands of (shareholding) booksellers from the late 1720s on (Harris 1978, 96).[33] Harris considers this development to be the result of financial exigencies: first, newspapers provided booksellers with a regular income; and second, newspapers were used as an advertising medium (ibid.; see Barker 2000, 97; Black 2001, 12).[34] An example from the *Alsatian Eccentricities* proves the mixing of news and advertising: following news about the executions of a confessing highwayman and of another non-confessing highwayman, the readers were informed, 'Their Confessions at large and Dying Words will be published next Monday Morning and may be had of any of the News Sellers' (*AE* 167: 1750). Some London newspapers (especially the bi- and tri-weekly papers that appeared on Tuesdays, Thursdays and Saturdays) depended on sales in the provinces (Barker 2000, 42-43), which made them the ideal medium for crime advertisements that had to reach a wider audience in geographical terms in order to be successful.

Circulation figures are difficult to establish, and when it comes to assessing who read the papers, even more problems arise. Barker points out that, even though the ratio between newspapers and population was low throughout the period, a single copy of a paper was read by more than one person (47).[35] She assumes that in 1750 about a quarter of the population in London read a newspaper and, by the 1780s, about one

32 Barker does not find that rises in newspaper circulation were linked solely to developments in domestic and foreign politics (2000, 36). For example, there was no significant rise in the 1760s, a period of insecurity, but newspaper production rose in the early 1770s and the late 1780s (37).

33 Michael Harris finds that 'for most of the eighteenth century the practice of group management [...] was of major importance in the conduct of all forms of London newspaper' (1978, 107). However, later research has modified this argument; see Barker 2000, 99.

34 Often, certain newspapers specialised in certain areas of advertising (Barker 2000, 97).

35 Barker suggests that 20-30 people might have read one copy (2000, 46-47). Black, who is not as positive about the impact of the newspaper as Barker (Black 2001, viii), stresses the marginality of printers (as newspaper producers) in the mid-eighteenth century and emphasises instead the influence of shareholding booksellers (19). Also, Black believes that the press 'was largely read by upper- and middle-class consumers' (ibid.).

third (ibid.).[36] As far as social status is concerned, some researchers maintain that the middle classes formed the chief readership (Harris 1996) while others, such as John Brewer, locate the readership predominantly in the elite (Brewer 1976, 143; see Barker 2000, 49).

The relatively high price of newspapers (see Barker 2000), which could serve as an alternative means of censorship by imposing economic restrictions on the readership, did not necessarily limit access to papers.[37] Neither did illiteracy – newspapers were read aloud, and there were even associations where papers were read and discussed by people from the lower classes (Barker 2000, 56). Barker maintains that newspaper readers were socially diverse and that, particularly in London, 'those fairly low down the social scale would have had some contact with the press' (63).

III. The Fielding Method of Detection as Presented through the *Alsatian Eccentricities*

In 1748 Henry Fielding was appointed to the Commission of Peace for Westminster as the successor of Thomas DeVeil; he took over the lease of the house in Bow Street, Covent Garden, and practised there from 2 November 1748. In January 1749, he assumed the County of Middlesex magistracy for financial reasons.[38] Fielding was a court Justice of the Peace with more financial support from the Government – and a greater workload – than the county JPs (see Langbein 1983, 58-60). In Middlesex a single 'principal magistrate' – Henry and later John Fielding – decided about half the cases, the other half was dealt with by the other Middlesex JPs (76-77). In the city, the institution of the 'sitting aldermen' had been introduced in December 1737 after the duties had become too heavy for the Lord Mayor (77).[39] Henry Fielding's blind half-brother John acted as his assistant and succeeded him in 1754.

Henry Fielding believed that the prevention and suppression of crime had to be based on an understanding of the causes, which he located in 'luxury' (Fielding 1988, 77; see Radzinowicz 1948, 405-406) and in the ineffectiveness of the Poor Law (Fielding 1988, 99; see Radzinowicz 1948, 406). Further, he blamed the virtual impunity of receivers of stolen goods (Fielding 1988, 126-130), 'inadequate control of the movement of potential criminals' (Radzinowicz 1948; Fielding 1988, 130-131), the backwardness in apprehending (Fielding 1988, 145-154) and prosecuting criminals

36 The figures for the provinces were significantly lower; Barker estimates that in 1750, 4%, and by the 1780s, around 8% of the population outside London read a paper (2000, 47).

37 See Black 2001, 10. In 1711 Robert Harley, later the first Earl of Oxford, supported moves towards the taxation of printed matter. In 1712 stamp duties were extended to newspapers. Harley's aim was to increase revenue, but perhaps also to exert censorship by increasing costs for the production of newspapers and, thus, limiting the number of readers (Feather 1988, 86). However, circulation was hardly affected in the first few years following 1712 (87).

38 According to Hay and Snyder, the office in Bow Street should not be analysed as the representative policing institution in the eighteenth century that led towards the new police (1989, 9).

39 For Fielding's duties, see Langbein 1983, 63; see also Langbein 1978; and, e.g., *AE* 390: 1777. Alternatively, Fielding encouraged out-of-court settlements (Bertelsen 1997, 338).

(also due to the practice of advertising, i.e., to the 'no-questions-asked' variety), fear of the offenders or of the costs (154-158), the difficulty in obtaining sufficient evidence (158-159), the number of pardons (which interrupted the chain of justice; Fielding 1988, 163) and the executions themselves which no longer served as a deterrent (167-168; see Radzinowicz 1948, 407).[40] Based upon his analysis, Henry Fielding proposed to strengthen control over criminals.[41] Control as envisaged by Henry Fielding and his successor, John Fielding, was to be achieved through a system of detection that Langbein characterises as: 'centralization of crime reporting and of the advertising of stolen goods; cooperation of the pawnbrokers; a shadowy police force for following up; and all of it supervised by the examining magistrate [...] who would build the prosecution for trial at the Old Bailey' (Langbein 1983, 67).

Ruth Paley points to some ambiguities in Henry Fielding's practices. While combating crime, Henry Fielding was involved with corrupt thief-takers such as Stephen McDaniel, who was arrested in 1745 (1989, 327, 336), and there is evidence that Fielding and other magistrates, such as John Gower and William Hammond, tolerated thief-takers and their conspiracies (which involved setting up innocent people to receive the statutory reward upon conviction, perjury, blackmail and extortion [309]) because 'to make any move against them was to risk exposing the corruption of the whole system of the administration of the criminal law in the metropolis' (334; see 302-303).[42] However, Paley does not imply that Fielding colluded with the thief-takers. His group, known as 'Mr Fielding's people', was changing fast: the old thief-takers had left the group by 1751 or 1752 and left Westminster (314). Still, Paley suggests that some of Fielding's 'policemen' were associated with the underworld and that the group as a whole was not above suspicion (337).

The evolution of the system of the Fielding brothers, especially as developed by John Fielding, can be illustrated through the *Alsatian Eccentricities*. Most categories introduced in the first part of the paper contain entries referring to the brothers. For example, in 1751 and 1752, there are advertisements for Henry Fielding's *Enquiry into the Causes of the Late Increase of Robbers* (first edition, *AE* 206; second edition, 300) and, in 1766, a book by John Fielding was advertised: the public would find the book useful because it would help them to decide whether to prosecute. Also, Fielding wanted to 'beget an Obedience to the Laws, by making them known', i.e., by publicising them (681: 1766; new edition, 843: Feb. 1769).[43] But by far the single largest group is constituted by news of and by Henry and especially John Fielding.

---

40 Similar complaints had been raised in 1725 by Bernard Mandeville (1964, 2-5).

41 For approval of Henry Fielding's scheme, see *AE* 1894: [Sept.] 1775.

42 For a list of thief-takers active in London in the mid-eighteenth century, see 'Appendix' in Paley 1989, 341.

43 In general, interest in legal matters was widespread. For example, an earlier advertisement from 1721 stated: 'Lately published, The Modern Justice; containing the Business of a Justice of Peace, in all its Parts: As an Abridgement of the Common Law, and of all the Acts of Parliament, relating to Justices of Peace, Constables, [...] Authentic Precedents, [...] Precepts, [...] Chairman's Charge in the Quarter Sessions, [...]. Third Edition, 1720, by Giles Jacob, Gent. Printed for B. Lintot at the Cross Keys in Fleet-street' (*AE* 73: 1721).

Reports of pre-trial hearings can be found regularly in the *Alsatian Eccentricities*: 'On Monday last was committed to Clerkenwell Bridewell, by Henry Fielding, Esq., one Solomon Smith, for picking the Pocket of Mr. John Mewburn, a Country Gentleman' (189: Feb. 1751). The impact of the Fieldings increased, and, by 1772, a regular column 'Proceedings Yesterday at the Public Office in Bow Street' appeared once a week (2224-2225: 12 Jan. 1780; 1228: April 1772).[44] Only a selection of the most important cases was reported;[45] typically, one matter-of-fact sentence sufficed, but sometimes a bit of humour was employed:

> A miserable one-legged, itinerant Fidler summoned a Mr. Hodges to give an Account of the Thief who stole his Fiddle. Mr. Hodges knew no more of it than the Man in the Moon, but the *Crowder's Stock in Trade*, Value 1s., 6 d., was returned after he had tuned it to prove that it was his own (*AE* 1282).

The following case is paradigmatic for the evolved Fielding method: Sir John Fielding's people received 'intelligence that Lawless, and the two other highwaymen that have lately infested the neighbourhood of London, were seen at Highgate' (1384: 1774). After having called in reinforcements, the 'policemen' pursued the offenders, searched them, found evidence of criminal activities and brought the highwaymen to the Public Office in Bow Street, where Fielding committed them to prison.[46] The announcement that the highwaymen would be re-examined ('today') is of importance because it carried an implied request for the public to come forward and to give evidence of crimes committed by the highwaymen. Fielding regularly held such 'public (and publicized) viewings of suspected persons and recovered goods' (Langbein 1983, 64). For example, Simpson, Martin, and Adwell, three sailors and footpads who belonged to a gang of nine, had been impeached by their accomplice Hunter and were re-examined before 'Sir John Fielding, Knt.', who found the accusation proven by both their accomplice and their own confessions (*AE* 552: 1762). But Fielding wanted to collect further instances of crimes committed by the gang and asked anyone who had been robbed on the roads near London to report crimes to the magistrate: 'It is earnestly requested that they will immediately apply to [Fielding], when their several informations will be taken, and the prisoners re-examined' (ibid.).

In turning their public office into a 'central clearing house for dealing with unsolved crime and for gathering evidence to be used at trial' (Langbein 1983, 64), the Fieldings

---

44 'Proceedings Yesterday at the Public Office in Bow Street' is a continuation of the 'Reports from the Public Office in Bow-street, relative to Felonies and Robberies during the Course of last week' (e.g., *AE* 719: 1767). 'Commitment of Offenders and Commission of Highway and Footpad Robberies during the Course of last Week' affords further information in the 1770s (e.g., 1044: 1770; 1060: 1770, 1068: 1770; 1072: 1770; 1076: 1770; see 1132: 1770; 1205: 1772).

45 Reports end, for example, like this: 'Several other Matters of inferior Consequence were heard and determined' (*AE* 2000: 2 April 1777); or 'No other Business worthy of Notice occurred Yesterday' (2004: 10 April 1777).

46 In a similar case, the neighbourhood of Hounslow was 'infested' by two daring highwaymen. Consequently, 'the vigilant magistrates of Bow-street have dispatched their active train in pursuit of them, but hitherto without success' (*AE* 2439: 1782).

depended on the press to a high degree.[47] In the following section, I will concentrate on the role of the press – especially in John Fielding's method of detection.

From 1752 on, the Fieldings co-operated with the *Public Advertiser*, which sold between 3,000 to 4,500 copies per day (Barker 2000, 32), and later with the *Gazetteer*, run by Mary Say from the 1770s until the 1790s (100; cf. Styles 1983, 136). John Brewer has shown that fluctuations in the sale of the *Public Advertiser* (between 1765 and 1771) suggest an elite readership.[48] The *Gazetteer*, on the other hand, did not follow a similar pattern in sales;[49] thus, one may deduce that the *Gazetteer* reached a non-elite audience (Barker 2000, 49; see Barker 1998, 22-42).[50] Since Fielding published advertisements in both papers, he could ask readers from various social strata to participate in the collaborative effort of detection.

For his detection, Fielding made extensive use of pawnbrokers, whom he asked to subscribe to the *Public Advertiser* (Langbein 1983, 66).[51] In January 1766, John Fielding announced in the *Public Advertiser* that, in order to reduce crime, the public should inform Fielding of any transgression; Fielding would insert advertisements in the *Public Advertiser*, and pawnbrokers and other shopkeepers should read these advertisements and act upon them.

> From the Police. The extensive Sale of the Public Advertiser; (joined to the Variety of Channel, thro' which it passes) has always been the Means of detecting of many Robberies, and of apprehending so many Offenders, that it may be proper to give this Public Notice, That, for the Future, all Informations of this Kind, sent to Bow-Street, will be constantly inserted in this Paper:

---

47 To summarise Lance Bertelsen's findings on Henry Fielding and his use of the *Covent-Garden Journal* (Feather 1988, 112) to publicise and to advertise his activities, analysing the proceedings described in the *Journal* during its short eleven-month existence in 1752, Bertelsen found that 'everyday activity in Fielding's court [...] was taken up primarily with idle and disorderly persons and small-time larcenists' (1997, 341). Bertelsen notices an ambiguity in Henry Fielding's descriptions of prostitutes and interprets this as Fielding's exertion of textual-sexual power over them (342, 344). Contemporaries, as well, remarked critically on the entertainment value derived from legal reports of that type (342, 345) and on Fielding's capacity for self-advertisement (344): 'Fielding the moralist and Fielding the journalist collide head-on' (346). According to Bertelsen, the dialectic of humanism and exploitation (the latter not necessarily as a conscious strategy [352]) becomes evident throughout his sample (347). In conclusion, he considers Fielding's legal writings not as authoritative and monosemic, but just as heteroglossic as his fictional writings (351). Ian Bell describes law as a 'univocal body of statue' (1991, 2) and literature as multi-vocal (46), but sees both as parallel discourses. With Henry Fielding, this division becomes blurred.

48 Circulation would reach a peak in February and March (before the end of the sessions in Parliament) and would decline afterwards. Sales would rise again in October or November, at the beginning of the parliamentary year (Brewer 1976, 143).

49 Barker (1998) analysed the circulation figures between 1784 and 1795.

50 As the century progressed, more staff was involved in producing a newspaper. Reporters, or rather 'newsgathers' and 'correspondents', were paid for contributions in London. Correspondents in the provinces often remained unpaid (Barker 2000, 104). The *Gazetteer* employed 14 correspondents in the 1770s, among them, those responsible for Guildhall and Bow Street news (101; see Haig 1960, 178-180).

51 'The gist of this scheme was to centralize and to bring within Fielding's domain the process by which citizens advertised for the return of stolen goods' (Langbein 1983, 66).

And if such informations are properly attended to, by Pawnbrokers, Jewellers, Silver-Smiths, Stable-Keepers, Buyers of second-hand Cloaths, etc., few Robberies will escape Detection, especially if all Persons robbed make use of this Paper to advertise their Losses in. J. Fielding (*AE* 643: 24 Jan. 1766)

Advertisements can be divided into three categories: 1) advertisements for stolen or lost property; 2) calls for owners to identify suspect goods, believed to be stolen (see 686: 27 Jan. 1766; 1429: 15 Jan. 1775; 1435: 16 Jan. 1775); and 3) advertisements for escaped offenders (see 582: 1765; 685: 1766; 2045: 1777; 2218: 10 Jan. 1780).[52] The (institutionalised) phrasing of advertisements in the first (and the largest) group included: 'If offered to be pawned or sold, stop it and the Party, and give Notice to Sir John Fielding, and you shall receive [specified amount of] Reward from the Owner on Conviction' (see entries 1772-1774: 1775).[53] The conditions for receiving rewards were detailed in Acts of 1717 (4 Geo. I, c.2) and of 1752 (26 Geo. II, c.36), which put a restriction on the practice of 'no questions asked' (Styles 1989, 60; Langbein 1983, 66). As a special incitement to co-operate, the following advertisement could be inserted: 'Sir John Fielding will pay the usual Reward of Five Guineas, over and above the Reward allowed by Act of Parliament' (*AE* 735: 1767).[54]

---

52 Styles placed the advertisements (in provincial newspapers) into three different categories: 1) advertisements for lost property (1989, 59-65); 2) advertisements for escaped offenders (65-67); and 3) threat of prosecution as a deterrent (67). The first category was by far the largest group and accounted for 98% in 1729-1730 and for 58% in 1784.

53 See also *AE* 597: 22 July 1765; for 1767, see 599-601, 741-742 and 750; for 1769, see 845-848; and for 1771, see 1183-1184; for 1771-1772, see 1184. Several advertisements can be found that are concerned with apprentices who ran away (e.g., for 1750, entries 169-170). A typical advertisement included a description of the apprentice, the offer of a sham reward and the threat of punishment if the apprentice would not be returned to his or her master.

54 Styles does not think that rewards (see Langbein 1983, 106-110) played a very important role; eighteenth-century people were willing to join in the detection of horse theft, which Styles analyses in detail. Such a type of crime was different from the 'kind of popular solidarities which sustained offences like smuggling or poaching' (Styles 1989, 92). On the other hand, Ruth Paley concludes that the chief effect of the 40-pound reward was not to encourage detection, but rather to encourage committing a crime, namely that of perjury to gain a reward (1989, 323). See the discussion of the McDaniel case and its impact on John Fielding in Langbein 1983, 110-114. Sometimes, the government increased the statutory reward by proclamation in order to 'create an atmosphere of suspicion' among criminals who, thus the reasoning, would fear the rise of informers among their midst (Paley 1989, 324). Proclamations can also be considered as catalysts of insecurity or as an attempt by authorities to spread fear in order to gain the public's co-operation. For example, the Black Boy Alley gang, a group of highwayman and street robbers, terrorised London in the mid 1740s when Sir Thomas de Veil – Henry Fielding's predecessor and 'London's principal acting justice' (325) – was ill for much of the time. Some of the gang were arrested, but in autumn 1748 members started to become active again, and in January 1749 a gang of 24 Irishmen stormed the Gatehouse Prison to secure the release of a fellow gang member (325-326). Paley believes that Henry Fielding's vigorous campaign against crime during that period 'created and maintained' the moral panic surrounding the attack on the Gatehouse Prison and the exposure of the McDaniel gang in 1753. The theme of 'moral panic' and its influence on criminal statistics is acknowledged by Hay 1982, 158.

In his case study on horse theft (Styles 1989, 76-82), John Styles has proved the effectiveness of the newspaper advertisement as an 'impersonal or indirect detective technique' (77; see 86). But the problems connected with prosecuting criminals, especially those who had removed themselves from the scene of the crime, were daunting in both time and cost,[55] and many victims were reluctant to insert advertisements. Therefore, John Fielding continually admonished the public to participate in prosecution by informing Fielding's office of any crime (*AE* 643-646: 1766; see Styles 1989, 92).

An indirect means to persuade the public to support Fielding was to spread news of success, in other word: self-advertising. In 1767 Fielding emphasised his expertise and claim to power:

> The collecting into one Point all Informations of Fraud and Felony committed in or near this Metropolis, by constant Advertisements, and the Correspondence opened and carried on from this Office for many Years past with the acting Magistrates in the Country, on the same Account, has constructed such an useful System of Police, as must ever be deemed a valuable Acquisition to this Country, when it is considered that by this means most of the notorious Offenders, whether in Gangs or otherwise, both in Town and Country, for these 15 Years past, have been apprehended, broke, dispersed, or brought to Justice. (*AE* 755, 1767)[56]

Fielding pointed out that the plan had received 'ready Assistance' by silversmiths, pawnbrokers, owners of clothes shops, etc., and that past advertising in the *Public Advertiser* and in the *Daily Gazetteer* and the notices and warnings sent from the Office had been successful in making it more difficult for criminals to operate. However, the continued success depended on the continued application of the same method, 'and this is in the Power of the Public only, by furnishing the above Office with all necessary Informations for that Purpose' (ibid.).

John Fielding tirelessly pointed out that he had extended his London system to the country and that he had thus tightened control over criminals. As readers knew, exchanging letters with county magistrates had already led to success in helping to arrest gangs and individuals. Fielding promised:

> and this useful Plan will of course become more and more so, in Proportion as this Correspondence is extended, as will also the Crimes of Highway and Footpad Robberies in particular, as well as other Offences in general, become more rare in Proportion as the Public shall continue to give the earliest Notice of the Commission of them in and near London. (762: 1767)

The success in London was beyond doubt. For example, according to Fielding in the same report, Richard Crouch, a burglar, had been caught because of immediate information to the Public office (ibid.).

Another report can also be considered as a form of self-advertising: Fielding claimed that his Office was most likely to know offenders and that it was most able to

55 See the ten stages of a criminal case in Hay and Snyder 1989, 25-26; and the case described by Styles 1983, 129-135. Styles writes that an advertisement in the *General Evening Post* cost about 7 shillings (for two appearances) in the 1730s (1983, 133). In provincial newspapers, placing an advertisement cost less than 2s. 6d. before 1723, and doubled to around 5s. by the 1790s due to an increase in tax (Styles 1989, 70).

56 The same advertisement also appeared in February 1769 (*AE* 844) and in March 1769 (*AE* 885).

deal with them by controlling and centralising the flow of information from other offices (863: 1769).[57] This plan was supported by the Duke of Grafton (1735-1811) (755: 1767), the First Lord Commissioner of the Treasury (from July 1766 to 28 Jan. 1770), and notice was given that on every Wednesday from eleven to two, several magistrates would sit in the office in Bow Street 'to hear Complaints relating to public Nuisances within their Jurisdiction, to order immediately to remove the same, if in their Power,' or to find other means of redressing grievances (863: 1769; see 1178: 1770).

News of Fielding's successes kept him in the public eye and perhaps aimed to create a favourable reception for measures of reform. For example, in 1769 Fielding's preventive plan involving sending poor, unsupervised boys to the merchant navy in order to preserve them from death received renewed publicity (862: 9 Feb. 1769).[58] In 1772, by which time his method of detection through advertisements, magistrates and 'policemen' (i.e., 'Mr Fielding's People) had become institutionalised in London, John Fielding proposed a 'General Preventive Plan' – an attempt to increase the efficiency of policing.[59] According to Styles, the innovative potential of the plan lay in its attempt to spread the system of gathering information on offenders to the whole country (1983, 136).[60] Fielding excited extreme admiration and praise:[61]

---

57 The advertisement stated that all offenders would be re-examined, as would be all felons and cheats brought in during the week by other magistrates in the County of Middlesex and the City and Liberty of Westminster. These criminals, Fielding argued, should be sent to the Public Office in Bow Street, 'where their Persons are most likely to be known, and where, from the many Informations of Frauds and Felonies transmitted to that Office, they may probably meet with the Parties they have injured; which Plan renders it impossible for real Offenders to escape Justice, and gives those who are falsely accused, an Opportunity of sending for their Friends, and defeating the Malice of their Enemies. J. Fielding' (*AE* 863: 1769).

58 The argument went like this: Fielding believed that unsupervised boys would turn to crime and would end at the gallows. Equipping them with clothes and sending them to sea was thought to offer the boys with a job opportunity that would keep them out of court (*AE* 862: 9 Feb. 1769). Boys had been sent to sea by Fielding since February 1756 (*AE* no number, after 886, third leaf). In about 1768, Fielding published ideas for the foundation of a society that would send boys to sea, but he did not get enough support. In 1769, he published his ideas again (*AE* 862: Feb 9, 1769). The Marine Society was thriving in 1780 and looked for boys to be sent to the Royal Navy, i.e., to serve on board war ships (after *AE* 886, second leaf: 1780).

59 See summary in Styles 1983, 135-136. The Fielding brothers are considered to be the founders of a reformed police; however, see Styles' criticism (148-149).

60 John Fielding extended his use of the press by including a thrice-weekly paper, the *London Packet or New Lloyd's Evening Post*. 'The General Hue and Cry' – a section of crime advertisements – was printed in large type and with a characteristic border on the front page on Mondays (Styles 1983, 137).

61 Once, a case of corruption in Fielding's public office linked to a denial of access to the public hearings was reported only to shed a positive light on Fielding. In principle, the pre-trial process was a public process; everyone was to get a free hearing. John Fielding was informed that some people with complaints had only been admitted to the office after paying a fee. During an interval in the proceedings, Fielding announced that if the persons who took the bribe were pointed out they would be dismissed. 'He observed that the Conduct of the Magistrates was open to the Censure or Approbation of the World; that [...] the Place where they sat to administer Justice was "free as Air;"

> A correspondent[62] observes, that the powers of Sir John Fielding are really amazing, and that his sensibility is as evident as his understanding is clear, manly and steady. [...] The same gentleman says, that the good sense, the equal temper, the steady and manly conduct of Sir John are so blended in the character of that worthy magistrate; and he displays the tender feelings of humanity so generously, that all who hear him are pleased, and indeed charmed with him. He is blind to the passions and prejudices which are so conspicuous in others [...] Happy would it be for society, if every Justice of the Peace had a head and heart like those of Sir John Fielding! (1416: 1774)

Yet Fielding's fame could not overcome traditional modes of thinking. In 1775, as a further stage in the 'General Preventive Plan', high constables in the country were to accept new duties, including the task of pursuing offenders (Styles 1983, 143-144). But such activities were deemed incompatible with the social position of high constables; thus, Fielding met with resistance from county magistrates because he had neglected to adapt his method to local conditions (148-149):[63] The 'General Preventive Plan' can be analysed in terms of a (partial) failure of an institution,[64] supporting the concept that institutions must be able to accommodate changes if they are to be successful in creating relatively stable and permanent procedures.

Countering an attack on magistrates who the public thought were not dealing with crime effectively, Fielding told readers that unless the public co-operated and provided the magistrates with information about offences, nothing could be done to improve the situation (*AE* 1178: 20 Dec. 1777). However, activities by the Fielding brothers and by other reformers gradually served to decrease the role of the public (Styles 1989, 93) as, in the nineteenth century, functions of the public were incorporated in new institutions controlled by the state.

---

and that so far from wishing to exclude respectable Company, they were happy in Proportion to the Number of Witnesses to the Integrity of their Proceedings' (*AE* 1998: 19 May 1777).

62 For the role of letters in newspapers, see Enkemann 1983, 10. Sometimes whole pages would be given over to letters from readers, who, thus, participated in a public debate.

63 Styles lists some of the reasons for the 'cool' reception of the 1775 proposals by magistrates: the expense of paying for increased levels of policing were to be raised locally; and high constables considered pursuing offenders beneath their position (1983, 143-144).

64 Fielding's failure foreshadows that of Chadwick's in 1839 (Hay and Snyder 1989, 11).

PRIMARY LITERATURE

Colquhoun, Patrick (1796). *A Treatise on the Police of the Metropolis*. London: Printed for C. Dilly.

Fielding, Henry (1988). *An Enquiry Into the Causes of the Late Increase of Robbers with some Proposals for Remedying the Evil*. In *An Enquiry Into the Causes of the Late Increase of Robbers and Related Writings*. Ed. Malvin R. Zirker. Oxford: Clarendon Press, 61-172. Original edition Dublin, 1751.

[Hitchen, Charles] (1718). *The Regulator; or, A Discovery of the Thieves, Thief-Takers, and Locks [...]. By a Prisoner in Newgate*. London: Printed for T. Warner.

Knapp, Andrew, and William Baldwin, eds. (1809-1810). *Criminal Chronology; or, the New Newgate Calendar; Being Interesting Memoirs of Notorious Characters, Who Have Been Convicted of Outrages on the Laws of England, during the Seventeenth Century, and Brought Down to the Present Time, and Chronologically Arranged. ... With Occasional Essays on Crimes and Punishments, Original Anecdotes, and Observations of Particular Cases; Explanations of the Criminal Laws; the Speeches, Confessions, and Last Exclamations of Sufferers*. 4 vols. London: Cundee; Liverpool: Dixon.

________ (1824-1826). *The Newgate Calendar; Comprising Interesting Memoirs of the Most Notorious Characters Who Have Been Convicted of Outrages on the Laws of England since the Commencement of the Eighteenth Century; with Occasional Anecdotes and Observations, Speeches, Confessions, and Last Exclamations of Sufferers*. 4 vols. London: J. Robbins.

Knight, Charles (1864-1865). *Passages of a Working Life*. 3 vols. London: Bradbury and Evans.

Mandeville, Bernard (1964). *An Enquiry into the Causes of the Frequent Executions at Tyburn*. Los Angeles: William Andrews Clark Memorial Library. Original edition 1725.

Purland, T[heodosius] (n.d.). *Alsatian Eccentricities*, 2 vols. Ms. London: British Library [1243.k.2-3].

Purland, Theodosius (1831). *Practical Directions for Preserving the Teeth; Advice to Parents; Growth and Structure of the Teeth; With an Account of the most improved Methods of Supplying their Loss. A Description of, and Remarks upon, every Operation Connected with the Teeth. And Strictures upon the Practice of Pretenders to Dental Surgery; including Crockery Teeth, Transplanting, Excision, &c.* London: William Henry Cox.

REFERENCES

Barker, Hannah (1998). *Newspapers, Politics, and Public Opinion in Late Eighteenth-Century England.* Oxford: Clarendon Press.

________ (2000). *Newspapers, Politics and English Society, 1695-1855*. Harlow: Longman.

Beattie, J.M. (1974). 'The Pattern of Crime in England 1660-1800.' *Past and Present* 63, 47-95.

Bell, Ian A. (1991). *Literature and Crime in Augustan England.* London: Routledge.

Bertelsen, Lance (1997). 'Committed by Justice Fielding: Judicial and Journalistic Representations in the Bow Street Magistrate's Office, January 3 - November 24, 1752.' *Eighteenth-Century Studies* 30, 337-363.

Black, Jeremy (2001). *The English Press, 1621-1861*. Phoenix Mill: Sutton.

Boase, Frederic (1897). 'Purland, Theodosius.' *Modern English Biography*. Vol. 2. Truro: Netherton and Worth, 1674.

Böker, Uwe (2001). 'The Institutionalisation of Legal Norms and Values in England (1500-1900).' In Uwe Böker and Julie A. Hibbard (eds.), *Processes of Institutionalisation: Case Studies in Law, Prison and Censorship*. Essen: Blaue Eule, 13-60.

Breuer, Horst (1996). 'Literarische Reflexe des englischen Freistättenrechts.' In Uwe Böker and Christoph Houswitschka (eds.), *Literatur, Kriminalität und Rechtskultur im 17. und 18. Jahrhundert: Tagung am 17. und 18. Juni 1994 an der Technischen Universität Dresden*. Essen: Blaue Eule, 184-198.

Brewer, John (1976). *Party Ideology and Popular Politics at the Accession of George III*. Cambridge: Cambridge University Press.

Brewer, John, and John Styles (1980). 'Introduction.' In John Brewer and John Styles (eds.), *An Ungovernable People: The English and Their Law in the Seventeenth and Eighteenth Centuries*. London: Hutchinson, 11-20.

Calcuttensis (1882). 'The Late T. Purland.' *Notes and Queries* 6 (19 Aug.), 154-155.

Curtis, T.C., and W.A. Speck (1976). 'The Societies for the Reformation of Manners: A Case Study in the Theory and Practice of Moral Reform.' *Literature and History* 3, 45-64.

Enkemann, Jürgen (1983). *Journalismus und Literatur: Zum Verhältnis von Zeitungswesen, Literatur und Entwicklung bürgerlicher Öffentlichkeit in England im 17. und 18. Jahrhundert*. Tübingen: Niemeyer.

Feather, John (1988). *A History of British Publishing*. London: Routledge.

Foucault, Michel (1992). *Überwachen und Strafen: Die Geburt des Gefängnisses*. Frankfurt/Main: Suhrkamp. Original edition 1975.

Gatty, Alfred, (1882). 'The Late T. Purland.' *Notes and Queries* 6 (22 April), 317.

Giovanopoulos, Anna-Christina (2002). '"This day is to be hanged the greatest rogue in England": Robert Walpole und Jonathan Wild.' In Stefan Müller, Gary Schaal, and Claudia Tiersch (eds.), *Dauer durch Wandel: Institutionelle Ordnungen zwischen Verstätigung und Transformation*. Cologne: Böhlau, 191-209.

Habermas, Jürgen (1994). 'The Emergence of the Public Sphere.' In *The Polity Reader in Cultural Theory*. Cambridge: Polity Press, 82-99.

Haig, Robert L. (1960). *The Gazetteer, 1735-1797: A Study in the Eighteenth-Century Newspaper*. Carbondale: Southern Illinois University Press.

Harris, Bob (1996). *Politics and the Rise of the Press: Britain and France, 1620-1800*. London: Routledge.

Harris, Michael (1978). 'The Management of the London Newspaper Press During the Eighteenth Century.' *Publishing History* 4, 95-112.

________ (1982). 'Trials and Criminal Biographies: A Case Study in Distribution.' In Robin Myers and Michael Harris (eds.), *Sale and Distribution of Books from 1700*. Oxford: Oxford Polytechnic Press, 1-36.

________ (1987). *London Newspapers in the Age of Walpole: A Study in the Origins of the Modern English Press*. London: Associated University Presses.

Hay, Douglas (1982). 'War, Dearth and Theft in the Eighteenth Century: The Record of the English Courts.' *Past and Present* 95, 117-160.

Hay, Douglas, and Francis Snyder (1989). 'Using the Criminal Law, 1750-1850: Policing, Private Prosecution, and the State.' In Douglas Hay and Francis Snyder (eds.), *Policing and Prosecution in Britain 1750-1850*. Oxford: Clarendon Press, 3-52.

Hellmuth, Eckhart (1996). 'To Make Sense of the Senseless: The Representation of Crime and Punishment in Eighteenth-Century England.' In Jürgen Klein and Dirk Vanderbeke (eds.), *Anglistentag 1995 Greifswald: Proceedings*. Tübingen: Niemeyer, 45-57.

Howson, Gerald (1970). *Thief-Taker General: Jonathan Wild and the Emergence of Crime and Corruption as a Way of Life in Eighteenth-Century England*. New Brunswick, NJ: Transaction.

Innes, Joanna, and John Styles (1986). 'The Crime Wave: Recent Writing on Crime and Criminal Justice in Eighteenth-Century England.' *Journal of British Studies* 25, 380-435.

J.R.D. (1882). 'The Late T. Purland.' *Notes and Queries* 6 (4 March), 168-169.

Jenkins, Robert (1912). *The Life of George Borrow*. E-Text from the 1912 John Murray edition. Internet. 16 November 2001. Available http://uiarchive.uiuc.edu/mirrors/ftp/ibiblio.unc.edu/pub/docs/books/gutenberg/etext02/lfgbr10.txt.

King, Peter (1984). 'Decision-Makers and Decision-Making in the English Criminal Law, 1750-1800.' *The Historical Journal* 27, 25-58.

Langbein, John (1978). 'The Criminal Trial before the Lawyers.' *The University of Chicago Law Journal* 45, 263-316.

_______ (1983). 'Shaping the Eighteenth-Century Criminal Trial: A View from the Ryder Sources.' *The University of Chicago Law Review* 50, 1-136.

Paley, Ruth (1989). 'Thief-Takers in London in the Age of the McDaniel Gang, c. 1745-1754.' In Douglas Hay and Francis Snyder (eds.), *Policing and Prosecution in Britain 1750-1850*. Oxford: Clarendon Press, 301-341.

Price, Richard (1999). *British Society, 1660-1800: Dynamism, Containment and Change*. Cambridge: Cambridge University Press.

Radzinowicz, Leon (1948). *A History of English Criminal Law and Its Administration from 1750*. Vol. 1: *The Movement for Reform*. London: Stevens and Sons.

Rehberg, Karl-Siegbert (1994). 'Institutionen als symbolische Ordnungen: Leitfragen und Grundkategorien zur Theorie und Analyse institutioneller Mechanismen.' In Gerhard Göhler (ed.), *Die Eigenart der Institutionen: Zum Profil politischer Institutionentheorie*. Baden-Baden: Nomos, 47-84.

_______ (1995). 'Die Öffentlichkeit der Institutionen: Grundbegriffliche Überlegungen im Rahmen der Theorie und Analyse institutioneller Mechanismen.' In Gerhard Göhler (ed.), *Macht der Öffentlichkeit – Öffentlichkeit der Macht*. Baden-Baden: Nomos, 181-211.

_______ (2001). 'Weltrepräsentanz und Verkörperung: Institutionelle Analyse und Symboltheorien – Eine Einführung in systematischer Absicht.' In Gert Melville (ed.), *Institutionalität und Symbolisierung: Verstetigungen kultureller Ordnungsmuster in Vergangenheit und Gegenwart*. Cologne: Böhlau, 3-49.

Styles, John (1983). 'Sir John Fielding.' *Transactions of the Royal Historical Society*, 5th series, 33, 127-149.

_______ (1989). 'Print and Policing: Crime Advertising in Eighteenth-Century Provincial England.' In Douglas Hay and Francis Snyder (eds.), *Policing and Prosecution in Britain 1750-1850*. Clarendon: Oxford, 55-111.

Wall, David S. (1998). *The Chief Constables of England and Wales: The Socio-Legal History of a Criminal Justice Elite*. Aldershot: Ashgate.

Weber, Harold (1996). *Paper Bullets: Print and Kingship under Charles II*. Lexington: University Press of Kentucky.

Zaret, David (2000). *Origins of Democratic Culture: Printing, Petitions, and the Public Sphere in Early-Modern England*. Princeton: Princeton University Press.

Eckhart Hellmuth

Criticising the Constitution; or, How to Talk about the Liberty of the Press in the 1790s

In the spring of 1792 Parliament passed Foxe's Libel Act. This meant that procedures in libel cases were brought into line with normal legal procedures. Foxe's Libel Act stated that in trials for seditious libel,

> [the] jury sworn to try the issues may give a general verdict of guilty or not guilty upon the whole matter put in the issue [...] and shall not be required or directed [...] to find the defendent or defendents guilty, merely of the proof of the publication [...] and of the sense ascribed to the same. (Quoted in Green 1985, 330)

This fulfilled one of the demands made by the reform movement during the 1760s, 1770s and 1780s (318ff.). But it would be wrong to assume that the passing of Foxe's Libel Act put an end to the discourse on the liberty of the press – on the contrary, the opposite was the case.

While Foxe's Libel Act was still being debated in the House of Lords, a royal proclamation was issued ordering all magistrates to find and prosecute the authors of 'divers wicked and seditious writings which had been printed, published and industriously dispersed, tending to excite tumult and disorder' (*Annual Register* 1792, 158-160). Thus, Pitt and his government declared war upon the radical press. But this was not all. In November 1792 the Association for Preserving Liberty and Property was formed under the leadership of John Reeves (see, among others, Dickinson 1960; Eastwood 1991; Dozier 1983). The declaration with which they launched their work in society contained the following statement:

> Considering the Danger to which the Public Peace and Order are exposed by the circulating of mischievous Opinions, founded upon plausible but false reasoning, and that this circulation is principally carried on by the industry of Clubs and Societies of various denominations in many parts of the kingdom: It appears to us, That it is now become the duty of all Persons, who wish well for their Native Country, to endeavour, in their several neighbourhoods, to prevent the sad effects of such mischievous industry; and that it would greatly tend to promote these good endeavours, if Societies were formed in different parts of the Kingdom, whose object should be to support the Laws, to suppress seditious publications, and to defend our Persons and Property against the innovations and depredations that seem to be threatened by those who maintain the mischievous opinions before alluded to. These opinions are conveyed in the terms – the Rights of Man – Liberty and Equality – No King – No Parliament – and others of the like impact: all of them, in the sense imposed on them, expressing sentiments in direct opposition to the Laws of the Land. (Association 1792)

In order to counteract tendencies of this sort, among other things, the society known as Friends to the Liberty of the Press was established in December 1792 (Rea 1961). It drew its members mainly from the rather elitist Friends of the People and the socially more open London Constitutional Society. The Friends to the Liberty of the Press to some extent represented a coalition between a parliamentary and an extra-parliamentary opposition. More than twenty MPs joined it, as did prominent representatives of the extra-parliamentary reform movement, among them Philip Francis, John Sawbridge, John Horne Tooke, George Tierney, John Thelwall, Samuel Whitbread, Major John Cartwright and Joseph Towers. The Friends to the Liberty of the Press engaged in all the activities that are so familiar from the late eighteenth century. They held meetings, passed resolutions, published pamphlets, and cultivated all the usual forms of political sociability. At times, they could mobilise between 700 and 900 supporters. And, it seems, similar societies were set up in Sheffield, Durham, Manchester and Derby. This prepared the ground for a new round in the public discourse on the liberty of the press. Within a very short time, the Association for Preserving Liberty and Property and the Friends to the Liberty of the Press, together with their respective sympathisers, were engaged in a vehement dispute.

I.

The debate on the freedom of the press in the 1790s[1] brought into prominence a subject which, despite its seriousness, had largely been ignored until then. This was the question of the legitimacy of criticising the constitution in the press. During the 1760s and 1770s, intellectual efforts had largely been directed towards determining the role of the press in relation to parliament and government, to defining it as an anti-governmental and anti-parliamentary agency (Hellmuth 1990). In the early 1790s, by contrast, a different problem came to the fore with unprecedented ferocity: to what extent was it legitimate publicly to question the constitution in its entirety?

A major factor in sparking off this process of reflection was the case brought against Thomas Paine for 'seditious Libel' because of the second volume of his *Rights of Man*. The trial took place *in absentia* in December 1792 (Keane 1995, 345 and passim). Paine had indeed launched a fundamental attack on the English constitution. This became very clear in Paine's criticism of the Bill of Rights, a constitutional document that, like the Magna Carta, was one of the sacred cows of the eighteenth-century constitutional debate. Paine believed that the Bill of Rights was no more than a myth of the English constitution. He regarded it as promoted by selfish interests, and saw it to be the result of a compromise between the Crown and the Convention Parliament, whose legitimacy he denied. What is the Bill of Rights, he wrote,

> but a bargain, which the parts of the government made with each other to divide powers, profits and privileges? You shall have so much, and I will have the rest: and with respect to the nation, it said, for your share, you shall have the right of petitioning. This being the case, the bill of rights is more properly a bill of wrongs, and of insult. (Paine 1969, 2: 215)

Paine's interpretation of the Glorious Revolution and the Bill of Rights was central to the charges levelled against him (Erskine 1810a, 60). Similarly, the Attorney General drew upon other passages from the *Rights of Man*. These included Paine's fundamental doubts about the legitimacy of the hereditary monarchy (55) and his description of

1 The present essay is a first approach to this debate. The author is preparing a more comprehensive treatment. Annotations are restricted to a minimum.

Parliament as an obsequious and obedient instrument of government (66). He was accused of 'a wilful, deliberate intention to vilify and degrade, and thereby to bring into abhorrence and contempt the whole constitution of the government of this country' (49). The jury agreed with this assessment of Paine and his *Rights of Man*, and found him guilty without even consulting. It could be argued that this verdict indicated the boundaries the loyalist political public wanted to see respected in the public discourse. In the face of a real, or even just assumed, internal or external threat, the King and Country faction took refuge in a rigid constitutional conservatism. Throughout the 1790s, they constantly praised the traditional English constitutional system and declared it sacrosanct.

These attempts to declare such a crucial area of public interest and political debate out of bounds met determined resistance from the radical and reformist camp. Although there was only limited sympathy for Paine and his republicanism, the principle that this sort of criticism of the constitution should not be subjected to criminal sanctions was undisputed. Thus, the declaration on the freedom of the press which the Friends of the Liberty of the Press regularly reproduced in their pamphlets was clearly designed to clear the ground for a debate on political fundamentals. It advocated 'that no writing ought to be considered as a public libel, and made the subject of criminal prosecution, unless such writing shall appear to be published with a design, to excite the People to resist the Civil Magistrate, or obstruct the execution of the existing laws' (*Proceedings* 1793, 1-2).

In determining what in fact was a libel, the crucial thing was to prove malicious intent, as Thomas Erskine explained during Thomas Paine's trial (Erskine 1810b, 96-97). What needed to be proved was that the author had deliberately set out to undermine social harmony. The Baptist preacher Robert Hall summed this up in his *Apology for the Freedom of the Press*: 'An enquiry respecting the comparative excellence of civil constitutions can be forbidden on no other pretence, than of its tendency to sedition and anarchy' (Hall 1793, 13-14).

But this indirect legitimation of fundamental criticism of the constitution was not the end of the story. Against the background of Paine's trial, it was also explicitly stated that republicanism was perfectly legitimate. Joseph Towers, for example, wrote in one of his tracts:

> But there may certainly be speculative men in the kingdom, who conceive, that a republic would be better than a limited monarchy. It is no crime for any man to entertain that opinion, if he be guilty of no illegal act in order to support it. There have always been such speculative men in this country, and there ever will be such men in it, till we are become a nation of slaves. (Towers 1793, 12)

And Robert Hall spoke out with equal vigour against all repressive measures directed against contemporary republican writing:

> Under pretence of its being seditious to express any disapprobation of the form of our government, the most alarming attempts are made to wrest the liberty of the press out of our hands. It is far from being my intention to step up a defence of republican principles, as I am persuaded whatever imperfections may attend the British constitution, it is competent to all the ends of government, and the best adapted of any to the actual situation of this kingdom. Yet I am convinced there is no crime in being a republican, and that while he obeys the laws, every man has a right to entertain what

> sentiments he pleases on our form of government, and to discuss this with the same freedom as any other topic. (Hall 1793, 8-9)

Behind declarations such as this lay a number of more fundamental justifications on which the advocates of free speech based their position. These included the idea that the existing constitution in England was a relative thing. This notion could take two forms. First, we find the argument that there was little agreement among contemporaries about the meaning of the term 'constitution', and it had been used to support a variety of clearly political ambitions:

> There are few words more equivocally employed or capable of a more abusive use than the Constitution. It has served equally the purpose of all parties; and scarce any two writers or speakers will be found to entertain exactly the same view of it. It is often used apparently with scarce meaning at all. (Bruce 1794, 68)

The consequences to be drawn from this sceptical position are clear: if there was no consensus about what the term 'constitution' actually meant, any attempt to control the public discourse on the subject by legal means was senseless.

More important in this context, however, was the thought that the English constitution in force at the end of the eighteenth century had evolved historically, over time, and was therefore something that could change in the future. It was assumed that the English constitution was being gradually perfected in a process which had largely been initiated by free public discussion. In the context of this sort of reasoning, George Rous put the following rhetorical question to a meeting of the Friends to the Liberty of the Press: 'If the right of discussion had not been used by those who lived in the old times, what would the government of England have been in the present moment?' (Erskine 1793, 4).

It was Thomas Erskine, however, who most fully developed the idea that the historical nature of the English constitution implied the right to criticise it. He started by looking at ideas on the permanence of constitutions, referring to, among others, Filmer, Burke, and Locke. He rejected Filmer's theory of the divine origins and sacrosanct nature of the authorities, as well as Burke's ideology of the status quo (Erskine 1810b, 126). Instead, Erskine turned to Locke. He quoted the passage from the *Two Treatises on Government* which stated that contracts entered into with governments, especially where they curtailed freedoms, could not be binding on later generations (134). Erskine also spoke of the 'great unalienable right of the people, to reform or to change their governments' (139). This theory of the legitimacy of constitutional change fed through to the problem of the freedom of the press. As far as Erskine was concerned, the freedom of the press was an indispensable instrument for effecting those revisions of the constitution which became necessary from time to time. In his view, the constitution owed its present state to this freedom:

> for had it not been for this inalienable right , how should we have had this constitution which we so loudly boast of? – If, in the march of the human mind, no man could have gone before the establishments of the time he lived in, how could our establishment, by reiterated changes, have become what it is? – If no man could have awakened the public mind to errors and abuses in our government, how could it have passed on from stage to stage, through reformation and revolution? (99)

It was this process of critically commenting upon and gradually perfecting the constitution that reformers and radicals wanted to see continuing in the present. Among the principles they appealed to were those of popular sovereignty and 'government by consent', which were expressed most clearly in Robert Hall's *Apology for the Freedom of the Press*. Hall derived the right to modify the constitution by means of public criticism from the maxim that the constitution should be based on the free consent of the people: 'Government is the creature of the people and that which they have a right to examine. The great Author of Nature having placed the right of dominion in no particular hands, hath left every point relating to it to be settled by the consent and approbation of mankind' (Hall 1793, 9-10). And elsewhere, he wrote,

> But if we allow the people are the true origin of political power, it is absurd to require them to resign the right of discussing any question that can arise either upon its form or its measures, as this would put it for ever out of their power to revoke the trust which they have placed in the hands of the rulers. (10-11)

However, a very different and rather unexpected note could be struck in this discourse on the freedom of the press and on criticising the constitution. This becomes evident in the case of *Reflections on the Freedom of Writing* (1794) by the Presbyterian clergyman Archibald Bruce. This text, one of the longest written on the subject in the 1790s, was permeated with Biblical language, and had a clearly millenarian dimension. For example, we read,

> Many striking symptoms are at present appearing that indicate some very memorable and general revolution in the system of governments, and in the constitution and public character of nations, to be fast approaching. The stupendous operations of that providence which rules in the kingdoms of men, and in the church, that has so often poured contempt on princes, and debased those who walked in pride, seem evidently to point that way. (Bruce 1794, 85)

Further, Bruce wrote of the 'last ages, as unfolded in the last book of inspiration', and of the 'restoration of truth, justice and universal peace' (85). The new Jerusalem dominated by the spirit of enlightened reason which Bruce envisaged seemed to him attainable in two different ways: either via the collapse of the existing political and social order; or – and this was the way he favoured – by a comprehensive dialogue between the authorities and their subjects on the reform of the constitution. Bruce passionately advocated free public discussion of this issue:

> There must still be reserved a power of discussing, of judging, objecting to, and of changing, by the laws of permanent reason and justice, not only the particular laws, but the discriminating form of its settled government, its very constitution upon sufficient grounds, as when any of them are radically bad, or are become grievous and oppressive; seeing they are ordinances or constitutions merely human, and have no claim to support when they either are incompatible with a higher and more sacred law, or with the immediate end for which they were appointed, [the] general good. (73)

Where, as in Bruce's case, the chord of divine right was also touched, any fears about possible negative consequences disappeared. Given the imminence of the Millennium, remodelling the constitution took absolute priority:

> In such cases neither the plea of long prescription, the venerable solemnity or sacredness supposed to belong to them, the engagements or oaths wherewith governors or subjects have in time past

> been bound to them, nor the fear of accidental dangers or convulsions that may attend the change, nor yet the negative of a part of the constituted legislature, or of the ordinary executive powers of the state, can be sufficient reason for postponing for ever the needful alteration. (73-74)

Ultimately, radicals and reformers were demanding the right to put the English constitution to a comprehensive and public test. They did not accept the argument, which loyalist propaganda so long insisted upon, of the superiority of the English constitution. However, they did not attack this view head-on; instead, they tried to undermine it. If, they argued, the English constitution really were as superior as the loyalists claimed, then it had no need to fear the test of publicity. Joseph Towers, for example, clearly had a polemical motive when he levelled the following accusation at the loyalist camp:

> And as to the apprehension of the dangers that may arise from what is called libelling the constitution, these appear to me the idle terrors of men, who are ignorant even of the first principles of civil government. If the constitution be good, it will bear the fullest and the freest investigation. Indeed, the greatest libellers of the constitution are many of the associators; they who suppose, that it will not stand the test of examination, and that it cannot be supported, but by suppressing the freedom of speaking and writing. We are sometimes told, that our constitution of government is the best in the world. If this be the case, is it possible that either the constitution, or the government, can be in any real danger from the publication of a few pamphlets? (Towers 1793, 11-12)

But this was not all. There were writers in the 'enlightened' camp who had thought the idea of testing the English constitution right through, and were prepared to allow positions which attacked the English system from the Right to be tolerated. Even though such criticism of the constitution from the 'Right' was diametrically opposed to their own political views, Charles Earl Stanhope believed that it had a legitimate place in the public discourse (Stanhope 1792, 142-143).

Alfred Cobban called the political debate of the 1790s the 'last real discussion of the fundamentals of politics in this country' (Cobban 1960, 31). While the generality of this often-quoted sentence makes it questionable, it nevertheless contains a great deal of truth. For, at least during the eighteenth century, there was really no other period when the established political order was questioned with the same degree of radicalism.[2] This situation inevitably had implications for the contemporary understanding of the notion of the freedom of the press. For reformers and radicals, it gained new connotations. Thus, the right 'to publish speculative Works upon the Constitution, whether they contain Praise or Censure' (Stanhope 1792, 144) was seen as a feature defining England's freedom of the press. Freedom of the press without the right to comment on the constitution was rejected as 'Russian Freedom of the Press' (143-144). And remarkably, Thomas Erskine defined a free press as the tribunal which could try the existing constitution and, above all, expose its faults and weaknesses:

> The proposition which I mean to maintain as the basis of the liberty of the press, and without which it is an empty sound, is this: that every man may address himself to the universal reason of a whole nation, that he may analyse the principles of its constitution, point out its errors and defects, examine and publish its corruptions, warn his fellow citizens against their ruinous consequences,

2 For further considerations on this topic, see Houswitschka 2002.

> and exert his whole faculties in pointing out the most advantageous changes in establishments which he considers to be radically defective, or sliding from their object by abuse. (Erskine 1810b, 95-96)

II.

This was by no means the end of the discourse on the liberty of the press and the criticism of the constitution. Discussion of this subject revived under somewhat unexpected circumstances a few years later, when loyalist writers became interested in the subject. This happened in 1795-96, when John Reeves was charged for 'seditious libel' and put on trial (this affair is comprehensively dealt with by Eastwood 1993, and Barrell 2000, 622).

The cause was his book, *Thoughts on the English Government* (1795), largely a polemic against the Foxite Whigs, whom he accused of making common cause with the extra-parliamentary radical movement. Further, Reeves' text was permeated with reflections on the constitution, including a passage in which he most bizarrely defined the monarchy as the centre of the English constitution, while regarding Lords and Commons as merely derivative powers. Despite the metaphorical style in which he clothed his arguments, it was quite clear that Reeves opposed the traditional idea of a balance of power within the framework of a mixed constitution. In doing so, Reeves certainly went beyond the existing consensus on the constitution. Given the prominence of its author, it was almost inevitable that *Thoughts on the English Government* would give offence. In the past, Reeves had unscrupulously accused radical authors of working to overthrow the established English constitution; now he himself stood accused of disloyalty to the constitution. Fox and his followers did not hesitate to bring the case before Parliament. With almost no opposition – indeed, with the approval of all parliamentary groups including the Tories – Parliament passed a petition on 14 December 1795 initiating criminal proceedings against Reeves for 'seditious libel'. Reeves was subsequently acquitted, but this is not of great interest to us here. More important is the loyalist propaganda that preceded the trial.

Loyalist authors such as George Chalmers and Joseph Cawthorne[3] of course tried to prove that Reeves' ideas were in line with the constitution and emphasised his work in the struggle against radicalism. But they also went beyond this rather pragmatic level of argument and addressed the fundamental problems of a free press and freedom of expression. And here we witness a certain convergence between radical and loyalist ideology: it seems to be 'the world turned upside down.'

At first sight, this might seem surprising, but in the light of recent research, it is not as astonishing as it appears. Scholars are, at present, becoming more sceptical about the idea of fixed, politically and ideologically clearly-defined camps in the late eighteenth century. They have become more open to the idea of inconsistency in

---

3 Cawthorne can only in a limited sense be described as a loyalist author. Barrell speaks of him as a 'pensioned Government pamphleteer of unusually independent views' (2000, 245).

political attitudes, and to processes of transformation within the intellectual stock of a society. In this sense, Mark Philp states,

> [we] find radicals becoming loyalists [...] and then radicals again [...], or loyalists becoming radicals [...]. The greater complexity we recognize in the ideological terrain of the period, and the more sophisticated our account of the motives behind people's expressions of commitment, the more porous and problematic become the ideological categories of radical and conservative. (Philp 1995, 68)

For the freedom of the press and criticism of the constitution, this means that loyalist authors developed rhetoric and arguments similar to those of their 'enlightened' opponents. Thus, it was possible for a writer such as George Chalmers to elevate the freedom of the press into a fundamental right in a way which would have done credit to any writer from the reformist or radical camp. Chalmers did not see the non-renewal of the Licensing Acts at the end of the seventeenth century as a simple modification of the English legal system; rather, he regarded the events of 1694 as the dawn of a new era:

> Then it was that the common law right, the Magna Charta right of free thinking, of free writing, and of free publishing, was again engraffed on the ancient stock; whereupon, being planted in a congenial soil, and cultivated by free hands, the tree of Liberty has since flourished luxuriantly, putting forth every season, goodly branches, which, I trust, will never be lopped off. (Chalmers 1796, 21-22)

And elsewhere he writes, with equal enthusiasm:

> If it be a genuine maxim of English law that every free hand may act freely, unless they be restrained by positive statute, it must be incontrovertible law that since the epoch of 1694, every man, every woman, and every child, has an indubitable right to think, write, and print freely. (22)

This position on fundamental rights gave rise to critical ideas that are, indeed, astonishing to find voiced by a loyalist author. Blackstone, the political and social Establishment's pet interpreter of the constitution, was condemned, quite correctly, for the fact that his 'classic' definition of the freedom of the press[4] merely described this right in legalistic terms (21). Even the Bill, or Declaration, of Rights was not spared. Chalmers, for example, complained that the freedom of the press was not enshrined in this document which was so central to England's constitutional development (ibid.). This, incidentally, was a position he shared with the non-conformist clergyman Joseph Towers (Towers 1793, 19-21, 24-25), one of the leading members of the Society for Constitutional Information.

We can find even more surprising points of contact between radicalism and loyalism. Loyalist authors pointed to prominent libel cases that counted as milestones in the establishment of the principle of freedom of the press, and which formed part of the ideological heritage of reformist and radical circles. Loyalists used these cases as precedents in order to demonstrate the obsolescence of the case brought against Reeves. They included the 1789 trial of John Stockdale, a London bookseller, who had been defended by Thomas Erskine. George Chalmers described this case in detail in

---

4 Blackstone's definition of the freedom of the press can be found in the fourth volume of his *Commentaries on the Laws of England* (Blackstone 1979, 153).

his *Vindication.* Among other things, he quoted Erskine's defence of Stockdale,[5] but changed the emphasis so that it appeared to be a plea in favour of Reeves (Chalmers 1796, 47-48). Thus, Thomas Erskine, one of the cult figures of the 'liberal' camp, was cast in the role of defending the arch-conservative John Reeves. And Joseph Cawthorne, who had provided the most well-founded contribution to Reeves' defence, did not hesitate to place a positive gloss on the General Warrants' Affair; that is, the episode from which John Wilkes, the most prominent radical of the 1760s, had emerged as the victor in the struggle against the authorities' attempts to limit public discourse (Cawthorne 1796, 75ff.).

It is no coincidence that loyalist authors picked on the Stockdale trial and the General Warrants' Affair, for in both cases Parliament had initiated criminal proceedings for 'seditious libel', and the parallel with Reeves' case was obvious. But there was more to it than that. Just as repeated attempts by Parliament to prohibit public debate on certain issues in the 1760s and 1770s had given rise to fundamental doubts about the extent of its powers, the events surrounding Reeves also provoked a re-thinking on fundamental issues. The difference was that it now came from the loyalist rather than the radical camp. Cawthorne described Parliament as follows:

> This legislative bugbear, which is often held out in terrorem to the people, under the hideous form of privileges undefined and incomprehensible (the description of discretionary and omnipotent power) puts me in mind of the Catholic carpenter, who was required to worship the wooden image he had made, as the people know what they have created. (18)

He went on to compare the behaviour of Parliament with that of the Catholic Inquisition and the Court of Star Chamber, comparisons which had generally been drawn by the radical camp in their struggle against the restrictions on freedom of the press and freedom of expression (11, 79). Cawthorne accused Parliament in such strong language because he believed that, in the action it was taking against Reeves' anti-parliamentary tract, *Thoughts on the English Government*, it had set itself up 'in the manner of an arbitrary Tribunal', to play the role of 'Judges and Jury in their own case' (110). Finally, he charged Parliament with undermining the division of power by its behaviour. It had arrogated to itself powers which the sovereign people had never granted it:

> When the people delegate their constitutional or legislative rights, they do not invest their Representatives with any judicial authority whatsoever. And since they possess no jurisdiction but what they receive from their constituents, for the general purposes of the people, from what source do they derive an inquisitorial capacity? It is an arbitrary assumption of power, and such an usurpation of power as plunges dagger in the bowles of the constitution. (5-6)

An attack on Parliament such as this was remarkable in itself. It gained added effect, however, by the fact that it was accompanied by wide ranging social criticism of the English aristocracy (89-98, 101).

---

5 Of course, this was a double edged-ploy. By appealing to Erskine, Chalmers hoped to be able to expose the radical or reforming milieu. He wanted to show that, while radicals and reformers claimed wide ranging freedom of the press and freedom of opinion for themselves, they denied the same right to their political opponents.

In order to prevent misunderstandings, I should point out that Cawthorne's aim was not a programme of 'liberal' reform. Although his support for the freedom of the press led over into criticism of Parliament's privileged position and the extent of its power, this does not mean that he advocated a more open parliamentary system or wider political participation. On the contrary, his constitutional ideal was a strong and efficient monarchy with extended powers (25, 26, 34). And although it may seem paradoxical, this desire for a 'conservative' revision of the constitution was linked with the origins of a comparatively 'modern' theory of the freedom of the press.

For Cawthorne, it was axiomatic that constitutions were not static, fixed entities, but that they changed over time. He regarded them as creations of the fallible human spirit. And he did not doubt that even the English constitution, although superior to other constitutions, had its defects (17). 'It is therefore', he concluded, 'the most preposterous in the English to account it Treason to dispute the eternity and immutability of their Constitution' (18-19). In his view, it was not in the nature of constitutions to be permanent; rather, they were in need of gradual perfection (45-46). And further: 'As Nations grow enlightened by experience and reflection they will adapt their Constitutions and their Laws to the wisdom of the age in which they live' (46). Ultimately, the question of which particular constitution was appropriate to the specific historical situation could only be clarified via public discussion: 'the proof of utility and expediency is left to the conviction and the judgement of the public' (13). Fully aware of the plurality of views that existed upon the subject, Cawthorne nevertheless advocated this sort of general public discourse: 'Upon this subject [reforming the constitution], so important to a free Nation, the sentiments of a Free and enlightened people will be as different as their Complexions' (84). These considerations led him to make a fervent plea for a free debate on political and constitutional issues:

> Englishmen have an inherent and constitutional right (that is, a natural right secured to them by the nature of their government) to speak of the principles and effects of government entirely monarchical, or an absolute monarchy of the nature and tendency of Aristocracy; and of the principles and effects of Democracy; either separately, or as they are connected with a monarchical system, commonly called a mixed government, or a limited monarchy. In treating of these subjects which so intimately concern all civilized human nature the contemplation would be useless to civilization were they not to give an opinion, and leave mankind to consider which system is best adapted to the genius and policy of their representative states; namely a government entirely monarchical; a limited monarchy; or a republican government. (13-14)

Positions such as those taken by George Chalmers and Joseph Cawthorne undoubtedly had an affinity with ideas that a few years earlier had been put forward by the radical camp. It seems that loyalism's potential for reflection went beyond demagogical reactions to the free public discussion of 1792-93. Although it is highly unlikely that loyalist writers wanted their plea for freedom of the press and the right to criticise the constitution to include 'radical' writers, it seems that a standardisation of norms was beginning. This situation casts doubt upon the sense of continuing to set up dichotomies between 'left' and 'right', or 'progressive' and 'traditional'.

REFERENCES

Annual Register, or A View of the History, Politics, and Literature, for the Year (1792). London: J. Dodsley.

Association for Preserving Liberty and Property Against Republicans and Levellers (1792). [Pamphlet of 4 December 1792]. London.

Barrell, John (2000). *Imagining the King's Death: Figurative Treason, Fantasies of Regicide 1793-1796*. Oxford: Oxford University Press.

Blackstone, William (1979). *Commentaries on the Laws of England: A Facsimile of the First Edition of 1765-1769*. Vol. 4: *Of Public Wrongs*. Chicago: University of Chicago Press. Original edition London, 1769.

Bruce, Archibald (1794). *Reflections on the Freedom of Writing; and the impropriety of attempting to suppress it by penal laws. Occasioned by the proclamation against seditious publications, and the measures consequent upon it ; viewed chiefly in the aspect they bear to religious liberty, and ecclesiastical reform*. Edinburgh.

Cawthorne, Joseph (1796). *A Letter to the King, in Justification of a Pamphlet, entitled 'Thoughts on the English Government', With an Appendix in Answer to Mr. Fox's Declaration of the Whig-Club*. London: J. Owen.

Chalmers, George (1796). *A Vindication of the Privilege of the People, in respect to the Constitutional Right of Free Discussion*. London: John Stockdale.

Cobban, Alfred (1960). 'Introduction.' In Alfred Cobban (ed.), *The Debate on the French Revolution*. London: Black, 1-32.

Dickinson, Harry T. (1960). 'Popular Loyalism in Britain in the 1790s.' In Eckhart Hellmuth (ed.), *The Transformation of Political Culture: England and Germany in the Late Eighteenth Century*. Oxford: Oxford University Press, 503-533.

Dozier, Robert R. (1983). *For King, Country, and Constitution: The English Loyalists and the French Revolution*. Lexington: University Press of Kentucky.

Eastwood, David (1991). 'Patriotism and the English State in the 1790s.' In Mark Philp (ed.), *The French Revolution and British Popular Politics*. Cambridge: Cambridge University Press, 146-168.

________ (1993). 'John Reeves and the Contested Idea of the Constitution.' *British Journal for Eighteenth Century Studies* 16, 197-212.

Erskine, Thomas (1793). *The Speech of the Hon. Thomas Erskine, at a meeting of the Friends to the Liberty of the Press, at Free-Mason's Tavern, Dec. 22 1792. With the resolutions, &c. of that Truly Patriotic Society*. London: Printed for James Ridgway.

________ (1810a). 'The Attorney General's Speech in Support of the Prosecution.' In *The Speeches of the Hon. Thomas Erskine When at the Bar, on Subjects Connected with the Liberty of the Press and against Constructive Treason*. Collected by James Ridgway. Vol. 2. London: Printed for James Ridgway, 46-86.

________ (1810b). 'Mr. Erskine's Speech for the Defendant.' In *The Speeches of the Hon. Thomas Erskine When at the Bar, on Subjects Connected with the Liberty of the Press and against Constructive Treason*. Collected by James Ridgway. Vol. 2. London: Printed for James Ridgway, 87-182.

Green, Thomas A. (1985). *Verdict According to Conscience: Perspectives on the English Criminal Trial Jury, 1200-1800*. Chicago: University of Chicago Press.

Hall, Robert (1793). *An Apology for the Freedom of the Press and for General Liberty: To which are prefixed remarks on Bishop Horsley's sermon, preache don the thirtieth of January last*. London: Printed for G.G.J. and J. Robinson.

Hellmuth, Eckhart (1990). '"The Palladium of all other English Liberties": Reflections on the Liberty of the Press in England during the 1760s and 1790s.' In Eckhart Hellmuth (ed.), *The*

Transformation of Political Culture: England and Germany in the Late Eighteenth Century. Oxford: Oxford University Press, 467-501.

Houswitschka, Christoph (2002). *Die Rechtskultur der High Treason Trials von 1794 und die Literatur der Demokratisierung.* [Forthcoming].

Keane, John (1995). *Tom Paine: A Political Life.* London: Bloomsbury.

Paine, Tom (1969). *Rights of Man.* Ed. Henry Collins. Harmondsworth: Penguin.

Philp, Mark (1995). 'Vulgar Conservatism, 1792-1793.' *English Historical Review* 110, 42-69.

Proceedings of the Friends to the Liberty of the Press, on December the 22^{d}, 1792, and January 17th, and March 9th, 1793 (1793). London: Printed by Order of the Committee.

Rea, Robert R. (1961). '"The Liberty of the Press" as an Issue in English Politics, 1792-1793. *The Historian* 24, 26-43.

Reeves, John (1795). *Thoughts on the English Government: Addressed to the Quiet Good Sense of the People in England. In a Series of Letters, Letter the First.* London: J. Owen.

Stanhope, Charles Earl (1792). *The Rights of Juries Defended; Together with Authorities of Law in Support of those Rights. And on the Objection to Mr. Fox's Libel Bill refuted.* London: P. Emsley.

Towers, Joseph (1793). *A Dialogue between an Associator and a well-informed Englishman, on the Grounds of the Late Associations and the Commencement of a War with France.* London: Printed for T. Evans.

________ (1788). *An Oration delivered at the London Tavern, on the Fourth of November, 1788, on Occasion of the Commemoration of the Revolution.* London: Printed for Charles Dilly.

Uwe Böker

The Prison and the Penitentiary as Sites of Public Counter-Discourse

I. The Eighteenth-Century Prison

According to Daniel Defoe's *Tour through the Whole Island of Great Britain* (1724-26), one might have found, at the beginning of the eighteenth century, 'more public and private prisons, and houses of confinement [in London], than in any city in Europe, perhaps as many as in all the capital cities of Europe put together' (Defoe 1971, 321). Defoe's long list of prisons includes the famous Newgate, which, for his fictional character Moll Flanders, was a 'dismal Place: [...] the hellish Noise, the Roaring, Swearing and Clamour, the Stench and Nastiness, and all the dreadful crowd of Afflicting things that I saw there [...] make the Place seem an Emblem of Hell itself.'[1] People in real life were of a similar opinion, comparing Newgate to 'Hell itself' or a 'tomb for the living' (Sheehan 1977, 229). Thus, for Capt. Alexander Smith, in his popular collection of criminal biographies, it was a 'place of calamity, [...] a confused Chaos [...] a bottomless pit of violence, and a Tower of Babel, where all are speakers and no hearers'.[2]

Eighteenth-century places of confinement in general were quite different from modern penitentiaries, but also from the older medieval dungeons (see Ignatieff 1978, 15ff.; McGowen 1998, 71-99). Contemporary gaols were primarily used to house people awaiting trial or execution, or to keep insolvents, felons, and debtors (and their families) – usually confined together.[3] A stylised illustration such as 'Debtors and Condemn'd Criminals Log'd Together', which can be found in Moses Pitt's *The Cry of the Oppressed* (1691), gives ample evidence of the conditions (see fig. 1 following), although there were luxurious rooms in King's Bench. But civil and criminal offenders often mixed close quarters in the old prisons.[4] The prison was not a governmental institution but an capitalist-based private venture: jailers derived their income from the fees they collected for room, board, bedding, and drink, as well as from visitors.

The prison, it is true, was commonly considered as a dismal place where no kind of 'solace' could be found.[5] Gaols had a definite function within the system of law enforcement and deterrence. English law was renowned for its so-called Bloody Code,

1 Defoe 1989, 349. On the physical conditions of prisons, see Sheehan 1977, 229-230.

2 Smith 1927, 108; see Babington 1971, esp. chs. 5-11; Sheehan 1977; Evans 1982, passim; Bender 1987a, passim; Linebaugh 1992, 28; as well as Hayward 1926, v-xix.

3 On the length of prison terms, see Sheehan 1977, 231f.

4 Bender 1987a, 16. On 'Prisoners for Debt,' see Babington 1971, 81ff.; and Innes 1980, 265.

5 For 'solace', see Sheehan 1977. For the longed-for romantic prison of distance from active life and society, see Brombert 1978.

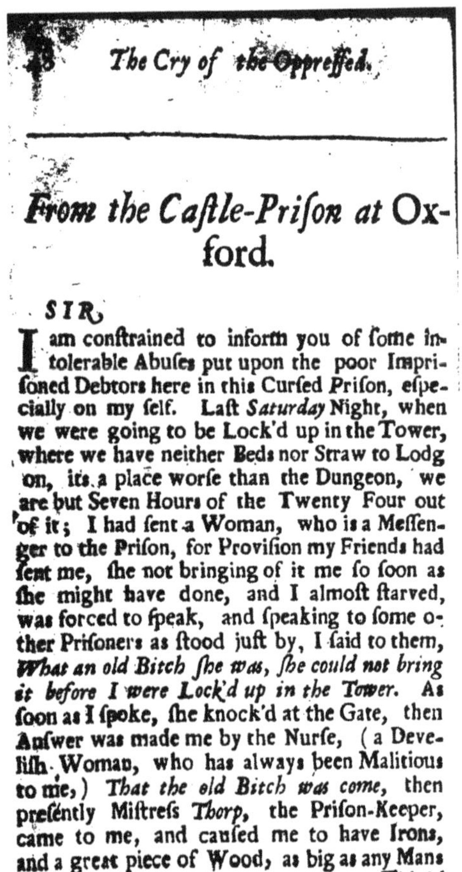
The Cry of the Oppreſſed.

From the Caſtle-Priſon at Oxford.

SIR,

I am conſtrained to inform you of ſome intolerable Abuſes put upon the poor Impriſoned Debtors here in this Curſed Priſon, eſpecially on my ſelf. Laſt *Saturday* Night, when we were going to be Lock'd up in the Tower, where we have neither Beds nor Straw to Lodg on, its a place worſe than the Dungeon, we are but Seven Hours of the Twenty Four out of it; I had ſent a Woman, who is a Meſſenger to the Priſon, for Proviſion my Friends had ſent me, ſhe not bringing of it me ſo ſoon as ſhe might have done, and I almoſt ſtarved, was forced to ſpeak, and ſpeaking to ſome other Priſoners as ſtood juſt by, I ſaid to them, *What an old Bitch ſhe was, ſhe could not bring it before I were Lock'd up in the Tower.* As ſoon as I ſpoke, ſhe knock'd at the Gate, then Anſwer was made me by the Nurſe, (a Develiſh Woman, who has always been Malitious to me,) *That the old Bitch was come,* then preſently Miſtreſs *Thorp*, the Priſon-Keeper, came to me, and cauſed me to have Irons, and a great piece of Wood, as big as any Mans Thigh

Figure 1: Copper-plate engraving and text from Pitt, *The Cry of the Oppressed* (1691).

prescribing capital punishment for all kinds of even minor crimes against property, although there were some non-capital offences (grand and petty larceny).[6] The gallows were therefore considered for a long time to be a primary means of deterrence, although contemporaries discussed the pros and cons of capital punishment. Tyburn, the customary place for public hangings, was frequently considered by the common people not to offer an event of terror but an occasion for a holiday. Henry Fielding, in *An Enquiry into the Late Increase of Robbers* (1751), was highly critical of the carnivalistic entertainments of the crowd. In order to secure the exemplary function of executions, they should 'be in the highest degree solemn. It is not the Essence of the Thing itself, but the Dress and Apparatus of it, which make an Impression on the Mind, especially on the Minds of the Multitude ' (Fielding 1980, 170).

Prisoners awaiting execution attracted much interest. They were, as a rule, visited by the prison chaplain, the Ordinary of Newgate, who was to offer spiritual help, but who also collected material for the *Ordinary Accounts*, which was published after the event (Linebaugh 1977). Convicts were also visited by relatives and friends, journalists and artists. When the Ordinary preached to the condemned prisoners the Sunday before their execution, the unfortunate candidates for the gallows had to sit in front of their black-shrouded caskets; tickets were sold to visitors (Sheehan 1977, 235-236). The first Sunday after the condemnation of the Irish highwayman James Maclaine, '3000 people,' according to Horace Walpole, 'went to see him; he fainted away twice with the heat of his cell. You can't conceive the ridiculous rage there is of going to Newgate; and the prints that are published of the malefactors, and the memoirs of their lives and deaths.'[7] In order to imagine the 'rage there is of going to Newgate,' one should have a look at the illustration entitled 'The London Rairey Shows or Who'll Step into Ketch's Theatre' (1750): it depicts a fanciful view of Old Newgate and the occasion for a street carnival. Jack Ketch, the executioner, appears at the upper left as master of a peep-show featuring Jack Sheppard and Jonathan Wild (see the reproduction in Bender 1987a, 15).

II. Pictorial Representation of Prisoners and Prisons

Graphic material such as this may be found in the *Catalogue of Political and Personal Satires Preserved in the Department of Prints and Drawings in the British Museum*, (Stephens and George 1978); there is also the Chadwyck-Healey microfiche edition of *English Cartoons and Satirical Prints, 1320-1832* (1978), as well as J.A. Sharpe's selection, *Crime and the Law in English Satirical Prints* (1986). Excepting the studies on Hogarth and P. Wagner's analysis of reading eighteenth-century graphic

6 On the types of property indictments for crimes of property between 1748 and 1800 at the Essex Quarter Sessions and Assizes, see King 2000, 137,. There was an apparently 'deliberate manipulation of offence definition by prosecutors' that seems to be responsible for a slight increase in non-capital indictments (136).

7 Walpole 1960, 199; Bender 1987a, 14, 168-169. See the illustration 'The trail at the Old Bailey in 1750 of highwayman James Maclaine' in Billett 1997, 90.

representations (Wagner 1995), to my knowledge, there is no systematic study of the popular prints Walpole refers to.[8]

One of the best-known early eighteenth-century graphic representations of a criminal condemned to death can be seen in Hogarth's 1733 print made after his painting of the murderess Sarah Malcolm (Clerc 1999). The print is a good example of Hogarth's self-advertising, his special style of deeply-bitten etching allowing for cheap reproduction:[9] it sold rapidly and was pirated. A coarser version was published in the *Gentleman's Magazine* in March 1733 (page 153), and a slightly changed version was used as a frontispiece for the first volume of Andrew Knapp's and William Baldwin's *Newgate Calendar* (1824; see fig. 2 following).

Hogarth had visited Sarah a few days before her execution, remarking, 'I see by this woman's features that she is capable of any wickedness' (quoted in Hinz and Krug 1986, 209). The account of the execution in the *Gentleman's Magazine* is printed alongside the woodcut:

> We have endeavoured to gratify our Readers with as near a Resemblance of the Face of this woman, who has made so much Noise, as this manner of printing will allow. She went to Execution neatly dressed in a Crape mourning gown, holding up her Head in the Cart with an Air, and looking as if she was painted, which some did no scruple to affirm. (*Gentlemen's Magazine* 1733, 153)

Other graphic representations of condemned criminals – less refined and highly stereotyped – carry the usual moral message, inculcating obedience, deference and submission to the elite. The thief-takers Stephen MacDaniel and Lodowick Campbell, the incendiaries John Collington and John Stone, or the murderer James Hall (see illustration following), all of whom were graphically represented around the middle of the eighteenth century, are examples of such an attitude on the side of the engravers.[10] An illustration such as 'A new Tenant for the old Room' (see illustration following) tells the message that prison and the cell – the institution – do not change; the innocents are discharged, but malefactors are going to encounter death by hanging and will suffer in hell.[11] This clear-cut iconography did not change much during the next

8 On pictorial representations as sources for historical criminology, see Hess 1981. On representations of law and justice in European art, see Pleister and Schild 1988; and Schild 1995.

9 See Wood 1994, 41ff. The Malcolm print might be compared with the portrait caricature 'Lord Lovat', picturing the recently arrested Scottish rebel; see Wood 1994, 47.

10 Reproductions of some of these prints may be found in an eighteenth-century collection of press cuttings in the British Library: *Alsatian Eccentricities 1700-1782*, comp. T. Purland; see Giovanopoulos' essay on this collection in this volume. For the thief-takers and the McDaniel gang, see Paley 1989. McDaniel's portrait was used as a frontispiece for Joseph Cox's *A faithful Narrative of the most wicked and inhuman Transactions of the Bloody-minded Gang of Thief-takers, alias Thief-makers, Macdaniel, Berry Salmon, Eagan alias Gahagan [...]*, London printed for Joseph Cox and sold by M. Mechell 1756. For Stone and Collington (incendiaries, executed in Canterbury, 7 April, 1749), see Crook 1926, 3: 161; and Knapp and Baldwin 1824-26, 2: 44.

11 For the expression of the passions in art and on the stage, see Kirchner 1991. There is, to my knowledge, no specific study of print materials portraying criminals; however, see Yonker 1969; and Smart 1965. For a general theory of the passions, see James 1997.

Figure 2: Sarah Malcolm; prints after Hogarth.

Left: woodcut from the *Gentlemen's Magazine* (1733).

Right: engraving by R. Page, frontispiece to vol.1 of Knapp and Baldwin's *Newgate Calendar* (1824).

JAMES HALL,
(Executed for Murder, 1741.)

LODOWICK CAMPBELL.
(Thief-Taker.)

A new Tenant for the old Room.

one hundred years, as woodcuts from sensational broadsheets published during the nineteenth century indicate.[12]

III. PRISON ESCAPE: JACK SHEPPARD

Ultimate death was not the only common lot to consider. As Peter Linebaugh has pointed out in his criticism of Foucault's *Surveiller et punir* (1975), the counter-cultural themes of freedom and escape ought to be emphasised; that is:

> the growing propensity, skill and success of London working people in escaping from the newly created institutions that were designed to discipline people by closing them in. [...] I see that activity [of excarceration] as a counter-tendency to [...] Foucault, who stresses incarceration in 'the great confinement' and who makes the rules of government and society seem all-powerful. (Linebaugh 1992, 3)

Here, Linebaugh is highly critical of Foucault's one-sided picture, which leaves no alternative to the criminal except to submit and suffer.[13]

Jack Sheppard was one of the early seventeenth-century idle apprentices 'turned robber at the age of twenty.'[14] But he also came to be known as one of the most renowned escapists of the early eighteenth-century. Sheppard had escaped from St Giles' Round-House, from Clerkenwell Prison, and twice from Newgate.[15] When finally caught, he was the talk of the town and was written about, although one is not quite sure about Daniel Defoe's authorship in *A Narrative of All the Robberies, Escapes &c. of John Sheppard* (1724); or *The History of the Remarkable Life of John Sheppard* (1724).[16] In this respect, the longer sections on Sheppard in Philip Rawlings' edition of *Drunks, Whores and Idle Apprentices: Criminal Biographies of the Eighteenth Century* (1992) are quite revealing. Sheppard was turned into a stage character, and was visited by James Figgs, the first English heavyweight boxing champion, and by the official court painter to George I, James Thornhill.[17] The escapist was a hero, though, at this time, a non-political one. Interestingly enough, in the fictitious dialogue between Julius Caesar and Sheppard (1725), Caesar (already)

---

12 See 'Accounts of Murders,' British Library, Printed Books, Shelfmark 1078.1.20; 'Murders, 1794-1860,' British Library, Printed Books, Shelfmark 1888.c.3. Further material and commentaries include James 1974 and 1976; Hindley 1968 and 1970; Neuburg 1973; Shepard 1969 and 1973.

13 For more recent evaluations of Foucault's *Surveiller et punir: naissance de la prison* (1975), see Sullivan 1996; Schriltz 1999; Alford 2000. For the Norbert Elias perspective on the prison, see Pratt 1999.

14 On Sheppard, see Bleackley 1933; Hibbert 1957; Linebaugh 1992, ch. 1. On contemporary biographies of Sheppard, see Linebaugh 1992, 8, n.3; Giovanopoulos 2002.

15 See 'The manner of John Shepherd's Escape out of the Condemn'd Hole in Newgate,' frontispiece to Smith's *Lives of the most Remarkable Criminals* (1927).

16 See Ellis' 'Bibliography' in Bleackley 1933, 127-136. According to Furbank and Owens (1997), Defoe's authorship cannot be definitively proved. On the disputed authorship of contemporary biographies, see Rawlings 1992, 43-44.

17 See 'G. White d'après J. Thornhill, *Jack Sheppard*, mezzotint, ca. 1724' (Clerc 1999, 213, fig. 3), unknown localisation. It had been published earlier in *Piccadilly Notes* 1934, 12; see Clerc's commentary, 213.

remarks: 'I perceive by your Discourse, that you are a Leveller, and not to be conversed with upon such Subjects' (quoted in Linebaugh 1992, 39). To be a 'Leveller' at that time meant being an unwanted revolutionary with radical democratic ideas stemming from the revolutionary 1640s.

Be that as it may, Sheppard's biography remained common knowledge throughout the century and was included in John Villette's *Annals of Newgate* and later editions of *The Newgate Calendar* (Villette 1776, 1: 253ff.; Knapp and Baldwin 1824-26, 1: 209ff.). And it was from January 1839 through February 1840 that the novelist W.H. Ainsworth's published his new work, *Jack Sheppard*, periodically in *Bentley's Miscellany*. The book was issued in October 1839 in three volumes, in part, at the same time as Charles Dickens's *Oliver Twist*; both were illustrated by Cruikshank. Three thousand copies were sold in a week. A second edition in one volume, reissued as an independent serial in fifteen shilling numbers, was dramatised – eight different versions produced in London (Hollingsworth 1963, 139).

According to the working class activist Francis Place (1771-1884), in debtor's prison himself, 'this notorious fellow was held in memory, spoken of and sung of with applause when I was a boy' (quoted in Linebaugh 1992, 3). Sheppard's story thus belongs to eighteenth and nineteenth-century popular culture. But he was not the only escapist hero: as Lorenz Eitner remarks, escapists generally met with universal sympathy, as was the case for the Abbé Bucquoy, Casanova, Linguet, Baron von der Trenck, or Henry Masers de Latude (Eitner 1978, 36).

IV. Prison, Prison Riots, and Political Excarcerations

Prisons, as we learn from the story of Jack Sheppard, were often in a bad state; complaints about the ruinous condition of Newgate were rather frequent (Rawlings 1992, 39, and 71, n.13). Still, the view of the prison presented by Alexander Smith or through Defoe's Moll Flanders was grounded in religious dichotomies of good and bad, heaven and hell.[18] But in the course of the eighteenth century, the 'controlling instruments and images of hegemony' shifted from the religious to the secular, and the awe-inspiring secular Law came to be the shaping force of everyday life (Thompson 1978; cf. Bender's criticism, 1987a, 264, n.26), and prisons were rebuilt in accordance with a secular *architecture parlante*, conveying messages of terror by means of awesome and sublime façades (Giebelhausen 1996).[19]

Popular criticism of the law in turn became more outspoken and aggressive. According to George Rudé, there had always been metropolitan riots, indicating some sort of opposition from the working classes. But the tendency to riot became, from the 1750s onwards, more politically motivated, and there were moments when rioting was

18 For the religious metaphors and dichotomies, see Fludernik's forthcoming essay on the images of the prison as world and the world as prison (2002).

19 See William Blackburn's 'Littledean Bridewell, entry lodge' (1785), in Giebelhausen 1996, fig. 5; and Bender 1987a, 241. See Bender 1987a, 19ff.

directed at prisons as symbols of the hegemonic order (Rudé 1974, 58; McLynn 1989, ch. 12).[20]

To give two contrasting examples: during the Wilkes' riots, the King's Bench was 'surrounded by a prodigious number of persons, [...] no disturbances happened till night, when the Rails which enclosed the footway were pulled up to make a fire.' But then nothing serious happened: 'a Captain Guard arriving soon after 12 the Mob dispersed' (Rudé 1974, 232) – this accounted for a rather harmless affair.

A few years later, the Gordon Riots of June 1780 – named after the Scottish peer Lord John Gordon, leader of the Protestant Association, a mass organisation that demanded the repeal of the Relief of Roman Catholics Act of 1778 – turned out to be more violent (268ff.; Kamphausen 2001) and it had a deep impact on contemporaries. It began as a manifestation of anti-Catholicism in mostly lower-class people; but when incited by Lord Gordon's attempt to petition the repeal of the Act, it soon became, according to McLynn, 'a broad river of social protest' (McLynn 1989, 234; Linebaugh 1992, 332ff.).

There were not only attacks on Roman Catholic chapels and on houses owned by Catholics, but also on London prisons. Newgate was set on fire (Rudé 1974, 272-273) and prisoners were set free – as one witness remarked, they 'marched out with all the humours of war, accompanied by a musical band of rattling fetters' (quoted in Linebaugh 1992, 334). The London working classes had long despised Newgate,[21] calling it 'King's Head Tavern', 'Sherriff's Hotel', 'Stone Tavern', 'Trib', 'Old Start', 'Little Ease' or 'Limbo' (335). On being asked during the trials why he had participated in the riots, Thomas Haycock referred the judge to 'The Cause', and explained: 'There should not be a prison standing on the morrow in London' (347).

William Gilchrist, William Blake's early biographer, remembered the radical Romantic poet having been in 'the front rank' of the rioting crowd, and Erdman adds: 'Blake shared the sentiments of Gilchrist's "triumphant black-guardism" insofar as "the mob" believed that freeing their fellows from Newgate was a step towards freeing Albion from an oppressive war.'[22] In addition, the radical writer Thomas Holcroft urged 'the necessity of [...] persevering and being united as One Man, against the infernal designs of the Ministry' (quoted in Erdman 1977, 10, n.16).

But there were others – people such as Crabbe, Walpole, Burke and even Bentham – who expressed anxiety and fear. Bentham had joined the Lincoln's Inn militia and

---

20 According to the 1715 Riot Act, it was a felony for more than twelve people to assemble and not to disperse within an hour after a magistrate had read out the Riot Act (McLynn 1989, 219).

21 See *The Whole Proceedings upon the King's Commission of Oyer and Terminer and Gaol Delivery for the City of London and also the Gaol Delivery for the County of Middlesex (1714-1800)* for 18 June 1780. For Haycock's remark, see Linebaugh 1992, 347. See also *The Proceedings of the King's Special Commission of Oyer and Terminer for the County of Surrey [...]*. London: printed for Joseph Gurney, 1780; printed in seven parts on 10 July 1780 and the following days; those who had anything to do with the attacks on the King's Bench were tried on the last day (see 123ff.).

22 Erdman 1977, 9, 10. See Linebaugh, who converts Erdman's hypothesis into a statement of fact: 'On 6 June 1780 Blake helped to deliver Newgate prison' (1992, 368). The 1780 drawing 'Albion Rose' might well be a direct outcome of Blake's experiences. For the question of Blake's sympathies for artisan rather than Whiggish radicalism, see Bindman 1993, 112-133.

was proud of having been 'a military hero for a night'.[23] Crabbe had witnessed the destruction of Newgate and the prisoners' escape from what he called the 'volcanoe'.[24] Almost fifteen years later, Burke still spoke of a 'wild and savage insurrection [that had] quitted the woods and prowled about our streets in the name of Reform.'[25] *The Newgate Calendar*, with its emphasis on the destruction of magistrates' property, public buildings and prisons, is evidence of the anxiety of the well-to-do and the elite and deserves to be quoted at length:

> The petition having been presented, the populace separated into parties and preceded to demolish the Catholic chapels [...]. After various other outrages the prison of Newgate was attacked. They demanded from the keeper, Mr Ackerman, the release of their confined associates. He refused to comply; yet, dreading the consequences, he went to the sheriffs to know their pleasure. On his return he found his house in flames, and the jail itself was soon in a similar situation. The doors and entrances were broken open with crowbars and sledge-hammers; and it is scarcely to be credited with what rapidity this strong prison was destroyed. The public office in Bow Street and Sir John Fielding's house, adjoining, were soon destroyed, and all their furniture and effects, books, papers, etc., committed to the flames. Justice Coxe's house in Great Queen Street, Lincoln's Inn Fields, was similarly treated; and the two prisons at Clerkenwell set open and the prisoners liberated. The King's Bench Prison, with some houses adjoining, a tavern and the New Bridewell were also set on fire, and almost entirely consumed.
>
> The mob now appeared to consider themselves as superior to all authority; the declared their resolution to burn all the remaining public prisons, and demolish the Bank, the Temple, Gray's Inn, Lincoln's Inn, the Mansion House, the Royal palaces, and the arsenal at Woolich. (Crook 1926, 4: 145; see also 144-148).

The Malefactors' Register (1796) has an illustration entitled 'Lord George Gordon and the Attack on Newgate' (Crook 1926, 4: facing 144; see illustration following), and another entitled 'Lord George Gordon and Mob in front of Newgate'. There are others about the destruction of Newgate on 7 June 1780 by the Gordon Rioters and the mob destroying King's Bench Prison.[26]

According to some historians, the Gordon riots were a 'revolution *manquée* – the nearest thing to the French Revolution in English history' (McLynn 1989, 240). After the event, the radical wing of the elite closed rank with the reactionaries, and most of the links between city radicalism and the London crowd were severed for some time (237). Lord Gordon's future career, however, indicates different developments. He was accused of high treason in January 1781, but the jury found him not guilty (see *Trial of George Gordon* 1781).

---

23 For Bentham, see Linebaugh 1992, 362: Bentham joined the Lincoln's Inn militia and wrote, 'I was a military here for a night.' See also Himmelfarb, 1995.

24 From Crabbe 1884, 1: 83; quoted in Linebaugh 1992, 334. For Crabbe's political attitude during the French Revolution and the subsequent anti-Jacobinism, see Edwards 1993.

25 Burke in his *Letter to a Noble Lord* (1796); quoted in Erdman 1977, 11.

26 See 'The destruction of Newgate on 7 June 1780 by the Gordon Rioters' (illus. 16) and 'The mob destroys King's Bench Prison (illus. 18) in McLynn, between pages 132 and 133.

Published by the Navarre Society, London.
LORD GEORGE GORDON.

Tried again in 1787 for his more political criticism of the country's methods of law enforcement, he was accused of 'libels; one of which tended to stir Mutiny and Dissention among the condemned Convicts, and those destined to Botany Bay.' At this second trial, Lord Gordon was accused of having

> wickedly and maliciously [...] compiled and written, printed and published, a wicked, seditious, and scandalous libel [...] the substance of which was: 'That during his present Majesty's reign, justice had not been administered; that the laws of England were contrary to the laws of God,' and that the judges were guilty of cruelty and oppression. In which said pamphlet, among other things, was the following false, scandalous, and malicious libel following, that is to say, 'But we have reasons to cry aloud from our dungeons and prisonships, in defence of our lives and liberties in this advanced period of the world.' (*Trial at Large* 1787, 2)

According to the Attorney General, the tendency of Lord George's pamphlet 'is of the most dangerous nature; for it excites the subject to rise in defence of those whose lives and liberties are forfeited. The liberty of the press in this country has great extent; but when they press into the minds of the nation, that the laws are insufficient and cruel, it must be corrected, and the printers are brought to the punishment they deserve' (3). The occasion of Lord Gordon's campaign was the governmental plans to send convicts to Botany Bay in New South Wales, which was allowed through the 1784 Transportation Act.

The second accusation was that Lord George had, on behalf of Count Cagliostro who had himself been imprisoned in the Bastille and afterwards exiled from France,[27] published some articles in the *Public Advertiser* in August 1786. These were said to affect 'the government of this kingdom. To such a pitch have our prints arrived, that no ambassador can come to London without being insulted by them' (8).

In his defence, Lord George remarked 'that Cagliostro wanted to sow dissentions in France – He must naturally be incensed against those who had persecuted him. He

27 Cagliostro had been implicated in the notorious Affair of the Diamond Necklace, which galvanised public opinion against the French royal family. He was suspected of having played a part in it, though no charges were proven. He was expelled from France in 1786. On the trials against Cagliostro, who was kept in the Bastille, see Lüsebrink and Reichardt 1990, 33-34; and Dumas 1981, 180-210. One has to bear in mind that after the lapse of the licensing act in 1695, the laws of libel were widely used as an instrument of political suppression under the motto 'the greater the truth, the greater the libel.' In the 1704 trial of John Tutchin for libels, Lord Chief Justice Holt declared in *The Observator*: 'This is a very strange doctrin to say, it is not a libel reflecting on the government, endeavouring to possess the people that the government is maladministered by corrupt persons, that are employed in such or such stations either in the navy or army. To say that corrupt officers are appointed to administer affairs, is certainly a reflection on the government. If people should not be called to account for possessing the people with an ill opinion of the government, no government can subsist. For it is very necessary for all government that the people should have a good opinion of it' (quoted in Schlenke 1963, 38, n.37). Prior to Fox's Libel Act of 1792, the jury could only decide on whether an accused had written, published, or sold a text in question, and whether or not the words had the meaning the government said it had; the truth or falsehood of a statement was not relevant to the verdict. See also Kropf 1982. According to Fox's Libel Act, 'the jury sworn to try the issue may give a general verdict of guilty or not guilty upon the whole matter put in issue upon such indictment and information; and shall not be required or directed by the court or judge'; quoted in Wickwar 1928, 42.

wished to level the infamous Bastille with the earth, and to make public walks upon it' (10). In the wake of this affair, the *Lettre du Comte de Cagliostro au Peuple Anglois* (1786) and the *Memoire pour Le Comte de Cagliostro* (1786), both attacking the Bastille, were addressed to the English reader in French; other publications with negative reference to the Bastille were published in London, addressing an English speaking audience; e.g., *Memorial, or Brief, for the Comte de Cagliostroy* (1786) and *Memorial for Comte de Cagliostro* (1786). Taken all together, Lord Gordon's story, his criticism on behalf of transportation and of the French Bastille, is an indication of a growing tendency towards a more fundamental criticism of the law and law enforcement. Thus, George Dyer could frankly remark in his *Complaints of the Poor People of England* (1793): 'Several poor men are now lingering in prison, when the men who have thrown them in are the criminals. But ignorance was the lot of the poor man, and their prosecutors and lawyers were, in broad English, KNOWING RASCALS' (Wu 1995, 42).

V. The Symbolism of the French Bastille in France and England

The Bastille had been for a long time, in France and abroad, as Lüsebrink and Reichardt have made clear (1990), the collective symbol of political cruelty, despotism and the suppression of political dissent. This is evident through a great number of texts – works such as Renneville's *L'inquisition françoise ou l'histoire de la Bastille* (1715), Voltaire's account in correspondence (1726-1729),[28] de Montgeron's *Letter from a councellor, of the Parliament of Paris* (1740), du Perray's *Historical remarks and anecdotes on the castle of the Bastille: for which he was confined in the Bastille, the night after he presented it to His Majesty* (1780), and Linguet's *Mémoires sur la Bastille, et sur la détention de l'auteur dans ce château royal* (1783)[29] – all of which were printed in London.

When the British prison reformer John Howard was not allowed to see the interior of the Bastille, he chose a French pamphlet of 1774 as his source of information, 'chiefly with the design of inculcating a reverence for the principles of a free constitution like our own, which will not permit in any degree the exercise of that despotism, which has rendered the name of Bastille so formidable.'[30] The Bastille thus had become the symbol of the *Ancien Régime*, although it was an outdated institution when it was stormed: none of the seven prisoners set free by the crowd were there for

28 See Lüsebrink and Reichardt 1990, 24. For Voltaire, see Voltaire 1913. Voltaire, himself incarcerated twice in the Bastille for several months, was the first to tell the story of the mysterious man in the iron mask in his *Le Siècle de Louis XIV* (Voltaire 1966); see Thompson 1987.

29 Linguet was a journalist who, after his release from prison, went into exile in London, publishing his memoirs in a political magazine; there are at least six French editions of the book and translations into several European languages. See Lüsebrink and Reichardt 1990, 29-33; Brombert 1978, 41-43.

30 See Howard 1929, 135; cf. Lüsebrink and Reichardt 1990, 26-27. On Howard, see McGowen 1998, 78-80.

political reasons. Such considerations highlight the contradictions between reality and the collective fantasy (see Lüsebrink and Reichardt 1990, 43; Brombert 1978, ch. 3).

After the storming of the Bastille, British radicals rejoiced over the revolutionary events. In November of 1789 at a meeting for the Commemoration of the Revolution (of 1688) Richard Price told the Friends of Freedom, 'Be encouraged, all ye friends of freedom, and writers in its defence! The times are auspicious', and 'Behold kingdoms [...] starting from sleep, breaking their fetters, and claiming justice from their oppressors' (Erdman 1977, 151).[31] At a grand dinner in celebration of the first anniversary of the fall of the Bastille, Sheridan praised 'the establishment and confirmation of liberty in France'; Horne Tooke, however, suggested that 'we feel equal satisfaction that the subjects of England, by the virtuous exertions of their ancestors, have not so arduous a task to perform as the French had; but have only to maintain and improve the constitution, which their forefathers have transmitted to them.'[32]

Eye-witness accounts of the events in Paris and the conditions in the Bastille tell gruesome stories; for example, Helen Maria Williams speaks about the great number of dungeons in her *Letters Written in France in the Summer of 1790*: 'Some skeletons were found in these recesses with irons still fastened on their decaying bones' (Williams 1989). In addition, there is a poem on the fall of the prison, 'The Bastille: A Vision', in her novel *Julia* (1790).[33] At the same time, London theatre-goers could watch the taking of the Bastille on stage in John Dent's *The Bastille* (1790), which ran for seventy-nine successive nights. The plot is as follows:

> Henry Dubois meets with his beloved Matilda whose father has been imprisoned in the Bastille. After scenes in which the people prepare their assault and the father faces torture, the masses finally storm the Bastille with Henry at their lead. They free Matilda's father, and the governor is led off to execution as his Cross of St Louis is stripped from him and given to Henry. The play concludes with a grand celebration of liberty which culminates in praises of England, as the figure

---

31 Price's address to the Revolution Society sparked off Burke's *Reflections on the Revolution in France* (1790). See Bewley and Bewley 1998, 93; and Prickett 1989, 3. On the English Revolution of the seventeenth century as a precedent for the events in France, see Bindman 1989, esp. cats. 49 and 64; and Bindman 1993, 113 and 114; Butler 1984, 32.

32 Tooke 1995, 5. See Bewley and Bewley 1998, 95ff. For the Birmingham riots on the second anniversary of Bastille Day, see Erdman 1977, 176.

33 See Wu 1997, 139-140. On Williams' poem, see Jones 1992, 178: 'History, in the form of a poem celebrating the fall of the Bastille, briefly disturbs the otherwise impeccably private world of Helen Maria Williams's sentimental novel *Julia*. It does so at a climactic moment of reconciliation when the "remorseless tyranny" of illicit desire has been subdued by a women's "open and ingenuous heart". Frederick Seymour, for whom the "paroxysm of passion" ultimately proves fatal, is reconciled to his wife Charlotte by her "generous affection", as she in turn reconciles herself to her friend and cousin Julia, the unwilling object of Seymour's attentions. This (feminine) moment of restored "cordiality and friendship" is interrupted – or confirmed – by the sublime moment of revolutionary violence: a visitor reads to the two women a "prophetic" poem on the Bastille which hails the goddesses Philosophy and Freedom: "Tis thine to love all nature's weal; / To give each gen'rous purpose birth / And renovate the gladden'd earth" (Williams 1790, 239, 267, 271).' See also Behrendt 1997a.

> of Britannia descends holding portraits of the English king and queen while a statue of liberty is seen trampling the figure of despotism. (Cox 1990, 242)

When Fr. Reynold prepared a play the same year on the fall of the Bastille, the Lord Chamberlain refused to license it. John St John's *The Island of St Marguerite*, a play centring upon the *Man in the Iron Mask*, was licensed after allusions to the Bastille were increasingly dropped. In consequence, references to the Revolution were deleted (see Cox 1990, 244-246). The Bastille had become a symbol of political oppression and its destruction, well-received by both English intellectuals and the working class,[34] was seen as the elimination of the *Ancien Régime*. But these were times when one had to be careful not to be too enthusiastic about the events on the other side of the Channel.

VI. HORNE TOOKE'S *PRISON DIARY*

The political situation was to change, however, with the Royal Proclamation against Seditious Writings and Publications (21 May 1792), and 'Terror was the order of the day' (Godwin 1988, 4; see Emsley 1985). England seemed to be, according to the British prime minister William Pitt, endangered by an 'enormous torrent of insurrection' (Tooke 1995, 1). In order to hinder oppositional groups from overthrowing 'Government, law, property, security, religion, order and every thing valuable in this country as they had already overturned and destroyed every thing in France' (ibid.), radicals were hunted down. Tooke, Thelwall, Hardy and others were arrested in May 1774 – even before the *Habeas Corpus* Suspension Act of 22 May – and were committed to the Tower on charges of high treason.[35] Tooke, under custody 'closer than was used in the Bastille' (quoted in Bewley and Bewley 1988, 156) was allowed to have pen, paper, and ink. His prison diary is a document of mental resistance:

> I shall certainly die With the principles which I have always professed; and I am very willing to dye For them. Whilst I live I will support and maintain them by every means within my power. 'I will resist argument by argument, reason by reason, legal means by legal means, force by force; but every man chooses to take that situation in which he can most advantageously employ his strength; and, as I have never professed any power but reason, I choose to take the field of argument.' (Tooke 1995, 32; see also Bewley and Bewley 1988, 161)

The next entry in his diary is a quotation from Chaucer's translation of Boethius' *De consolatione philosophiae* (ca. 523).[36] Boethius had been a public servant under and

---

34 On the English Romantic poets' reaction to the Revolution in France, see the general studies Smith 1984; Prickett 1989; Hanley and Selden 1990; Jones 1993a and 1993b; Wood 1994; and Behrendt 1997b.

35 Bewley and Bewley 1988, 151ff. See also Barrell 2000; Pfau 1997. See the broadside entitled 'Treason' in Vernon 1996, 102. The *Habeas Corpus* Act was again suspended in 1798 and in 1817; see Worral 1992.

36 See Tooke 1995, 80. According to Bewley and Bewley, Tooke 'worked hard at his Chaucer from which he intended to cite examples in the *Diversions*, and made critical comments on poems with a revolutionary flavour which Bonney had composed' (1988, 160). Tooke had only a small library of

political adviser to Theodoric, who eventually had Boethius imprisoned and executed as a traitor. It was in prison that he wrote *De consolatione philosophiae*, one of the most influential books of the Middle Ages. Tooke was in need of the lesson learned by the prisoner Boethius, who, complaining about his severe lot and the tyranny of princes, learns from Dame Philosophy that true happiness may be found within the human soul.[37] The illustration from a thirteenth-century Codex preserved in the Staatsbibliothek of Munich[38] tells the story of the victimised, of worldly power, and of spiritual hope. According to Victor Brombert, the Romantic prisoner's mind, too, quite often attains freedom from the imperatives of time and space, retreating into an inner world (Brombert 1978, 3-17). Such was the case for Boethius in the sixth century. Coming back to Tooke, whereas Dyer's poor uneducated prisoners ironically 'linger' in their places of confinement, Tooke, in the tradition of Boethius, and ultimately of Plato's prisoners,[39] receives his strength from the power of reason and argument, as indicated in the first entry in his diary.[40] Tooke's trial ended in a verdict of not guilty.[41] For the rest of his life, Tooke kept a stone from the Bastille on his desk to remind him of his spirit of resistance (Bewley and Bewley 1988, 118).

VII. John Thelwall's Prison Poems

Another reformer to be arrested was John Thelwall, according to one critic, 'the most outspoken radical orator of the day' (Wordsworth 2000, n.p.; see also Roe 1998; and Houswitschka 2002). His *Poems Written in Close Confinement in the Tower and Newgate* (1795) are headed by an epigraph from John Milton: 'Fool, do not boast: /

---

valuable books (119). He later gave his Chaucer edition to Samuel Rogers. While in the Tower, Tooke made many notes in the margin of the first book of *De consolatione* (156); he also worked on his *Diversions of Purley* for a forthcoming second edition.

37 About the place of Boethius' imprisonment, Dame Philosophy says: 'So that I seie that the face of this place ne moeveth me noght to muchel as thy owene face, ne I ne axe nat rather the walles of thy librarye, apparayled and wrought with yvory and with glas, that after the sete of thi thought, in whiche I put noght whilom bookes, but I putte that that maketh bokes wurthy of prys or precyous, that is to seyn the sentence of my bookes' (Chaucer 1987, 397-469; here 405: 1.5.36-45). Cf. Boethius 1997, 55. On Boethius and prison, see Göller 1990, 25-53. On the general literary influence of Boethius, see Patch 1935; and Courcelle 1967.

38 Codex Latinus Monacensis 2599, Staatsbibliothek Munich (thirteenth century). Cf. Boethius 1997, 183-184.

39 Klinger points to Boethius' indebtedness to Plato's *Republic*, Book 7, 514a-518a (Boethius 1997, xx).

40 Tooke 1995, 39. Tooke was allowed to read several of the London newspapers (40). There were two warders, iron bars were put up at the window, letters sent to Tooke were opened, but on the other hand, he was able to read and write approximately seven or eight hours every day.

41 The verdict was in part due to Godwin's essay 'Cursory Strictures on the Charge Delivered by Lord Chief Justice Eyre to the Grand Jury', which was first published in the *Morning Chronicle* on 21 October 1794. Godwin had, with the help of the medievalist Joseph Ritson, gone back to the statute of Edward III, and argued that the extension of the law by the public prosecutor was a case of *ex post facto* legislation. Also, Thomas Erskine was able to show the irrelevance of the prosecution evidence.

Thou can'st not touch the freedom of my mind, / – Altho' this corporal rind / thou hast immanacled.'[42] According to Thelwall's 'Advertisement', his poems are:

> sketches of the state of mind [...] and [...] a breviary of the sentiments and principles which occasioned my persecution, they may perhaps gratify the curiosity of those who wish to know what the feelings of men are in situations the most perilous and awful, when supported by the consciousness of suffering for a virtuous principle. (Thelwall 2000, i)

His poems are, as Thelwall later remarks, 'generally transcripts of the heart, rather than flights of the imagination; – rather intended to rouse the patriotic feeling, than calculated to amuse the admirer of poetical enthusiasm' (ii). He is not, as he says, writing from a personal point of view but as a 'Patriot, immured in the walls of a bastille', being 'called upon, by important duties, to repel every enervating sensation, and cultivate those habits of reflection only which may increase the energy of his mind, and enable him to render his sufferings ultimately beneficial to mankind' (iii).

Thus, 'The Feelings of a Parent' (written in the Tower on 12 July 1794) is an attack on 'tyranny' and 'the despot's rod' pursuing 'Liberty' by means of incarceration. The poet scorns 'Each fierce opposing danger – the fell steel / Of ruthless Janissaries – the stern Bastille – / Its bars, its iron doors, and caves forlorn' (Thelwall 2000, 1). In his 'Ode II', he speaks about:

> [...] the Dungeon's gloom,
> The gale impure that round the sullen walls
> Creeps noxious, and, and deathful whispers, calls
> The fiend Contagion to assure the doom
> Which Tyranny pronounces? (19-20)

In 'The Cell' (written in Newgate 24 October 1794), Thelwall refers the reader to the patriot's 'dauntless breast' and 'cheerful aspect'. Although he complains about the 'damp foul floor, the ragged wall, and shattered window, grated high', he is looking 'inward to his heart, and sees / The objects that must ever please' (9). In 'Ode II', the poet again praises the incarcerated individual turning inward and outward, overcoming the constraints of the prison:

> ... what are dungeons? – what the gloom
> Of Solitude, to him who thus can turn
> From *Self* to *Sentient Nature* – to the doom
> Of myriads yet in embrio [...]. (22)

In Tooke's *Prison Diary* as well as in Thelwall's *Poems*, the concepts of incarceration and of inner freedom are linked with one another. But one has to bear in mind that the texts are more or less a direct outcome of the cultural conditions in prisons such as the Tower or Newgate, or of prison culture in general.

42 I am grateful for Dr Anne-Julia Zwierlein, Bamberg, for locating this quotation, which is from Milton's *Comus*, lines 664-666 (Milton 1874, 2: 317). Because of her inner strength, the Lady succeeds in resisting Comus' power till there is outside help.

VIII. Tower and Newgate Counter-Cultures

According to Monika Fludernik, the topoi of the prison as world and of the world as prison are generally related in English literature (see Fludernik 2002). Both topoi, however, reproduce – implicitly or explicitly – hegemonic cultural values, as in the case of William Godwin's *Caleb Williams*: the 'master trope of "the world is a prison" is established metonymically by scene after scene of imprisoned humanity' (Fludernik 2002). But the prison may be, from the inmates' point of view, more than a homologous counter-world; rather, it may be a counter-world generating excarcerating ideas and values that evade or try to overcome disciplinary control.

Even when they were confined in the Tower, Tooke and Thelwall were allowed to get some air outside their cells by walking on the leads at the top of the round tower and the ramparts. After three month's imprisonment, they were able to speak to one another with their doors open, and by degrees they were eventually permitted to enter each other's cells (Bewley and Bewley 1988, 160). Thus, they were, even under the restrictive custody of the Tower, able to exchange ideas, revise or write books, and make plans. Tooke gave, as Bewley and Bewley remark,

> a courageous and unwavering lead to his younger and less seasoned companions. Thelwall, who said that it was from Tooke that he had principally derived 'that energy which enabled him to preserve a calm fortitude of mind when persecuted,' wrote 'Of the philosophic firmness or the playful vivacity of Tooke's mind no one will be surprised to hear; but a delightful conversation [...] stolen while our guards were asleep, I shall to the last moment of my life remember.' At midnight, while the moon shone on the river between the mass of the vessels, they talked with the freedom of men, having nothing to conceal, had nothing to fear from what might be overheard. [...] 'We rejoiced in the conduct we had already persued [...] we paid discriminating tribute of approbation to the memory of those murdered patriots who had been the preoccupants of our dungeons, and comparing the fate of Sydney and Essex, rejected the cowardly subterfuge of suicide [...] I will, said Tooke, either live to be useful or die usefully,' which Thelwall thought a maxim for all seasons. Before they left the Tower, Tooke said through the grating of his cell, 'I fear these bloodhounds mean our death.'[43]

When transferred to Newgate, the situation changed again. According to McCalman, conditions in Newgate were helpful for the emergence of a radical counterculture (McCalman 1998). During the eighteenth century, the most effective way to guarantee the custody of the incarcerated was to chain prisoners to the wall, thereby allowing not only legal advisers but other visitors, too, access to places of confinement. Thus, one can speak of an 'easy commerce between the prison world and the street' (Ignatieff 1978, 35). As keepers were private contractors, independent of the state and relying on the fees from inmates for their income, prisoners had the opportunity – given they were able to pay – to have everything from wine, gourmet tables, books and newspapers to the pleasures of sex. This situation was due to the fact that Newgate's interior was divided into the overcrowded and dismal 'Common Side' for those who

43 See Bewley and Bewley 1988, 161-166; the quotations within the quotation are from *The Life of John Thelwall* (Thelwall 1837, 190). One of the other political prisoners, Kyd, was even able to write the second volume of his *Treatise on the Law of Corporations* while imprisoned in the Tower, which he dedicated to Tooke (Bewley and Bewley 1988, 162).

were unable to pay and the 'Master Side' for affluent prisoners (Sheehan 1977, 230). In addition, prisoners were allowed to police themselves, and a debtor's access to the outside world could not be limited.[44]

These conditions contributed to the emergence of an inmate subculture of its own that made possible the radical Newgate counter-culture – a separate legal culture.[45] Newgate was 'an entrenched inmate netherworld, [...] an institution of the state with its own officers, its own customs, and its own rituals.'[46] Lord Gordon, for example, had a number of privileges,[47] and through the open society within the prison microcosm, Gordon became associated with the radical counter-culture of people such as Holcroft, Hardy, Tooke, Richter, Thelwall, and Joyce. Richard Newton's etchings, 'Soulagement en Prison, or Comfort in Prison' and 'Promenade on the State Side of Newgate' of August and October 1793, depict Lord Gordon side-by-side with future Romantic treason trialists and radical publishers and printers (see the reproductions in McCalman 1998, and 107, n.4). Newgate was 'a notorious prison republic', generating ideas and discourses that, 'under attack, cohered gradually into an "alternative" culture that appealed to both literati and radical artisans' (McCalman 1998, 96). Publishers worked together in order to print polemical, satirical, and philosophical works of prisoners. Political prisoners were visited by people such as William Godwin, the classical scholar Gilbert Wakefield, the Welsh poet Iolo Morganwyg, and the author Robert Southey.[48] McCalman has indicated further links between the Newgate radicals of the 1790s, the mixture of Enlightenment ideas, millenarianism, the 'Cercle Social drive for physical, moral, and social regeneration' and women's-rights advocacies.[49] Dyer, Mary and Percy Shelley, Peacock, de Quincey – these are names associated with the Newgate counter-culture.

---

44 Ignatieff 1978, 37. For the debtors' prison and its regulations, see Innes 1980.

45 On the inmates' legal aid in the form of 'mock tryals' or other forms of mocking symbolic inversion, see Ignatieff 1978, 40-41. For literary and law books as popular readings, see Sheehan 1977, 237. For 'gaol lawyers' in debtors' prisons, see Innes, 1980, 256-57. For Wilkes, 'whose prison cell became the central press office for a propaganda campaign,' see Wood 1994, 54. On prisoners writing pamphlets, autobiographies, and even scholarly studies, see Sheehan 1977, 238. On William Penn writing some of his pamphlets in prison, see Böker on the courtroom as a place of public discourse (in this volume).

46 Ignatieff 1978, 42. Such was the state of things not only at the time John Howard conducted his census of the British prisons in the 1770s, but continuing until the Commons inquiry of 1813 and the prison inspectors' report in 1836.

47 Lord Gordon was allowed books, personal wardrobe, a luxurious table, a servant, and unlimited number of visitors; see Ignatieff 1978, 123. See also Babington: 'I am become one of the shows of London for strangers and foreigners to stare at' (1971, 139). Gordon completed his sentence in January 1793, but was recommitted to Newgate for an indefinite term. He died of 'gaol fever' in November 1793.

48 See McCalman 1998, 98-99. For Wakefield, see Ignatieff 1978, 125. Southey brought the manuscript of his new poem 'Wat Tyler'.

49 E.g., James Lawrence's utopian gynocracy or Dr William Hodgson's *The Female Citizen*, dedicated to promoting 'the rights of women, as members of society' (McCalman 1998, 101-103). On Wakefield's classical studies in Dorchester penitentiary and his correspondence with the opposition leader Charles James Fox, see Ignatieff 1978, 125-126.

IX. Prison Reform, the Penitentiary Idea, and the New Prison

McCalman's analysis, however, gives a one-sided picture of the situation. There had been, since the 1780s, considerable changes in prison administration. Newgate and the entire system of punishment had been under severe criticism since the middle of the century. Such criticism intensified with the English publication of Cesare Beccaria's book, *Dei delitti e delle pene* (1764), in which Baccaria argued that punishments ought to be proportional to crimes.[50] The allegorical engraving on the frontispiece to his influential book[51] significantly depicts Justice turning away from capital punishment in horror and looking benignly on the instruments of socially useful hard labour. Two years later, Goldsmith's *The Vicar of Wakefield* (1766) likewise emphasised the necessity of penal reform (Bender 1987b). In addition, there always had been doubts about the deterrent value of transportation and of the death penalty.

It was in 1773 that John Howard, gentrified son of a Dissenting family, began to visit prisons in England and Wales, the outcome of which was his book *The State of Prisons* (1777). After having visited various European institutions of this sort, Howard made proposals for a reform that resulted in the Penitentiary Act, or Hard Labour Bill, of 1779, drafted by William Eden and William Blackstone.[52] From this point on, the aim of confinement would be the reform of the criminal, making it possible to substitute penitentiary imprisonment for transportation:

> If many offenders, convicted of crimes for which transportation hath been usually inflicted, were ordered to solitary imprisonment, accompanied by well-regulated labour, and religious instruction, it might be the means, under providence, not only of deterring others from the commission of the like crimes, but also of reforming the individuals, and inuring them to habits of industry. (Quoted in Bender 1987a, 23)

Although the idea of solitary confinement was nothing new in England, it was Howard who succeeded in propagating the idea that there should be a general prison reform on the understanding that criminals were capable of reformation. Howard was of the opinion that routinisation and regimes of disciplines could be internalised in order to reshape the mind of the criminal. Solitary confinement was to be the instrument to remould the prisoner by inducing him or her to think about his situation and the reasons for banishment from society. As Jeremy Bentham remarks on the opening page of his book on his model prison: 'Morals reformed, health preserved, industry invigorated, instruction diffused, public burthens lightened, Economy seated, as it

50 On Beccaria, see Bellamy 1995.

51 As reproduced in Beccaria 1995, 2.

52 Eden and Blackstone used the obsolete term 'penitentiary', which originally referred to a monastic cell as a place of penitence and remorse for sinful monks; see Evans 1982, 119. For commemorative poems on Howard, see Eitner, who refers to, among other examples, Erasmus Darwin's 'The Love of Plants', where the prison is called 'sister to the tomb' (Canto 2.439ff.; quoted in Eitner 1978, 33).

were upon a rock, the gordian knot of the Poor-Laws not cut but untied – all by a simple idea in Architecture' (Bentham 1962, 4: 39).[53]

Solitary confinement had been adopted in the United States and in Revolutionary France.[54] But the new places of confinement soon began to be used in England for political prisoners (see Ignatieff 1978, 121ff.; and Evans 1982, 187ff.). After the triumphant acquittals of Tooke, Thelwall and Hardy in 1794, the Pitt administration found it more convenient to confine political opponents by warrants under the *Habeas Corpus* Suspension Act than to bring them to trial or to sue them for libel. According to Ignatieff, several hundred political prisoners were confined during the next ten years in penitentiaries that had the facilities for their isolation (Ignatieff 1978, 122). Jacobins, it is true, were exempt from hard labour, and they were allowed books and visits, but contact with one other was restricted.[55] The public began to mobilise against the penitentiary system, castigating solitary confinement as 'an ingenious mode of intellectual torture' (quoted in Ignatieff 1978, 129.) Thus, the sixteen members of the London Corresponding Society and those of the Manchester Society knew what to expect when they were sent to the London Coldbath Fields House of Correction in 1798 (126ff.; Babington 1971, 190ff.). In December of the same year, they began a campaign openly criticising Coldbath Fields. Conditions were so bad that in 1800 there were disturbances by the convicts singing 'Pull down the Bastille' (Ignatieff 1978, 134). The state of the prisons was the top political issue during the ensuing Middlesex election, one propagandist declaring:

> when the people are taught to view the magistrates with contempt or hatred and consider every gaol a Bastille, annexing to that appellation some indefinite idea of severity and tyranny, it is greatly to be feared that their indignation will next be turned against the laws of the land: and the state of the country, the prosperity of which is so inseparably connected with a due respect for its laws and legal institutions will then be deplorable indeed. (Quoted in Ignatieff, 137)

The penitentiary system remained associated in the popular imagination with the Bastille. The slang word 'steel' or 'stile', short for Bastille, became the poor people's expression for houses of correction and for Coldbath Fields, and after Pentonville Prison was opened in 1842, it was eventually called Bastille, too (141; Evans 1982, 387.) Pentonville was the meticulously contrived, model Victorian prison in which solitary confinement and control were the leading concepts. Control was achieved through abolishing personal identity by emblazoning numbers on uniforms and cell doors, requiring that faces always to be covered with a mask of brown cloth with slots

---

53 On Bentham's idea of the Panopticon (from Greek 'all seeing'), see Himmelfarb 1995, 33ff. Bentham's Panopticon was a circular building with the cells at the circumference and the keeper in a tower at the centre. On the law of solitude, see Himmelfarb 1995, 36f. On the Penitentiary Act and on William Blackburne's architectural plans of a penitentiary, see Evans 1982, 118ff.; on the principle of separation and solitary confinement, see 169ff.; on Bentham's Panopticon, see 195ff.

54 For the new prisons on the other side of the Atlantic and de Tocqueville's opinion, see Evans 1982, ch. 7, 318ff.

55 On some members of the London Corresponding Society who were in prison at the same time and on the impossibility for extended contact, see Ignatieff 1978, 124.

for the eyes.[56] Separate and solitary confinement – thought to be the reason for some prisoners' madness as early as December 1843 – was meant to break down the structure of the mind and to make the moral character 'plastic by the discipline', as one writer said. 'It is not that the faculty of volition is enfeebled, but that the bad influence by which the will has been previously actuated is withdrawn or abated and the will is bent in its direction; it is broken in its resistance to virtue.'[57] Since the 1850s, reform was devoted more and more to problems of housing; but prison nevertheless remained an institution in which individuals were, through intrusion into their innermost recesses, made plastic and broken down – as in the case of Oscar Wilde (Böker 2001).

X. The Romantic and Man's 'Unconquerable Mind'

The introduction of the silent system around 1790 thus resulted in a transformation of prison culture, though it took some time to institutionalise the new methods of incarceration. This transformation, however, went unnoticed by the English Romantics poets who were attracted to a different discourse – that of the dungeon.

The dungeon was, according to Evans, an invention attributed by Mabillon to Abbot Athuei Prieur,

> who dug a subterranean sepulchre into which he threw a monk who he considered incorrigible [...] it had been common practice since medieval times to consign malefactors, political enemies and heretics to chambers cut into the depth of tower walls, in the footings of bailey, to undercrofts and cellars. (Evans 1982, 76ff.)

Dungeons were associated with absolutism and arbitrary power. Seventeenth and eighteenth-century theatre and its tradition of including prison scenes contributed to the stereotype (Eitner 1978, 20). But, as Evans remarks, in late-eighteenth-century England,

> the dungeon was not consciously recreated in prison architecture as it was in France [...] the dungeon was not admitted as an ingredient of contemporary prison architecture. It might be evoked as the symbol of imprisonment but real dungeons were nonetheless relics to be rediscovered in old gaols and exposed to lurid and unsentimental light. (Evans 1982, 82)

One major influence on the Romantic dungeon discourse was the Italian artist B.B. Piranesi who had etched fourteen imaginary prisons (ca. 1745). As has been convincingly shown, Piranesi's *Carceri* have no direct relationship with the gaol architecture of their time, nor even with theatrical stage imagery, except for the prison interior of *Carcere oscuro* (Eitner 1978, 20f., 23). Horace Walpole, however, the author of the first Gothic novel, remarked that Piranesi 'has imagined scenes that would startle geometry, and exhaust the Indies to realise. He piles palaces on bridges and temples on palaces, and scales Heaven with mountains of edifices' (quoted in

---

56 See Evans 1982, 346ff., esp. 361. See Evans, fig. 191, 'The Model Prison, prisoners exercising, 1856' (362); and fig. 192, 'The Model Prison, the chapel as seen from the pulpit, 1856' (364). For Charles Dickens' opinion of the 'Model Prisoner', Uriah Heep, see his *David Copperfield* (1848/1850).

57 According to J.T. Burt in his book *The Results of the System of Separate Confinement* (1852); quoted in Evans 1982, 387.

Eitner 1978, 23). As his continual revisions indicate, Piranesi tried to 'to escape the limitations of the Vitruvian classical grammar by an almost mannerist flouting of the conventions of classical architectural design' (Wilton-Ely 1993, 48). The startling geometry, mentioned by Walpole, was based on Piranesi's despair at the impotence of modern architecture which has, as he says in connection with the designs of the *Prima parte*,

> fallen from its high perfection in the period of the Roman Republic's splendour and the times of the all-powerful Emperors who came after [...] The fact is that we have not seen in our day buildings equalling the cost of the Forum de Nerva, the Amphitheater of Vespasian, the Palace of Nero. (Quoted in Eitner 1978, 23)

Piranesi, lacking adequate patronage, used his imagination to conjure up images of authority, identifying with naked force and power, bare of all sympathy with the imprisoned (25).

In his effort to produce terror, Piranesi anticipates Edmund Burke's concept of the sublime: 'power derives all its sublimity from the terror with which it is generally accompanied' (quoted in Eitner 1978, 26; Burke 1958, 59). Different from Piranesi, the new late eighteenth-century prison architecture turned to reality, aiming at experimenting with forms of penitentiary imprisonment based on the new concepts of Cesare Beccaria and John Howard. Piranesi's *Carceri* had only slight influence on prison builders. Nevertheless, the architectural rhetoric of the sublime sought to convey similar ideas of grandeur and terror, prison façades symbolising the power and the authority of law. John Howard, inspecting the newly built Newgate Prison, was told that 'criminals who had affected an air of boldness during their trial, and appeared quite unconcerned at the pronouncing sentence upon them, were struck with horror, and shed tears when brought to their darksome solitary abodes' (quoted in Eitner 1978, 28).

If we interpret the Burkean concept of the sublime as a fantasy of 'endangered subjectivity' (Milbank 1998, 228), then there were also artists and writers dramatising this danger from the point of view of the incarcerated individual and making use of the symbols of the dungeon and the solitary captive as well as the anti-absolutist dungeon discourse. Thus, in his *A Sentimental Journey* (1768), Laurence Sterne has Yorick imagine the figure of a 'single captive [...] shut up in his dungeon [...] his body half wasted away with long expectation and confinement [...] pale and feverish' (Sterne 1984, 71ff.; Bender 1987a, 234ff.; Eitner 1978, 30). There are elements of ironic distancing, and Sterne's character even gets a passport of limitless freedom in the country of the Bastille.

Slightly different reactions to Piranesi-like Italian buildings are to be found in William Beckford's epistolary travelogue of 1783, *Dreams, Waking Thoughts and Incidents*, as well as in his novel *Vathek* (1786).[58] When Beckford, who had studied architecture with Sir William Chambers, becomes aware of the fact that the doge's

58 I am grateful to Michael Meyer for providing me with the text of his essay on 'William Beckford's Real and Imaginary Travels', to be published in 2003. The subsequent quotation from Beckford's *Dreams* is quoted in this essay.

palace in Venice is built on top of the prison caverns below the canals, he is scandalised, though his terror is toned down by irony:

> Sometimes, by way of clemency, it [the Doge's tribunal] condemns its victims to perpetual imprisonment, in close, stifling cells, between the leads and beams of the palace; or, unwilling to spill the blood of a fellow-citizen, generously sinks them into dungeons deep under the canals which wash its foundations; so that, above and below, its majesty is contaminated by the abodes of punishment (Beckford 1972, 96-97).

Nevertheless he still feels haunted: 'I drew chasms and subterraneous hollows, the domain of fear and torture, with chains, racks, wheels, and dreadful engines in the style of Piranesi' (98).

But it was ultimately Sterne's sentimentalism that inspired pre-Revolutionary artists such as John Hamilton Mortimer and Joseph Wright. In Wright's two painted versions of Yorick's imagined captive in Sterne's *A Sentimental Journey*, the emphasis is on the suffering victim (Eitner 1978, 34; on other artists, see Bender 1987a, 233).[59] This is the case, too, in the frontispiece etching to W.L. Bowles' *Sonnets, and Other Poems* (1802; see illustration following), which is an illustration to his 'Verses on Reading Mr. Howard's Description of Prisons, &c.' (1802, 55). Howard is apostrophised as 'Charity', who seeks:

> the prisoner's gloom,
> Where ghastly Guilt implore her ling'ring doom;
> Where Penitence unpity'd sits, and pale,
> That never told to human ears her tale. (56-57)

His 'tender look' has visited 'the darksome vaults profound, / The caves, hid fathoms deep beneath the ground / [...] / In horror's realm the voice of peace is heard!' (57). The frontispiece shows a lone prisoner sitting on his bed of straw, leaning against the cold stone column, nearly naked except for a torn blanket, his feet and hands menacled. The caption underneath quotes from the poem:

> But oh! For him, who, to yon vault confin'd,
> Has bid a long farewell to human kind;
> His wasted form, his cold an bloodless cheek,
> A tale of sadder sorrow seems to speak. (58)

Although the frontispiece was first published in February 1798, there is no indication of the social or political conditions under which the prisoner is languishing.

Nevertheless, after the storming of the Paris prison, the plight of lone captives, a topos in Gothic fiction,[60] was both terrifying and hope-inspiring for the Romantics,

---

59 Wright's two paintings *The Captive* (ca. 1775-77; Derby Art Gallery) and *Prisoner* (ca. 1787-90; Yale Center for British Art, Paul Mellon Collection) are reproduced in Bender 1987a, 234 and 237.

60 See Fludernik 2002: 'the Gothic novel fails to make its potent schema of metonymic incarceration politically useful and retreats into the fantasy worlds of characters' psychology, catering to readers' love for the sensational and horrific. In typically sentimentalist fashion, our compassion for these incarcerated creatures is muted by the knowledge of our safe distance from that ugly world of Catholic and ancien régime cruelty.'

Frontispiece.

—But oh! for him, who, to yon Vault confin'd,
Has bid a long farewell to human kind;—Page 57.
Published Feb. 1.1791. by C. Dilly, —Cadell & Davies, London,
—— and R. Cruttwell, Bath. ——

who tried to imagine physical and mental excarceration. The Romantics were, due to the repercussions of the French Revolution on the British Isles, more interested in poetic 'dungeons' of absolutist European descent than in the actual debates on prison reform. The dungeon was for them a symbol of the unenlightened past as well as of the terror of absolutism, especially after the storming of the Bastille, which was, according to Thomas Paine, 'the downfall of Despotism'. Paine tells Edmund Burke to imagine what his fate might have been: 'Mr Burke might have been in the Bastille his whole life, as well as under Louis XVI as Louis XIV and neither of the one nor the other have known that such a man as Mr Burke existed' (Paine 1971, 70; see Bindman 1993, 114). Poets were full of sympathy for the lone captives dealing with their terrifying plight in solitary cells; but this plight was also hope-inspiring as it allowed the Romantics to imagine mental excarceration and political freedom. We should, however, be aware of the fact that the political disputes about liberty were to a large extent considered to be solely a male property (see Bruder 1997, 125-126). All the prisoners in the poems by male Romantic poets mentioned here are male.

One of the earliest examples showing the fusion of the dungeon and the Bastille discourse is Samuel Taylor Coleridge's 'The Destruction of the Bastille' (presumably written in 1789, but first published in 1834). It is a straightforward political-utopian vision, written in hope that 'every land from pole to pole / Shall boast one independent soul!' (Coleridge 1964, 11). It might be read in conjunction with Coleridge's 'France: An Ode,' first published in the *Morning Post*, 16 April 1798 (343-347) and 'La Fayette' (1796): 'Thou, FAYETTE / [...] in they Country's triumphs shalt rejoice / And mock with raptures high the Dungeon's might' (82), as well as 'The Dungeon' (from the fithe act of *Osorio*, reprinted in *Lyrical Ballads*; Coleridge 1964, 185).[61]

The British writer Helen Maria Williams –an exception from the male domination of the discourse on liberty – had herself been imprisoned in Paris; taking refuge in looking out of her window onto the Luxembourg Gardens, she found solace in 'the beauties of nature [...]. When such dispositions are excited in the mind, resignation to suffering, which in the sacred words of scripture "are but for a moment," becomes a less difficult duty' (quoted in Jones 1993b, 148). Chris Jones hints at the similarities between Williams' experience and Mrs Radcliffe's scenes of imprisonment in *The Mysteries of Udolpho* (1794) and especially in *The Italian* (1797), where the imprisoned heroine looks from her turret-room unto 'sublime view, which allows her to achieve similar transcendence and strength to bear her persecution.' For Williams, some sort of comfort seemed to have come from communication with other prisoners. In her *Letters from France* (1792/1793), the 'lonely dungeon in the caverned ground' is associated with 'the work of ages past', whereas the French, American, and British flags in the Hall of the Jacobins promise future liberty.[62]

61 William Cowper gives an account of prisoners in the Bastille in *The Task* (1785). In Southey's edition of Cowper's *Life and Works*, Cowper's Bastille passage is glossed with a footnote quotation from Coleridge's 'The Dungeon'; see Roe 1998, 193.

62 See Jones 1993b, 139-140. Jones indicates that Williams' letters of 1793 are less optimistic, detecting in Robespierre 'some deep and extraordinary malignity' (Jones is quoting from *Letters from France*; Williams 1796, 2: 12).

William Blake's prophecy in *The French Revolution* (1791-93)[63] and in *America: A Prophecy* (1793) is addressed likewise to the 'inchained soul, shut up in darkness and in sighing, / whose face has never seen a smile in thirty weary years': but now 'his chains are loose, his dungeon doors are open.'[64] Nevertheless we should be aware of the fact that Blake's central heroes in *America*, female Oothon and male Orc, are highly ambiguous characters: as Bruder remarks, 'it is Orc's ability to rape which allows him liberty, it is Oothon's capacity to be raped that facilitates her bondage'.[65]

William Wordsworth's 'The Convict' (composed in October 1796, published in 1798) is about the poet's visit to a British prison, giving solace to a captive in his 'dungeon' that is surrounded by 'thick-ribbed walls' and guarded by 'the jail-mastiff [howling] at the dull-clanking chain' (Wordsworth 1965, 484). Wordsworth is here advocating transportation that will give a second chance to convicts. In the end, the poet is able to imagine more humane conditions of law enforcement: 'My care, if the arm of the mighty were mine, / Would plant thee where yet thou might'st blossom again' (485). 'To Toussaint L'Ouverture' again depicts a man lying 'Alone in some deep dungeon's earless den'; the poet tells him not to despair, because 'thou hast great allies; / Thy friends are exultations, agonies, / And love, and man's unconquerable mind' (Wordsworth 1965, 242-243).[66] The idea of the poet being able 'to transcend his

---

63 There is a letterpress volume of *The French Revolution* (dated 1791) as 'a poem in seven books'; only the first book of this version of Blake's poem is preserved in a single copy in the Huntington Library see Bindman 1993, 113. According to Bindman, *The French Revolution* is a 'Bastille' poem, 'belonging to a well-established genre, encompassing dramas, operas (Beethoven's *Fidelio* being the best-known example), in the years immediately following the prison's destruction' (113). The Bastille genre depends upon an absolute contrast between 'despotism', hideous cruelty towards the innocent, and a vision of 'liberty' in which man may reach joy and perfection after his release from prison. Blake's Bastille has seven towers, each of which contains an exemplary prisoner condemned to rot for a righteous challenge to the political or religious hegemony of the French State.

64 From *America*, Blake 1957, 198; also quoted in Bindman 1993, 118. Bindman refers the reader back to Sterne's Captive and the mythical Comte to Lorges; see Bindman 1989, 32-42: 'the prisoner has been imprisoned indefinitely, and could only hope for release through revolution.' On the relationship and/or influence of Paine on Blake, see Bindman 1993, 114-115. Whereas Price and Paine identified the creation of a new American Republic with a state of democracy, Blake is historically less specific: 'The post-revolutionary state is [...] a pastoral paradise which follows the removal of the chains of the old order and is also a return to the "original" happy state before their imposition' (114).

65 Bruder 1997, 124. As Bruder suggests, the 'American Revolution was even less oriented towards enfranchising women than the French one which followed. [...] it is interesting to note that the very concept of liberty, of which the revolution's sympathisers were so proud, was itself utterly compromised by [...] often unconscious sexism' (125-126).

66 The poem was composed in August 1802 and is dedicated to a Negro slave who had become Governor of San Domingo, but was imprisoned in Paris for resistance to Napoleon, where L'Ouverture died in April 1803. See also Wordsworth's poem 'Captivity – Mary Queen of Scots' (Wordsworth 1965, 212). On the relationship between H.M. Williams and Wordsworth, see Jones 1993b, 141ff. For Wordsworth's later attitude, see, e.g., Book 10 of *The Prelude* (1804). See also Jonathan Wordsworth: 'Clearly Wordsworth now feels, with Burke, that the crash of the Bastille

confinement through imaginative transport' is at the heart of these poems as well as Coleridge's 'This Lime-Tree Bower My Prison' (1797).[67]

The best-known prison poem is without doubt Lord Byron's 'The Prisoner of Chillon' (1816), presenting another example of the Romantics' 'unconquerable mind'. In *A Tour in Switzerland* (1798), H.M. Williams had already written about the castle of Chillon from a different point if view, calling it the:

> Swiss Bastille [...] guarded by a stern soldiery. The tear of sensibility which has so often been shed over this spot for the woes of fiction, may now fall for sorrows that have the dull reality of existence. It is not the imaginary maternal shriek that pierces the air, it is the groan of the patriot rising from the floor of his damp dungeon that rends the heart. (Williams 1798, 2: 180; quoted in Jones 1993b, 156)

After having paid a visit to the Castle (Dangerfield 1978, 33-34),[68] Byron tells the story of François Bonivard, the Genovese priest with democratic sentiments, praising the 'Eternal Spirit of the chainless Mind' (Byron 1978, 115, line 1). In the end, the prisoner is sure that:

> my very chains and I grew friends,
> So much a long communion tends
> To make us what we are: – even I
> Regained my freedom with a sigh. (ll. 389-392)

'The Prisoner of Chillon' has been called Byron's first 'tale of a real people' (Trueblood 1977, 76-78). Considering the historical subject, this is certainly true. But, in fact, Byron's treatment of the topic is a melodramatic dramatisation of transpolitical utopianism, highlighting a kind of unfettered spiritual freedom. This strange variety of utopianism fits well into the pattern of melodrama that historians have detected in mid-nineteenth-century politics in general. According to James Vernon, it:

> instilled in its subjects a sense of agency and purpose by moralising the world into a narrative of struggle between the forces of good and evil, one which held out the utopian promise of the restoration of a 'golden age' before the fall of all that was good – innocence, honesty, virtue. (Vernon 1996, 14)

Byron, who was, according to John D. Jump, a 'Whig aristocrat with certain Radical sympathies, but [...] with little sympathy with Radicals who had risen from the lower orders' (1978, 360), does not seem to be interested in the subversive middle-class or even artisanal prison counter-culture. It was precisely because the emancipatory promise of the French Revolution remained unfulfilled that poets such as Blake, Coleridge, Williams, Wordsworth and Byron nevertheless subscribed to 'the redemptive social function [as] the mainstay of Romantic aesthetic theory' (McCann 1999, 4). Whereas Tooke, Thelwall, and others had had some experience with prison

---

made in falling – the destruction of long-established tradition – should have been heeded. The Revolution in this account must inevitably be portrayed as a false hope' (1990, 215).

67 See Simpson 1999, 26. According to Roe, Wordsworth's 'The Convict', Coleridge's 'The Dungeon', and Thelwall's prison poems 'explore the psychological effects of imprisonment, and the inner resources of memory and imagination which may dispel 'the Dungeon's noxious gloom' (1998, 193).

68 See the contemporary picture of the Château de Chillon from 1820 in Dangerfield 1978, 32.

and prison counter-culture, the Romantic poets moved in varying degrees away from public politics to the sphere of transcendental (predominantly male) freedom grounded in the excarcerating and liberating, but nevertheless private and transpolitical imagination. It is true that P.B. Shelley, living through a period of repression that only showed some signs of hope at the end of his life-time, was convinced of the practical necessity to 'make justice cheap, certain, and speedy, and extend the institution of juries to every possible occasion of jurisprudence' (Shelley 1970, 136). But the general concept of the poets as the 'unacknowledged legislators of the world' (ibid.) seems to have been more important, poets partaking, during the times of political repression, in a discourse that conveys ideas of freedom by means the image of the dungeon.

One should, however, bear in mind conservative Wordsworth's retrospective loss of faith in political radicalism and his uneasiness while remembering, in *The Prelude* (versions of 1805 and 1850), his stay in Paris and:

> Revolutionary Power
> Toss like a ship at anchor, rocked by storms
> Where silent zephyrs sported with the dust
> Of the Bastile, I sate in the open sun
> And from the rubbish gathered up a stone,
> And pocketed the relic, in the guise
> Of an enthusiast; yet, in honest truth,
> I looked for something that I could not find,
> Affecting more emotion than I felt;
> For 'tis most certain, that these various sights,
> However potent their first shock, with me
> Appeared to recompense the traveller's pains
> Less than the painted Magdalen of Le Brun,
> A beauty exquisitely wrought, with hair
> Dishevelled, gleaming eyes and rueful cheek
> Pale and bedropped with everflowing tears.
> (Wordsworth 1965, 556; IX, 50-51, and 67-80)[69]

---

69 Wordsworth is referring here to a picture of the weeping Mary Magdalene, painted by Charles Brun (1616-1690), which is now in the Louvre; see Wordsworth 1979, 316, n.4. For Wordsworth's growing conservatism and his changing reactions to the Revolution in France, see Gassenmeier 1987. See also Wordsworth's late *Sonnets upon the Punishment of Death*, published in the *Quarterly Review* in December 1842; especially 'Sonnet IX' and 'Sonnet XII', reminding the reader of 'Law's dispassionate voice' as represented by the 'State':

> See the Condemned alone within his cell
> and prostrate at some moment when remorse
> Stings to the quick, and, with resistless force,
> assaults the pride she strove in vain to quell.
> Then mark him, him who could so long rebel,
> The crime confessed, a kneeling Penitent
> Before the Altar, where the Sacrament
> Softens his heart, till from his eyes outwell
> Tears of salvation. Welcome death!
> (Wordsworth 1965, 406 and 407).

In fact, the contemporary British poet Tony Harrison was recently wondering, in his verses about a relic from the French dungeon:

> if that bit of stone
> Wordsworth had from the Bastille
> ever got itself rethrown
> against repressive steel,
> or was it tossed into a lake,
> the poet watching from the bank,
> seeing what ripples it would make
> and go on making while it sank?
> (Harrison 2000, 82)

(Wordsworth 1965, 406 and 407).

PRIMARY LITERATURE

Beccaria, Cesare (1995). *On Crimes and Punishments* [*Die delitti e delle pene*, 1764] *and Other Writings*. Ed. Richard Bellamy. Trans. Richard Davies, Virginia Cox and Richard Bellamy. Cambridge: Cambridge University Press.
Beckford, William (1972). *Dreams, Waking Thoughts and Incidents: The Travel-Diaries of William Beckford of Fonthill*. Ed. with a memoir and notes by Guy Chapman. Vol. 1. New York: Kraus.
Bentham, Jeremiah (1962). *The Works of Jeremy Bentham*. Ed. John Bowring. Vol. 4. New York: Russell and Russell. Original edition London, 1843.
Blake, William (1957). *The Complete Writings of William Blake with Variant Readings*. Ed. G. Keynes. London: Oxford University Press.
Boethius (1997). *Trost der Philosophie*. Trans. and ed. Karl Büchner. Intro. Friedrich Klinger. Stuttgart: Reclam.
Bowles, Rev. W.L. (1802). *Sonnets, and Other Poems [...] To which is added, Hope, An Allegorical Sketch on Recovering slowly from Sickness*. 8th ed. London: Printed for T. Cadell, Jr, et al.
Burke, Edmund (1958). *A Philosophical Enquiry into the Origin of our Ideas of the Sublime and Beautiful*. Ed. J.T. Boulton. London: Routledge and Kegan Paul. Original edition 1756.
Byron, Lord George Gordon (1978). *Byron's Poetry*. Ed. Frank D. McConnell. New York: Norton.
Chaucer, Geoffrey (1987). *The Riverside Chaucer*. Ed. Larry D. Benson. 3rd ed. Boston: Houghton Mifflin.
Coleridge, S.T. (1964). *The Poems of Samuel Taylor Coleridge*. Ed. Ernest Hartley Coleridge. London: Oxford University Press.
Crabbe, George (1884). *Poetical Works*. Vol. 1 London: Murray.
Crook, G.T., ed. (1926). *The Complete Newgate Calendar*. 5 vols. London: For the Navarre Society.
Defoe, Daniel (1971). *A Tour through the Whole Island of Great Britain*. Abridged and ed. with intro. and notes by Pat Rogers. Harmondsworth: Penguin. Original edition 1724-27.
________ (1989). *Moll Flanders*. Ed. David Blewett. London: Penguin. Original edition 1722.
English Cartoons and Satirical Prints, 1320-1832 (1978). Microfiche edition. Cambridge: Chadwyck-Healey.
Fielding, Henry (1980). *An Enquiry into the Causes of the Late Increase of Robbers and Related Writings*. Ed. Melvin R. Zirker. Oxford: Clarendon Press. Original edition Dublin, 1751.
Gentleman's Magazine 3 (March 1733). Online: *Internet Library of Early Journals*. Internet. 21 February 2002. Available http://www.bodley.ox.ac.uk/ilej/.
Godwin, William (1988). *Caleb Williams*. Harmondsworth: Penguin. Original edition 1794.
Harrison, Tony (2000). *Laureate's Block and Other Poems*. Harmondworth: Penguin.
Howard, John (1929). *The State of Prisons*. Intro. K. Ruck. London: Dent. Original edition 1777.
Knapp, Andrew and William Baldwin, eds. (1824-1826). *The Newgate Calendar; Comprising Interesting Memoirs of the Most Notorious Characters Who Have Been Convicted of Outrages on the Laws of England since the Commencement of the Eighteenth Century; with Occasional Anecdotes and Observations, Speeches, Confessions, and Last Exclamations of Sufferers*. 4 vols. London: J. Robbins.
Memorial for Comte de Cagliostro, Plaintiff [...] (1786). London: Printed for J.W. Galabin.
Memorial, or Brief, for the Comte de Cagliostro, Defendant [...] (1786). London: Printed for J. Debrett.
Milton, John (1874). *The Poetical Works of John Milton*. Ed. David Masson. 2 vols. London: Macmillan.
Paine, Thomas (1971). *The Rights of Man*. Ed. with an intro. Henry Collins. Harmondsworth: Penguin. Original edition 1791/92.
Sharpe, J.A., ed. (1986). *Crime and the Law in English Satirical Prints*. Cambridge: Chadwyck-Healey.

Shelley, P.B. (1970). *Political Writings including* A Defence of Poetry. Ed. Roland A. Duerksen. New York: Appleton-Century-Crofts.

Smith, Capt. Alexander (1927). *Lives of the Most Remarkable Criminals [...]*. Ed. Arthur L. Hayward. London: Routledge. Original edition 1735.

Stephens, Frederick G., and Mary D. George, comps. and eds. (1978). *Catalogue of Political and Personal Satires Preserved in the Department of Prints and Drawings in the British Museum*. 11 vols. London: British Museum Publications.

Sterne, Laurence (1984). *A Sentimental Journey Through France and Italy By Mr. Yorick with The Journal to Eliza and A Political Romance*. Ed. Ian Jack. Oxford: Oxford University Press. Original edition 1768.

Thelwall, John (2000). *Poems Written in Close Confinement in the Tower and Newgate, under a Charge of High Treason*. Washington, DC: Woodstock Books. Original edition 1795.

Thelwall, Mrs John (1837). *The Life of John Thelwall, by His Widow*. London: John Macrone.

Tooke, John Horne (1995). *The Prison Diary (16 May-22 November 1794)*. Ed. with intro. and notes by A.V. Beedell and A.D. Harvey. Leeds: Leeds Philosophical and Literary Society.

Trial at Large of The Hon. George Gordon, commonly called Lord George Gordon [...] (1787). London: Printed for R. Randall.

Trial of George Gordon, Esquire, commonly called Lord George Gordon, for High Treason, at the Bar of the Court of King's Bench (1781). 4th ed. London: Sold by G. Kearsley.

Villette, John (1776). *The Annals of Newgate; or, the Malefactor's Register [...]*. 4 vols. London: Printed for J. Wenman.

Voltaire (1913). *Correspondance de Voltaire (1726-1729): La Bastille, L'Angleterre, Le Retour en France*. Ed. Lucien Foulet. Paris: Hachette.

________ (1966). *Le Siècle de Louis XIV*. 2 vols. Paris: Garnier-Fammarion.

Walpole, Horace (1960). *Correspondence*. Vol. 20: *Correspondence with Sir Horace Mann*. Ed. W.S. Lewis, Warren Hunting Smith and George L. Lam. New Haven: Yale University Press.

Williams, H.M. (1790). *Julia*. 2 vols. London: T. Cadell.

________ (1796). *Letters from France*. London.

________ (1798). *A Tour in Switzerland; or, A view of the present state of the governments and manners of those cantons; with comparative sketches of the present state of Paris*. 2 vols. London.

________ (1989). *Letters Written in France: 1790*. Intro. Jonathan Wordsworth. Oxford: Woodstock Books.

Wordsworth, William (1965). *The Poetical Works*. Ed. with intro. and notes by Thomas Hutchinson. New ed. rev. Ernest de Selincourt. London: Oxford University Press.

________ (1979). *The Prelude 1799, 1805, 1850: Authoritative Texts, Context and Reception – Recent Critical Essays*. Ed. Jonathan Wordsworth, M.H. Abrams and Stephen Gill. New York: Norton.

Wu, Duncan, ed. (1995). *Romanticism: An Anthology*. Oxford: Blackwell.

References

Alford, C. Fred (2000). 'What would it matter if everything Foucault said about prison were wrong? *Discipline and Punish* after Twenty Years.' *Theory and Society* 29, 125-146.

Babington, Anthony (1971). *The English Bastille: A History of Newgate Gaol and Prison Conditions in Britain 1188-1902*. London: Macdonald.

Barrell, John (2000). *Imagining the King's Death: Figurative Treason, Fantasies of Regicide 1793-1796*. Oxford: Oxford University Press.

Behrendt, Stephen C. (1997a). 'British Women Poets and the Reverberations of Radicalism in the 1790s.' In Stephen C. Behrendt (ed.), *Romanticism, Radicalism, and the Press*. Detroit: Wayne State University Press, 83-102.

_______, ed. (1997b). *Romanticism, Radicalism, and the Press*. Detroit: Wayne State University Press.

Bellamy, Richard (1995). 'Introduction.' In Cesare Beccaria, *On Crimes and Punishments* [*Die delitti e delle pene*, 1764] *and Other Writings*. Ed. Richard Bellamy. Trans. Richard Davies, Virginia Cox and Richard Bellamy. Cambridge: Cambridge University Press, i-xlix.

Bender, John (1987a). *Imagining the Penitentiary: Fiction and the Architecture of Mind in Eighteenth-Century England.* Chicago: University of Chicago Press.

_______ (1987b). 'Prison Reform and the Sentence of Narration in *The Vicar of Wakefield*.' In Felicity Nussbaum and Laura Brown (eds.), *The New Eighteenth Century – Theory, Politics, English Literature.* London: Methuen, 168-188.

Bewley, Christina, and David Bewley (1998). *Gentleman Radical: A Life of John Horne Tooke 1736-1812.* London: Taurus Academic Studies.

Billett, Michael (1997). *Highwaymen and Outlaws.* London: Arms and Armour.

Bindman, David (1989). *Shadow of the Guillotine: Britain and the French Revolution.* London: British Museum.

_______ (1993). '"My own mind is my own church": Blake, Paine and the French Revolution.' In Alison Yarrington and Kelvin Everest (eds.), *Reflections of Revolution: Images of Romanticism.* London: Routledge, 112-133.

Bleackley, Horace (1933). *Jack Sheppard, with an Epilogue on Jack Sheppard in Literature and Drama, a Bibliography, a Note on Jonathan Wild, and a Memoir of Horace Bleackley, by S.M. Ellis.* Edinburgh: Hodge.

Böker, Uwe (2001). 'The Institutionalisation of Legal Norms and Values in England (1500-1900).' In Uwe Böker and Julie A. Hibbard (eds.), *Processes of Institutionalisation: Case Studies in Law, Prison and Censorship.* Essen: Blaue Eule, 13-60.

Brombert, Victor (1978). *The Romantic Prison: The French Tradition.* Princeton: Princeton University Press.

Bruder, Helen P. (1997). *William Blake and the Daughters of Albion.* Houndsmills: Macmillan.

Butler, Marylin, ed. (1984). *Burke, Paine, Godwin, and the Revolution Controversy.* Cambridge: Cambridge University Press.

Clerc, Marianne (1999). 'Sarah Malcolm en Prison de William Hogarth: Essay sur la représentation du condemné à mort.' *Gazette des Beaux Arts* 141, 211-218.

Courcelle, Pierre (1967). La Consolation de Philosophie *dans la tradition littéraire.* Paris: Etudes Augustiniennes.

Cox, Jeffrey N. (1990). 'Romantic Drama and the French Revolution.' In Keith Hanley and Raman Selden (eds.), *Revolution and English Romanticism: Politics and Rhetoric.* Hemel Hempstead: Harvester Wheatsheaf, 241-260.

Dangerfield, Elma (1978). *Byron and the Romantics in Switzerland 1816.* London: Ascent Books.

Dumas, François Ribadeau (1981). *Cagliostro, homme de lumière.* Paris: Editions Philosophiques.

Edwards, Gavin (1993). 'Crabbe's Regicide Households.' In Alison Yarrington and Kelvin Everest (eds.), *Reflections of Revolution: Images of Romanticism.* London: Routledge, 83-94.

Emsley, Clive (1985). 'Repression, "Terror" and the Rule of Law in England during the Decade of the French Revolution.' *English Historical Review* 100, 801-825.

Eitner, Franz (1978). 'Cages, Prisons, and Captives in Eighteenth-Century Art.' In (eds.), *Images of Romanticism: Verbal and Visual Affinities.* New Haven: Yale University Press, 13-38.

Erdman, David V. (1977). *Blake – Prophet Against Empire: A Poet's Interpretation of the History of His Own Times.* 3rd ed. Princeton: Princeton University Press.

Evans, Robin (1982). *The Fabrication of Virtue: English Prison Architecture, 1750-1840.* Cambridge: Cambridge University Press.

Fludernik, Monika (2002). 'The Prison as World – The World as Prison: Theoretical and Historical Aspects of two Recurrent Topoi.' *Symbolism* 2/2, in press.

Foucault, Michel (1975). *Surveiller et punir: naissance de la prison.* Paris: Gallimard.

Furbank, P.N., and W.R. Owens (1997). 'The Myth of Defoe as "Applebee's Man."' *Review of English Studies* NS 48, 198-204.

Gassenmeier, Michael (1987). '"Twas a Transport of the Outward Sense": Wordsworth's Own Account of His Visions and Revisions of the French Revolution.' In Michael Gassenmeier and Norbert H. Platz (eds.), *Beyond the Suburbs of the Mind: Exploring English Romanticism*. Essen: Blaue Eule, 116-136.

Giebelhausen, Michaela (1996). '"More terrors than reason could justify": Zur Bedeutung der Fassade in der Gefängnisarchitektur um 1800.' In Uwe Böker and Christoph Houswitschka (eds.), *Literatur, Kriminalität und Rechtskultur im 17. und 18. Jahrhundert*. Essen: Blaue Eule 1996, 199-240.

Giovanopoulos, Anna-Christina (2002). '"This day is to be hanged the greatest rogue in England": Robert Walpole und Jonathan Wild.' In Stefan Müller, Gary Schaal, and Claudia Tiersch (eds.), *Dauer durch Wandel: Institutionelle Ordnungen zwischen Verstätigung und Transformation*. Cologne: Böhlau, 191-209.

Göller, Karl Heinz (1990). 'Das metaphorische Gefängnis: Zum Verhältnis von Literatur und Weltbild im Mittelalter.' In Heinz-Joachim Müllenbrock and Alfons Klein (eds.), *Motive and Themen in englischsprachiger Litreratur als Indikatoren literaturgeschichtlicher Prozesse: Festschrift zum 65. Geburtstag von Theodor Wolpers*. Tübingen: Niemeyer, 25-53.

Hanley, Keith, and Raman Selden, eds. (1990). *Revolution and English Romanticism: Politics and Rhetoric*. Hemel Hempstead: Harvester Wheatsheaf.

Hayward, Arthur L. (1926). 'Introduction.' In Alexander Smith, *A Complete History of the Lives and Robberies of the Most Notorious Highwaymen, [...], for the Common Benefit of Mankind*. Ed. Arthur L. Hayward. London: Routledge, v-xx.

Hess, Albert G. (1981). 'Pictorial Representations as Sources for Historical Criminology.' *Criminal Justice History* 2, 63-84.

Hibbert, Christopher (1957). *The Road to Tyburn: The Story of Jack Sheppard and the Eighteenth-Century Underworld*. London: Longmans Green.

Himmelfarb, Gertrude (1995). 'The Haunted House of Jeremiah Bentham.' In *Victorian Minds*. Chicago: Elephant, 32-81.

Hindley, Charles (1968). *The Life and Times of James Catnach (Late of Seven Dials), Ballad Monger*. Detroit: Singing Tree Press. Original edition London: Reeves and Turner, 1878.

________ (1970). *Curiosities of Street Literature*. Foreword by Michael Hughes. New York: Kelly. Original edition 1871.

Hinz, Berthold, and Hartmut Krug, eds. (1986). *William Hogarth 1697-1764*. 2nd ed. Giessen: Anabas.

Hollingsworth, Keith (1963). *The Newgate Novel 1830-1847: Bulwer, Ainsworth, Dickens, & Thackeray*. Detroit: Wayne State University Press.

Houswitschka, Christoph (2002). *Die Rechtskultur der High Treason Trials von 1794 und die Literatur der Demokratisierung*. [Forthcoming].

Ignatieff, Michael (1978). *A Just Measure of Pain: The Penitentiary in the Industrial Revolution, 1750-1850*. New York: Pantheon Books.

Innes, Joanna (1980). 'The King's Bench Prison in the Late Eighteenth Century: Law, Authority and Order in a London Debtors' Prison.' In John Brewer and John Styles (eds.), *An Ungovernable People: The English and Their Law in the Seventeenth and Eighteenth Centuries*. London: Hutchinson, 250-298.

James, Louis (1974). *Fiction for the Working Man 1830-1851: A Study of the Literature Produced for the Working Classes in Early Victorian Urban England*. Harmondsworth: Penguin.

________, ed. (1976). *Print and the People, 1819-1851*. London: Lane.

James, Susan (1997). *Passion and Action: The Emotions in Seventeenth-Century Philosophy*. Oxford: Clarendon Press.

Jones, Chris (1993a). 'Radical Sensibility in the 1790s.' In Alison Yarrington and Kelvin Everest (eds.), *Reflections of Revolution: Images of Romanticism*. London: Routledge, 68-82.

________ (1993b). *Radical Sensibility: Literature and Ideas in the 1790s*. London: Routledge.

Jones, Vivien (1992). 'Women Writing Revolution: Narratives of History and Sexuality in Wollstonecraft and Williams.' In Stephen Copley and John Whale (eds.), *Beyond Romanticism: New Approaches to Texts and Contexts, 1780-1832*. London: Routledge, 178-199.

Jump, John D. (1978). 'Byron: The Historical Context.' In Frank D. McConnell (ed.), *Byron's Poetry*. New York: Norton, 351-360.

Kamphausen, Christoph (2001). 'Emancipation and Violence: On the Interpretation of the Anti-Jewish Riots in the German Vormärz.' In Richard Bonney and Franz Bosbach (eds.), *Religion und Politik in Deutschland und Großbritannien. Religion and Politics in Britain and Germany*. Munich: Saur, 63-82.

Kirchner, Thomas (1991). *L'expression des passion: Ausdruck als Darstellungsproblem in der französischen Kunst und Kunstheorie des 17. und 18. Jahrhunderts*. Mainz: Von Zabern.

Kropf, C.R. (1982). 'Libel and Satire in the Eighteenth Century.' In Wolfgang Weiss (ed.), *Die englische Satire*. Darmstadt: Wissenschaftliche Buchgesellschaft, 334-351.

Linebaugh, Peter (1977). 'The Newgate Ordinary and his Account.' In J.S. Cockburn (ed.), *Crime in England 1550-1800*. London: Methuen, 246-269.

________ (1992). *The London Hanged: Crime and Society in the Eighteenth Century*. Cambridge: Cambridge University Press.

Lüsebrink, Hans-Jürgen, and Rolf Reichardt (1990). *Die 'Bastille': Zur Symbolgeschichte von Herrschaft und Freiheit*. Frankfurt/Main: Fischer.

McCalman, Iain (1998). 'Newgate in Revolution: Radical Enthusiasm and Romantic Counterculture.' *Eighteenth-Century Life* 22, 95-110.

McCann, Andrew (1999). *Cultural Politics in the 1790s: Literature, Radicalism and the Public Sphere*. London: Macmillan.

McGowen, Randall (1998). 'The Well-Ordered Prison: England, 1780-1865.' In Norval Morris and David J. Rothman (eds.), *The Oxford History of the Prison: The Practice of Punishment in Western Society*. New York: Oxford University Press, 71-99.

McLynn, Frank (1989). *Crime and Punishment in Eighteenth-Century England*. London: Routledge.

Meyer, Michael (2003). 'William Beckford's Real and Imaginary Travels.' In Werner Huber (ed.), *Alternative Romanticisms: Exploring Romantic Locations and Genres*. Essen: Blaue Eule, forthcoming.

Neuburg, Victor E. (1973). 'The Literature of the Streets.' In H.J. Dyos and Michael Wolff (eds.), *The Victorian City: Images and Realities*. Vol. 1 London: Routledge and Kegan Paul, 191-209.

Paley, Ruth (1989). 'Thief-Takers in London in the Age of the McDaniel Gang, c. 1745-1754.' In Douglas Hay and Francis Snyder (eds.), *Policing and Prosecution in Britain 1750-1850*. Oxford: Clarendon Press, 301-341.

Patch, Howard Rollin (1935). *The Tradition of Boethius: A Study of His Importance in Medieval Culture*. New York: Oxford University Press.

Pfau, Thomas (1997). 'Paranoia Historicized: Legal Fantasy, Social Change, and Satiric Meta-Commentary in the 1794 Treason Trials.' In Stephen C. Behrendt (ed.), *Romanticism, Radicalism, and the Press*. Detroit: Wayne State University Press, 30-64.

Pleister, Wolfgang, and Wolfgang Schild, eds. (1988). *Recht und Gerechtigkeit im Spiegel der europäischen Kunst*. Cologne: DuMont.

Pratt, John (1999). 'Norbert Elias and the Civilised Prison.' *British Journal of Sociology* 50, 271-296.

Prickett, Stephen (1989). *England and the French Revolution*. London: Macmillan.

Rawlings Philip, ed. (1992). *Drunks, Whores and Idle Apprentices: Criminal Biographies of the Eighteenth Century*. London: Routledge.

Roe, Nicholas (1998). '"Atmospheric Air Itself": Medical Science, Politics and Poetry in Thelwall, Coleridge and Wordsworth.' In Richard Cronin (ed.), *1798: The Year of the Lyrical Ballads*. Houndsmill: St Martin's Press, 185-202.

Rudé, George (1974). *Paris and London in the 18th Century: Studies in Popular Protest*. London: Fontana/Collins.

Schild, Wolfgang (1995). *Bilder von Recht und Gerechtigkeit*. Cologne: DuMont.

Schlenke, Manfred (1963). *England und das Friderizianische Preußen, 1740-1763: Ein Beitrag zum Verhältnis von Politik und öffentlicher Meinung im England des 18. Jahrhunderts*. Munich: Alber.

Schriltz, Karl von (1999). 'Foucault on the Prison: Torturing History to Punish Capitalism.' *Critical Review* 13, 391-411.

Sheehan, W.J. (1977). 'Finding Solace in Eighteenth-Century Newgate.' In J.S. Cockburn (ed.), *Crime in England 1550-1800*. London: Methuen, 229-245.

Shepard, Leslie (1969). *John Pitts: Ballad Printer of Seven Dials, London 1765-1844, With a short account of his predecessors in the Ballad & Chapbook Trade*. London: Private Libraries Association.

________ (1973). *The History of Street Literature: The Story of Broadside Ballads, Chapbooks, Proclamations, News-Sheets, Election Bills, Tracts, Pamphlets, Cooks, Catchpennies, and other Ephemera*. Newton Abbot: David and Charles.

Simpson, Michael (1999). 'Coleridge's Swinging Moods and the Revision of "This Lime-Tree Bower My Prison."' *Style* 33, 21-42.

Smart, Alastair (1965). 'Dramatic Gesture and Expression in the Age of Hogarth and Reynolds.' *Apollo* (August), 90-97.

Smith, Olivia (1984). *The Politics of Language 1791-1819*. Oxford: Oxford University Press.

Sullivan, Robert R. (1996). 'The Birth of the Prison: Discipline or Punish?' *Journal of Criminal Justice* 24, 449-458.

Thompson, E.P. (1978). 'Eighteenth-Century English Society: Class Struggle without Class?' *Social History* 3, 133-165.

Thompson, Harry (1987). *The Man in the Iron Mask: A Historical Detective Investigation*. London: Weidenfeld and Nicolson.

Trueblood, Paul G. (1977). *Lord Byron*. 2nd ed. Boston: Twayne.

Vernon, James (1996). *Re-Reading the Constitution: New Narratives in the Political History of England's long Nineteenth Century*. Cambridge: Cambridge University Press.

Wagner, Peter (1995). *Reading Iconotexts: From Swift to the French Revolution*. London: Reaktion Books.

Wickwar, William Hardy (1928). *The Struggle for the Freedom of the Press 1819-1832*. London: Allen and Unwin.

Wilton-Ely, John (1993). *Piranesi as Architect and Designer*. New York: Pierpont Morgan.

Wood, Marcus (1994). *Radical Satire and Print Culture 1790-1822*. Oxford: Clarendon Press.

Wordsworth, Jonathan (1990). 'Wordsworth's Dim and Perilous Way.' In Keith Hanley and Raman Selden (eds.), *Revolution and English Romanticism: Politics and Rhetoric*. Hemel Hempstead: Harvester Wheatsheaf, 205-223.

________ (2000). 'Introduction.' In John Thelwall, *Poems Written in Close Confinement in the Tower and Newgate, under a Charge of High Treason*. Washington, DC: Woodstock, n.p.

Worral, David (1992). *Radical Culture: Discourse, Resistance and Surveillance, 1790-1820*. New York: Harvester Wheatsheaf.

Yonker, Dolores Beck (1969). *The Face as an Element of Style: Physiognomical Theory in Eighteenth-Century British Art*. PhD diss. University of California, Los Angeles.

York-Gothart Mix

'*Ubi libertas, ibi patria*': The Interculturality of German-American Popular Almanacs of the Eighteenth and Nineteenth Centuries[1]

I. The Research Topic

The only fairly recent general article investigating the literary relationships between North America and Germany, published in 1993 in Walter Killy's *Literaturlexikon*, does not account for an important textual source placed at the core of daily discourse and dealing with questions of cultural identity and differences: the German popular almanacs published in Pennsylvania (from 1731 onward) and in other parts of North America. Ignoring these periodicals helped to shape the idea that 'the emigrants', similar to the German Americans influential after 1848, did not participate in the 'American cultural discourse'. It also led to the conclusion that the cultural transfer was due to the 'travels of the educated Europeans' (Schmitz 1993, 165, 166). Such conclusions are questionable in consideration of *Meyer's Groschen-Bibliothek der Deutschen Classiker*, a small book series that had been created for emigrants. Published in Hildburghausen and New York, it was distributed for mass consumption. In addition to this series, there was the literary program of the *Amerikanische Tractat-Gesellschaft*, listing more than 160 titles, the numerous German periodicals, and at least thirty-nine German almanac series published in eastern North America. Karl Goedeke provides a 142-page overview of German-American literature in volume 15 of the *Grundriß zur Geschichte der Deutschen Dichtung* (1966).[2]

The North American German publishing industry was originally based in Pennsylvania, and the popular almanacs produced there are of particular interest. They came out what had been, at the beginning, a British colony. In 1775, the number of German-speaking emigrants living in Pennsylvania by far extended 100,000; a non-English culture proliferated in Germantown, Lancaster and Philadelphia.[3] The earliest

---

1 This paper developed out of a DFG sponsored project, together with Hans-Jürgen Lüsebrink (Saarbrücken), under the title 'Cultural Transfer and Process of Autonomisation: Comparative and Intercultural Studies of German-American and Franco-Canadian Eighteenth and Nineteenth-Century Popular Calendars and Almanacs.'

2 The series *Meyer's Groschen-Bibliothek der Deutschen Classiker* was made up of hundreds of small volumes; the publisher's notes were identical throughout: 'Hildburghausen: Druck vom Bibliographischen Institut. New-York: Hermann J. Meyer.' According to the cover, this series was sent to all 'substantial bookshops in Germany and abroad' and was sold at a discount. According to the publisher's advertisements, the New York based *Amerikanische Tractat-Gesellschaft* offered a great number of 'Erbauungs-Bücher von ausgezeichneten theologischen Schriftstellern, sowie 140 evangelische Tractate und 20 Kinder-Tractate.' For the periodicals and the German-American books, see Goedeke 1966, 518-661. Emigration as a theme in contemporary fiction is dealt with by Mikoletzky 1988.

3 As early as 1800, printers and booksellers such as Jacob Hütter in Lancaster offered a selection of '8000 volumes' of the 'latest and best German books' (Goedeke 1966, 519). The francophile readership in Philadelphia was served by 'Boinod and Gaillard', who had published a *Catalogue des*

German-American almanac included in Karl John Richard Arndt's and May Evelyn Olson's authoritative bibliography, the *Deutsch-Amerikanische Zeitungen und Zeitschriften 1732-1955* (1961), was published in 1731; its title was *Der Teutsche Pilgrim, Mitbringende einen Sitten-Calender*. Goedeke's *Grundriß zur Geschichte der deutschen Dichtung* (1966), edited by Herbert Jacob, takes the Arndt-Olson work into account, listing thirty-nine series of popular almanacs in German. Most of the complete annual publications originated in the decades after 1776. The bulk of these publications – thirty-four series – was published in Pennsylvania, another five series were published in Ohio (Cincinnati and Lancaster) and Maryland (Hagerstown and Baltimore). About a quarter of these periodicals were issued over a considerably long period: *Der Neue Nord-Americanische Stadt- und Land Calender* (Hagerstown) from 1797 until 1818; yet older, *Der Americanische Stadt- und Landcalender*, (Philadelphia) between 1784 and 1860; *Der Neue Gemeinnützige Landwirtschafts Calender* (Lancaster) also from 1784 to 1860; and, 'definitely the most important' series (Goedeke 1966, 541), *Der Hoch-Deutsche Americanische Calender* (Germantown and Philadelphia), published from 1739 to 1833.

Besides the almanac columns, all the publications mentioned by Jacob in Goedeke's summary included a literary section, usually featuring 'poems and prose' (540). These included items from German almanacs, *Taschenbücher*, almanacs and periodicals, translations from English and French, and excerpts from German novels or *Volksbücher* as well as original contributions from the producers of the almanacs or from German-speaking authors in North America. The range of literary genres was similar to that of the *Hinkende Boten* which were distributed in the south of Germany, eastern France and Switzerland. Its intellectual aims were educational and emancipatory, with an egalitarian – often also abolitionist – attitude (Mix 1996, 16f.).

From the outset, these almanacs dealt with definitively American topics not only in their travel writings, anecdotes, biographies and contemporary reports, but also in the poetry and fiction. These texts in particular illustrate the process of cultural autonomy, which was not a straightforward transitional process but which, at times, could even be reversed, as may be seen in the biography of Friedrich Kapp, a book trade historian who returned to Germany (Brauer 1984, B152f.). Thus, at times it proved difficult to clearly determine if these publications belong to a German or a North American culture (Goedeke 1966, 519). Karl Kurt Klein's question, in *Literaturgeschichte des Deutschtums im Ausland* (1939), as to what extent German-American culture was based on the 'German *Volkskörper*', is useless due to its racist and organicist presuppositions (Klein 1939, 87).

To focus on the aesthetic quality of German-American texts, as Jacob demands (Goedeke 1966, 518), proves unsatisfactory as, with this approach, the socialisation of symbolic cultural transfer[4] is marginalised.

The very name and concept of *Der Hinckend- und Stolpernd- doch eilfertig-fliegend- und laufende Americanische Reichs-Bott*[5] illustrates the tensions and

livres since 1784, with an unusually large quantity of titles of French authors (see Stern 1984, A408).

4 See Bollenbeck 1994, 193; Döring 1998, 75ff.; Jurt 1998, 101ff.

contradictions between cultural transfer and autonomy. As the contemporary reader was able to see, this project was based on the almanac published (since at least 1698) in the German town of Offenbach, entitled *Der Hinckend- und Stolpernd- doch eilfertig fliegend- und lauffende Bott; Das ist: Neu-Verbesserter Reichs- Staats-Geschichts- Kriegs- Siegs- und Friedens-Calender*. It was similar to *Der Cincinnatier hinkende Bote*, published almost a century later, which was intended to be a *vademecum* in German 'for the United States of North America' (*Der Cincinnatier hinkende Bote* 1865, title page). What appeared to be a strictly traditional periodical proved to be significantly different, even ostensibly so, in spite of similarities in respect to lay-out, concept and contents.

The limping messenger of the title figure was no longer providing rulers or their subjects with the latest news; instead, the news was transmitted to settlers who sought productivity and independence under the protective wings of the American Eagle, encircled by stars. Instead of the typical historical panoramas of the *Hinkender Bote* – peopled with princes, soldiers and warlords of eastern France, southwest Germany and Switzerland – the frontispiece of *Der Cincinnatier hinkende Bote* showed a large uncultured plot of land and a newly built log cabin. The iconography of the title page clearly illustrates a transition of the socio-cultural identity. In spite of the common language and a 'tendency to persist' that is typical of this medium, *Der Cincinnatier hinkende Bote* is a manifestation of the relativising of the characteristic 'relevance of tradition' (Schenda 1970, 325) which functioned as a norm for cultural integration. Through the image of the settler and the eagle under the firmament, the life of the intended reader of almanacs was placed in a regional as well as a global order, evoking its own past, present and future, and integrating the individual range of experience into the collective symbolism of a shared history. More so than in novels and short stories, these almanac contributions, oscillating between fact and fiction, referred to historical events which were interpreted in various ways, depending on the prevalent concepts of history.

Historical complexity was reduced through selection and combination of singular facts and identity-forming events, thus creating new areas of experience: 'Man perceives himself as placed within the context of history, and, in narrating it to himself, he re-creates it for himself according to his own laws' (Koselleck 1992, 640; Döring 1998, 75ff.). The personification of the almanac, in accordance with the familiar example of the Old World, as *Der Cincinnatier hinkende Bote* allowed the periodical to thematicise itself in a way that corroborated the truth of the things reported, reflecting an intention to transform anything strange, in a double sense, into a familiar pattern. It was of no consequence whether it concerned exemplary stories of emigrants, juridical and political problems, reports from the American War for Independence, or episodes dealing with native Indian history: the texts always referred to a pattern that made a new awareness of history and culture popular in spite of the 'tendency to persist', as diagnosed by Rudolf Schenda (1970, 325). In *Der Hinckend-*

5 See Drake 1962, 963; for the German-American calendars and almanacs, see also Goedeke 1966, 540-544. *Der Hinckend- und Stolpernd- doch eilfertig- fliegend- und laufende Americanische Reichs-Bott* was distributed in Pennsylvania in 1777 and is listed in Milton Drake's bibliography, *Almanacs of the United States* (1962).

und Stolpernd- doch eilfertig fliegend- und lauffende Bott, as in *Der Cincinnatier hinkende Bote*, reality was not interpreted in accordance with aesthetic simulations or mirrored as reality, but was constructed in a media-specific manner (Luhmann 1996, 16f.).

In correlation with its own history, conceived to be a collectively singular culture, the legitimisation of identity within the discursive dynamics of a different social and political sphere ultimately received the stamp of distinction. Due to its ties with republican ideals, for the European world it evoked different concepts of the duties to be performed by the citizens and of their respective places in society and history, which soon had an impact on the old country. This can be seen, for example, by the fact that a 'Moralischer Artikel', published in the *Pennsylvanischen Haushaltskalender* of 1770, continued to be considered a decisive influence: it was reprinted in the *Hannoverisches Magazin* in 1771 and again, with great approval, in the Hermannstadt *Siebenbürgischer Allmanach* in 1781 (see Haefs and Mix 1986, 184). On the other hand, Heinrich Heine rejected the concept of a positive America as envisaged even by Johann Wolfgang Goethe in his *Zahmen Xenien* and *Wilhelm Meisters Wanderjahre*. In his polemical treatise, 'Ludwig Börne', Heine objected to Goethe's image of America encompassing an 'unlimited scope for general questions of ethics and morality' and an 'unconditional will to work' (Goethe 1989, 343), instead, using negative catchwords such as 'ruthless dominion', 'slavery', 'brutality', 'hypocrisy', 'egoism' and 'injustice' (Heine 1978, 37f.). Heine concluded: 'Wordily profit is their real religion and money their God, their sole omnipotent God' (38). August Heinrich Hoffmann von Fallersleben associated the demagogical stereotype of an all-pervading commercial spirit with the British mentality in his satirical poems 'John Bull, der Enthusiast' and 'Time Is Money', published in 1844 and 1871 (Hoffmann von Fallersleben 1974, 317f. and 350).

Set against the background of Weimar classicism, an 'aesthetic ennobling of the prosaically-formless bourgeois existence' was propagated (Borchmeyer 1994, 295), and the ideal of education was celebrated as a 'national characteristic' (Bollenbeck 1994, 160). In the writings of literary history, the final goal of culture was seen as a matter of a decidedly national purport. German culture in North America, however, developed under different conditions. The immigrants had never imagined the state to be 'the highest developed collective product of education' (Jeismann 1987, 4), as Georg Wilhelm Friedrich Hegel suggested; rather, the absence of the state was perceived as a guarantee of 'free speech' and 'thought' (Hoffmann von Fallersleben 1974, 302; Ritter 1999, 39f.). Therefore, there never was a cultured bourgeois class in support of the state, nor was there a dramatic cultural crisis in reaction to the uncritical idealisation of the educational utopia, which occurred after 1871 (Mix 1995, 26ff. and 185ff.). Instead, the reception of German and Austrian elite culture in the German societies (Conzen 1984, 27ff.) was centred on popular German literature (Doerris 1984, 81ff.; Yoder 1984, 94ff.; Bentzel 1987, 9ff.; Conner and Roberts 1988) in the communicative structures of a 'civilisatoric network' which had been derided in Germany for many decades, attesting to the 'fatal antithesis between *Kultur* and culture' (Adorno 1977, 695 and 697).

When travelling through the USA in 1827, Alexis de Tocqueville claimed that the North Americans had, 'strictly speaking, no literature yet' – apart from the many writings of journalists, politicians and missionaries (Tocqueville 1987, 342). This claim was formalised in light of the mass distribution of popular almanacs and periodicals, the continuous reception of canonised works of European authors, and the late emergence of an original American literature. As opposed to Europe, in the USA, national identity did not grow out of an integrative culture supported by the state, but from the belief that a national identity 'descends from human communities', which were considered 'natural' to the extent that they merely 'needed to affirm themselves in order to define who they were' (Hobsbawm 1998, 115). Thus, the cultural ties between the emigrants and their countries of origin were evaluated according to different criteria. Within this framework, Germany – a country that was culturally, confessionally, politically and territorially divided – was certainly not idealised but seen as ambivalent. In a political and social sense, the 'American' was considered to be 'a new being' already in the eighteenth century; however, the cultural traditions of the German homeland continued to exert an influence that shaped identity. On the eve of the French Revolution, Hector St. John de Crèvecœur wrote about the German immigrants in Pennsylvania:

> Their astonishment at their first arrival from Germany is very great – it is to them a dream; the contrast must be very powerful indeed; they observe their countrymen flourishing in every place; they travel through whole counties where not a word of English is spoken; and in the names and the language of the people, they retrace Germany. They have been an useful acquisition to this continent, and to Pennsylvania in particular; to them it owes some share of its prosperity: to their mechanical knowledge and patience it owes the finest mills in all America, the best teams of horses, and many other advantages. The recollection of their former poverty and slavery never quits them as long as they live. (Crèvecœur 1981, 84-85)

The seemingly paradoxical combination referred to here – cultural traditionalism, a sense of regional identity as well as an economic and political modernity in society – could be thematised as part of daily life by the popular almanac as no other medium could. Considering its content, which covered a broad spectrum and was both instructive and diverting, almanacs such as the *Hinkender Bote* or *Haushaltungs-Kalender* (Wiedemann 1984, 51f.) had proven to be successful ethno-cultural integrative media in Europe, reaching not only the literate but also the illiterate public. Since only 'few German immigrants were in command of the English language when they came to the United States' (Mikoletzky 1988, 253), the almanac continued to be an important guide in the New World: in areas where English dominated, cultural adaptation and, above all, assimilation were at first subjected to strict limits (Esser 1980, 20f.). Like the emigrant novels of the nineteenth century, many popular almanacs told their readers that forced cultural adaptation was not an important goal:

> Only characters harbouring criminal intentions adapt themselves quickly and voluntarily to the American lifestyle; the *positive* heroes, however, show themselves particularly [...] reluctant; on the other hand, holding on to habits and objects brought along from Germany is generally used to favourably describe the characters. (Mikoletzky 1988, 272)

When the revolutions of 1848 failed, the anti-American attitudes, shown by authors of the Young Germany school such as Heinrich Heine, crystallised into an idea of 'cultural superiority'; ultimately, this was the basis for a 'fear of foreign elements for many Americans' (277).

As in the emigration novels, the almanacs presented a positive self-image based on allegedly German qualities such as integrity, industry, honesty, and abiding the law. For many emigrants, to insist on distinctive norms and values strengthened the awareness of an ethno-cultural otherness. This was eventually consciously directed against the homeland, considered to be backward.

Within the context of a totally different political reality, in the New World, a divergent collective identity developed. Favouring the attitude of 'clannishness' (300), it was a decisive attitude of self-protection that engendered the idea that they were the ones who, for the first time, embodied what was *actually* German. Friedrich Gerstäcker, an author of travel books who left the USA to return home in 1843, wrote in his book *In America*, published in 1879 and consisting of several volumes:

> Those of us here in America are a completely different people from those at home, we did not only change physically but probably also spiritually – in a rather astonishing manner. What we have never been in Germany, we have become all of a sudden over here: real Germans – without all that miserable prejudice from the homeland, which could not survive the journey. We became not only Germans, but also people with a awareness of equality for all, who accomplish something; and, together with that, there emerged something that many of us back home had hardly known by name: our self-respect. (Gerstäcker 1872, 233)

II. Questions for Future Research

The context outlined above presents four topics that will be of utmost importance to future research. First, we will have to investigate the media-specific characteristics and genre differences manifest in the German-American almanac; second, the collective patterns of identity encapsulated in these periodicals; third, the possible forms of intercultural communication; and, finally, the relationship between cultural adaptation and autonomy.

The first complex of problems includes the analysis of the sociology of readership and of the history of the book trade that made a literary mass-communication in the German speaking areas of the USA possible. The focus should be on the differences from the traditional patterns of popular European almanacs. Taking into account the material shape, structure, and function of the almanac, the following aspects should be explored: the profile of the implicit and explicit reader, the spectrum of textual genres, the image of the almanac man, the relationship between text and illustration as well as the editor's intentions. The German almanacs of North America omitted or re-designed traditional topics – such as lists of European dynasties and summaries or cursory reports on wars in the Old World. In their practical section, almanacs focused on everyday American life; they put a greater emphasis on texts with a moral and didactic purport; they preferred new genres, such as dialogues between emigrants; and they constructed a new view of history. Thus, they constructed a different identity which correlates to the collective identity patterns popularised by the almanacs.

Considering the formation of an American history of their own, one should also look into the relationship between histories and history, since the '*communicative memory* – living, communicated and represented in contemporary testimonies – extends its significance beyond the personal carriers of memory, due to the institutions and media of a *cultural memory*' (Schmidt 2000). Within this context, reports on daily life of emigrants that reflected the individual but which were also considered paradigmatic, for example, 'Die traurige Geschichte der Manheimischen Familie, welche 1799 an dem Fluß Mohawk ein Opfer indianischer Grausamkeit geworden', should be seen as constituting collective patterns of identity as well as traditional symbolic forms of codification; for example, the notice about 'General Waschington's Geburtstag', the first 'Sitzung des Congreßes' (1775), or the 'Erklärung der Unabhängigkeit der Vereinigten Staaten von Amerika' (see *Der Neue Hoch Deutsche Americanische Calender* 1798; *Der gemeinnützige Americanische Calender* 1803). Inevitably, the time frame of the American almanac was narrowed down to a few generations; the images and stories derived from a mythical pre-historic time (Langewiesche 1996, 58; Blitz 2000, 361ff.), which were popular in the context of the construction of a German nationhood, do not play a role in the German-American almanacs.

The belief in a momentous new beginning stimulated a 'unification' (Schmidt 2000, 35) within the scope of memory that was almost unknown in Europe: beyond the range of confessional, territorial-historical, state-administrative or monarchical conflicts, *Der Hoch-Deutsche Americanische Calender* or *Der Americanische Stadt- und Land Calender* functioned as a *perpetuum mobile* for historical and ethno-cultural patterns of identification. The modified collective symbolism could be given concrete shape, on the one hand, by listing anniversaries and people in the *calendarium*, and, on the other hand, through persons and events mentioned in the anecdotes, jokes, and historical tales that were claimed to be based on actual facts. Decisive socio-cultural values and symbols can be clarified through the 'proverbs and aphorisms' which were inserted into the almanac and the text 'with the particular goal of conveying moral values' (Masel 1997, 170). In the process of analysing the contents, one has to concentrate on questions concerning the construction of powerful historical subjects, the relationship between historical events and fiction, the focus on teleological-historical categories, the stereotypes of a generalised interpretation of the universe, as well as the texts' possible soliciting character. Embedded in everyday life and festive traditions, the German-American almanacs, in spite of their enormous distribution, did not address the lower classes (difficult to define), but *all* social groups within a readership defined through ethnicity and culture. The anecdotes, jokes, aphorisms and historical tales printed in the almanacs were meant to be read aloud and told, rather than enjoyed, in the quiet seclusion of individual reading. The borders between oral and written language, usually so manifest, were consciously blurred.

Thirdly, the patterns of identification codified under these pre-conditions allow for an elucidation of both intra-cultural reference to tradition and inter-cultural inter-relationships. This latent competitive relationship manifests itself in orthography, syntax, vocabulary, anglicisms and idiosyncratic germanisms as well as in examples of textual migration, translations, bureaucratic instructions, and book advertisements typical for almanacs. For example, spellings such as 'Germantaun', 'Kutztaun', 'Yorktaun', 'Courthaus', 'Courten' and 'Fären' are widespread; there are advertisements for 'allerley Deutsche Schulbücher'; one may find the 'Sprüche von Benj. Franklin', lyrics entitled 'Yänkie-Dudel',[6] and the presentation of the *Freyschütz* in *Der Americanische Stadt und Land Calender Auf das 1834ste Jahr Christi* or Schiller's 'An die Freude' in the *Readinger Calender* in 1806. The German-American almanacs do not merely represent the margins of written daily communication; they illustrate how texts that were typical for their time or highly esteemed came to represent, in the course of a multi-faceted historical process of reception and assimilation, an integral part of popular culture as exemplified by recitals, ballroom dances, concerts, and recitation. In contrast to the emigrants originating from England and Ireland,

> most Germans brought far more of their traditional modes of recreation with them into the industrial age and to America, expecting to continue to enjoy a convivial glass of beer or wine, gathering with their womenfolk as well as in purely male assemblies to sing, dance, and drink, and doing so on their one day of leisure, Sunday, should they so choose. These lifestyle conflicts were evident by the 1840s, as German Americans rallied in defence of *personal liberty* and added *Geselligkeit und Gemütlichkeit* to the list of cultural differences that they saw separating themselves from Americans and defining their *Deutschtum*, the fundamental set of values and observances that delineated their ethnic identity in America. (Conzen 1984, 27)

The conflicts addressed here point to a *fourth* complex of problems involving the relationship between culturation and autonomy. Even if the 'Hessians, Franconians, Westphalians, Hannoverians and Oldenburgers', who followed the 'Rhinelanders, Badenese and Württembergers', at first did not possess a group identity beyond that of the status of emigrants, they were regarded in the USA 'simply as *Germans*' (Conzen 1984, 20 and 25). However, this tendency to schematise the concept of the self and the alien was reciprocal: opposed to a comparatively differentiated self-presentation, there was the fractional image, due to lack of information, of the North American who was not of German descent. Cultural autonomy grew from the awareness of difference, which, according to Carl Schurz's motto *ubi libertas, ibi patria,* also clearly distanced itself from the motherland. The 'definition of the ethnicity was essentially cultural' (Conzen 1984, 29), but it was not under the auspices of an 'extension of German territory' (Klein 1939, 91) as Klein, ideologically blind, surmised in 1939. Emigration was not stimulated by imperial ambitions of power; it was a clear 'protest against the political conditions in the homeland, a kind of voting carried out by their feet, as it were' (see Ottomeyer 1988, 551).

In relation to the German discussion on education, it should therefore be argued whether the German interpretation of cultural identity by Georg Bollenbeck, powerful in its impact on the nineteenth century, is as apodictic and free of contradictions as it is a consequential amalgamation of education and reactionary modernisation; moreover, whether it might be specified as the 'awareness of an exceptional task to fulfil' (Bollenbeck 1994, 162). As preference was given to a universal concept of education rather than to a training program geared towards the needs of the market, the preliminaries of stable cultural symbols and images emerging in the USA were of an entirely different political and social nature:

---

6 See *Der Hoch-Deutsch Americanische Calender* (1748), n.p.; *Americanischer Stadt und Land Calender* (1830), n.p.; *Der Americanische Stadt- und Land-Calender* (1852), n.p.; *Americanischer Stadt und Land Calender* (1840), n.p.

> German Americans constantly defended their difference by arguing that they wished to preserve certain values in order to make them part of a new and truly American culture, and they succeed only too well. By the early 20th century, American schools and universities were purveying a higher culture barely differing from that of their German counterparts. (Conzen 1984, 33)

'National characteristics' were determined by means of a concept of education that included a dual perspective of self and otherness. Bollenbeck's criterion of a 'politically deficient function' (Bollenbeck 1994, 162), however, is by no means an inescapable consequence of a collective understanding of culture. The idea of the formation of self and individuality is inherent in the contributions to German-American almanacs, based on the concept of harmonious and individual self-realisation, ultimately taking shape under the influence of idealism as a vision of autonomous education. In terms of literary research, the process can be illustrated by means of examples, such as the prose text 'Der deutsche Patriot' (1801) or the genre of the political programmatic treatise (see 'Der Zustand der Deutschen in Pennsylvanien 1825', 1786), as well as by dialogues of emigrants or by almanac texts alluding to historical events.

PRIMARY SOURCES: ALMANACS

Americanischer Stadt und Land Calender Auf das 1830ste Jahr Christi, Welches ein Gemeines Jahr ist von 365 Tagen (1830). Philadelphia: Gedruckt und zu haben bey Conrad Zentler, in der Zweyten Strasse, unterhalb der Rehs-Strasse.

Americanischer Stadt und Land Calender Auf das 1840ste Jahr Christi, Welches ein Schalt-Jahr ist von 366 Tagen (1830). Philadelphia: Gedruckt und zu haben bey Conrad Zentler, in der Zweyten Strasse, unterhalb der Rehs-Strasse.

Der Americanische Stadt- und Land-Calender auf das Jahr 1852 (1852). Philadelphia: Herausgegeben von Ch. G. Sauer.

Der Cincinnatier hinkende Bote: Ein Kalender für die Vereinigten Staaten von Nordamerika, auf das Jahr unsers Herrn 1865, welches ein gemeines Jahr von 365 Tagen ist (1865). Cincinnati: Verlag von Gebrüder Benzinger, Cincinnati, im Katholischen Institut. New-York, No. 9 Dey Str.

'Der deutsche Patriot' (1801). *Der gemeinnützige Americanische Calender Auf das Jahr Christi 1801.* Reading: Gedruckt und zu haben bey Jacob Schneider und Comp.

Der gemeinnützige Americanische Calender Auf das Jahr Christi 1803 (1803). Reading: Gedruckt und zu haben bey Schneider und Ritter.

Der Hoch-Deutsch Americanische Calender, Auf das Jahr Nach der Gnadenreichen Geburt unsers Herrn und Heylandes Jesu Christi 1748 (1748). Germantown: Gedruckt und zu finden bey Christoph Saur.

Der Neue Hoch Deutsche Americanische Calender, Auf das Jahr Christi 1798, Welches ein Gemein Jahr von 365 Tagen ist (1798). Baltimore: Gedruckt und zu finden bey Samuel Saur.

'Der Zustand der Deutschen in Pennsylvanien im Jahr 1825: Wenn sie Wollen' (1786). In *Der Hoch-Deutsche Americanische Calender, Auf das Jahr 1786.* Germantaun: Gedruckt und zu finden bey Leibert und Billmeyer, n.p.

REFERENCES

Arndt, Karl J.R., and May E. Olson (1961). *Deutsch-Amerikanische Zeitungen und Zeitschriften 1732-1955: Geschichte und Bibliographie*. Heidelberg: Quelle and Meyer.

Adorno, Theodor W. (1977). 'Auf die Frage: Was ist deutsch'. In *Gesammelte Schriften.* Vol. 10/2. Ed. Rolf Tiedemann. Frankfurt/Main: Suhrkamp, 69-701.

Bentzel, Curtis C. (1987). 'Calligraphy and Linguistics: A Different Look at the F&M Fraktur.' In *Fraktur: A Selective Guide to the Franklin and Marshall Fraktur Collection*. Lancaster: Franklin and Marshall College, n.p.

Blitz, Hans-Martin (2000). *Aus Liebe zum Vaterland: Die deutsche Nation im 18. Jahrhundert*. Hamburg: Hamburger Edition.

Bollenbeck, Georg (1994). *Bildung und Kultur: Glanz und Elend eines deutschen Deutungsmusters*. Frankfurt/Main: Insel.

Borchmeyer, Dieter (1994). *Weimarer Klassik: Portrait einer Epoche*. Weinheim: Beltz Athenäum.

Brauer, Adalbert (1984). 'Friedrich Kapp und die Geschichte des deutschen Buchhandels.' *Buchhandelsgeschichte* 4, B150-B156.

Conner, Paul, and Jill Roberts, comp. (1988). *Pennsylvania German Fraktur and Printed Broadsides: A Guide to the Collections in the Library of Congress*. Washington, DC: Library of Congress.

Conzen, Kathleen Neils (1984). 'Patterns of German-American History.' In Randall M. Miller (ed.), *Germans in America – Retrospect and Prospect: Tricentennial Lectures Delivered at the German Society of Pennsylvania*. Philadelphia: German Society of Pennsylvania, 14-36.

Crèvecœur, J. Hector St John de (1981). *Letters from an American Farmer* and *Sketches of Eighteenth-Century America*. Ed. with an intro. Albert E. Stone. Harmondsworth: Penguin. Original edition 1782.

Doerris, Reinhard R. (1984). 'Immigrant Culture and Religion: Church and Faith among German Americans.' In Randall M. Miller (ed.), *Germans in America – Retrospect and Prospect: Tricentennial Lectures Delivered at the German Society of Pennsylvania*. Philadelphia: German Society of Pennsylvania, 75-91.

Döring, Sabine A. (1998). 'Vom "nation-building" zum Identifikationsfeld: Zur Integrationsfunktion nationaler Mythen in der Literatur.' In Horst Turk, Brigitte Schultze and Roberto Simanowski (eds.), *Kulturelle Grenzziehungen im Spiegel der Literaturen: Nationalismus, Regionalismus, Fundamentalismus*. Göttingen: Wallstein, 63-83.

Drake, Milton, comp. (1962). *Almanacs of the United States: Part II*. New York: Scarecrow Press.

Esser, Hartmut (1980). *Aspekte der Wanderungssoziologie: Assimilation und Integration von Wanderern, ethnischen Gruppen und Minderheiten – Eine handlungstheoretische Analyse*. Darmstadt: Luchterhand.

Gerstäcker, Friedrich (1872). *In Amerika: Amerikanisches Lebensbild aus neuerer Zeit – Im Anschluss an 'Nach Amerika'*. Vol. 1. Jena: Costenobel.

Goedeke, Karl (1966). *Grundriß zur Geschichte der deutschen Dichtung aus den Quellen*. Vol. 15. Ed. Herbert Jacob. Berlin: Akademie Verlag.

Goethe, Johann Wolfgang (1989). *Wilhelm Meisters Wanderjahre*. In *Sämtliche Werke*. Part 1, vol. 10. Ed. Gerhard Neumann and Hans-Georg Dewitz. Frankfurt/Main: Deutscher Klassiker Verlag.

Haefs, Wilhelm, and York-Gothart Mix (1986). 'Der Musenhort in der Provinz: Literarische Almanache in den Kronländern der österreichischen Monarchie im ausgehenden 18. und beginnenden 19. Jahrhundert.' *Archiv für Geschichte des Buchwesens (AGB)* 27, 171-194.

Heine, Heinrich (1978). 'Ludwig Börne: Eine Denkschrift.' In *Historisch-kritische Gesamtausgabe der Werke*. Vol. 11. Rev. Helmut Koopmann. Hamburg: Hoffmann and Campe, 9-132.

Hobsbawm, Eric (1998). 'Das Erfinden von Traditionen.' In Christoph Conrad and Martina Kessel (eds.), *Kultur & Geschichte: Neue Einblicke in eine alte Beziehung*. Stuttgart: Reclam, 87-118.

Hoffmann von Fallersleben, August Heinrich (1974). 'Time is money'; 'John Bull, der Enthusiast.' In *Gedichte und Lieder*. Ed. Hermann Wendebourg and Anneliese Gerbert. Hamburg: Hoffmann and Campe, 317-318, 350.

Jeismann, Karl-Ernst (1987). 'Zur Bedeutung der "Bildung" im 19. Jahrhundert.' In Karl-Ernst Jeismann and Peter Lundgreen (eds.), *Handbuch der deutschen Bildungsgeschichte*. Vol. 3. *1800-1870: Von der Neuordnung Deutschlands bis zur Gründung des Deutschen Reiches*. Munich: Beck, 1-21.

Jurt, Joseph (1998). 'Das Konzept des literarischen Feldes und die Internationalisierung der Literatur.' In Horst Turk, Brigitte Schultze and Roberto Simanowski (eds.), *Kulturelle Grenzziehungen im*

Spiegel der Literaturen: Nationalismus, Regionalismus, Fundamentalismus. Göttingen: Wallstein, 84-103.

Klein, Karl Kurt (1939). *Literaturgeschichte des Deutschtums im Ausland: Schrifttum und Geistesleben der deutschen Volksgruppen im Ausland vom Mittelalter bis zur Gegenwart*. Leipzig: Bibliographisches Institut.

Koselleck, Reinhart (1992). 'Geschichte.' In Otto Brunner, Werner Conze and Reinhart Koselleck (eds.), *Geschichtliche Grundbegriffe: Historisches Lexikon zur politisch-sozialen Sprache in Deutschland*. Vol. 2. 3rd edition. Stuttgart: Klett-Cotta, 593-717.

Langewiesche, Dieter (1996). 'Kulturelle Nationenbildung in Deutschland des 19. Jahrhunderts.' In Manfred Hettling and Paul Nolte (eds.), *Nation und Gesellschaft in Deutschland: Historische Essays*. Munich: Beck, 46-64.

Luhmann, Niklas (1996). *Die Realität der Massenmedien*. Opladen: Westdeutscher Verlag.

Masel, Katharina (1997). *Kalender und Volksaufklärung in Bayern: Zur Entwicklung des Kalenderwesens 1750 bis 1830*. St Ottilien: EOS-Verlag.

Mikoletzky, Juliane (1988). *Die deutsche Amerika-Auswanderung des 19. Jahrhunderts in der zeitgenössischen fiktionalen Literatur*. Tübingen: Niemeyer.

Mix, York-Gothart (1995). *Die Schulen der Nation: Bildungskritik in der Literatur der frühen Moderne*. Stuttgart: Metzler.

——— (1996). 'Lektüre für Gebildete und Ungebildete: Einleitende Bemerkungen zu H.C. Boies "Musenalmanach", J.P. Hebels "Rheinländischem Hausfreund" und anderen literarischen Begleitern durch das Jahr.' In York-Gothart Mix (ed.), *Almanach- und Taschenbuchkultur des 18. und 19. Jahrhunderts*. Wiesbaden: Harrassowitz, 7-19.

Ottomeyer, Hans, ed. (1988). *Biedermeiers Glück und Ende: ... die gestörte Idylle 1815-1848*. Munich: Hugendubel.

Ritter, Alexander (1999). 'Grenzübertritt und Schattentausch: Der österreichische Priester Carl Postl und seine vage staatsbürgerliche Identität als amerikanischer Autor Charles Sealsfield – Eine Dokumentation.' *Freiburger Universitätsblätter* 143, 39-71.

Schenda, Rudolf (1970). *Volk ohne Buch: Studien zur Sozialgeschichte der populären Lesestoffe 1770-1910*. Frankfurt/Main: Klostermann.

Schmidt, Thomas (2000). *Kalender und Gedächtnis: Erinnern im Rhythmus der Zeit*. Göttingen: Vandenhoeck and Ruprecht.

Schmitz, Walter (1993). 'Nordamerikanisch-deutsche Literaturbeziehungen.' In Walther Killy (ed.), *Literaturlexikon*. Vol. 14. Gütersloh: Bertelsmann Lexikon Verlag, 162-170.

Stern, Madeleine B. (1984). 'Ursprung und Entwicklung des Antiquariatsbuchhandels in Philadelphia.' *Aus dem Antiquariat* 11, A405-A420.

Tocqueville, Alexis de (1987). 'Über die Demokratie in Amerika.' In Heinz Förster (ed.), *Was ist ein Amerikaner? Zeugnisse aus dem Zeitalter der amerikanischen Revolution*. Leipzig: Kiepenheuer, 324-347.

Wiedemann, Inga (1984). *'Der Hinkende Bote' und seine Vettern: Familien-, Haus- und Volkskalender von 1757 bis 1929 – Katalog der Kalendersammlung des Museums für Deutsche Volkskunde*. Berlin: Museum für Deutsche Volkskunde.

Yoder, Don (1984). 'The Palatine Connection: The Pennsylvania German Culture and Its European Roots.' In Randall M. Miller (ed.), *Germans in America – Retrospect and Prospect: Tricentennial Lectures Delivered at the German Society of Pennsylvania*. Philadelphia: German Society of Pennsylvania, 92-109.